HAMLET WITHOUT HAMLET

"Hamlet" without Hamlet sets out to counter the modern tradition of abstracting the character Hamlet from the play. For over two centuries, Hamlet has been valued as the icon of consciousness, but only by ignoring the hard fact of his dispossession. By admitting that premise, this book brings the play to life around man's relation to land, from graves to estate to empire. Key preoccupations are thereby released, including the gendered imperatives of genealogy, the rhythms of world history, and man's elemental affinity to dust. As de Grazia demonstrates from the 400 years of Hamlet's afterlife, such features have disappeared into the vortex of an interiorized Hamlet, but they remain in the language of the play as well as in the earliest accounts of its production. Once they are reactivated, a very different Hamlet emerges, one whose thoughts and desires are thickly embedded in the worldly, and otherworldly, matters of the play: a Hamlet within *Hamlet*.

MARGRETA DE GRAZIA is Joseph B. Glossberg Term Professor in the Humanities, Department of English, University of Pennsylvania. She is co-editor, with Stanley Wells, of *The Cambridge Companion to Shakespeare* (2002); co-editor, with Maureen Quilligan and Peter Stallybrass, of *Subject and Object in Renaissance Culture* (1996); and author of *Shakespeare Verbatim: The Reproduction of Authenticity and the 1790 Apparatus* (1991). Her work has appeared in many books and journals including *Shakespeare Survey*, *Shakespeare Quarterly*, *Modern Language Quarterly*, and *Textual Practice*.

D1596913

HAMLET WITHOUT HAMLET

MARGRETA DE GRAZIA

CAMBRIDGE
UNIVERSITY PRESS

CAMBRIDGE UNIVERSITY PRESS
Cambridge, New York, Melbourne, Madrid, Cape Town, Singapore, São Paulo

Cambridge University Press
The Edinburgh Building, Cambridge CB2 2RU, UK

Published in the United States of America by Cambridge University Press, New York

www.cambridge.org

Information on this title: www.cambridge.org/9780521690362

First published 2007

Printed in the United Kingdom at the University Press, Cambridge

A catalogue record for this publication is available from the British Library

ISBN-13 978-0-521-87025-2 hardback
ISBN-10 0-521-87025-9 hardback
ISBN-13 978-0-521-69036-2 paperback
ISBN-10 0-521-69036-6 paperback

For Colin Thubron

Contents

Illustrations

Acknowledgments

If writing were not for me such a hard act of self-absorption, this book would have come out better, and earlier. I hold Hamlet in part responsible. I mean the modern metaphysical Hamlet, the Hamlet this study would do without: the Wittgensteinian fly in the fly-bottle, endlessly spinning its cogitative wheels against the glass.

There are three friends who know the problem: Howard Zeiderman who always stood ready to help with muddles; Peter Stallybrass whose instruction to "Just print it out" still rings in my ears; and Colin Thubron who assured me again and again that there really was nothing left to be understood.

But a number of others also deserve thanks: John Parker who was the manuscript's first and aptest reader; Maureen Quilligan who has a gift for imbuing the work of others with her own brilliance; and the many who entertained in print or conversation some part of the book: Crystal Bartolovich, Rita Copeland, Joe de Grazia, Andrew Gurr, Juliet Fleming, Jay Grossman, Peter Holland, Rayna Kalas, David Kastan, Suvir Kaul, Sean Keilen, Paulina Kewes, Carla Mazzio, Jeff Masten, Gordon Mcmullan, Stephen Orgel, Patricia Parker, Tyler Smith, Jack Spivack, Gary Tomlinson, David Wallace, and Valerie Wayne.

If it weren't for her inimitable stylistic sparkle, Emma Smith's comments would have remained anonymous, as must those of the Cambridge readers, to whom I am also grateful. I wish also to thank Andrew McNellie for early encouragement of the book and Sarah Stanton for wafting it through its final stages. My copy-editor, Caroline Howlett, must also be singled out, for her exacting and gracious attention.

Special thanks are due to Georgiana Zeigler of the Folger Library in Washington, DC; Dan Traister, Michael Ryan, and John Pollack of the Van Pelt Library at the University of Pennsylvania; and Robert Yorke of the College of Arms. Stephanie Elsky, Cathy Nicholson, and Brian Kirk were invaluable in pulling together innumerable loose ends in the preparation of the manuscript.

The John Simon Guggenheim Memorial Foundation gave me the year in which to lay down the foundation for this book, and the Rockefeller Foundation highlighted that year with a residence at the Bellagio Study and Conference Center.

Austin Zeiderman and Page Bertelsen are in a category all their own.

Versions of Chapters 1 and 2 have appeared in *Modern Language Quarterly*, *Textual Practice*, and *Shakespeare Quarterly*, and parts of Chapters 5 and 6 were published in collections published by Oxford University Press and Routledge. I am grateful to the editors of these publications for permission to reprint these materials here.

Note on text used

Except when otherwise indicated, I have quoted from a modern edition: that is, a composite of the two substantive early texts of *Hamlet* (the 1604/5 Quarto and the 1623 Folio), in modernized spelling and punctuation, within an editorial frame consisting of an introduction, stemma, notes, and appendices. I have chosen Harold Jenkins' compendious Arden *Hamlet* published in 1982.

It might be expected that a book purporting to counter the modern tradition would avoid editorial mediation altogether and return to the two substantive early texts. Quoting from the early Quarto or Folio would have had the distinct advantage of defamiliarizing what is, to be sure, the most familiar play in the language. But what then would prevent us from applying to the unedited text the same old interpretative procedures encouraged by the edited? This project would heighten rather than avoid the familiar by drawing attention to the editorial and critical maneuvers that have made Hamlet the supreme modern presence he continues to be. For this purpose, it is not the text stripped-bare that is required, but rather the edition most saturated with the modern critical tradition.

Though quotations are taken from the 1982 Arden, I frequently draw on the facsimile reproductions of the 1604/5 Quarto (Q2) from the Huntington Library and the 1623 Folio (F) from the Folger Library, as well as the truncated 1603 Quarto (Q1) from the British Library. I take the liberty of interspersing variants from these early texts whenever they open up possibilities limited or foreclosed by the modern edition. Such eclecticism, I would argue, is warranted by their relationship: although separate, they are by no means discrete, much less mutually exclusive. Furthermore the vagaries of textual production as well as of lexical and grammatical usage allow for considerable convertibility among their particulars.

Introduction

To suppose, as the title of this book implies, that *Hamlet* could be considered without Hamlet is obviously absurd. After all, little would remain: Hamlet either speaks or is spoken about for most of the play. And why eliminate the most valued character in our cultural tradition?

The Hamlet this book would do without is the modern Hamlet, the one distinguished by an inner being so transcendent that it barely comes into contact with the play from which it emerges.

The book would do without this Hamlet for the simple reason that, for some two hundred years, history has done so. As is frequently noted, Hamlet's deep and complex inwardness was not perceived as the play's salient feature until around 1800. Earlier generations appreciated the play, as is well documented, but – it has been said – for the wrong reasons: "Seeing they saw not." Hamlet's singular importance passed unnoticed until a good two centuries after the writing of the play. Genius, it would appear, is always in advance of history. Shakespeare was ahead of his time and history took centuries to catch up. Only after the auroral advances of the Enlightenment was it possible to perceive the phenomenon of Hamlet's intransitive inwardness.

Hamlet without Hamlet maintains precisely the opposite. It was not sharper vision that brought Hamlet's complex interiority into focus. Rather, it was a blind spot. In order for Hamlet to appear modern, the premise of the play had to drop out of sight. The premise is this: at his father's death, just at the point when an only son in a patrilineal system stands to inherit, Hamlet is dispossessed – and, as far as the court is concerned, legitimately.

The promise of the patronymic is broken: Prince Hamlet does not become King Hamlet; Hamlet II does not step into the place of Hamlet I. The kingdom does not pass to the (adult and capable) only son of the dead king. This is a remarkable turn of events. In an hereditary monarchy like England's, it would have been unthinkable. Yet the critical tradition has mainly ignored the upset, as if dispossession were of no consequence. Hamlet's bereavement at the play's start has been considered in light of his father's sudden death and his mother's hasty remarriage, but without acknowledgment of how both events have left him disentitled.

And yet surely the loss of the kingdom affects what Hamlet has within. A prince bereft of his prospective kingdom, like any man deprived of his expected estate, must feel the injury. That the blow has been dealt legally – approved by the Danish Council, consolidated by marriage to the Queen – hardly lessens the damage.

At Elsinore, Hamlet has no choice but to keep his resentment to himself: "Break, my heart, / For I must hold my tongue."[1] If at court Hamlet were to protest the election of another over himself, he would be guilty of the highest crime in the land: treason. Only in jest does he venture complaint, "I lack advancement" (3.2.331). Only in private does he confide that the same man who has killed his father and married his mother has "[p]opp'd in between th'election and my hopes" (5.2.65). To early readers and audiences, the evasion that has mystified so many modern critics – "I have that within which passes show" (1.2.85) – might have been quite transparent. Transparent, too, for the characters within the play. The king calls for an investigation at court to determine the cause of Hamlet's distraction; but might it not, like an open secret, be obvious to all?

When under the protection of his antic disposition, Hamlet no longer needs to hold his tongue; it is perhaps not irrelevant that, in the words of the great jurist Edward Coke, "he that is *non compos mentis* . . . cannot commit High Treason."[2] So immunized, he is free to hint broadly at the cause of his transformation. Time and again he refers to himself in terms of lack: he is a starving horse; a castrated capon; a thankless beggar; a hollow reed; a trapped prisoner; a disgruntled menial; a contumacious poor man, dreadfully attended, who can remunerate only with a half-pennyworth of thanks. His purse has been cut and pocketed by another man; the hands he swears by are retaliatory "pickers and stealers" (3.2.327). In the letter he writes upon return from his sea-faring voyage, he characterizes himself as "Naked" and "Alone" (4.7.42, 50, 51).

In a world in which men fight and kill for land – "A poisons him i'th'garden for his estate" (3.2.255) – the importance of the realm to Hamlet might well be a given. It does more than give substance to his state of dejection at the play's start: it knits him into the fabric of the play. The play opens with threatened invasion and ends in military occupation. Framed by territorial conflict, it stages one contest over land after another.

Fortinbras I and Hamlet I clash over crown lands, Hamlet I and Claudius over the garden kingdom, Gonzago and Lucianus over the "bank of flowers" or "estate," Norway and Poland over a garrisoned "patch of ground," the boy and adult companies over the commercial stage, the Crown and the Church over the churchyard, Laertes and Hamlet over the flower-strewn grave pit of Ophelia, and the actor who plays Hamlet and any other actor who challenges him over the performative arena of the stage.

The language of the play itself upholds the attachment of persons to land, human to humus. Flesh and earth repeatedly coalesce through overlaps of sound and sense, as they do in the name of the first man, called after not his father but the dust from which he was fashioned, *adamah*, the Hebrew word for clay; Hamlet plays on the primal cognomen when he refers to that clayey "piece of work" (2.2.303) as a "quintessence of dust" (2.2.308). *Mole* and *mold* are interchangeable spellings for the word designating not only loose soil, but also both a subterranean mammal and a dark skin growth. Hamlet accuses his mother of battening on a *moor* (3.4.67), implying an appetite for both blackened flesh and wasteland. One substance can be used to repair another: holes in earthen walls are patched with the pulverized flesh of Caesar ("that earth which kept the world in awe," 5.1.208) and pocks on the skin are smoothed over with cosmetic plaster ("an inch thick," 5.1.187–8). The *weeds* which clothe bodies also cover turf: Ophelia falls down into the brook with her "weedy trophies" and is pulled down further, "[t]o muddy death," by her sodden garments (4.7.173, 182). Her brother hopes her dead body will, like a flower bed, sprout violets. Men are commensurate with the acreage they possess, as if their bodies were literally extended by the tracts of land they hold by inheritance, purchase, or conquest. And however enlarged in life, even if to imperial proportions, bodies at death shrink to the size of a grave plot, or to smaller still: to the dimensions of the deed by which lands are conveyed, one stretch of parchment coterminous with another.

As Hamlet's dispossession has been ignored, so, too, has *Hamlet's* investment in land. The connection between character and plot has thereby disappeared: the play has been seen as a mere pretext for the main character, quite literally so when it is assumed that the play's structure derived from an earlier revenge play, the hypothetical *Ur-Hamlet*, while Hamlet's character issued purely from Shakespeare's creative imagination. Scholarship has been content to treat the plot as inert backdrop to the main character who can readily leave it behind to wander into other and later works, no strings attached. Thus for the better part of its critical history, Hamlet (to invert this book's title) has existed without *Hamlet*. Indeed one of the great sources of Hamlet's enduring cultural prominence is his free-standing autonomy. Existing independently of the play in which he appears, he glides freely into other texts, both fictional and theoretical. Nor does he stop there. In numerous allusions and accounts, he leaves his fictionalized textual provenance altogether to appear in the ranks of historical personages. Like Germany's Luther, France's Descartes, Italy's Machiavelli, and England's Bacon or Hobbes, he is accorded epochal status for inaugurating a distinctly modern consciousness.

As we shall see, Hamlet's disengagement from the land-driven plot is the very precondition of the modernity ascribed to him after 1800. Adrift from the plot, he assumes the self-determining autonomy that opens him to later projections. Yet as Chapter 1, "Modern Hamlet," demonstrates, during the first century of its production the play was deemed old-fashioned and even barbaric. Only after the turn of the eighteenth century did the play take on its modern cast, and in response to a radical critical maneuver: the main character was abstracted from the exigencies of the plot.

Chapter 2, "'Old mole': the modern *telos* and the return to dust," shows how the onset of the modern epoch was itself imagined as a disembedding or deracination. In the grand periodizing narratives of both Hegel and Marx, the affinity between persons and land must be dissolved before history can break into the modern period. For ideational Hegel, the release occurs when the Reformation severs faith from the Holy Land. For materialist Marx, it happens when Primitive Accumulation evicts peasants from the soil.

The next three chapters demonstrate how the play counteracts such narratives by affirming the attachment their historical programs would dissolve. Indeed, the temporal schema of the play will not allow for its dissolution. Chapter 3, "Empires of World History," shows how the play situates the fall of Denmark within both an imperial history of territorial transfer (ancient and modern) and Britain's own history of conquest in the eleventh century by both Danes and Normans. Chapter 4, "Generation and Degeneracy," focuses on the generational interval that organizes the devolution of estate in family history or genealogy. Chapter 5, "Doomsday and Domain," demonstrates how the lay of the land is fixed or altered in anticipation of the world's end, the consummation of salvational history.

The final Chapter 6, "Hamlet's Delay," circles back to the auroral breakthrough of 1800 when criticism fixed on a duration more personal than those marked by empire, genealogy, and eschatology: the time it takes Hamlet to act. The question of his delay has driven critical inquiry deep into Hamlet's psyche where it has discovered an inexhaustible hermeneutic resource from which some of the most brilliant readings in the entire critical tradition have been fashioned. And yet irregularities – of speech, behavior, comportment – which modern readings take as symptoms of psychic disorder were once the signature stunts and riffs of the Clown, madman, Vice, and devil: all stock figures of privation and therefore suitable role models for the dispossessed prince.

Hamlet without Hamlet makes a sweeping claim: a 200-year-old critical tradition has been built on an oversight (and of the play's premise, no less). It supports that claim by illustrating what happens when what has been overlooked is brought back into view. This is not, it must be said, the same as retrieving *Hamlet* as intended by Shakespeare or as experienced by its first readers and audiences. (Unmodernizing the play is not the same as restoring its original meaning.) For the project is not to identify what the play was in 1600 but rather what it could not possibly be after 1800 and as long as Hamlet's interiority was taken as the vortical subject of the play. In the process, Hamlet will not lose his centrality or his complexity, but they will be a function not of his intransitive and unfathomable depth but of his worldliness as dramatized by the play's dialogue and action. What he will lose is the monadic exclusivity that alienates him from the play. "What goes on inside" Hamlet, of course, will always be a challenge in a play in which even his monosyllabic disclaimer "I know not 'seems'" (1.2.76) is fraught with ambiguity. But whether the category of the psychological will remain the best hermeneutic for meeting the challenge depends on whether it can survive the demystification. If there is any test for such a radical reconfiguring of the play, it can only be in the details of its readings. When newly contextualized, words, passages, even props passed over by the editorial and critical tradition should take on new life.

Thus in the graveyard scene amidst so much commentary on tracts of land, from graves to empires, it has not been noted that a *hide* denotes a measure of land as well as the skin of a man ("a tanner's hide") or of a beast (parchment of sheep or calves), or that *Doomsday* conjoins *domain* and *doom*, land and judgment, a pairing that twice recurs when *land* and *law* appear as textual alternatives. As might be expected, references to heraldry, the system that encodes dynastic identity, have been under-glossed. They multiply in the avenger Pyrrhus who blazes forth like a coat-of-arms, in Laertes' call for an heraldic panel to reinstate his father's honor after his disgraceful burial, and in the armigerous boast of the grave-maker. The play's allusions to mythical and biblical women – Niobe, Hecuba, Jepthah's daughter – all pertain to the cutting off of progeny or lineage. In the Mousetrap play, the prop of *a bank of flowers* gives material form to the dynastic fantasy of a flourishing and fruitful estate; its dark double is the lethal "wharf" from which a *mountebank* has gathered the toxic weeds for the poison that wipes out the entire dynastic line. Aslant a similar bank grows the downcast willow that Ophelia drapes with weeds, in grotesque parody of the abundantly fruitful genealogical oak. Appropriately it is this play which coins a toponym, *groundlings*, for those who pay ground rent to the theater for a place to stand. Other names similarly encode relations to land: of ownership, of labor, of vagrancy.

In a play that has generated more commentary than any other, it is surprising to find any textual strains that have eluded editorial and critical scrutiny. Yet even this small sampling suggests a certain bias. Amidst so many instances of the close kinship between human and humus, man and manor, titles and entitlement, *dominus* and *domus*, even the protagonist's name begins to resonate. *Hamme*, as the earliest dictionaries establish, derives from the Germanic word for home. A hamlet is a cluster of homes: a kingdom in miniature.

CHAPTER I

Modern Hamlet

No work in the English canon has been so closely identified with the beginning of the modern age as *Hamlet*. The basis of the identification is so obvious now that it hardly needs to be stated. By speaking his thoughts in soliloquy, by reflecting on his own penchant for thought, by giving others cause to worry about what he is thinking, Hamlet draws attention to what is putatively going on inside him. In recognition of his psychological depth and complexity, Hamlet has been hailed as the inaugural figure of the modern period: "the Western hero of consciousness," "[a]n icon of pure consciousness," "a distinctly modern hero," providing "the premier Western performance of consciousness."[1]

Yet early allusions to *Hamlet* suggest that in its own time the play was considered behind the times rather than ahead of them. To begin with, Shakespeare's *Hamlet* was a recycling of an earlier play. Even the supposed original or *Ur-Hamlet* was remembered not for its novelty but for its tired formulas and stock devices.[2] A remark from 1589 satirizes the play for its dependence on the ancient Senecan elements of murder, madness, and revenge, and for its studied diction fraught with commonplaces ("good sentences") and set-pieces ("handfuls . . . of tragical speeches").[3] Another reference, from 1596, indicates that the play was already so familiar that the Ghost's injunction – "Hamlet, revenge!" – registered as a byword.[4]

These responses to the *Ur-Hamlet* might just as well have greeted Shakespeare's *Hamlet* when it was first staged several years later. Like its predecessor, it was set in the remote times of Nordic saga. It, too, depended on the Senecan formula of murder, madness, and revenge. It, too, was made up of old-fashioned stage conventions (the dumb show and the play-within-the-play), stiff set-pieces (like the Player's speech), and a grab-bag of *sententiae* (for example: "all that lives must die," 1.2.72, "to thine own self be true," 1.3.78, "There's a divinity that shapes our ends," 5.2.10).[5] And, of course, it retained the most archaic feature of all – a ghost returning from an old-faith

Purgatory, enjoining the retaliative ("an eye for an eye") revenge of the
Old Testament. Shakespeare's *Hamlet*, it might then be said, was old on
arrival. Its sententious rhetoric and venerable topoi may explain why,
according to Gabriel Harvey's marginal note, the play particularly
appealed to "the wiser sort."[6] In all events, as the majority of the
allusions from the seventeenth century indicate, it was the hoary old
Ghost rather than the bright young Hamlet who stole the show.[7]

In 1604 one author, Anthony Scoloker, did credit the play's popularity
to the prince and wished a like fortune on his own work, "Faith it should
please all, like Prince Hamlet."[8] Yet the pleasure Hamlet gave derived not
from what he had with*in* ("that within which passes show," 1.2.85) but
from what he had put *on*: his "antic disposition" (1.5.180). Concluding
that such popularity would cost him his sanity, Scoloker reconsiders: if to
"please all" is to be "moone-sicke" and "runne madde," perhaps it would
be better to have "displeased all." Several allusions suggest that Hamlet's
lunatic racing – the physical counterpart to his "wild and whirling words"
(1.5.139) – might well have been what pleased all. In two separate works,
Dekker alludes to entrances by Hamlet in distracted motion: "break[ing]
loose like a Beare from the stake" and "rush[ing] in by violence."[9] In
Chapman, Jonson, and Marston's *Eastward Ho*, a madcap character named
Hamlet makes a similarly disruptive entrance: "Enter Hamlet, a footman,
in haste," reads the stage direction, and as an attendant's response indicates,
his haste is quite frantic, "'Sfoot, Hamlet; are you mad? Whither run you
now . . . ?"[10]

These spoofs were no doubt inspired by Shakespeare's play which
explicitly calls for excited or violent motion from Hamlet. For example,
he tears himself away from the clutches of Horatio and the guards in order
to follow the Ghost; "By heaven, I'll make a ghost of him that lets me,"
he threatens (1.4.85). So, too, he zigzags maniacally about the stage in
response to the Ghost's intonations from beneath the floorboards
(1.5.156–71). He also holds Rosencrantz and Guildenstern in chase when
they come to fetch him for England; "Hide fox, and all after" (F 4.2.30), he
taunts, as he darts wildly off stage.[11] Hamlet's outrageous behavior at Ophelia's graveside might also be included in this zany repertoire, especially his
salient leap into her grave, the only detail from the play remembered in
the anonymous elegy (1618) to Richard Burbage, the first actor to play the
role.[12] In the early decades of its performance, Hamlet's signature action
may have been not paralyzing thought but frenzied motion. Like his
dancing a jig and playing on a pipe after the success of the Mousetrap
play (3.2.265ff.), his hyperactivity would have linked him more with the

roustabout clown of medieval folk tradition than with the introspective consciousness acclaimed by the modern period.[13]

Hamlet appeared old for different reasons after 1660 when Charles II upon returning from exile in France reopened the commercial theaters – after a hiatus of almost twenty years – with the formation of two theatrical companies. When the stock of extant English plays was divided between them, the plays of Shakespeare, consisting of "antiquated manners, morals, language and wit," were considered more old-fashioned than those of Jonson, Beaumont and Fletcher, and Shirley. John Evelyn after seeing a performance in 1661 jotted in his diary that he found *Hamlet* tediously outmoded: "the old playe began to disgust this refined age."[14] In the "refined age" of the Restoration, *Hamlet*, like all Elizabethan and Jacobean plays, belonged to the cruder previous period or "last age" before the great interregnal divide separating Charles I from Charles II.[15] English letters during this period were deemed backward or even barbarous, as Samuel Johnson noted: "The *English* nation, in the time of *Shakespeare*, was yet struggling to emerge from barbarity."[16] Shakespeare, according to David Hume, was the product of such benighted times: "born in a rude age, and educated in the lowest manner, without any instruction, either from the world or books."[17] The basis of the later period's contempt for the earlier was clear. Before the Interregnum, the English stage had largely lacked or ignored the civilizing canons of Aristotle, Horace, and their sixteenth-century Italian and seventeenth-century French redactors. The playhouses were imagined to have followed their own rustic native traditions, those of the medieval artisanal guilds, the "Carpenters, Cobblers and illiterate fellows," who had performed the early mysteries and miracle plays.[18] Written without the benefit of classical models, these earlier dramatic efforts were considered *gothic*: in the manner of the Goths, the barbarian hordes who had destroyed the Roman Empire. A minority insisted that Shakespeare was perfectly capable of having written *Hamlet* in the classical style; it was his regrettable desire to satisfy vulgar taste that drove him back to the "old Gothic manner."[19] Pope concluded the Preface to his edition of Shakespeare by comparing Shakespeare's works to "an ancient, majestick piece of *Gothick* Architecture" in contrast to "a neat Modern building" based on classical models, like Wren's St. Paul's Cathedral.[20]

Thus *Hamlet*, timeworn on arrival, was regarded after the Restoration and well into the eighteenth century as *antiquated, old, barbarous,* and *gothic*. So when did the play, or rather the main character of the play, acquire this historically precocious modernity?

In what may be our earliest reference to Shakespeare's *Hamlet*, the play is classified as "modern." In a marginal note made sometime after 1598, Gabriel Harvey discusses the best works in English, "auncient & moderne": Chaucer and Lidgate represent the ancient, while *Hamlet* along with other works by Shakespeare and his contemporaries make up the modern.[21] In this earlier and still current sense of the word, *Hamlet* was "modern" at its inception.[22] Our frequent use of "modern" to designate a period concept with defining features tends to obscure the term's original main usage. The word's primary function was deictic: its signification, like that of "today," "now," "at present," "within recent memory," depended on the time of its enunciation. In 1555 Mary was the "queen moderne," but only until succeeded by Elizabeth in 1558.[23]

In this sense, Shakespeare like all his contemporaries was once modern, at least temporarily. From the other side of the epochal watershed of the Interregnum, however, Shakespeare showed signs of age. In catalogues of English authors after the Restoration, he was considered "our old Dramatick Poet," in contrast to such dramatists as Dryden, Congreve, and Rowe.[24] By the early 1700s, quartos printed in Shakespeare's time were thought *"ancient"* and in need of restoration by *"modern"* editions like those of Pope and Theobald. Indeed Shakespeare's earliest claim to the rank of *classic* came with the recognition that his works, like those of Homer or Horace, had decayed with time. Rife with obsolete vocabulary, forgotten allusions, unfamiliar diction, and errors of transmission, their state "resembled that of a corrupt *Classic*."[25]

In another sense, however, Shakespeare's status as modern was more stable. Throughout the eighteenth century and beyond, whenever the age-old rivalry between ancient and modern authors cropped up, Shakespeare was chosen to represent the moderns. In a 1699 treatise, *The Antient and Modern Stages Survey'd*, Sophocles is set against Shakespeare, "the Proto-Dramatist of England."[26] In this sense, however, any contemporary might have qualified as modern as long as he or she wrote in the vernacular: in a modern language rather than Hebrew, Greek, or Latin. But Shakespeare's particular claim to being modern resided in his ostensible independence from the ancients. As the front matter to the 1623 Folio edition of his plays emphasized, his literary achievement was to be credited to nature not art, to his native gifts rather than his acquired learning.[27] Ben Jonson's pronouncement that Shakespeare had "small Latin and less Greek" underscored his rival's casual relation to the ancients. Shakespeare's reputation for "rudeness" extended to the Continent; English theatre was said to receive "From all their neighbors, the reproach of barbarism," especially from France where Voltaire notoriously panned *Hamlet* as "grossière et barbare," the work of a drunken savage.[28] In the neo-classical climate of the Augustan age, critics were mystified by his neglect of the Greek dramatists, "How comes it then that we hear nothing from him of the *Oedipus*, the *Electra*, the *Antigone* of *Sophocles*, of the *Iphigenia's* [sic], the *Orestes*, the *Medea*, the *Hecuba* of *Euripides*?"[29] Even when he drew on ancient topoi, as in the Player's recitation from "Aeneas's tale to Dido" (2.2.443–4), Shakespeare was blamed for having turned to accounts "daub'd and bungled by one of his Countrymen" rather than to their Virgilian source.[30] Without the guidance of the ancient languages, canons, and models, his writing was routinely termed *irregular, unruly, extravagant,* and *wild.* It thereby provided the perfect material for the emergent art of criticism whose business was, after all, to cultivate taste by being *critical.* "The great contention of criticism is to find the faults of the moderns, and the beauties of the ancients."[31] His works were compared to a garden in need of weeding, a mine in which gold had to be sifted from dirt.

Shakespeare's plots especially were thought to have suffered from his neglect of the ancients.[32] That his characters were often found to be superior did not altogether offset the criticism, for, as neo-classically minded critics frequently repeated, Aristotle had stressed the primacy of plot: "plot is the origin and as it were the soul of tragedy, and the characters are secondary."[33] Shakespeare's plots, derived from the wrong sources – from what Pope described as "the common *Old Stories* or *Vulgar Traditions*" of the crude earlier age[34] – hopelessly violated the neo-classical dramatic unities of action, time, and place. In this context, the discovery of an ancient analogue for one of his plots was quite a breakthrough. In the first eighteenth-century edition of Shakespeare (1709), Nicholas Rowe announced, "*Hamlet* is founded upon much the same Tale with the *Electra* of Sophocles."[35] In both plays, he explains, a son must avenge his father's death upon the murderer who has married his mother. But it is not the similarity of plots that impresses Rowe so much as the superiority of Shakespeare's characterization of the protagonist: unlike Orestes, Hamlet refrained from killing his own mother, thereby demonstrating Shakespeare's greater respect for "the rules of manner proper to Persons." In this one instance, at least in respect to character, Shakespeare proved more decorous than his ancient predecessors.

Critics continued to debate the relative merits of *Electra* and *Hamlet* throughout the eighteenth century, holding both up to the Horatian standard of decorum (or its anglicized cognate, "decency"). Indeed their comments on the analogy constitute a kind of small-scale replay of the grand debate between the ancients and the moderns in late-seventeenth-century France.[36] Both sides had their supporters. Charles Gildon denied the superiority of Shakespeare's play (with its "abundance of Errors" of both character and plot), and defended Sophocles against the charge of "barbarity" by pointing out that matricide was a requirement of the legend and not the dramatist's invention.[37] George Stubbes, on the other hand, faulted Sophocles for overstepping the bounds of tragic horror ("there is something too shocking in a mother's being put to Death by her Son, although she be never so guilty"), but commended Shakespeare for his "great Delicacy" in having the Ghost caution Hamlet to spare his mother.[38] As with the French *Querelle*, the debate leads toward the recognition that the same standard cannot be applied to works so disparate in time.[39] How can a modern work be held up to ancient standards of unity, decorum, and genre? For defenders of the modern, the critical task shifts: it is not so much a matter of determining superiority as of defining difference. In the ongoing debate over the Orestes/Hamlet parallel, alternative criteria for modern drama begin to emerge. The ascendant criterion of emotive appeal clearly tips the critical scale in Hamlet's direction when Henry Mackenzie weighs in on the contest. While Orestes is a mere instrument of plot, Hamlet is a character – indeed a person in his own right – and readers and spectators respond accordingly, with affection.

> The *Orestes* of the Greek . . . interests us for the accomplishment of his purpose; but of him we think only as the instrument of that justice which we wish to overtake the murderers of Agamemnon . . . but when *Horatio* exclaims on the death of his friend, "Now crack'd [sic] a noble heart" we forget the murder of the King, the villainy of *Claudius*, the guilt of *Gertrude*; our recollection dwells only on the memory of that "sweet prince".[40]

That the plot is overshadowed by Hamlet's affective appeal is also noted by two of Mackenzie's contemporaries. William Richardson dismisses Shakespeare's plot as of "slight importance" and insists that our involvement with the play "exclusively spring[s] from our attachment to the person of Hamlet."[41] Thomas Robertson imagines that in writing the play Shakespeare became so absorbed by the character that he left "Hamlet, in his sole person, predominating over, and almost eclipsing the whole action of the drama."[42]

By the time of Coleridge's lectures in 1811, there is no need for Robertson's qualifying "almost": Hamlet *does* eclipse the plot. Coleridge imagined Shakespeare heaping one provocation upon another in order to dramatize his protagonist's utter indifference to them:

Shakespeare places him in the most stimulating circumstances that a human being can be placed in: he is the heir apparent of the throne: his father dies suspiciously: his mother excludes him from the throne by marrying his uncle. This was not enough but the Ghost of the murdered father is introduced to assure the son that he was put to death by his own brother. [What is the effect upon the son? – instant action and pursuit of revenge? No: endless reasoning and hesitating.][43]

Instead of being crushed by such a series of blows, the protagonist remains unmoved. Hermetically sealed-off by his "excessive thought" or "ratiocinative meditativeness," Hamlet is plot-resistant.[44] So, too, is Coleridge's criticism of *Hamlet*. Plot is hardly mentioned in his scattered but numerous comments on the play. And why should it be? What happens in the play has no bearing on Hamlet's character. His penchant for thought predates the play's action. Indeed, for Coleridge, it is congenital, having issued from the "germ" of his character. Programmed by that inborn germ to do what he does (or does not), he is entirely self-determining. What need for a plot "among such as have a world within themselves" (1:386)?

Coleridge does consider plot, however, when defining the difference between ancient and modern drama. His interest focuses on the problem of the dramatic unities, "the iron compulsion of space and time" (1:350). According to him, ancient drama had to submit to their regulation in order to avoid intolerable contradiction. The Chorus' consistent presence on stage required that time and space be fixed; if the plot required their fluctuation, the audience would experience "too great an Extravagation from nature" (1:226). Once the Chorus was eliminated, however, temporal and spatial shifts could be indicated by the clearing of the stage (or the dropping of a curtain). Scene divisions dispelled the need for continuity, thereby releasing performance from the "bondage of time and space" and consigning it to "the arbitrary control" of the imagination (1:467). In this respect, Coleridge maintained, "The advantage is indeed vastly on the side of the modern" (1:350). For the unities had been a concession to the senses, "the meanest part of our nature"; they were instated because of the senses' inability to reconcile physical presence with abstract leaps in time and space (1:467). Shakespeare, however, had understood what Coleridge had recently learned from Kant's *Critique of Pure Reason*, that the imagination organizes perception of time and space in accordance with its own *a priori* categories.

For Coleridge, Shakespeare's indifference to the unities represented such a radical departure from the ancients that it called for a new generic classification: "[W]e must emancipate ourselves of a false association from

misapplied names – & find a new word for the Plays of Shakespear – they
are in the ancient sense neither Tragedies nor Comedies, nor both in one –
but a different genus, diverse in kind not merely different in Degree"
(1:466). And he does find a new word for the new genus, "I have named
the true genuine 'modern' Poetry the 'romantic'" (1:467). His use of
"romantic" is not to be confused with "romanticism", the period concept
(or intellectual movement) for which he himself would become a defining
figure. The "romantic" he applies to Shakespeare reverts back to the middle
ages. It invokes the time between the fall of Rome and the humanistic
revival of its culture. Yet for Coleridge, this interval is not the dark and
fallow interval of the later Burckhardtian scheme, but rather a period in
which cultural forms are free to develop without subscribing to ancient
strictures. With Roman influence at its weakest after the Nordic invasion,
new cultural forms began to arise with only vestigial relations to their
decadent antecedents. The vernacular Romant tongue resulted when the
"decomposed Latin became amalgamated . . . with the Gothic or Celtic"
(1:481); distinctive *romance* forms soon emerged, like the chansons and
fabliaux (1:519). In the aftermath of Rome's decline, both the Romant
language and romance forms developed organically, from within, unfet-
tered by mechanical rules. The etymology of the new term conferred a new
prestige on Shakespeare's drama by assigning it a history. As the neo-
classical could trace its mechanical heritage back to antiquity, so the
romantic could derive its organic origins from medievalism. Like Dryden,
he supported the distinction with an architectural analogy: as the Pantheon
was to Westminster Abbey so Sophocles was to Shakespeare (1:517).

The new nomenclature was no doubt intended to release Shakespeare
from the ancient/modern dyad in which "modern" signified only as
antithesis to "ancient". When applied to Shakespeare, "modern" had come
to denote the absence of ancient principles of order, decorum, and unity.
According to Coleridge, Shakespeare's reputation suffered from the bias:
not only was it the basis of a "national Prejudice" (1:494), but "whole
Nations have combined in unhesitating condemnation of our great Dramatist, as a sort of African Nature" (1:495). The new term for Shakespeare's
plays – "romantic Dramas, or dramatic Romances" (1:466) – designated an
absolute rather than a relational status. No less than the "ancient", the
"romantic" or Shakespearean drama possessed its own "very essence":

[B]ut once more let me repeat what can never be too often reflected on by all who
would intelligently study the works either of the Athenian Dramatists or of
Shakespere: that the very essence of the former consists in the sternest separation
of the diverse in kind [and disparate in degree, whilst the latter delights in

indissoluble combinations; all opposites, nature and art, poetry and prose, seriousness and jest, recollection and anticipation, spirituality and sensuality, the earthly and the heavenly, life and death, are blended together intimately with each other] (1:467).[45]

While Schlegel famously paired "romantic" with classical, Coleridge preferred to use the new term without its counterpart as if to preserve its incomparable autonomy.

The need to differentiate Shakespeare from the ancients drove Coleridge to inaugurate another term, again in relation to the dramatic unities, but this time focusing on the Horatian unity of character. In his *Treatise on Method*, to support his thesis that poetry no less than science is methodical, Coleridge offers the example of Shakespeare, the poet who had long been judged "eminently *immethodical*."[46] The problem was not that Shakespeare had no method but that his method had not yet been identified. Coleridge labels it *psychological*, an unfamiliar word to his readership, as is revealed by his apologetic footnote: "We beg pardon for the use of this *insolens verbum*: but it is one of which our language stands in great need. We have no single term to express the Philosophy of the Human Mind."[47] While the first use of *psychological* recorded by the *OED* is from 1812, Coleridge had been using the term in his lectures since 1800 to refer to Shakespeare's singular insight into character: his power to discern "the habits of the mind." He applauds his "psychologic portraiture" (1:126), "psycological" or "psychological" genius (1:306, II:490), and "psychological . . . mode of reasoning" (1:253).[48] Coleridge's own commitment to the same method is evident in his rationale for discussing Shakespeare's works in "psychological" rather than "historical" or chronological order. Ignoring recent attempts to determine when they were written on the basis of material evidence – title-pages, external references, topical allusions – he pursues them instead "as they seemed naturally to flow from the progress & order of [Shakespeare's] mind" (1:253).

As might be expected, among dramatic characters the *psychological* method is "peculiarly characteristic of Hamlet's mind."[49] As example, Coleridge in his *Treatise on Method* quotes a long passage from Act 5 in which Hamlet narrates to Horatio his adventures at sea, reporting how aboard ship he discovered the King's commission ordering his execution and replaced it with a forged commission commanding instead the execution of its two bearers.[50] The account is exemplary because Hamlet, rather than relating events in the accidental order in which his senses perceived them, organizes them by relations of "mental contiguity and succession."[51] It thereby represents both functions of the mind: its passive receiving of impressions and its active reflection upon them. In the reproduction of Hamlet's 45-line report, these two functions are indicated typographically. The lines recording the mind's passive registering of outward circumstances and events are in roman, while those giving voice to the mind's "internal activity" or reflection are in italics. Hamlet's account of the sea episode thus illustrates the ideal psychological "balance between the passive impression received from outward things, and the internal activity of the mind in reflecting and generalizing."

But the balance is not quite ideal. Hamlet's omission of an important detail about the forged commission suggests too casual a response to the outside world. He must be prompted to provide it by a direct question from Horatio: "How was this seal'd?" (5.2.47).[52] As Coleridge explains, the mind's reflective capacity can be overbearing, "the prerogative of the mind is stretched into despotism." Under its peremptory sway, discourse can degenerate into "the wayward or fantastical,"[53] as when in the grave-yard Hamlet dwells upon the decomposition of emperors to spongy loam. Hamlet's antic outbursts are attributed to the same imbalance. As Coleridge maintains elsewhere, his "wild and whirling words" after encountering the Ghost are not a rehearsal of the antic role he is about to assume, but a "temporary mania" (II:541–2), the side-effect of meditation taken to extremes. The antic role is only partly pretended: "Hamlet's Wildness is but *half-false* – O that subtle trick to pretend to be *acting* when we are very near *being* what we act" (II:541). The antics that were in 1600 a throwback to popular stage traditions are in 1800 instantiations of recent "mental philosophy." Old theatrical stunts are taken for newly identified psychological symptoms of a mind diseased by "surplus meditation."

Unlike "romantic," Coleridge's "psychological" connected Shakespeare not to the bygone time of the Provençal troubadours but to the very contemporary present of German idealist philosophy, particularly that of Kant. As Coleridge allowed, it was *Hamlet* which drove him to "philosophical criticism";[54] only after reading Kant's account of the primacy of mind in the *Critique of Pure Reason* did he recognize "Shakespeare's deep and accurate science in mental philosophy" – what he termed his "psychological genius." Coleridge's own familiarity with that philosophy explains why his understanding of Shakespeare's psychological method surpassed that of previous English editors and critics. It explains why it trailed upon Schlegel's. Being German, Schlegel had the advantage of a native language "incomparable in its metaphysical and psychological force" (I:291) and a tradition "driven into speculation: all the feelings have been forced back into the thinking and reasoning mind" (1:354). The English, by contrast, "a busy commercial people," had become "a mighty empire, one of the great nations of the world" (II.515).

As *Hamlet* criticism turns to German speculative philosophy, so German speculative philosophy turns to *Hamlet*. In Hegel's *Aesthetics*, all of the arts follow the progress of World History toward the freedom of absolute consciousness, from East to West, from symbolic art (India, Persia, Egypt), to classical (Greece), and ending with romantic (Europe). The last of the arts to be discussed in this progression is poetry, the most developed of all the genres.[55] Recognizing no drama in the symbolic stage,[56] Hegel focuses his discussion of drama on its development from classical to romantic and addresses some of the familiar topics of the ancient/modern debates, including the old parallel between *Hamlet* and *Electra*. *Hamlet* is "rooted in a collision similar to that treated by . . . Sophocles in the *Electra*" (II:1225). The nature of that collision points to a key difference between the two dramas. For ancient Orestes, the collision is ethical: his mother's complicity in his father's slaughter requires that he either kill his mother or neglect to avenge his father. For modern Hamlet, however, his mother's innocence eliminates the ethical conflict, "Therefore the collision turns strictly here not on a son's pursuing an ethically justified revenge and being forced in the process to violate an ethical order, but on Hamlet's personal character" (II:1225–6). The arena of the conflict has shifted, from outside Orestes in the impersonal realm of ethics, to the inner life of Hamlet. If "[t]he true content of romantic art is absolute inwardness" (1:519), Hamlet is perfectly representative, "His beautiful heart is indrawn" (1:231). Classical characters possessed no such inner life. The vacuity in the eyes of Greek sculpture shares the same defect: "the light of the eye" is absent; "their inner being does not look out of them as self-knowing inwardness" (1:520–1). In the ancient drama, this same absence is evident in the tight identification of characters with their intentions and actions: "they . . . *are* what they will and accomplish" (II:1214). In modern drama, however, a gap separates a character from his intentions and actions: "[H]e may swither irresolutely from this to that and let caprice decide. From this swithering the Greek plastic figures are exempt; for them the bond between the subject and what he wills as his object remains indissoluble" (II:1214). The separation between intention/ knowledge and action in the modern character opens up a space for "the swithering of reflection" (II:1228). It is here, of course, that Hamlet serves as representative; his "beautiful inwardness" pulls him away from compromising externals. And yet, because he fails to make contact with "the external march and turn of events" (I:217), he remains "sunk into himself" (I:584). Incidents in the plot relate to him only as contingency and accident in a series of setbacks rather than dialectical advances. External events continue to withstand him as he is "bandied from pillar to post" (II:1226). "[H]e persists in the inactivity of a beautiful inner soul which cannot make itself actual or engage in the relationships of his present world" (I:584).

Because forever withdrawn into himself, Hamlet fails to develop through external encounters and falls short of the independence and freedom toward which consciousness strives in the modern phase of Hegel's World History. In this respect, it is helpful to compare him to another Wittenbergian: Martin Luther, the great epochal figure of Hegel's *The Philosophy of History* who ushers in the modern period by turning faith inward. Hamlet's "inwardness" is the dramatic counterpart to the historical Luther's "introversion of the soul upon itself." Yet Luther's inner state was "actualized" through nothing less than the historical movement of the Reformation. Hamlet, however, could not get beyond his "beautiful inwardness," perhaps born too soon to benefit from the philosophical advances of Descartes, Spinoza, Kant, and, of course, Hegel himself. But his inner struggle, though it comes short of reconciling itself with the outward world, still marks an advance in the Hegelian history of consciousness. However haltingly, Hamlet is headed in the right direction of an indefinitely progressing future.[57]

It is now that *Hamlet* or rather Hamlet (and it is easy to see how the former has been subsumed by the latter) might be called "modern" in its present sense: that is, in possession of interiority or subjectivity, whether imagined in terms of Coleridge's psychology or Hegel's consciousness. Accounts of the play's reception have assumed that an interiorized Hamlet had been in the wings for two centuries, waiting to be discovered, postponing his debut until around 1800 when the right audience came along. Yet when situated in the context of the effort to distinguish the modern from the ancient, the emergence of his interiority seems less a critical discovery than a final solution to the problem of how to clear a critical space for Shakespeare. For two centuries, Shakespeare's dramas had been deemed *unruly* and *wild* by the biases of the ancients. While the category of the "romantic" allowed for an alternative genealogy, it is that of the *psychological* which lifted Shakespeare out of the dramatic contest with the ancients altogether, and primarily through the character of Hamlet. The focus of the play moved inward, and expressed itself not by the action primary to ancient drama, but by the withdrawal from action into the depths and interstices of character. With the tie to the past dissolved, Hamlet was newly opened to the future. Accompanying his subjectivity is what we might term a "futurity effect," a proleptic predisposition to times to come. Freed from the determinants of plot, Hamlet is available to every advancing construal of what goes on inside.

Once perceived as psychological, Hamlet begins to look contemporary, with a slightly futuristic tilt. Hazlitt marvels that Shakespeare could have taken Saxo's remote Amleth, "who lived . . . five hundred years before we were born," and converted him into such a familiar character that "we seem to know [his thoughts] as well as we do our own." He ascribes to the play "a prophetic truth, which is above that of history," emanating from Shakespeare's "prophetic soul," which could foresee as in a crystal ball Hazlitt's own present, "It is we who are Hamlet."[58] German critics similarly hail Hamlet as epoch-making, providing a "mirror of our present state as if this work had been first written in our own day."[59] For Emerson, the entire nineteenth-century's "speculative genius is a sort of living Hamlet," whose "mind is the horizon beyond which, at present, we do not see."[60] At the turn of the nineteenth century Georg Brandes notes that Hamlet will always be at the vanishing point of our perception: "Hamlet in virtue of his creator's marvelous power of rising above his time . . . has a range of significance which we, on the threshold of the twentieth century, can foresee no limit."[61] And Bradley in 1904 takes stock of Hamlet's enduring futurity, noting that Hamlet only began to be visible with the dawn of romanticism: "[I]t was only when the slowly rising sun of Romance began to flush the sky that the wonder, beauty and pathos of this most marvelous of Shakespeare's creations began to be visible!"[62] It was during "the great ideal movement which began toward the close of the eighteenth century" (126) that it was possible to start understanding Hamlet from "the psychological point of view" (125) and, a century later, Bradley reaches out to what at the beginning of the twentieth century was a new area of inquiry, *pathology*; to those who would learn more about Hamlet's "pathological condition" (125), he recommends recent work on "mental diseases" (120). That such a modern science should be applicable to a character created three centuries earlier is evidence of Hamlet's anachronistic futurity: "so far from being a characteristic product of the time, [he] was a vision of 'the prophetic soul / Of the wide world dreaming on things to come'" (95).

For Freud, Bradley's near contemporary, Hamlet opened up even greater vistas. His importance to Freud's discovery of the Oedipus complex is well known. What has not been noted, however, is the degree to which his discovery emerged from a newly configured version of the ancient/modern context. Oedipus had certainly appeared in this context before; Hegel, for example, turns to Oedipus to illustrate his theory of the inseparability of ancient characters from their actions. Oedipus cannot be judged independently of his crime: whether he intended it or not, whether he knew of it or not, he is still responsible for his parricidal and incestuous deeds. But in Germany, as in England, it had been Orestes not Oedipus who was repeatedly contrasted to Hamlet. Hegel undoubtedly knew Herder's reference to Hamlet as the "thoughtful Orestes" as well as Schlegel's use of the contrast in his discussion of the classical and romantic opposition.[63] The substitution of Oedipus for Orestes made for an unlikely comparison. Until Freud hypothesized that all men desired to sleep with their mothers and kill their fathers, what did Oedipus and Hamlet have in common? The parallel depended on the postulation of a new region of character. And Freud here does Hegel one better: what differentiates the ancient from the modern is not just inwardness but sub-inwardness. The place of conflict drops down a level, from consciousness to the unconscious.

Freud's analysis is accompanied by the same sense of the play's proleptic powers. As he records in his "Autobiographical Study," "*Hamlet* . . . had been admired for three hundred years without its meaning being dis-covered or its author's motives guessed."[64] And as his disciple Ernest Jones reiterates, "Shakespeare's extraordinary powers of observation and pene-tration granted him a degree of insight that it has taken the world three subsequent centuries to reach."[65] Three hundred years would have brought the time up to 1900, the very year in which Freud published his analysis of Hamlet in *The Interpretation of Dreams*. (The book was in fact published in 1899, but Freud postdated the title-page to the more portentous 1900.) The reason Hamlet's meaning could not be known before 1900 was that Freud had not yet discovered the theory of the unconscious: "It was a novelty, and nothing like it had ever before been recognized in mental life."[66] Freud's discovery yielded an entirely new understanding of the division between the two great epochs of human civilization: in the ancient epoch, patricidal and incestuous desires were enacted; in the modern epoch, they were repressed. The shift from enactment to repression marked an advance "in the emotional life of humanity";[67] and Freud's psychoanalysis through transference promised to advance it further still.

Jacques Lacan, another of Freud's disciples, also finds Hamlet ahead of Shakespeare's time, as well as Freud's. What Hamlet reveals is not the symptoms of repressed desire but rather of inexpiable loss; it is a play about mourning, not guilt: "I know of no commentator who has ever taken the trouble to make this remark . . . from one end of *Hamlet* to the other, all anyone talks about is mourning."[68] It is no coincidence that Hamlet's problem is also that of "modern society" (40). The truncated and furtive rites of mourning in the play (the death of King Hamlet without final unction, Polonius' "hugger-mugger" burial, Ophelia's abbreviated service) all gesture toward the present abandonment of the rites and ceremonies by which loss was once compensated. Death, when not repaired by rituals, leaves a gap or "hole in the real" (37) that activates the "scar of castration" (47), the primary oedipal loss of the phallus. The mourner tries in vain to patch the loss with imaginary projections or mirages (signifiers, images, symbols, embodiments), but it can never be made good. It is because Freud never gauged the permanence of the injury that his successor Lacan can boast of having gone "much further than anyone has ever gone by any route" (29).[69]

So, too, does another Freudian disciple, Nicolas Abraham, who sets out to pursue what Freud began by undertaking "a fresh psychoanalysis of the hero."[70] Abraham subjects Hamlet to an analysis that locates guilt not in the son's desires but in the father's crimes. Abraham's treatment requires the appending of a Sixth Act in which the truth is finally extracted from the prevaricating Ghost: old Hamlet overcame old Fortinbras not by chivalric might but with a poisoned sword. What afflicts Hamlet in the dramatic realm of 1600 – "the phantom effect" – brings to light a post-Holocaustal transgenerational neurosis, so that only in its wake can the "secret" be discerned which "spectators and critics alike have, for nearly four hundred years, failed to consider."[71]

As *Hamlet*, in order to be understood, must await Freud's theory of repression, Lacan's language of the Other, and Abraham's "phantom effect," so, too, it must tarry for Derrida's deconstruction. In *Specters of Marx*, Hamlet slips out from the past to indicate a future direction for Marxism after the collapse of communism. Hamlet's hesitation in this convoluted configuration prescribes for the present (defined by its "non-contemporaneity with itself") not a course but a stance: "a waiting without horizon of expectations" for an alternative justice to that of global democratic liberalism.[72] It is a justice that has nothing to do with the retribution of revenge tragedy. If it did, Hamlet would execute it without hesitation, automatically, for the logic of tit for tat requires no deliberation. The incommensurate justice of a future-yet-to-come, however, demands hard calculation.

"Thou art a scholar, speak to it" (1.1.45), says Marcellus to Horatio at the appearance of the Ghost. But Horatio, like all traditional scholars, is too grounded in the language of ontology, the logic of being, to know the language of *hauntology*, the logic of specters. The dilatory scholar at the close of the second millennium has no use for the Latin once used to exorcize ghosts; he needs instead to speak (or better, to *write*) a language that will conjure them up – the language of Derrida's deconstruction that eludes the innumerable binaries (past/present, dead/alive, matter/spirit, and so on) which keep specters securely in place. It is not until almost four centuries later (in 1994) that the right scholar finally does come along, as Derrida wryly intimates: "Marcellus was perhaps anticipating the coming, one day, one night, several centuries later, of another 'scholar.'"[73]

Hamlet remains proleptically in tune with the latest present. Since 1800, he has proven capable of accommodating each new modification of inwardness, including the unconscious and the unconscious that is structured like language. But no new construal of his inwardness can last long. For the modern as a period concept still retains something of the transience of its earlier deictic function. It is only a matter of time before any given modern is superseded. There is now something of a tradition in which critics reach beyond their predecessors with newly available insights and theories into Hamlet's interiority. And yet there is no catching-up. Indeed Richard Halpern's discussion of Hamlet in terms of mechanical failure rather than psychological breakdown prepares him for a brave new world of technological readings to come.[74] Hamlet remains perennially in the critical forefront as new (and newer still) explanations emerge to account for his singular interiority. By definition the "modern" must always look new, up-to-date, or better yet, a bit ahead of its time, and Hamlet – once severed from plot and internally configured – remains open indefinitely to future modernization.[75]

And yet for the first couple of centuries after its publication, *Hamlet* was modern not because of its intimation of things to come, but because of its problematic relation to what had gone before. Inwardness emerges on the literary scene as the defining trait of the modern that ostensibly dissolves its ties to the past and opens it up to the future. At the end of the twentieth century, Hamlet continued to possess this strange futurity, still gesturing beyond its most recent site of reception, so that Terry Eagleton could observe that Hamlet inaugurates, however tentatively, a subjectivity of which we are the "end-products" and "beyond which we can only gropingly feel our way."[76] So, too, at the threshold of the twenty-first, Harold Bloom can continue to value the play for revealing "the internalization of the self" at a time "before anyone else was ready for it," still confident that Hamlet remains at the extreme limit of what we know about interiority: "Hamlet himself is a frontier of consciousness yet to be passed."[77]

CHAPTER 2

"Old mole": the modern telos and the return to dust

> The word "land" includes not only the face of the earth, but everything under it or over it.
>
> Blackstone

At the end of his *History of Philosophy*, Hegel looks to *Hamlet* for a phrase by which to describe his subject: the 2,500-year course of world history, the long, hard, dialectical journey toward absolute consciousness. He finds it not in one of Hamlet's philosophizing soliloquies, as we might expect, but rather in one of his antic wisecracks. As Hamlet enjoins his attendants to take an oath of secrecy, the Ghost of his father from underground intones, "Swear"; Hamlet shifts to another spot and renews the oath; the Ghost follows him below and urges again, "Swear."[1] Hamlet exclaims, "Well said, old mole. Canst work i'th'earth so fast?" (1.5.170). It is this gag which Hegel selects to illustrate the movement of world history:

[I]nwardly opposed to itself, [Spirit] is inwardly working ever forward (as when Hamlet says of the ghost of his father, "Well said, old mole! Canst work i'the ground so fast?") until grown strong in itself it bursts asunder the crust of earth which divided it from the sun . . . so that the earth crumbles away.[2]

Like a mole tunneling its way through earth toward light, the spirit of consciousness advances dialectically at an ever-accelerating pace toward its end of self-realization. At some point in the near future it will break through the crust of the earth dividing it from the enlightening sun and attain at long last its emancipatory end – like an "old mole" emerging from long and dark confinement.

Hegel's quotation from *Hamlet* is followed by a quotation from another literary masterpiece, and one which also figures in *Hamlet*. In the *Aeneid* (1.33), Virgil famously summarizes the hardships Aeneas suffered on the journey that finally led to the founding of Rome: *Tantae molis erat Romanam condere gentem*: "So vast was the effort to found the race of Rome."[3] For Hegel, the labor ends in a different goal: *Tantae molis erat, se ipsam cognoscere mentem*: "All this time was required to produce the philosophy of our day."[4] *The Philosophy of History* describes the arduous struggle on the "long track" of history to establish "the empire of Thought."[5] The tunneling mole and the journeying Aeneas – like the rising sun, the gliding owl, Napoleon charging on horseback – are Hegel's metaphors for the movement of world history, for the long trajectory charted in his *The Philosophy of History* from East to West through the four successive empires he identifies as the Oriental, Greek, Roman, and Modern.

Another great historical narrative uses the same passages from both Virgil and Shakespeare in recounting the founding of a much less aureate realm. Marx in *Capital* describes the three centuries of struggle, bloodshed, exploitation, and oppression that culminated in the emergence of capitalism. This is the period of extended struggle he names after what it accomplished: the primitive accumulation of capital. After recounting this long ("bloody and filthy") process from the fifteenth century up until the eighteenth, Marx concludes, "this is the entire history: *Tantae molis erat.*"[6] Here, as so often, Marx has followed Hegel ("coquetted" with his terminology, 103) by inverting his priorities, and inflecting them with irony. Hegel, as Marx likes to point out, had things precisely upside down in putting "bubble-blowing" philosophical consciousness before the "earthy conditions" of economic production.[7] The modern equivalent of imperial Rome is the empire not of consciousness but of capitalism, and it was attained through the ordeal not of philosophical dialectic but of class struggle. So, too, in quoting *Hamlet*, Marx changes Hegel's ideational mole to a materialist one. When it finally breaks through the crust of the earth, it will be to attain not absolute consciousness but rather the utter overthrow or "inevitable breaking up" of the capitalist system. At this world-shattering event, "Europe will leap from her seat and exultantly exclaim, Well grubbed, old mole!"[8] Marx's substitution of "grubbed" for Shakespeare's "said" inverts Hegel's emphasis on transcendent faith, as well as Jesus' credo after his forty-day fast: "Man shall not live by bread alone, but by every word that proceedeth out of the mouth of God" (Matt. 4:4). It is not longing for spiritual sustenance that the materialist mole would satisfy but hunger for the basics of subsistence. In place of Hegel's speculative philosopher, Engels puts the representative proletarian laborer who in the mid-nineteenth century was quite literally mole-like: the coal-miner who burrowed into the mine-shafts, sometimes on all fours, tossing up slag heaps, fueling the capitalist industry which the working class would one day unite to bring down.[9]

In the grand periodizing narratives of both nineteenth-century thinkers, the mole is featured as the epic hero of world history; like Aeneas, it braves hardship while moving toward a promised future. And in each narrative the mole's activity applies with particular force to the last stretch of that history. The onset of that period is marked in each case by a ground-breaking event of an almost literal kind. The break occurs in Hegel's *The Philosophy of History* when the Reformation turns devotion away from the Holy Land and in Marx's *Capital* when primitive accumulation dissolves economic ties to the land. By locating divinity in the soul rather than in any remains of Christ's earthly existence, Hegel's Luther frees the individual from the mediation of the Church, fastening him instead to inner faith. Marx's wage-earner, no longer accountable to lord or guild, is the owner of his own labor: the worker "could dispose of his own person only after he had ceased to be bound to the soil, and ceased to be the slave or serf of another person" (875). Both breaks release history from an encumbering and restrictive past and set it on an advancing trajectory toward an emancipatory end. And in the process, subjects come closer to attaining the freedom Hegel identifies with self-determination and Marx with self-activity. The land that is left behind represents the restricting hold of the past, the material investments of Catholicism for Hegel, the exploitative work relations of feudalism for Marx.

At the onset of the final section of *The Philosophy of History*, Hegel marks the arrival of the modern age with Luther's Great Schism. It is Luther who conclusively breaks from the medieval past, with the "simple doctrine" that divinity resides inwardly in spirit rather than in any external form (414). While "Christendom had formerly sought [the deity] in an earthly sepulchre of stone," at the time of the Reformation "we find a simple Monk" looking for that deity elsewhere: "in the deeper abyss . . . in the Spirit and the Heart" (414). The Crusades epitomize the misguided desire of the past to locate Christ in the lands and shrines of the East. For Hegel, Christendom's burning concern was "simply and solely the conquest of the Holy Land" (391); "every pious Christian wished to be in possession of such sacred earthly remains" (378). Devotion sought out the actual sites of Christ's passion. It was only by visiting Bethlehem, Gethsemane, Golgotha, and the Holy Sepulchre that the mysteries of Christ's birth, transfiguration, crucifixion, and resurrection could be known. The desire to experience Christ through the land he frequented incited pilgrims as well as Crusaders; they desired to worship the very physical ground Christ had trodden: "veritably to walk unobstructed in the footsteps of the Saviour" (392). As Europe migrated to the Holy Land, so too the

Holy Land made its way to Europe: "Whole shiploads of earth were brought from the Holy Land to Europe."

The Reformation put an end to this earthbound devotion, however, and at the very place where Christ's remains had been thought to lie: "The West bade an eternal farewell to the East at the Holy Sepulchre" (393). This is "the real point of retroversion" (392) where the "revolution" or "rupture" from the past took place. Christendom saw that it could not find its "ultimatum of truth in the grave" (393). As the Psalmist foresaw, the Incarnation did not extend to the grave: "Thou wouldst not suffer thy Holy One to see corruption" (Psalms 16:10). Christ's incarnate body had never been subject to the penalty incurred by Adam's fall of the return to dust. Though interred, he had risen leaving no material traces behind. "*Non est hic*," as the three Marys discovered who sought him in the sepulchre in the earliest dramatization of the Christian liturgy.[10] The Crusades were a "sham" (588); it was futile to seek his presence in the land, however sanctified. Nor was it to be recovered in the Eucharist, that "daub" of matter or piece of "dough" in which Christ was also believed corporeally to reside. At this climacteric point, in turning from contingent earth to limitless soul, Christendom came to understand the boundless capacity of soul or consciousness. There it "gained a comprehension of its own principle of subjective infinite freedom," and it is toward the realization of that principle that modern history has since then continued to advance.

The allegory of the mole's flight from earth applies to the turning-point in Marx's historical narrative as well. As with Hegel, the break occurs in the sixteenth century, and while England is the subject of his narrative, Germany is as much his primary concern as it was Hegel's: "*De te fabula narratur*" (90), he instructs his German readership. It is above all a dissociation of the population from the land which marks the turn from the medieval past to the modern present, from feudalism to capitalism. Here, again, Marx turns Hegel on his metaphysical head by locating the turning-point in a bodily and enforced break rather than in the spiritual and voluntary one of Hegel's Reformation. The Reformation also figures in Marx's account, but it involves not the Church's renunciation of the Holy Land but the state's confiscation of Church lands, "a great part of the soil of England." The dissolution of the monasteries, "the spoliation of the Church's property" is only one part of the "pre-history of capital" (928). "The expropriation of the great mass of the people from the soil" included other forms of deracination as well: "the fraudulent alienation of the state domains, the theft of the common lands, the usurpation of feudal and clan property under conditions of ruthless terrorism, all these things were just so many idyllic methods of primitive accumulation" (895). The landed remained just that, while peasants, retainers, and soldiers were thrust off from the land that formerly yielded them their subsistence and were consigned to a state of "vagabondage." Without any means of production, they became itinerant wage-earners, selling their labor to those with the capital to buy it, and in such numbers that they formed a class unto themselves.

Capitalism, then, begins in the wake of widespread uprooting. Through the dissolution of the monasteries, the disbanding of retainers from the great houses, and the enclosure of common lands for pasture, men are expelled from the land and subject to new forms and degrees of exploitation. It is this removal that suggests to Marx an analogy between primitive accumulation and another "primitive" event. In the Genesis of salvational history, as well as in the "historical genesis" of capitalism (927), an expulsion from land marks the epochal divide: between unfallen aevum and fallen history, between feudalism and capitalism. And in both cases, a violent rupture precipitates the break: original sin exiles man from paradise; primitive accumulation deprives him of his means of subsistence – "primitive accumulation plays approximately the same role in political economy as original sin does in theology" (873). As the expelled Adam, sentenced to labor, exits Eden into the fallen world of history empty-handed and with no destination, so the deracinated worker with no workplace or means of production sets out into the smutty world to earn wages through the labor that is his only resource.

The uprooting of the population is Marx's economic equivalent to Hegel's leave-taking at the sepulchre. It severed the medieval ties that bound men to the soil and released them into the alienated forms of labor on which capitalism depended for its development. And in both cases, the dissolving of the attachment to land is followed by accelerated movement. The mole's velocity ("Canst work i'th'earth so fast?" 1.5.170) is paralleled by both the increased strides ("seven-league boots"[11]) of post-Reformation history (and post-Cartesian philosophy) and the ever-increasing exploitative productivity of capitalism. And the movement is resolutely future-oriented. Hegel's Reformation and Marx's revolution have both abandoned the reiterative force of their prefixes. Both terms, though once designating recursivity, are now taken to delineate irreversible linearity. Hegel's hero Luther saw the Reformation as a reversion back to the period of the pristine Apostolic Church, before the corruptions of new-fangled Catholicism. Hegel, however, identified the Reformation as a "rupture" rather than a return. He terms it a "revolution" not because it turns *back* (re-volvere) but because it turns *in*: "introversion of the soul upon itself." Marx even more deliberately ignored the force of the prefix in *The Eighteenth Brumaire* in insisting that future revolutions must no longer look back to the past for their inspiration. In the sixteenth-century Reformation, Luther had reverted to Paul; in the seventeenth-century English Revolution, Cromwell had gone back to the Hebrew prophets; in the eighteenth-century French Revolution, the new regime had returned to the Roman Republic and Empire. For Marx, the approaching "modern revolution" must tolerate no such regress. It must break radically with the past, effecting what Marx had earlier termed "the forcible overthrow of all existing conditions," the rupture which would make "all turning back impossible."[12] "Let the dead bury their dead" (Matt. 8:22) Marx intones, quoting what may be Christ's most radical precept.[13] The past should be left to look after itself, while the future aims toward something unprecedented – "the revolutionary point of departure."

The old mole's flight from earth nicely encapsulates the dialectical trajectory of world history in the two great movements, roughly contemporaneous, which, in the two grand nineteenth-century narratives, usher in the modern period. Once broken off from medieval Christendom and feudal serfdom, the trajectory is free to head toward the ultimate goal of either ideational absolute consciousness or material classless "self-activity." A radical and irreversible break with the past must occur before the advance into the modern can proceed, and in both cases it takes the form of a dissociation from the land. But why do both narratives draw on the "old mole" in *Hamlet*? Why will not any old mole do? What does the advancing dialectical old mole of Hegel and Marx have to do with the Ghost of Hamlet's father?

As Hegel's comments on *Hamlet* in his *Aesthetics* make clear, his "old mole" refers not to the Ghost who slips beneath the ground as dawn approaches but rather to Hamlet himself. It is he who is perceived as struggling to move forward, his delay itself a testimony to that struggle. Like Hegel's spirit of consciousness, Hamlet is both driven ahead and held back, not by outward circumstances but by the conflict within himself. The play dramatizes Hamlet's attempt to advance as a series of "collisions" or "colliding factors."[14] He forges ahead until his loss of self-determination leaves him the plaything of contingency and chance, and he is "bandied from pillar to post."[15] His progressive advance is blocked by the pillars, posts, sandbanks of his own uncompromising resistance. He continues to push against these obstacles until fatally stopped in his tracks, his infinite spirit mired in necessity, "the sands of time" or the "sandbank of his finite condition."[16] The very features that distinguish Hamlet's character – his doubts, hesitation, backsliding, failures of resolve, "swither[ing] irresolutely from this to that" – are all manifestations of the inward struggle that determines his wavering course of action.[17] Critical attention focuses on his progress toward his end. What is he thinking? What is he doing? How does his thinking determine what he does or does not do? For Hegel, because his revenge is accomplished through chance (the shuffling of the swords that enables him to kill Claudius with the poisoned blade), Hamlet fails to attain the self-determination toward which he strives. That he falls short of his goal in no way invalidates his epochal role in the history of consciousness. The year 1600 puts Hamlet just on the threshold of the final stretch of its trajectory. Before the philosophical advances of Descartes, Spinoza, Kant, and, of course, Hegel himself, Hamlet can get only so far.

There is, it has to be said, something catachrestic about the use of the old mole's tunneling as a figure for the trajectory of world history and the action of Prince Hamlet. In nature, the mole burrows to seek not an exit but food; once out of its element, it is exposed to predators and cannot survive long. In order to bring the metaphor into alignment with the emancipatory movement of history, Hegel took the liberty of redesigning its trajectory, straightening out its helter-skelter burrowing and pointing it straight for open light. Once recast as a progressive struggle against earth and toward liberating air and sun, the mole's naturally erratic course looks unnaturally teleological. Hegel's metaphor runs into problems with philology as well as natural history. In 1600 the liberating movement Hegel requires of the mole would have been precluded by the word's homonymic kinship with *mold*. The spelling and pronunciation of *mole* and *mold* were interchangeable in 1600; *mole, mould, moulde,* and *moule* could refer to both the burrowing mammal and the earth in which it burrowed. Edward Topsel, in the entry on moles in *The History of Four-Footed Beasts* (1606), refers to his subject as both *moles* and *mouldes*, sometimes alternating spellings in the same paragraph. The etymology of the word explains the overlap: mole is an abbreviation of the Anglo-Saxon compound *mouldewarpe* (or *molewarpe*), compounding *moulde* (earth) and *warpen* (to throw). The abridgment leaves the "mole" phonetically and orthographically indistinct from the "mold" it tosses up.

If we follow this philological lead, the mole is the creature embedded in earth rather than fleeing from it. Its philological affinity to *mold* prompts an analogy to man, who is also verbally linked to earth. William Camden notes the linkage in reporting that in Latin the "last and most perfect worke" of the Almighty is called "*Homo*, for that he was made of *Mold*."[18] The *homo/humus* linkage was born out by two classical myths of man's creation. Ovid's account allows for the possibility that Prometheus engendered man by tempering earth with spring water: "And thus the earth which late before had neyther shape nor hew,/ Did take the noble shape of Man, and was transformed new."[19] Plutarch similarly derives man from earth in the *Moralia*: "The primitive generations came first from the earth";[20] so, too, does Lucretius whose first generation of human beings were "children of tough earth."[21] But the most authoritative overlap was to be found in Hebrew, the language whose names were thought to enshrine the essences of things. Adam, the first man, was named for the element from which he was made (*adamah* = clay).

The kinship of flesh and earth explains why the same name is given to small burrowing mammals and dark growths on human skin. Both kinds of moles disfigure moldy surfaces, topographical and epidermal. Horatio concludes that the Ghost's visitation "bodes some strange eruption to our state" (1.1.72). The Ghost's armor might indicate that the "eruption" will take the form of invasion from Denmark's inveterate enemy, for it is "the very armour [King Hamlet] had on" (1.1.63) in the combat Norway now threatens to avenge. But Norway's aggression is deflected to Poland, and the "eruption" Denmark suffers turns out to be "interial" rather than "exterial," to use the distinction introduced by a sixteenth-century medical treatise in diagnosing various outbreaks on the skin.[22]

The pathology infecting the body politic is reflected in the numerous outbreaks on Danish bodies, particularly royal ones. King Hamlet had broken out in leprous scabs, "most lazar-like" (1.5.72): an "instant tetter" (71) overspread his skin as poison coursed through the arterial "gates and alleys of [his] body" (67). In Hamlet's imagination at least, the queen's body is also infected; her "ulcerous place" signals the "rank corruption" festering within (3.4.149, 150). The ulcerous lesions hint at venereal disease, as do the syphilitic pocks or pustules which, according to the Grave-digger, cause bodies to decompose before they hit the grave. Hamlet's account of the "vicious mole" (1.4.24) that spoils a man's reputation similarly signals a sinister cause beneath the skin, at best a humoral imbalance, at worst a tumor or cancer. A single flaw is able to "soil" the reputation of a person, just as a dark raised mole can blemish the smooth pale surface of the skin. In a wonderful blend of homonymy and homeopathy, mole-paste was prescribed as the remedy for mole-marks. Outbreaks on the surface warn of sinister activity below, unlike the fatally malignant "impostume" or in "imposthume" (Q2) that swell invisibly within: "That inward breaks, and shows no cause without" (4.4.27–8). The same homonymic cluster linking flesh and earth pertains to a third kind of mole: the fleshy mass or fetus aborted from the womb. Such discharges were often thought to be the result of coition during menstruation when the "filthy" matter of the uterus or "mother" overwhelmed the form-giving seed of the father. As King James' physician explained, under such conditions, "the matter is naught and unfit to receive a decent and proper figure."[23] The result is moldy issue: "fleshy Mole[s]" of monstrous shape or else mole-like spots on the infant. *Mould* also participated in this homonymic cluster by signifying the opposite of shapeless or misshapen matter: Ophelia remembers the earlier Hamlet as the model courtier with the pleonastic epithet, "the mould of form" (3.1.162).

These semantic overlays between man and clay, human and humus, point toward another world history, long predating the nineteenth-century narratives, and one which prescribes a very different relation of man to earth. Genesis tells of man's beginning in dust, "And the Lord God formed man of the dust of the ground, and breathed into his nostrils the breath of life" (Gen. 2:7).[24] Raleigh in his *History of the World* (1614) elaborates on man's primal ingredient:

The externall man God formed out of the dust of the earth, or according to the signification of the word, *Adam* of *Adamath*, of redde earth, or, *ex limo terrae*, out of the slime of the earth, or a mixed mater of earth and water . . . not that God made an image or statue of clay, but out of clay, earth, or dust God formed and made flesh, blood, and bone, with all parts of man . . . That man was formed of earth and dust, did *Abraham* acknowledge, when in humble feare he called unto God, to save *Sodome. Let not my Lord now be angrie, if I speake, I, that am but dust and ashes: And in these houses of clay, whose foundation is in the dust, doe our soules inhabite* (Gen. 18:27; Job 4:27).[25]

After the fall, Adam and Eve's disobedience was punished with a lifelong bondage to dust. Taken from dust, man was to return "unto the ground"; "for out of [the ground] wast thou taken, for dust thou *art* and unto dust shalt thou return" (Gen. 3:19). During the interim, Adam was to work the ground by the sweat of his brow, expelled "from the garden of Eden, to till the ground from whence he was taken" (Gen. 3:23). All the days of a man's life were consigned, by penalty, to work the earth which in Eden needed only to be tended and dressed. As a result of his disobedience the earth had been cursed into recalcitrance: "cursed is the ground for thy sake" (Gen. 3:17). After the fall, then, the significance of Adam's name extended beyond his autochthonous origin in clay to include a lifetime of working the earth before finally dying back into it.

Every burial service performed in compliance with Elizabeth's *Book of Common Prayer* served as a reminder of this elemental affinity: "Earth to earth, ashes to ashes, dust to dust," the priest is instructed to say after the body has been laid in the earth and as earth is cast upon it. So, too, the formulaic wording of last wills and testaments, after commending the soul to God, consigned the body to "the earth whereof it is made."[26] As God raised man from the dust, so death reduced him back to it. *Hamlet* recalls the process again and again by both referring to interment and staging it. King Hamlet was "quietly interr'd" (Q1, Q2) before being cast up again. Ophelia weeps to think of her father laid to rest in the "cold ground" (4.5.70); "the people [are] muddied" (4.5.81) by the king's decision "[i]n hugger-mugger to inter him" (4.5.84). But it is Ophelia's committal to earth which receives the most attention. Even before burial, she suffers inhumation when pulled to a "muddy death" (4.7.182) at the bottom of a stream. The ground into which she will finally be laid to rest is a subject of debate at the level of both clown and king. Her interment is staged: her "corpse" (F,Q1) or "coffin" (Q2) is lowered into the earth and the sexton, about to shovel earth upon her, is instructed first to "hold off" and then to "pile" it on (5.1.242, 244). In order to make room for her body, the remains of the dead are removed in a material form closer to dust than flesh. The skeletal bits and pieces give Hamlet occasion to consider the body's moldering, "too curiously" (5.1.199) according to Horatio. His mother speaks metaphorically when she bids Hamlet, "Do not for ever with thy vailed lids/ Seek for thy noble father in the dust" (1.2.70–1). But in the graveyard he seems to be conducting just such a search, though notably not for his "noble father." In fingering the crumbling remains of the dead, he imagines the persons they might once have been. "This might be the pate of a politician . . . [o]r of a courtier . . . This might be my Lord Such-a-one . . . Why, may not that be the skull of a lawyer? . . . Hum, this fellow might be in's time a great buyer of land" (5.1.76–102).

This sequence of hypothetical persons – statesmen, courtiers, landlords, lawyers – now disintegrating into earth, in life strove to acquire and retain tracts of land. Death reduces them to bits of the element they once lived to amass. Whether they held estates like Lord-such-a-one, or empires, like Alexander and Caesar, they end up themselves specks of dust. Hamlet explicitly invokes the cycle, "To what base uses we may return" (5.1.196). He traces the cycle of history's two great conquerors beyond the return to dust, as if seeking extreme forms of abasement or humiliation for those who possessed the largest dominions: "Alexander returneth to dust" and ends up loam to "stop a beer-barrel" (5.1.202–5); Caesar, "that earth which kept the world in awe" (208), once "dead and turn'd to clay" (206) ends up patching a wall. Earlier Hamlet had followed another imperial body beyond decomposition: after returning to dust, the king's body is eaten by worms and then by a fish which in turn passes through the guts of a beggar.

In life as well as death, the kinship between man and dust is in evidence. In the Danish legend, Amleth or Hamblet convinces the court of his idiocy by wallowing in filth. In Saxo's *Historiae Danicae*, Amleth can be found "flinging himself in the ground and bespattering his person with foul and filthy dirt," and in the anonymous *The Hystorie of Hamblet* (1608), Hamlet appears "lying in the durt and mire, his face all filthy blacke."[27] It has been suggested that traces of the legend survive in the "dishabille" of his appearance, as described by Ophelia, particularly his "foul'd" stockings (2.1.79).[28] But with Shakespeare's Hamlet, dirt is more than skin deep. He finds his own flesh soiled or "sullied,"[29] his imagination "as foul / As Vulcan's stithy" (3.2.83–4), his reason like a wasteland "fust[s] . . . unused" (4.4.39), his mettle or spirit "muddy" (2.2.562). Man, in Hamlet's estimation, however much idealized as angel, god, or paragon, is only the most rarified form of the earth from which he was extracted, an autochthonous sublimation or "quintessence of dust" – a sophisticated piece of earthenware.

The metaphorics of the play insist upon the interchangeability of the two materials, flesh and clay. "Moor" (3.4.67), Hamlet's epithet for Claudius, is a double slur, identifying his moral depravity with both black skin and unarable land. A woman's face, like a wall, can be mended with plaster and beautified with color: a "plaster'ing art" (3.1.51) teaches her how to coat her face "an inch thick" (5.1.187–8) with a poultice of lime and clay to fill up wrinkles and pock-marks; cosmetic "paintings" are then applied, like wall frescoes. As flesh can be improved with clay, so clay is repaired with flesh: "flaw[s]" (5.1.209) and "bung-hole[s]" (5.1.198) in the wall are patched with the "clay" or "earth" of Alexander (5.1.206, 208). The return to dust begins even before the body is interred. Polonius "stowed" (4.2.1) in the lobby is already imagined to be "compounded . . . with dust, whereto 'tis kin" (5). "How long will a man lie i'th'earth ere he rot?" (5.1.158) Hamlet asks the sexton, and is told that some are rotten before they die; "pocky corses" (160) eaten up by disease decompose before interment ("scarce hold the laying in," 160–1). The poison which kills King Hamlet has the effect of accelerating the process of

natural deterioration. Coursing through his blood system, it eats away
at his "smooth body" (1.5.73) and covers it with crusty scabs. As the
sexton observes, water also hastens disintegration: "water is a sore
decayer of your whoreson dead body" (5.1.165–6). Ophelia's water-
logged body seems a case in point. No sooner is she buried, than her
brother imagines flowers sprouting from her corpse, as from a flowerbed.

> Lay her i'th'earth,
> And from her fair and unpolluted flesh
> May violets spring.　　　(5.1.231–3)

Hamlet earlier had entertained a similar, though less savory, conceit of the
fecundity of Ophelia's "carrion" when he – "sole son" of a king likened to
Hyperion (3.3.77) – warned her father of exposure to the sun, "Let her not
walk i'th'sun": "Conception is a blessing, but as your daughter may
conceive – friend, look to't" (2.2.184–6).

In a semantic setting in which *human* and *humus* are cognate, ambition for
land is a form of self-aggrandizement. The body extends itself through the
acquisition of territory. The greatness of persons as well as of nations is
measured by the expanse of their terrain. The great conquerors Alexander
and Caesar find their debased modern counterpart in the courtier Osric: he is
"spacious in the possession of dirt" (5.2.88–9). He displays his spaciousness
by both physically and rhetorically taking up more room than he needs. His
hat is disproportionately large and is perhaps extended further by an outsized
ostrich feather.[30] Horatio and Hamlet might have to keep their distance from
the sweeping gesture with which he takes it off, perhaps with an exaggerated
sprawling bow. Designated a "Bragart Gentleman" in Q1, his diction is
inflated to the point of incomprehensibility (glossing or edification in the
margin is required); Hamlet describes his overblown phrasing as "a kind of
yeasty collection," a swelling frothy concoction: "do but blow them to their
trial, the bubbles are out" (5.2.187–8, 190–1). His extravagant dress, gestures,
and speech are the pretenses of someone who, though he has "much land
and fertile" (5.2.86) can never be "to the manner born" (1.4.14). His manners
are all wrong, and the "native" (14) Hamlet sees through them to the rusticated
origins they are designed to conceal. However much Osric plays the courtier,
Hamlet recognizes the boor beneath: he is a "chuff," farm-born, foremost
among livestock, "lord of beasts" (5.2.87–8).[31] Nowhere is one's breeding more
obvious than at the table: "his crib shall stand at the king's mess."

As a man is enlarged in life by the lands he owns, he is in death
downsized. The grave he occupies is not much larger than the measure

of his body and, as the sexton's exhuming activity reveals, the plot he is allotted is neither exclusive nor permanent. In clearing the grave for Ophelia, he chucks out a number of previous occupants. In the graveyard, Hamlet marvels at how the "great buyer of land" (5.1.102) ends up in the grave holding land no larger than one of his legal instruments, "the length and breadth of a pair of indentures" (5.1.107–8). The material on which these deeds and conveyances are drawn is a fleshly alloy,

HAM.   Is not parchment made of sheepskins?
HOR.   Ay, my lord, and calveskins too.
                                        (5.1.112–13)

Land ownership is made official on the prepared flesh of livestock or cattle which are themselves a form of property or chattel. As Hamlet maintains, only fools would find "assurance" (5.1.114) in such documents; even tanned skins deteriorate, only more slowly.

HAM.   How long will a man lie i'th'earth ere he rot?
CLOWN   ... A tanner will last you nine year.
HAM.   Why he more than another?
CLOWN   Why, sir, his hide is so tanned with his trade that a will
              keep out water a great while.
                                        (5.1.158–65)

The parchment which determined land ownership in due course will go the way of all flesh and itself pulverize. Talk of plots, land, and deeds, may trigger a pun on "hide," a unit of land measurement dating back to the Domesday Book: "The usuall account of land at this day in England is by acres, yardes, carewes, hydes."[32] The measurement varied, but it was often equated with the amount of land needed to support one free family with dependents: so much humus per human.

On stage, the plot of Ophelia's grave is blocked out by the open trap in the middle of the stage. Another plot of land is materially designated. The stage directions to the dumbshow indicate that the king "lies him down upon a bank of flowers." We can assume that Shakespeare's company owned such a flowery bank; the Lord Admiral's men list "ii mose banckes" in their inventory.[33] Like the throne or bed, the flowery bank could be carried on and off stage as needed. In the dumbshow, it would represent the "orchard" (1.5.35, 39) or garden in which, according to the Ghost's report, the king was sleeping at the time of his poisoning.[34] But the flowery bank does more than set the scene of the crime: it also stands for its motive. The crime is committed *for* that flowery bank; it symbolizes fruitful terrain, the happy combination of land and seed that forms the basis of dynasty. As Hamlet exclaims at its climax when Lucianus poisons the King, "A poisons him i'th'garden for his estate" (3.2.255).[35] Claudius poisons the King for the same reason: for the royal estate that is the kingdom itself. Like the play-within-the-play, the plot of the play is driven by the desire for a plot.[36]

The garden setting, complete with guilty serpent, also suggests Eden. ("'Tis given out that, sleeping in my orchard, /A serpent stung me . . . The serpent that did sting thy father's life / Now wears his crown," 1.5.35–6, 39–40). It is not, however, the original sin of disobedience that is enacted there, but rather the crime of fratricide, the crime that occurred after the Fall just east of Eden. Cain slew Abel not over land, but over God's favor; though God subsequently came to show his favor to his chosen people in the form of land, or, rather, the promise of it. In Genesis, Abel's blood speaks out accusingly at Cain, "his blood crieth unto me from the ground" (Gen. 4:10). In Q1 Claudius admits to being haunted by that same subterranean cry, "The earth doth still crie out upon my fact / Pay me the murder of a brother" (Gv). The play three times invokes Cain's fratricide, in each case assigning it primacy: the crime was the "first murder" (5.1.76); it produced the "first corse" (1.2.105) and received the "primal eldest curse" (3.3.37).[37] In the graveyard, Cain is also the first to be imaginatively fleshed out from the anonymous exhumed remains, and appropriately, for his act of violence introduced death into the world. Exiled and cursed for his crime, he went on to be the founder of cities as well as of a long line of emulous successors, the sons of Cain. The persons Hamlet pieces out from the remains might have been among them, having obtained what they wanted through guile rather than force: a politician through prevarication ("one that would circumvent God," 5.1.178), a courtier through flattery ("Lord Such-a-one, that praised my Lord Such-a-one's horse," 5.1.83–4), and a lawyer through technicalities ("Where be his quiddities now, his quillities, his cases, his tenures, and his tricks?" 5.1.97–8).

Performance allows for another means of representing land besides the "bank of flowers," and one that requires no transporting. The stage floor itself can stand for earth. It is generally assumed that the platform is purely functional, serving as the surface on which players stand in order to be widely visible. A demonstrative pronoun accompanied by a gesture, however, can at any point attach a specific identity to those floorboards.[38] There are numerous occasions when the soil of Denmark might be indicated underfoot, as when the sentries claim to be "friends to *this* ground" (1.1.16, emphasis added) and when the Prince of Denmark boasts of being "native *here*" (1.4.14, emphasis added). When the sexton is asked "[u]pon what ground" was Hamlet sent to England and replies, "Why *here* in Denmark" (5.1.155–6, emphasis added) – he might localize that *here* with a thump of the foot or shovel, to distinguish the immediate *here* from the faraway *there* – the land where it will not matter whether or not Hamlet recovers his wits: "'tis no great matter *there* . . . 'Twill not be seen in him *there. There* the men are as mad as he" (5.1.147, 149–50, emphasis added). (If the sexton were to gesture toward the space of the audience, the border between the *here* of Denmark and the *there* of England would be the rim of the stage.) In Q2, when Fortinbras' army is granted "quiet pass" through Denmark's "dominions" (2.2.77, 78) to Poland, a captain explains that the aim of the campaign is "to gain a little patch of ground" (4.4.18). The captain might use the parameters of the stage to indicate just how small that "little patch" is. The size of the contested territory is again mentioned when Hamlet concludes that the "plot" is not even large enough – "not tomb enough and continent" (4.4.62, 64) – to bury all the soldiers who will die fighting for it. The platform of the stage (often called the *plat* or plot) might again be indicated. The desire of nations to expand themselves through territory yields no more than a burial ground for the army which fought for it, just as the desire of individuals to enlarge themselves through land in the end amounts to no more than a grave plot.

In the graveyard scene, everything – props, dialogue, gesture – combines to convert the floorboards to elemental earth. Two Clowns enter with spade and mattock; the sexton goes through the motions of digging a pit that, of course, already exists if the trap door is open. Along with earth, remains from former corpses are shoveled up for Hamlet's inspection. If the sexton listens to Laertes' order delivered from the "pit of clay" (5.1.94, 118) into which he has leapt to embrace the dead Ophelia – "Now pile your dust upon the quick and dead" (5.1.244) – he must again pretend to shovel out earth. This concave rectangle at the center of the stage repeatedly serves to represent the object of conflict. As we learn from both the sexton's companion and the priest, Church and Crown have debated over who should be buried in the consecrated ground of the churchyard. Hamlet's question to the sexton also raises the issue of proprietorship:

HAM.   Who's grave's this, sirrah?
GRAVE.   Mine, sir.

(5.1.115–17)

And a frenzied physical struggle over that grave occurs between Hamlet and Laertes when the flower-strewn body of Ophelia is laid to rest there. Like the flowery bank, the garden, and the Polish "patch of ground," this plot sets off a violent struggle.

The stage floor can also stand for itself and as such be contested like any other expanse. Its status as ground is unexpectedly foregrounded when Hamlet diagnoses his melancholic disposition. Both objective world and his subjective perception of it are illustrated by the material features of the stage. The earth is a "goodly frame," like the scaffolding supporting the stage, but seems to him a "sterile promontory" (2.2.298–9) like the protruding bare platform where the Ghost, for example, has been seen to promenade: "thrice he walk'd" (1.2.203). Like other plots of ground, the "promontory" of the stage sets off territorial rivalries. That the Players are on tour rather than in residence is the result of the competition for that stage between adult troupe and boy acting company. *Hamlet* itself was first performed on one of those "common stages" (2.2.340). Indeed an allusion to the signpost of the Globe picturing Hercules shouldering the world implies that the Players were ousted from the very stage on which they are in reality about to appear.[39]

HAM.   Do the boys carry it away?
ROS.   Ay . . . Hercules and his load too.
                    (2.2.357–8)

The "frame" or "promontory" of the stage, then, is like the flowery bank, "patch of ground," or "pit of clay": all ground spaces spurring male rivalries. Hamlet notes that by supplanting their elders, the boy actors "exclaim against their own succession" (2.2.349). For in time the boy players will become adult players, and will have set the precedent for their own overthrow.

It is competition between theatrical companies that brings the Players to Elsinore; but the important competition as far as the audience is concerned may be that between actors in the same company. Though Hamlet does not occupy the throne, he certainly does dominate the stage. On stage he is unquestionably the commanding presence, and not only when he has it all to himself. His instructions to the Players mainly warn them off any form of excess. His golden rule is, "o'erstep not the modesty of nature" (3.2.19), as if his mastery were threatened by all forms of over-acting: voices that are too loud (like the town-crier's), gestures that are too broad (like the sawing of the air), gaits that are too affected (like outland-ish strutting). While critics have typically taken these precepts as evidence of Hamlet's elitist allegiance to Horatian decorum, they could equally well reflect his desire to suppress all forms of upstaging.

At the same time that Hamlet urges moderation, he goes quite over-the-top himself, as in his diatribe against bombastic acting: "O, it offends me to the soul to hear a robustious periwig-pated fellow tear a passion to tatters, to very rags" (3.2.8–10), a mouthful that hardly lends itself to the "temperance" and "smoothness" (3.2.7–8) he has just recommended. "I would have such a fellow whipped" (3.2.13), he histrionically claims. Indeed in voice, gesture, movement, Hamlet's role seems to require that the actor playing Hamlet violate the principles he urges on the Players. He is not infrequently projecting like the "town-crier," even in the intimate space of his mother's closet: what act has she committed, his mother asks, "That roars so loud and thunders in the index?" (3.4.52). His behavior in this scene is nothing if not "robustious"; he so roughly holds his mother in place ("you shall not budge," 17) that she fears violence: "What wilt thou do? Thou wilt not murder me? Help, ho!" (20–1). Certainly his antic part requires him to "o'erstep . . . the modesty of nature." He warns his confidantes to expect quirky comportment, "Arms encumber'd thus, or this head-shake" (1.5.182), and Ophelia bears witness to it: "thrice his head thus waving up and down"; his sighs seemed to "shatter all his bulk / And end his being" (2.1.93, 95–6). We know that early spectators were im-pressed by Hamlet's maniacal motion, his "running mad," perhaps when he breaks away from Horatio and the guards to follow the ghost, perhaps when in flight from Rosencrantz and Guildenstern. Claudius' orders to restrain Hamlet's "liberty" (4.1.14) and fetter the fear "[w]hich now goes too free-footed" (3.3.26) may be intended quite literally.

Hamlet most outrageously violates his own dicta at Ophelia's funeral. As he himself admits in apologizing for his wild behavior there, he felt compelled to outdo Laertes' graveside ostentation: "But sure, the bravery of his grief did put me / Into a tow'ring passion" (5.2.78–9). It is not a matter of who loved or mourns Ophelia most but of who can better rise to the rhetorical and histrionic challenge: "Dost come here to whine, / To outface me with leaping in her grave?" (5.1.272–3). Hamlet succeeds in outdoing Laertes in both word and deed. "Forty thousand brothers / Could not with all their quantity of love, / Make up my sum" (5.1.264–6), he insists. When Laertes leaps into Ophelia's grave and orders that earth be piled in after him to exceed the double-decker mountain by which the Giants hoped to scale Olympus, Hamlet bests him, perhaps with a higher leap, certainly with a higher land mass – one so colossal that Laertes' formation dwindles from an oversized peak to a tiny "wart"

(5.1.278) – from a swell on the earth's crust to a bump on the skin's surface. (Here, too, the topographical and the dermatological intermesh.) This is clearly a contest between two performers, in which Hamlet out-Laerteses Laertes; indeed, he even out-Hamlets himself: "I forgot myself," he later allows (5.2.76).

Hamlet is himself upstaged by the player who is designated *Clown* in all three early texts. Hamlet had singled out the Clown in his instructions to the Players, warning against his "most pitiful ambition" (3.2.44) in disrupting the course of the play by provoking contagious laughter. He has good reason to rein in the Clown, for hitherto the antic role had been his own. But in the graveyard, the role passes from prince to rustic. In all of their exchanges, it is the rustic who comes out on top, as Hamlet himself concedes, "How absolute the knave is. We must speak by the card or equivocation will undo us" (5.1.133–4). It is the precision of the rustic's responses that gives him the edge over the Prince's ambiguous wording. Who is to be buried in the grave? asks the Prince; it is not a man or a woman but "One that was a woman" (5.1.131), answers the rustic. Upon what ground did Hamlet lose his wits? "Why, here in Denmark" (156). The Clown gets all the laughs, and at Hamlet's expense. In an earlier contest, the rustic fared less well. Yorick, the court jester, once "poured a flagon of Rhenish" (173–4) over the Clown's head, as if to assert his sophisticated superiority over the rustic buffoon. Empowered in the graveyard, the rustic Clown gets his revenge on the "whoreson mad fellow" (5.1.170) by banging his skull with a spade. One capital crime deserves another.

There is another character who upstages Hamlet, not with jests or dialogue, for he says nothing in their first encounter. Rising from the ground, clad in armor, bearing a truncheon, moving in stately martial strides, he presides over the stage, "majestical" (1.1.148) as is fitting for the "majesty of buried Denmark" (1.1.151). When alone with Hamlet, the Ghost finally speaks, to deliver his captivating narrative, and Hamlet holds his peace, nearly dumbfounded. It is only after the Ghost has sunk back into the earth, safely underfoot and out of sight, that Hamlet takes over again – but only until the Ghost makes four monosyllabic comebacks with his resounding subterranean imperative, "Swear" (1.5.163). Early audiences were particularly impressed by this scene; as Paul Conklin notes in his study of seventeenth-century allusions to the play, the Ghost's phrases were as frequently quoted as any of Hamlet's.[40] There are numer- ous liftings of Hamlet's frenzied interjections ("hillo, ho, ho" [118], "truepenny" [158], "*hic et ubique*" [164]) as well as of the Ghost's lugubrious narration ("Like quills upon the fretful porpentine" [20] and the glow-worm's "uneffectual fire," [90]).[41] The parts of Antic and Ghost were well-established theatrical favorites, and would have been relished all the more if performed by company stars. According to Shakespeare's first biographer, Shakespeare himself played the part of the Ghost; Nicholas Rowe records that the only information he could obtain about Shakespeare's acting career was "that the top of his Performance was the Ghost in his own *Hamlet*."[42] If that is true, then Shakespeare in his "top" performance would have shared the stage with Richard Burbage in his celebrated role as Hamlet. Another early account pits the two players against one another, over a woman rather than the stage; Sir John Manningham records in his *Diary* that Shakespeare, upon discovering that both he and Burbage had been granted audience with the same woman at the same time, entitled himself by maintaining that his William the Conqueror took precedence over Burbage's Richard III.[43]

The encounter between Hamlet and the Ghost culminates in the swearing scene. As Hamlet attempts to swear his companions to secrecy, the Ghost breaks in, intoning from directly below: "Swear." "Rest, rest, perturbed spirit" (1.5.190) responds Hamlet, echoing the *requiem in pace*, but the Ghost underground will keep neither quiet nor still. Hamlet four times relocates the ceremony – "we'll shift our ground" (164), "Once more remove, good friends" (171) – and the Ghost follows their movement, repeating the injunction, "Swear." Hamlet compliments the Ghost on both his diction and action, "Well said, old mole. Canst work i'th'earth so fast?" (170). But the Ghost's intervention disrupts the ceremony. When underground, occupying the region theatrical tradition continued to reserve for devils, the Ghost falls into the ranks of the damned and diabolic. It is for this reason, it appears, that the swearing ceremony over the cross of the sword cannot proceed. Two forces are in conflict. While the cross-like sword sanctifies the spot, the Ghost's presence beneath hexes it. The swearing ceremony replays the old contest between heaven and hell for the middle zone between. The same metaphysics requires that the nocturnal Ghost "hies to his confine" (1.1.159–60) with the arrival of dawn and that evil spirits absent themselves ("dare [not] stir abroad," 166) during the season of the "Saviour's birth" (164). As editors have noted, ubiquity ("*hic et ubique*") is predicated to two beings only, God and the devil, and the two cannot occupy the same space at the same time.[44]

The very vertical structure of the Globe stage recalled the perpetual contest of the medieval moralities between heaven and hell over the middle region of earth.[45] Above the stage floor was the painted starry roof of the "heavens," and beneath lay the cavernous underworld accessed through the trap door. That audiences were still keen to see the two moral forces contend is demonstrated by the hoax advertisement from 1602 of a play promising a show of pure souls being wafted up to heaven while "blacke and damned souls" writhed in torment.[46] At several points, the dialogue, perhaps accompanied by gesture, activates the stage's eschatological layout. After the Ghost's disclosure, Hamlet does not know what region to summon: "O all you host of heaven! O earth! What else? / And shall I couple hell?" (1.5.92–3). Claudius at prayer admits that his "words fly up" while his "thoughts remain below" (3.3.97). Laertes, maddened by his father's death, repudiates both heaven and hell: "both the worlds I give to negligence" (4.5.34). Hamlet recommends that Claudius locate Polonius' body by sending messengers up to heaven or by seeking him down "i'th'other place" himself (4.3.34).

The up-down symbolism of the stage also operates on a social level. With the "old mole" epithet, Hamlet notoriously talks down to his father as if his father once beneath him spatially were his social inferior. When he was above ground, Hamlet had addressed the person of his father with reverence, "I'll call thee Hamlet, / King, father, royal Dane" (1.4.44–5) and "What would your gracious figure?" (3.4.104–5). But once the spirit has dropped below, Hamlet insults him, referring to his father as "boy" (1.5.158), to his king as his subordinate "fellow" (159), and to the great commander with truncheon in hand as "worthy pioneer" (171) – a lowly foot soldier who dug trenches around fortifications. Even the term "truepenny" (158) suggests a decline, from the highest currency in the land – "sovereign Highness" and "royal Dane" – to the common penny. At the Globe, "truepenny" might have referenced the penny a groundling would pay for standing room or ground-rent for the duration of the performance. Some commentators have suggested that the entire swearing scene was designed to give groundlings their penny's worth. The tearing about the stage and the Ghost's eerie cries do indeed seem to cater to their taste for what Hamlet identifies as "inexplicable dumb-shows and noise" (3.2.12). Yet the stage effects may have afforded groundlings a more sophisticated pleasure. The area beneath the stage boards, the floor of the cellarage, is level with the surface of the yard. Having been lowered via the trap door, the actor playing the Ghost would be standing literally on the same level as the groundlings. His descent leaves him about five feet below the stage, with only thin panels separating him from the lowest members of the audience.[47] All of these epithets – *boy, fellow, worthy pioneer, truepenny* – underscore one of the play's basic premises: status depends on station. "Old mole" is only the most humiliating of Hamlet's many put-downs, reducing the king who ruled over the land to a subterranean creature synonymous with base earth.

In both Hegel's idealist and Marx's materialist accounts, the tunneling of the mole represents the long hard forward movement of history toward an emancipatory end, particularly as it accelerates into the latest stretch of the modern age. Both metanarratives mark the start of that latest stretch with a rupture from the land: the former with the Reformation and the renunciation of the Holy Land and the latter with primitive accumulation and the expropriation of a population from the land. In this tradition, *Hamlet* has served to accommodate a parallel trajectory, dramatizing the struggle of consciousness, through halting advances, to attain self-determination, and its tragic failure to do so. In that modern context, land has no place: the mole is in flight from mold. The play, however, subscribed to the biblical narrative in which man's life is rounded in dust. Man issues from earth, returns to it, and during the interim is involved in its acquisition (through inheritance, purchase, conquest) or working (gardeners, ditchers, grave-makers, pioneers). The play dramatizes one conflict over land after another: Fortinbras I and Hamlet I over crown lands, Hamlet I and Claudius over the garden kingdom, Gonzago and Lucianus over the "bank of flowers" or "estate", Norway and Poland over "a patch of ground", the boy and adult companies over the commercial stage, the Crown and the Church over the churchyard, Laertes and Hamlet over Ophelia's flowered body, and the actor who plays Hamlet and any actor whose role challenges Hamlet's command over the stage.

The critical tradition that has identified *Hamlet* with the onset of the modern period has ignored the centrality of land. For this tradition, it makes little or no difference that Claudius, "a cutpurse of the empire" (3.4.99), has dispossessed Hamlet of the realm to which his birth all but entitled him. If anything, the loss is imagined to have left him, as Coleridge and Hegel both assumed, free to be himself. Yet it is not clear that personal identity can survive deracination or disentitlement. Sir Edward Coke, the great expounder of the common law, insisted on an etymological link between an heir and his inheritance: "*Haereditas* (inheritance) and *haeres* (heir) are so called from *haerendo* (adhering), that is, firmly sticking, either because he who is an heir adheres [to his inheritance] or because the inheritance adheres to him who is the heir."[48] As is stressed by a number of key words in this play, names of persons reference their relation to land. King and kingdom are designated by the

same name: "buried Denmark" (1.1.51) recalls the late king of Denmark; "th'ambitious Norway" (64) refers to the king of Norway; "Do it, England" (4.4.68) is addressed to the king of England. The names of counts, earls, and dukes are similarly interchangeable with those of their estates. The territories of counts are *counties*, of marquesses are *marches*, of barons are *baronies*. Commoners are also named for their relation to land, through work or bondage. Goodman Delver's name connects him to the soil he digs. So, too, does the name he is assigned by the play's prefixes and stage directions: *clown* derives from *colonus*, a tiller of the soil. He is also termed a *peasant*, a term which, like rustic, can be traced back to the countryside (*rus, païs*). Hamlet's insult "villain" (1.5.106) or *villein* also points to a status in relation to the land, a serf who works on a *villa* or farm and cannot be separated from the lord's land except by manumission. The semantics of Hamlet's term of self-abuse, "muddy-mettled rascal" (2.2.562) recalls the name of the biblical first man: *rascaille* is French for mud and *adamah* is Hebrew for red earth or clay. The *rabble* which storms the palace derives its name from the same word: it is the collective form of *rascal*. Hamlet himself is credited with naming the lowest-paying part of the audience after the muddy ground on which they stand: groundlings (3.2.11). In this context, it is tempting to connect the landless Hamlet with the humble unit of land whose name he shares. A hamlet is a diminuitive *ham*, the Saxon word for a settlement, often marked off by a ditch, with too few dwellings to warrant a church. Sir Edward Coke, in his authoritative gloss of Littleton's *Tenures* (c. 1470), the treatise on the having, holding, and transfer of land, provides an ascending list of estates: "a hamlet, a towne, a burgh, a city, a mannor, an honor, an hundred, and a county."[49] A variant of this list appears in Shakespeare's last will and testament which bequeaths to his only child all of his holdings "within the townes and Hamletts, villages, ffieldes and groundes" in Warwick.[50] Minsheu's 1617 dictionary defines the area in terms uncannily apposite to *Hamlet*'s most famous landscape:

Hamme. a little plot of ground growing by the river or Thames side beset with many willow trees or osiers.[51]

CHAPTER 3

Empires of world history

Within two years of its publication, *Hamlet* was cited in the report of a recent, almost concurrent, event in world history: the fall of Boris God-unov, the Tsar of Russia. In 1605, the anonymous author of *Sir Thomas Smithes Voiage and Entertainment in Rushia* likened the demise of Russia's regime in 1605 to the tragedy of *Hamlet*. At the time of writing, Boris Godunov, who had obtained the throne in 1598 after allegedly poisoning the rightful heir, died suddenly, and the empire passed to his own son Theodor. Within a month's time, a young man claiming to be the rightful heir appeared from obscurity to avenge Godunov's usurpation by slaying his relations and supporters. To the anonymous English reporter, the episode possessed all the makings of an Aristotelian tragedy.

[H]is fathers Empire and Government [was] but as the *Poeticall Furie in a Stage-action*, compleat yet with horrid and wofull Tragedies: a first, but no second to any Hamlet; and that now *Revenge*, just *Revenge* was comming with his Sworde drawne against, his royall Mother, and dearest Sister, to fill up those Murdering Sceanes, the *Embryon* whereof was long since Modeld, yea digested (but unlawfully and too-too vive-ly) by his dead selfe-murdering Father: such and so many being their feares and terrours.[1]

Springing from the "Embryon" of Godunov's treachery and driven toward its fatal dénouement by peripatetic revenge, the downfall of the Godunovs comprised a "compleat" action. The collapse of an imperial regime appeared as dramatic as tragedy itself, "a first, but no second to any Hamlet."[2] Like the "Stage-action" of *Hamlet*, the contemporary event featured usurpation, a dispossessed prince, revenge, self-slaughter, and dynastic collapse. Horatio's sensationalized synopsis at the conclusion of *Hamlet* applies as well to the Russian upheaval as the Danish: "So shall you hear / Of carnal, bloody, and unnatural acts" (5.2.385–6).[3] The resemblance between events in the world historical arena and on the professional stage suggests the close association between tragedy and history. As Aristotle's

Illustration 1. *The Four Great Kingdoms as prophesied by Daniel*: Ninus (Babylon), Cyrus
(Persia), Alexander (Greece), Julius Caesar (Rome). A series of plates by Marten de Vos
engraved by Adriaen Collaert (1600).

Illustration 1 (*cont.*).

redactors had maintained, tragedy commonly looked to history for its materials. And as this traveler's account indicates, history turned to tragedy to give form to tumultuous political upheaval.

That this allusion to the demise of Godunov has received scant critical attention is not surprising, for it highlights a feature of *Hamlet* rarely noted in modern discussions: its preoccupation with the stuff of history – the fall of states, kingdoms, and empires. The play begins with the threat of invasion and ends with foreign occupation. Its action blocks out the major event punctuating one of the earliest schema for organizing world history: the fall of empire. From the days of the early church, exegetes schematized history into a series of four monarchies, kingdoms, or empires, each one rising from the ashes of its predecessor until all would be subsumed by a final fifth. Although the theory had pagan precedents, Christian exegetes found a basis for the schema in the prophet Daniel's interpretation of King Nebuchadnezzar's dream.[4] A statue with a head of gold, shoulders of silver, stomach of brass, and legs of iron and clay is smashed by a falling stone which then expands into a mountain so vast as to cover the face of the earth (Dan. 2:36–45). Daniel interprets the dream as a prophecy: the statue's head stands for Nebuchadnezzar's Babylon, the other three body parts represent the three great kingdoms yet to come, and their smashing by the stone foretells the eventual subsuming of them all by the final and eternal heavenly kingdom.[5] By the start of the fifth century, Jerome in his commentary on Daniel was able to identify the statue's four parts with the four great monarchies which had emerged since the time of Abraham: Babylon, Media-Persia, Greece, and Rome, as illustrated in the series of magnificent engravings by Marten de Vos (1600) (Illustration 1). Prevalent throughout the middle ages, the schema survived in England well into the seventeenth century, as is testified by the emergence after the execution of Charles I of the Fifth Monarchy Men, a radical millenarian sect determined to bring Daniel's prophecy to fulfillment by preparing the way for the everlasting fifth kingdom.[6]

A number of world histories published in England during the sixteenth and seventeenth centuries adopt Daniel's schema. In *A Briefe chronicle of the foure principall Empyres: To witte, of Babilon, Persia, Grecia, and Rome* (1563), John Sleidan organizes all of world history up to his present according to Daniel's prophecy.[7] Thomas Heywood's *Troia Britanica: or, Great Britaines Troy* (1609) begins with a four-page *Proemium* intended to "instruct [the reader's] memory" of the Four Monarchies of ancient history.[8] Sir Walter Raleigh's *The History of the World* (1614) traces "the beginning and end of the three first Monarchies of the world," breaking off his history with the fourth, Rome, still flourishing, though in full knowledge that after "long continuance," it, too, did decline, "and a rabble of barbarous Nations enter the field, and cut her downe."[9] In his *A Briefe Chronicle, of the Successe of Times, from the Creation of the World, to this Instant* (1611), Anthony Munday dedicates a chapter to each of the Four Monarchies, and extends the succession or "successe" to include modern empires and kingdoms of both the East and West.

Protestant historiographers tended to see the Reformation as the final fifth epoch which would eventually culminate in the promised kingdom come. John Foxe's *Actes and Monuments* (1563), for example, culminates in a fifth period of history, beginning with John Wycliff, England's first champion against the Pope, and extending up to the reign of Elizabeth, a period of liberation from the shackles of Rome or "from the Loosing out of Satan."[10] As Norman Cohn has maintained, the schema had a particular appeal to seventeenth-century millennial sects for whom the expected arrival of a fifth kingdom or monarchy served as "the central phantasy of revolutionary eschatology."[11] Though some historians, including Bacon, rejected the fourfold schema, insisting on the need to separate world history from eschatology, they certainly acknowledged its authority. Jean Bodin, for example, in *Method for the Easy Comprehension of History* (1566), allowed that the theory had persuaded "men well read in ancient history and things divine," including Luther, Melancthon, and Sleidan.[12] Louis Leroy, in *Of the Interchangeable Course, or Variety of Things* (trans. 1594), broke from Daniel's fourfold schema, but continued to organize history into the waxing and waning of successive empires from the Egyptians, Assyrians, Persians, Greeks, Romans, and Saracens up through his own period whose onset was marked by the fall of Constantinople in 1453.[13] Sixteenth-century kingdoms, it was assumed, were subject to the same "alternations," "vicissitudes," or "revolutions" as their predecessors. Leroy ends his account of the achievements of modern European nations by anticipating their eventual demise.

[Since] memorie and knowledge of that which is past, be the instruction of the present, and advertisement for that which is to come . . . I foresee alreadie in my mind, many strange Nations . . . rushing into Europe as did in old times the Gothes, Hunnes, Lombardse, Vandales, and Saracens; which will distroy our Townes, Cities, Castles, Palaces, and Temples.[14]

As with the Four Monarchies schema, the arrival of another kingdom was imminent, but it was not expected to be European, despite the imperial ambitions of such rising powers as Spain and Portugal:

Now if we identify monarchy with force of arms, or with great wealth, or with fertility of areas, or with the number of victories, or with the size of population, or with the etymology of the name [?], or with the fatherland of Daniel, or with the seat of the Babylonian empire, or with the amplitude of sway, it will be more appropriate certainly, to interpret the prophecy of Daniel as applied to the sultan of the Turks.[15]

Luther had assigned the same eschatological significance to the Turks: "If we fight off the Turks, so is Daniel's prophecy fulfilled, and the Final Judgment will be at the door."[16] More than a half-century later, the threat of the Ottoman Empire still looms large; in his *The History of the World* (1614), after tracing the successive Four Monarchies, Raleigh warns of its ambition "to joyne all *Europe* to *Asia*."[17]

As several studies have demonstrated, a cluster of plays in the late sixteenth and early seventeenth centuries addressed the lingering fear of Ottoman infiltration by staging the conversion from Christian to Muslim, a prospect popularly dubbed "turning Turk."[18] The turn or conversion in matters of faith was often dramatized in sexual terms. To be converted to Islam was to be sexually penetrated by the Turk. At stake was the body of a Christian woman – would she keep the faith when assailed by the infidel? In Hamlet's use of the expression, the female in question has already yielded to the Ottoman: Lady Fortune has turned Turk. Her proverbial fickleness is translated into promiscuity – she is twice called "strumpet" (2.2.235–6, 489), her symbolic wheel changed into her gyrating "waist" or "secret parts" (2.2.232, 235). No longer in her favor, Hamlet has fallen from prince to player. After such a rough ride with Lady Fortune, he seems after his Mousetrap success to settle for an all-male "fellowship" of players: "Would not this . . . if the rest of my fortunes turn Turk with me . . . get me a fellowship in a cry of players?" (3.2.269–72). When Hamlet later accuses his mother of a similarly perverse sexualized turn from one man to another, he resorts to the same racialized opposition, as the Folio's capitalization inadvertently underscores: "Could you on this faire Mountaine leaue to feed / And batten on this Moore?"[19]

If modern empires follow the same alternating course as the ancient, past knowledge could be expected to cast light on things to come. When the mysterious Ghost appears in the play's opening scene, the scholar Horatio recalls a precedent from ancient history. "In the most high and palmy state of Rome" similar prodigies had been observed (Q2, 1.1.116). As in ancient Rome, so in modern Denmark: "even the like precurse of fear'd events . . . Have heaven and earth together demonstrated / Unto our climatures and countrymen" (Q2, 124–8). Versed in Roman history,

Horatio knows that the dread event "precursed" by the Roman prodigies was the fall of Caesar. The present ghost, he prognosticates, portends no less for Denmark: "This bodes some strange eruption to our state" (72). The play's end delivers what the Ghost portended. The state collapses, as it had in Caesar's Rome, as it would in Godunov's Russia. It is no accident that the play makes occasion to reference the transience of other emperors and empires – Troy (Priam), Macedon (Alexander), Imperial Rome (Augustus Caesar), Vienna (Charles V) – and that, at the start of its final act, the two greatest "Imperious" [Q2] or "Imperiall" [F] (5.1.206) conquerors should be invoked in the shadow of Doomsday, as if all history in this world were in preparation for the kingdom promised in the next.

Hamlet's concern with the fall of state may have been more recognizable when the play appeared under the rubric designated on its quarto title-pages.[20] All five early quartos (1603, 1604/5, 1611, n.d. [1622?], 1637) entitle the play not *The Tragedy of Hamlet*, as does the Folio, but *The Tragicall Historie of Hamlet*. This is not to say that these quartos classified the play as history rather than tragedy, for that would presuppose that the two classifications were already generically distinct.[21] Numerous plays of the period were termed 'histories,' but not necessarily because they drama-tized historical materials.[22] For example, no historical source has been found for *The Most Excellent Historie of the Merchant of Venice*. "History" was applied as loosely and broadly to playtexts as to other kinds of texts to signify a narrative or story. As D. R. Woolf concludes, "[Histories] tell stories, true or false, about real or imaginary men and women who lived in the remote or the recent past."[23] This would explain why, for example, the verse narrative from which Shakespeare drew his tragedy of star-crossed lovers bears the title *The Tragical History of Romeus and Juliet* (1562). The same rubric was shared by both the Latin and the French sources for *Hamlet*: the late-twelfth-century Saxo Gramaticus' *Historiae Danicae* (first printed in 1514) and Belleforest's translation of Saxo in his frequently reprinted *Histoires Tragiques* (1570). It was also adapted by the anonymous English translation of Belleforest, *The Hystorie of Hamblet*, conjectured to have circulated in manuscript before its printing in 1608. In these last three cases, however, the use of "history" is informed by the later more restricted use of the term to designate writing about a nation's past. *Historiae Danicae* was intended as an account of Denmark's past, from its founding to the time of the account's writing. As has been noted, it served the same function for Denmark as Geoffrey of Monmouth's

Historiae Regum Britanniae had for Britain. Drawing on genealogies, legends, and historical documents, as well as pure invention, Monmouth provided a continuous history from the founding of England up to his present; historiographers continued to consult it through the seventeenth century, including John Milton in his *History of Britain.*

Sidney himself would have been hard pressed to classify works like Saxo's or Monmouth's as either "history" or "poesie": did they pertain to what "was" or to what "should be"?[24] It is significant that the earliest English tragedy, *Gorboduc,* turns to Monmouth's *Historiae* for its tragic content, for it is in history that grand personages and consequential acts are to be found. As numerous historical narratives indicated, from Boccaccio's *De Viribus Illustrium* to Lydgate's *Fall of Princes* to the *Mirror for Magistrates,* the lives of the highborn had a cadential structure.[25] The two plays *Hamlet* references, the one Hamlet chiefly loved and the one in which Polonius performed, both climax in the fall of a great man. Priam topples and Troy comes crashing down; Caesar is assassinated and Rome erupts in civil war. The interdependency of king and kingdom is axiomatic, as Rosencrantz stresses through a string of commonplaces – "The cess of majesty / Dies not alone" (3.3.15–16), "Never alone / Did the King sigh, but with a general groan" (22–3) – and through the ekphrastic image of a king on top of a wheel, falling from "the summit of the highest mount" (18) taking with him "ten thousand lesser things" (19) to "boist'rous ruin" (22). There is no separating tragic action from historical events: both tend toward catastrophe. And both can appear to be divinely precipitated: "There is special providence in the fall of a sparrow" (5.2.215–16).

As its title indicated – *Mr. William Shakespeares Comedies, Histories, & Tragedies* – the 1623 Folio wedged a group of plays it termed *Histories* between the two classical dramatic genres. The tripartite division was boldly indicated in the table of contents or "Catalogue of the seuerall Comedies, Histories and Tragedies contained in this Volume" (Illustration 2). A frame of solid lines rendered each of the three genres spatially and typographically distinct. The middle category appears to have been something of an innovation in 1623. The title-pages of earlier quartos had no particular use for it; only one of the Folio Histories is tagged as such in quarto, the *History of Henry IV,* but so too, as we have seen, is one of the Comedies. In the first known generic division of Shakespeare's plays, the two ancient dramatic genres suffice. In *Palladis Tamia* (1598), Francis Meres divides the twelve plays he attributes to Shakespeare equally

A CATALOGVE

of the feuerall Comedies, Hiftories, and Tra-gedies contained in this Volume.

Illustration 2. A Catalogue, *Mr. William Shakespeares Comedies, Histories, & Tragedies* (1623).

between the two. Indeed the introduction of a third genre would have defeated his purpose. Subtitled *A Comparative Discourse of our English Poets with the Greeke, Latine and Italian Poets,* his text is based on the assumption that English poets can be compared with their ancient and modern rivals precisely because they all work within the same genres. For Meres, the great distinction of modern Shakespeare is that while ancient Plautus excelled in comedy and ancient Seneca in tragedy, "*Shakespeare* among ye English is the most excellent in both kinds for the stage."[26] On the basis of Meres' classification of both *1 Henry IV* and *King John* as tragedy, recent critics have assumed that he must not have known their content; and yet if the criterion for tragedy is high matters featuring noble personages and momentous events, those two plays would certainly qualify. (*The Tragedy of Romeo and Juliet* would then be the anomaly.)

The Folio's grouping of ten of Shakespeare's plays into a discrete unit would not have been as obvious before 1623 as it has been since. It took some effort on the part of the Folio compilers to affiliate them, as is illustrated by the following comparison of the titles of the Histories as they first appeared in quarto (or when no quarto is extant, in the earliest reference) to their listing in the Folio. The Folio unified the group by

Titles before 1623	Titles in 1623 folio
The Life and Death of King John	The Life and Death of King John
The Tragedy of King Richard the Second [+]	The Life & death of Richard the second [#]
The History of Henry the Fourth	The First part of King Henry the fourth
The Second Part of Henry the Fourth	The second part of K. Henry the fourth
The Life of Henry the Fifth	The Life of King Henry the Fift.
Harey the vj	The first part of King Henry the Sixt
The First Part of the Contention betwixt the Two Famous Houses of York and Lancaster [*]	The second part of King Henry the Sixt
The True Tragedy of Richard Duke of York [*][+]	The Third part of King Henry the Sixt
The Tragedy of Richard the Third [+]	The Life & Death of Richard the Third [#]
All is True [*]	The Life of King Henry the Eight

both standardizing and serializing individual titles. It assigned a monarch's name to the three titles which had appeared without one on their quarto title-page (see *). It also prefixed the title *King* to all the names, except in the two cases where spacing would not permit (see [#]). *Tragedy* is dropped from the title of the three plays labeled as such in quarto (see [+]). Once adjusted, all titles indicate a regnal period, either in part (*The First Part*, etc.) or in whole (*The Life*), sometimes extending up to the moment of the sovereign's death ("*Life and Death*"). Unlike the other two generic groupings, these ten plays are given in chronological order. It was not, however, the same chronological order followed by the only precedent for the 1623 Folio, Jonson's 1616 Folio, where the plays were catalogued and printed in the order of their performance. Nor was it, as it came to be in the nineteenth century, in the order of their composition. Instead the ten plays followed the order of regnal succession, thereby conforming to the chapter divisions of their primary source, the third volume of Holinshed's *Chronicles* (1587), beginning with William the Conqueror and "*descending by degrees of yeeres* to all the kings and *queens* of England in their orderlie successions."[27]

This was not the order in which Shakespeare wrote them, however. As modern editors must explain, Shakespeare began with three plays dramatizing the Wars of the Roses and then several years later backtracked with three plays dramatizing the events leading up to those wars. Less generally noted, however, is that Shakespeare continued to retreat back into Britain's chronicle history; to the eighth century BC for *King Lear*, to the eleventh century AD for *Macbeth*, and to the first century AD for *Cymbeline*. For two of these plays, we have evidence from an early playgoer that their historical setting mattered. Simon Forman entered in his diary that he had seen both *Macbeth* and *Cymbeline* at the Globe in 1610/11. As Stephen Orgel has suggested, his summary of *Macbeth* seems to have been mediated by his reading of Holinshed's *Chronicles* (1587): "Mackbeth and Bancko 2 noble men of Scotland Ridinge throrowe a wod ther stode befor them 3 women feiries or Nimphes."[28] Two of these details are to be found not in Shakespeare's play but in Holinshed's narrative: Macbeth and Banquo appear on horseback only in a woodcut in the *Historie of Scotland* and only there are they confronted by "Nimphes or Feiries" rather than bearded witches. Forman also coordinated the reign of Macbeth in Scotland with a reference point familiar to Holinshed's English readers: "yt was in the dais of Edward the Confessor." He also situates *Cymbeline* with a reference to an early regnal period, registering that it occurred "in Lucius tyme."

Remember also the storri of Cymbalin king of England, in *Lucius* tyme, howe *Lucius* Cam from Octavus Cesar for Tribut, and being denied, after sent *Lucius* with a greate Arme of Souldiars who landed at Milford haven, and Affter wer vanquished by Cimbalin, and *Lucius* taken prisoner [italics added].

Scholars have assumed that all three Luciuses italicized above refer to the character Caius Lucius who figures in the play as Roman ambassador and general. But what sense does it make to identify the historical moment by *any* fictional person? "In Lucius time" should function like "in the dais of Edward the Confessor" to situate the play in historical time. It is more probable that the first-named Lucius refers not to the character Lucius but to the historical British king Lucius who ruled in the final decades of the second century AD. But how could the story of one historical British king (Cymbeline, 23 BC to AD 2) take place in the "tyme" of another (Lucius, AD 180–200)? The anachronism may be the result less of confused genealogy than of the interchangeability of the two kings who ruled during periods when chronicle history intersected with ecclesiastical. In the reign of Cymbeline, as Holinshed stressed, Jesus was born.[29] In the reign of Lucius, as Holinshed also highlighted, Britain converted to Christianity, Lucius himself having been "the first king of the Britains that receiued the faith of Jesus Christ."[30] So, too, in *Actes and Monuments*, John Foxe follows upon his first period, beginning with the birth of Christ, with a second, "From the Time of King Lucius," which includes "The First planting of the Christian faith in England" and "Lucius first christened king of the Britons."[31] In both diary entries, then, Forman's recollection of plays the Folio catalogues as Tragedies is filtered through his encounter with the historical record.

Had *Macbeth* and *Cymbeline* survived in quarto, they might have been titled Histories, as was the quarto *Lear*. Like the plays the Folio classifies as such, *King Lear*, *Cymbeline*, and *Macbeth* all draw on Holinshed's *Chronicles*. (Indeed, in the case of *Cymbeline*, in which the eponymous king neither suffers nor dies and which ends in happy reconciliation of both nations and families, History seems a fitter term than Tragedy.) The Folio excludes *Cymbeline* as it does *Lear* and *Macbeth* (not to mention the Roman plays) from the *Histories* not because they are not part of the historical record but because they are set in a time before 1066, before the rule of William I from whom, in theory, all twenty-five subsequent kings had descended, "in their orderlie successions." In Holinshed's 1587 *Chronicles*, the break is unmistakable. In the first volume, England's history stops just before the Conquest and does not resume until the third volume; the second volume contains the description and histories of Ireland and Scotland. When the third volume begins, a new format is introduced. "*Beginning at duke William the Norman, commonlie called the Conqueror*" and extending to the twenty-fifth year of Elizabeth's reign, each chapter corresponds to and is titled after a reign. Shakespeare's Folio also follows the *Chronicles* by signaling the epochal break with a change in format. A new generic unit is introduced, cordoned off on the "Catalogue" page, and differentiated from the other two genres within the volume by its own pagination (1–232).

In Holinshed, the period before 1066 is divided into a series not of English rulers but of foreign Rules, as its title-page announces: "*The Historie of England, from the time that it was first inhabited, until the time that it was last conquered.*" At its conclusion, a "summe of all the foresaid historie" is provided on half of a page. The marginal rubrics read as follows: "Britaine inhabited by Brute. 1 Britaine conquered by the Romans. 2 Britaine conquered and ouercome by the Saxons. 3 Britaine conquered and ouercome by the Danes. 4 Britaine conquered and possessed by the Normans."[32] After its legendary founding by the eponymous Brut, Britain's history fell into four periods of colonization, "the foure great and notable conquests of this land," each one occurring after a foreign invasion: by the Romans, Saxons, Danes, and Normans. In both John Speed's *The Theatre of the Empire of Great Britain* (1611) and Michael Drayton's *Poly-Olbion* (1612), these four "Rules" or "Regiments" were represented on the title-page engraving by four conquering figures (Illustration 3).[33] Samuel Daniel in his *Historie of England* explains why the fourth period was distinct from the others:

I come to write of a time . . . an alteration, and generally an innovation in most things, but Religion. So that from this mutation, which was the greatest it euer had, we are to begin, with a new accompt of an *England,* more in dominion abroad, more in State, and ability at home, and of more honour, and name in the world, then heretofore.[34]

For Daniel, the unprecedented and extensive changes ushered in by the Norman Conquest called for "a new accompt." England experienced "innovation in most things" – in law, government, language, and custom – in everything but religion, which would have to await the Reformation.[35] In 1600, England could still consider itself in the Fourth or Norman Rule, and its submission to a fifth was not unimaginable. Fulke Greville speculated that had the Spanish Armada succeeded, England would have passed into a fifth rule: "*Albion* / Hath fyve tymes byn assaild, fowre tymes o'recome."[36] It is this history of being overcome four times over that is lost to the processional history of royal lineage after 1066.[37] In the Folio Histories, England is threatened by internal strife rather than attacked from abroad, and, consolidating its forces, it becomes itself an invader, extending its "dominion abroad," in Daniel's words, to Ireland, Scotland, the Holy Land, France, and eventually the New World. "More in dominion abroad" and no more dominated by foreign powers, Britain

Illustration 3. *The Four Rules of British History,* Frontispiece to Michael Drayton, *Poly-Olbion* (1612).

steps from the role of ruled to that of ruler, and history is represented by a succession not of foreign rules but of English monarchs.

After the Folio's dispensation, genre served to differentiate the pre-Conquest from the post-Conquest plays. The pre-1066 plays are tragedies: remote, legendary (if not fictional), and pertaining to the suffering of individuals; the post-1066 plays are histories: immediate, relevant, and concerning the vicissitudes of state. The generic divide cut England's history off from that of Britain, for *Cymbeline*, *Lear*, and *Macbeth* all feature the reigns of British kings. Written in the early years of James' reign and performed by the newly liveried King's men, these plays may have been an attempt to provide the new king with a more broadly based history that could be shared by England, Scotland, and Wales. By 1623, however, James' project of union had long been forgotten. By removing the reigns before William I from those after, the Folio Catalogue represented not the British history of the Four Rules but the English history of royal succession, from the coronation of King John (1199) to the baptism of Elizabeth I in the reign of her father (1533). While the Histories themselves emphasize the indirections by which the crown is obtained and retained (King John's contested rule, Richard's deposition, the Wars of the Roses), the Folio's serializing of these reigns gave the impression of the orderly tenure and transfer of the crown, not to mention its indefinite extension into the future.

With the introduction of a genre called Histories, the Folio dissolved the kinship between tragedy and history. The tragedies, traditionally drawn from historical materials, appeared ahistorical when segregated from the new genre. Plays from chronicle history before 1066 are cast into mythical time or aevum. Indeed the Folio's generic division definitively split off England's post-1066 history of sovereign autonomy from Britain's approximately 1,000 years of having been conquered and dominated. If *Cymbeline, King Lear*, and *Macbeth* had been included among the Folio Histories, the chronological line-up would have been considerably more extensive: beginning with the pre-Roman "Inhabitation" under *King Lear*, continuing with the First Rule under King Cymbeline, skipping to the Third with King Macbeth in Scotland and King Edward the Successor in England, before continuing the sequence with King John in the last Fourth Rule. From William I's epochal ascension, the jump back to the tragedy *Macbeth* is shorter in years than the one forward to the history *King John*.

It is worth noting that eighteenth-century editors did not adopt the Folio's generic dispensation. Pope classified *Lear* as an "Historical Play,"

Macbeth and *Cymbeline* as "Tragedies drawn from History" as distinct from "Tragedies drawn from Fable" like *Othello*. Subsequent editors from Theobald through Malone lead off the Histories with *King Lear* or *Macbeth* or both. Only after the 1821 Boswell/Malone edition are the two tragedies permanently returned to the generic niche assigned by the Folio. And yet, had Boswell followed his senior editor's instructions, the 1821 edition would have been the first to change the order of the Histories, for Malone urged him to arrange the plays in all three Folio genres in the conjectured order of composition Malone had himself provided.[38] Boswell obliged with the tragedies and comedies, but refused to "break the historical chain,"[39] so the procession of English kings prevailed until the twentieth century when in some editions the author's development took precedence over the nation's regnal history and the Histories for the first time were printed in the order in which Shakespeare was thought to have written them. Several twentieth-century editions, notably *The Norton Shakespeare*, in violation of both ordinal logic and regnal history, begin the Histories with *2 Henry VI* and proceed to *Henry IV* and *Henry V*.[40]

The historical divide of 1066 has thus come to double as a generic determinant, splitting plays which dramatize the same chronicle material into Histories and Tragedies. And yet, as we have seen, the three pre-1066 chronicle plays are set in the more capacious British history of the Four Rules. This may account for their common thematic feature of foreign invasion. France invades England to restore Lear to the throne, Rome storms Wales in order to exact tribute from the English, England attacks Scotland to oust the bloody tyrant Macbeth. (And here *Othello*, though originating in fable rather than history, is true to kind in featuring the specter of Turkish invasion.) *King John*, the History which takes place closest to the 1066 watershed, glances back to this earlier history; the possibility of attack from France hovers over the play, though it ends with a boast of England's invincibility, "Come the three corners of the world in arms / And we shall shock them."[41]

At the turn of the nineteenth century, A. C. Bradley devised the category of "pure" tragedy in order to explain why his *Shakespearean Tragedy* focused on four plays alone: *Hamlet, Lear, Macbeth,* and *Othello*. What makes them "pure" is their dissociation from history. Disencumbered of matters of state, the "pure tragedies" are free to concentrate on the suffering of great individuals. But post-Kantian transcendence was nowhere on the horizon of the Folio's compilers.[42] Their concerns were more practical: how to stake a cultural claim for Shakespeare's Folio to rival that of its only precedent, *The Workes of Beniamin Jonson* (1616). If

Jonson was hailed as the "English Horace," what claim to fame could be made for the poet with "small Latin and less Greek"? The 1616 Folio was formatted to celebrate Jonson's accomplishment as the ancient English poet: the triumphal monument that comprises the title-page, its Latin inscriptions, the allegorical statues representing the classical genres sub-titled in Latin (*Tragi Comoedia, Tragoedia, Comoedia, Satyr,* and *Pastor*), and the scholarly marginal glosses. The 1623 Folio, by contrast, billed Shakespeare as the modern English poet. Without mediating classical apparatus, the author himself appears in contemporary dress, enframed not in a classical roundel but in a modern quadrilateral. Unlike Jonson's *Workes,* Shakespeare's texts make no pretense to being like classical *Opera.* They are instead "Comedies, Histories, & Tragedies," all plays, including one kind that is exclusively modern. The new genre of Histories imparts a fresh contemporaneity to the volume, and one that is distinctly English, especially when made up of a series of plays dealing with what might be termed "modern English history," history since 1066, the history England chose to recognize as the beginning of its own present, stretching from the crowning of King John to the birth of its last monarch, Queen Elizabeth.

But where does *Hamlet* fit in?

When Pope edited *Hamlet* in 1725, no source for the play had yet surfaced: "This Story was not invented by our Author; tho' from whence he took it, I know not."[43] Certain that the source was fictional, he classified the play as a "Tragedy from Fable," like *Romeo and Juliet* and *Othello,* rather than a "Tragedy from History," like *Julius Caesar* or *Coriolanus.* The decision might have been more complicated later in the century after Theobald had discovered Saxo's *Historiae Danicae* and Capell had tracked down Belleforest's *Histoires Tragiques* as well as the anonymous *The Hystorie of Hamblet.*[44] In all events, *Hamlet* after the Restoration was unequivocally a tragedy. The 1676 quarto broke with the quarto tradition of calling the play the *Tragical History of Hamlet* and switched to the Folio nomenclature: *The Tragedy of Hamlet.* All subsequent quartos followed suit. Performances conformed to the classification by omitting the very passages that would have signaled its historical affiliations. The 1676 *Tragedy of Hamlet* downplayed the Norwegian element, reducing Horatio's account of Denmark's victory over Norway, eliminating the Norwegian and English ambassadors, and cutting Claudius' explanation of England's homage to Denmark. In 1718, the Hugh-Wilkes version dehistoricized the play further still, eliminating not only the ambassadors but Fortinbras too, and transferring the play's final words from Denmark's conqueror to

Hamlet's friend Horatio. Not until 1898 did Fortinbras return at the play's end to take over the Danish throne.[45] For some 200 years of its performance history, no invasion was threatened at the start and no foreign takeover occurred at the end. The Ghost ceased to augur the fall of state; the lines describing it as a "portentous figure" (1.1.112) are cut, along with those from Q2 comparing it to Roman prodigies. No Norwegian army crosses the stage; no exchange between Hamlet and the Norwegian captain occurs. In short, all of the features that signify the play's involvement in the history of governments and nations are abbreviated or removed.

Like *Lear*, *Cymbeline*, and *Macbeth*, *Hamlet* is notionally set in the preregnal history of the Four Rules. In Saxo Grammaticus, Amleth's adventures occur during the eleventh century when England's and Denmark's histories were entwined. The French redactor and English translator had no interest in this history, and vaguely set the narrative in pre-Christian times, "long time before the kingdome of Denmark received the faith of Jesus Christ."[46] Shakespeare's play is notably more specific about England's role in the Danish narrative. English ambassadors arrive in Denmark, and England is invoked by name nineteen times, more often than in any of the post-1066 regnal plays with the exception of *King John*, *Henry V*, and *2 Henry VI*. At three separate points, Claudius resolves to send Hamlet to England, each time with increasing conviction that his madness conceals treachery. Doubtful that Hamlet's aberrant behavior is symptomatic of love, Claudius resolves to deport him: "he shall with speed to England" (3.1.171). After the incriminatory Mousetrap play, he again determines to do so, and arranges for his conveyance by Rosencrantz and Guildenstern: "And he to England shall along with you" (3.3.4). When the slaying of Polonius reveals that his own life is at risk – "It had been so with us had we been there" (4.1.13) – he finally dispatches him: "We will ship him hence" (4.1.30); "everything is bent / For England . . . For England? . . . [B]ut come, for England . . . [C]ome, for England" (4.3.45–6, 47, 51–2, 55–6).

That the King wishes to eliminate Hamlet is obvious, and he explains why he cannot do so himself: for "the great love the general gender bear him" (4.7.18). But why ship him to England rather than any other nearby country? (Hamlet incognito will later ask this very question: "Why was he sent into England?" [5.1.145].) In Belleforest, as in Saxo, the king takes advantage of his friend, prefering rather "that his friende should defile his renowne with so great wickednesse, then himself to fall into perpetuall infamie."[47] But Shakespeare assigns a less personal motive. England is

Denmark's "faithful tributary" (5.2.39). Hamlet can be sent there quite plausibly on the pretense of collecting "our neglected tribute" (3.1.172). The tribute, as editorial glosses routinely explain, refers to the *Danegeld* or land tax paid by the Anglo-Saxon kings to fend off the marauding Danish. Because of England's tributary status, Denmark's king is confident that his command for "[t]he present death of Hamlet" will be satisfied (4.3.68). "Do it, England" (4.3.68), he enjoins, and knows England would not dare do otherwise.

> And England, if my love thou hold'st at aught –
> As my great power thereof may give thee sense,
> Since yet thy cicatrice looks raw and red
> After the Danish sword, and thy free awe
> Pays homage to us – thou mayst not coldly set
> Our sovereign process[.]   (4.3.61–6)

Still smarting from conquest by the "Danish sword," England will readily perform the Danish king's command.[48]

Because *Hamlet* has been read as timeless tragedy, the specificity of its historical setting has been overlooked.[49] As the references to England indicate, however, Shakespeare set the play sometime after Denmark's invasion of England in 1017, the beginning of the Third Rule, just after the Danish King Canute's defeat of the English, dramatized in the anonymous *Edmund Ironside* (c. 1632). Conquered by Denmark, Britain retained its tributary status until conquered again in 1066 by the Normans. Indeed the Norman invasion occurred so fast upon the Danish, that some chroniclers consolidated the two, considering them "a double blow as it were in the necke one after another within a few yeares," "a two-fold conquest of the land."[50] The proximity of the two invasions might shed light on the gratuitous introduction of the mysterious Norman horseman.

KING   Two month since
          Here was a gentleman of Normandy . . .
LAERTES   A Norman was't?
KING   A Norman.
LAERTES   Upon my life, Lamord [*Lamound* F].
KING   The very same.
LAERTES   I know him well. He is the brooch indeed
          And gem of all the nation.
                    (4.7.80–1, 89–93)

The "gentleman of Normandy," by Claudius' report, is the equestrian marvel who piqued Hamlet's envy by lavishly praising Laertes' skill at fencing. His praise "[d]id Hamlet so envenom with his envy / That he could nothing do but wish and beg / Your sudden coming o'er to play with you" (4.7.102–4). But why must Laertes' praises be sung by a Norman? The Folio's name for the Norman, *Lamound*, has led some editors to take the horseman as a "personal allusion" to a cavalier in Castiglione's *The Courtier*, Pietro Monte or, in Hoby's translation, Peter Mount. But why cast the Italian cavalier as a Norman? Another strain of commentary finds allegorical significance in Q2's rendition of his name. Harry Levin has identified *Lamord* as the apocalyptic rider from Revelation (6:2), "a vision of Death on a pale horse," and Margaret Ferguson also argues for his association with death, a subtle "*memento mori* admonition" intended for the reader.[51] But, again, why should this mysterious figure originate in Normandy? Here it may be helpful to distinguish Normandy from modern France, the location of Paris, the city to which Laertes is keen to return, the fashion capital where the best in rank are "rich, not gaudy" (1.3.71) in their dress, where even rapiers and poiniards are stylishly attired (5.2.146–7). The Normandy of *Lamord/Lamound* belongs to an earlier time frame, after the region was conquered by the eponymous Norsemen in the tenth century and before they charged across the Channel to conquer England in the eleventh. It was their skill on horseback that gave them the advantage over the English at the Battle of Hastings, as is commemorated by the Bayeux tapestry. As Claudius remembers of the Normans, "they can well on horseback" (4.7.83). The horseman's association with the invading Normans by no means rules out Revelation as his provenance. Norman and apocalyptic horsemen are both conquerors. The deathly resonance of *Lamord* is appropriate to both. So, too, are the two senses of *mound* in *Lamound*: a burial tumulus and the globe-like orb mounted with a cross, often featured in imperial portraits.

Extraneous to the plot, Claudius' fifty-line disquisition on the Norman makes for a clean theatrical cut. Even Laertes seems puzzled by its purpose: "What out of this, my lord?" (4.7.105). Claudius's response suggests that it is intended to warm Laertes up to duel with Hamlet, but surely the incensed Laertes needs no fueling. The ambiguous horseman, belonging to both England's eleventh century past and its unprescribed eschatological future, is an anachronous composite. He serves the same admonitory and premonitory function as the Ghost, who simultaneously references the historical past of ancient Rome's "sheeted dead" (1.1.118) as well as the looming future of the rising dead. Both specters presage fatality to the state and its prince.

In an attempt to identify topical allusions, scholarly attention has focused on England's relation to Denmark around 1600. Scholars have determined that the Baltic Sea was then infested by pirates, that a Danish embassy arrived in Edinburgh to demand the return of the isles of Orkney and Scotland, that negotiations were underway for the marriage of James VI to Anne of Denmark. Yet England is pulled into the play through a much earlier relation to Denmark. A period of English history was named after it: the fifty-year period just before the Norman Conquest known as the Rule of the Danes. The long tradition that has seen *Hamlet* as the inaugural work of the modern period has been blind to the historical moment in which the play situates itself. But it has also ignored the play's own preoccupation with the process of history, the alternations of state that punctuate world history, as one kingdom gives way to another in what might be called a premodern imperial schema that assumes the eventual fall of all kingdoms and their final subsumption by the apocalyptic kingdom-to-come.

Set within the fifty-year period in which Britain fell first to the Danes and then to the Normans, the play alludes to the most famous imperial falls of ancient history. The speech Hamlet "chiefly loved" derives from Virgil's great imperial epic. Extracted from Aeneas' extended account of the Trojan War, it was widely translated and imitated during Shakespeare's time in both school exercises and poetic set-pieces. The speech climaxes when Pyrrhus, after wending his way through burning Troy, comes upon his royal victim and slays him as the towers of Troy come crashing down. King and kingdom go down together, the felling of Priam and fall of Troy. The fall marks the extinction of a great race, as Thomas Heywood concludes in his great poem, "Thus is King *Priam* and Queene *Hecubs* race, / Extinct in dust," and the beginning of a new, as Aeneas flees Troy to found what by Virgil's time was imperial Rome.[52] The context in which Aeneas narrates the fall of Troy is also important: he recounts it to Dido, the Queen of an emergent empire, on his voyage to found a new empire. As he surveys the newly erected edifices of Carthage, he thinks back on the destruction of his native kingdom and looks ahead to the long task of founding a new one. At the time of Aeneas' recounting, Troy was the kingdom of the past, Carthage of the present, and Rome of the future. By the time Virgil wrote his great epic, however, Carthage had been reduced to salty ashes by Rome's infamous Carthaginian peace. Carthage had followed the course of Troy; and, in due time, Rome would cede to the same fate. Even at the height of its power, historically minded Romans knew what the future held in store. In an account in Appian's *History of Rome* which Shakespeare may have known, at the very moment of Rome's victory over Carthage, Scipio Africanus at once remembered the fall of Troy, foresaw the fall of Rome, and wept:

After being wrapped in thought for long, and realizing that all cities, nations, and empires, just like men, must meet their doom, that this was what the once fortunate city of Troy suffered, as did the might of the Assyrians, the Medes, the Persians, and the very recent and brilliant empire of Macedonia, he uttered, whether voluntarily or otherwise, the words of the poet: "The day shall come when sacred Troy shall perish; as also Priam, with the people over whom spear-bearing Priam rules."[53]

When asked by his tutor what he meant by quoting from the *Iliad* (6.448–90), Scipio allowed that he feared the same fate would befall Rome.[54] Recollection and prolepsis produce the same narrative of the "precurse of fear'd events" (1.1.124). As Carthage fell, so, too, had past kingdoms and so, too, would future ones. In his *History of the World*, Raleigh observed the same pattern in commenting on Carthage's decline: "So this glorious citie, ranne the same fortune, which many other great ones have done, both before and since." As in the history of the Four Monarchies, the long series of imperial falls would finally culminate in the end of the world portended by every fall: "The ruine of the goodliest pieces of the world foreshews the dissolution of the whole world."[55]

The great example of imperial collapse is featured in the "excellent play" (2.2.435) from which the Player recites. Within the speech Hamlet "chiefly loved" (442), Aeneas' tale to Dido, lies the passage he "especially" loved of "Priam's slaughter" (443–4). The relevance of the speech is generally seen through Hamlet's eyes: he seeks inspiration from the bloodthirsty avenger Pyrrhus. But the importance of the speech extends beyond Hamlet's personal situation. The death of Priam was the foundational moment of England's own history. Like Virgil's Rome, Britain traced its origins back to "Priam's slaughter" or the fall of Troy. From Caxton's *Chronicles of England* (1480) to Holinshed's *Chronicles* (1586), the event was routinely present at the threshold of British chronicle history. Gyles Godet's pictorial account of British kings opens with a woodcut of the burning of Troy.[56] The Historical Preface to *The Mirror for Magistrates* takes the same starting point, "When Troy was sackt, and brent, and could not stand."[57] As Jeffrey Knapp has shown, the story of Britain's founding as narrated by Geoffrey of Monmouth both extended and patterned itself after Virgil's great epic.[58] After the fall of Troy, Aeneas fled to found Rome; from there his great-grandson Brut was also thrown into exile (for the accidental killing of his father) and into multiple adventures while sailing around the Mediterranean before arriving, as prophesied, to the land over which he and his descendants would rule. *Nomen est omen*: embedded in the name given that isle was its link to that history: "Brute did first inhabit this land, and called it then after his owne name, Britaine."[59] A punning reference to Britain's founder has been heard in Hamlet's quip to Polonius when he boasts of having played Caesar at the university, "It was a brute part" (3.2.104).[60]

But the play is more interested in the brutal part played by the Roman Brutus. Polonius recalls having played the part of Caesar in a university production, "I did enact Julius Caesar" (3.2.102). The scene he remembers represented the very "fear'd events" (1.1.124) portended by the prodigies in the "high and palmy state of Rome" (1.1.116). "I was killed i'th'Capitol" (3.2.102), says the man who played Caesar. As Stephen Orgel has noted, the reference to Caesar's assassination in the Capitol refers to Shakespeare's own *Julius Caesar*, written shortly before *Hamlet*, for in Plutarch it occurs elsewhere, in Pompey's Theatre.[61] Named according to Pliny after the *caput* or head, the Capitol better suited Caesar's offending ambition to be alone at the top, in the position his name posthumously came to signify. As Polonius emphasizes, though all the conspirators set upon Caesar, the fatal stab was dealt by Brutus, the man he valued as a son, as his final words in Plutarch record, "*Et tu, mi fili, Brute.*" "It was a brute part of him to kill so capital a calf" (3.2.104–5), quips Hamlet, who will end up playing that brutish part himself when he stabs the former impersonator of Caesar behind the arras, mistaking him for the King ("Is it the king?" 3.4.26). His victim, however, turns out to be not the head of state but only a "capital" calf. The drop from Caesar to calf is one from ruler to slave, both types of movable property or cattle/chattel, deriving from the Latin for the chief source of wealth, *capitale* or property. In a repertory theatre that ran the two plays in close proximity, the link between Hamlet and Brutus would have been more apparent still if, as has been suggested, Richard Burbage (the English counterpart to the Roman Roscius, 2.2.386) played the parts of both Brutus and Hamlet and John Heminge of both Caesar and Polonius.[62] As Cassius and Brutus had predicted in Shakespeare's dramatization of Caesar's assassination, the deed would be reenacted, time after time, in other states and other tongues, on stage and off.

The play relates Hamlet to another Brute or Brutus, Lucius Junius Brutus, the ancestor of Marcus Brutus. Whether he came to know the story of Hamlet from the fifth volume of the French *Histories Tragiques* or from a manuscript version of the English translation, *The Hystorie of Hamblet*, Shakespeare would have found that the model for Hamlet's feigned idiocy was Lucius Junius Brutus. In the English translation, Hamlet is said to have known how to counterfeit madness because he "had been at the schoole" of this Brutus. It was from him that he learned how to bide his time by playing the fool: "running through the streets like a man distraught," begriming himself, speaking nonsense, "all his actions and jestures" proper only to a man deprived of his wits, "fitte for nothing but to make sport."[63] Hamlet adopts an ancient model, as is intimated by the unusual adjective he uses to describe his "disposition": "antic" shared both spelling and pronunciation with "antique."[64] One of the printed marginal notations of *The Hystorie of Hamblet* instructs the reader where to look for a fuller account of Brutus' "counterfeiting the foole" or "antic": "Read Titus Livius."[65] In the recently translated *The Romane Historie* (1600), Livy explained that this Brutus counterfeited "a noddie and a verie innocent" in order to conceal his conspiracy against the tyrannous king Tarquin, enduring the indignity of being called *Brutus*, "a name appropriate to unreasonable creatures." His disguise enabled him to "abide the full time and appeare in due season."[66] At the end of Shakespeare's *The Rape of Lucrece*, at the moment when Tarquin's crime is disclosed, Brutus casts off his "folly's show" and "shallow habit" and sparks an insurrection against Tarquin, ending in his "everlasting banishment."[67] In Livy, the very historian the reader of the English narrative is instructed to read, this event put an end not only to the Tarquinian line of kings, but to monarchy itself, thereby clearing the way for the rise of the Roman republic.[68] In his republican commentary on Livy, Machiavelli also describes Lucius Junius Brutus' dilatory folly and hails him as founder of the Roman republic and father of Roman liberty.[69]

Junius Brutus figured as consequentially at the beginning of republican Rome as his descendant did at its end. As the elder Brutus inaugurated the Republic so the younger Brutus attempted to preserve it by eliminating the man who aspired to the sovereignty that became synonymous with his name. The two Brutuses were often paired, one at either end of the 500-year duration of the Republic. Plutarch connects them in the opening sentence of his Life of the younger Brutus, "Marcus Brutus came of that Junius Brutus."[70] Lucan in his *Pharsalia* has the ghost of Junius Brutus anticipating the success of his descendant and namesake in the assassination of the absolutist Caesar.[71] Depending on their constitutional position, commentators either credited or blamed the Brutuses for felling kings. In the early 1600s, both Samuel Daniel and William Fulbecke wrote Roman histories condemning "the two Bruti," centuries apart, as haters of monarchy; for Fulbecke, the assassination was an act of "regicide," for once he had assumed sovereign power, Caesar was a *de facto* monarch.[72] Shakespeare stresses their kinship in *Julius Caesar* by having Cassius remind Brutus of his ancestor's hatred of kingship ("There was a Brutus once . . .") and Brutus takes that reminder to heart in reflecting on his predecessor, "My ancestor did from the streets of Rome / The Tarquin drive when he was called a king."[73]

Hamlet could be said to play the part of both Brutuses. He adopts the "antic disposition" of the former and the "brute part" of the latter. Might he also have shared their politics? As many scholars have pointed out, the circle forming around the Earl of Essex had a particular interest in Livy's *History of Rome*.[74] One member of this circle paired two Shakespearean works as the particular favorites of the learned. In a note to his edition of Chaucer's *Works* (1598), Gabriel Harvey maintained that *The Rape of Lucrece* and *Hamlet* both "haue it in them, to please the wiser sort."[75] Could "the wiser sort" have been those who like Harvey pored over Livy, readers who heeded the marginal instruction in the *The Hystorie of Hamblet* – "Read Livy" – and were sympathetic with the political leanings of the republican historian?[76] In the same note, Harvey cites one of the most celebrated readers of Livy, the Earl of Essex, whose fatal uprising against the monarch in February 1601 has often been identified with the civic disturbance or "late innovation" (2.2.331) Rosencrantz associates with the Players' flight from the city.[77]

Although bent on one in particular, Hamlet seems to take pleasure in the death of sovereigns in general. His favorite speech, as we have seen, describes the slaughter of a king. In both silent and spoken versions, the performance he sponsors requires that a king be poisoned. He stabs the man he thinks is king ("Is it the King?" 3.4.26); he considers, "too curiously" (5.1.199), the reduction of kings to dust, as well as their passage through "the guts of a beggar" (4.3.31). All these regicides – represented, mistaken, reflected upon – resemble rehearsals for the final debacle when he first stabs and then poisons the King of Denmark, to the frantic cry of "Treason! treason!" (5.2.328).

The play, too, targets monarchs with unusual frequency, in word and deed. It features a long graphic description of a king's poisoning, as well as an extended exposition on the dire consequences attending the end of kings or "cess [cease F] of majesty" (3.3.15). Sentries strike with their partisans at the "majestical" figure (1.1.148) they have just identified with the King: "Looks a not like the King?" (1.1.46) and "Is it not like the King?" (61). Backed by a "riotous head" (4.5.101), Laertes, "arm'd" as the Folio stage directions specify, breaks through the King's bodyguards – "Where is my Switzers?" (97); "The doors are broke" (111) – and draws on the King, "O thou vile king" (115). The messenger describes the violence of this outbreak as unprecedented, "as the world were now but to begin" (103). In this respect, it qualifies as an "innovation" (2.2.331), the term used to describe the civil disturbance that forced the "inhibition" (330) or ban on playing in the city. After so many assaults on the King's person and office, represented or enacted, the play leaves Denmark with no king on the throne, at least no Danish king.

In Q1, the Norwegian conqueror, upon spotting the heap of royal bodies strewn on the palace floor, cries out, "O imperious death!" (I4r). The carnage bears witness to both the death of an empire and the imperial sway of Death. The death of "so many princes at a shot" (5.2.371) leaves the empire without a ruling family. As with Priam's slaughter and Caesar's assassination, the "cess of majesty" takes the state with it. As the English Ambassador is moved to observe in Q1, "O most most unlooked for time! unhappy country" (I4r). Denmark has fallen, without a fight, into the hands of Denmark's inveterate enemy. Horatio knows full well what this means, "I am more an antique Roman than a Dane" (5.2.346). Editors stop short of a full gloss here, identifying his "antique" Romaness with a preference for suicide over dishonorable life without explaining that the source of dishonor derives from submission. Cato the younger and Brutus and even Portia chose death by their own hands in order to avoid the indignity of subjection. The import of these lines has been missed because tragedy has been defined to play down, if not rule out, historical events like a regime's downfall or foreign occupation. Also ignored are the multiple references to the pattern of imperial succession set in the ancient world by the four kingdoms and extended or translated into the present by the modern imperial ambitions of Europe and the East whose expir- ation was expected to coincide with the apocalyptic ushering in of a new heaven and new earth.

The same prodigies which presaged the fall of empire, in ancient "palmy Rome" and modern "pursy" Denmark, were also expected to herald the eschaton.[78] Horatio's description of the eclipse foreshadowing Caesar's death has precedents in both Plutarch and Lucan. Yet neither Roman would have recognized the phrase used to indicate the degree of darkness – "the moist star . . . Was sick almost to doomsday with eclipse" (1.1.121–3) – for it echoes the biblical prophecy in Isaiah that "the moon

shall not cause her light to shine" (13:10) as well as Christ's predictions of
his own Second Coming in both Mark (13:24) and Matthew (24:29).[79] So,
too, the evacuated graves – "the graves stood tenantless" (118) – that
preceded Caesar's fall also prefigure the rising of the dead at Judgment
Day. As we shall see in Chapter 5, in the graveyard scene, the remains of
imperial Alexander and Caesar are contemplated in the shadow of
Doomsday. The grave-digger makes "houses" to last until Doomsday,
while the great imperial houses (of Alexander, Caesar, and King Hamlet)
terminate in dust. These overlaps recall the celebrated point in time when
imperial history and salvational history converged. During the *pax
Romana*, the seven-year duration when the Roman Empire was at peace,
Christ was born. Prophecies of the auspicious concurrence were retro-
spectively identified in both classical and biblical texts, in Virgil's fourth
eclogue and Isaiah's prophecy in 2:4. The "time of peace" invoked to
comfort the watch after the eerie disturbance of the Ghost is Christmas,
"that season / Wherein our Saviour's birth is celebrated" when "this bird
of dawning singeth all night long" (1.1.163–5); "So hallow'd and so
gracious is that time" (1.1.169). Christmas marks the beginning of the
salvational history which ends with the Second Coming or Doomsday.
Eusebius and other Church historians believed that the two histories were
coterminous: when the Roman Empire expired, so too would the world
come to an end. Yet the world did not end when Rome fell in 476.[80] Nor
did the history of empire. The Danielic process began all over again.
Through the mechanism of *translatio imperii*, imperial power was transferred first to the Eastern Roman Empire at Byzantium (the "new
Rome"), then to the Franks with the crowning of Charlemagne as Holy
Roman Emperor in 800, and then through the Habsburgs to the Vienna
of Charles V in 1555; its destination after Charles' abdication was a major
European concern.[81]

Hamlet goes out of his way to specify that *The Murder of Gonzago* "is
the image of a murder done in Vienna" (3.2.232–3). It has been conjectured that Vienna may be a compositor's misreading of *Urbino* in an
alphabet in which V and U were interchangeable. Indeed Urbino would
be a more plausible location for a play which was purportedly "written in
very choice Italian" (256–7) and which scholars have identified with a
crime documented in 1538: the poisoning of the Duke of Urbino through
the ear by a Gonzago.[82] And yet in the context of the play's concern with
ancient and modern empires, the appearance of Vienna is not implausible, especially when backed by a punning allusion to Charles V's empire.
When asked the whereabouts of the slain Polonius, Hamlet says he is "At

supper" (4.3.17), or more accurately he *is* supper: "A certain convocation of politic worms are e'en at him. Your worm is your only emperor for diet" (4.3.19–21). A transposition of Hamlet's response allows for a more specific reference: to the convocation or Diet at Worms presided over by the emperor Charles V. At this momentous assembly in 1521, Luther was condemned by the Holy Roman Emperor for refusing to recant. It was this standoff at Worms between Vienna's Holy Roman Emperor and Wittenberg's protesting monk that split Christendom in two.[83] Foxe's detailed account of the Diet at Worms illustrated "how, and by what means this reformation of the church first began, and how it proceeded, increasing by little and little unto this perfection which now we see, and more I trust shall see."[84]

Another German city is woven into the play's imperial backdrop. Wittenberg was considered the "German Rome," the Protestant alternative to the great papal city. Hamlet, Horatio, Rosencrantz, and Guildenstern have all studied at Wittenberg, the university which had "growen famous, by reason of the controversies and disputations of religion, there handled by Martin Luther, and his adherents: the Doctors thereof at this day the greatest propugnators of the confession of Ausburge, and retaine in use the meere Lutherane religion."[85] Luther held an appointment at the University of Wittenberg, and famously posted his incendiary 95 theses on the Castle Church door. It was at Wittenberg, according to Foxe, that Luther repudiated the material presence of Christ in the Eucharist. "The mass [was] laid down first at Wittenberg," and on the advice of the learned, it was determined there that "the use of the mass [was] to be abrogated through [Duke Frederic's] dominion."[86] The context of supping on a corpse sharpens the reference since it was Luther's position on the substance of the Last Supper's bread and wine that posed the greatest threat to the established Church. From the vantage of the Protestant historiographers like Foxe, the Reformation witnessed the same convergence of the imperial and salvational as the Incarnation. For Samuel Daniel, too, it marked the beginning of the final fifth period before Doomsday which by reforming "religio" would complete the political and cultural "alternation" ushered in by the Norman Conquest.

There is no denying that the play produces a sense of contemporaneity: the university at Wittenberg (founded in 1502) is foregrounded, various types of cutting-edge weaponry (rapiers, petards, ordnances, Swiss mercenaries) are in view, recent or concurrent theatrical practices (jigs, chopines, boy acting companies) are mentioned, and topical events are referenced, like the theatrical flare-up between the rival boy and adult companies in 1600 and, more conjecturally, Essex's political "innovation" or insurrection in 1601. And yet through scattered allusions, tropes, and puns, the play also references events of world historical magnitude, all bearing on England's own remote and recent history, from the ancient Fall of Troy from which Britain claimed its own origins to the modern breakup of Christendom at Worms and Wittenberg from which it marked its spiritual Reformation. While the play is set in Denmark, England is drawn into the picture by the time period shared by the two nations, the Danish Rule preceding the great epochal divide of the Norman Conquest from which regnal succession traced its beginnings. Rather than a continuous time line running through this play we have a temporal jumble. A heavy Roman presence is created by the high number of Latinate names circulating in the play. Some are borne by characters (Lucianus, Cornelius, Reynaldo, Barnado, Francisco), including one belonging to an Augustan poet (Horatio) and another to a Roman emperor of the same dynasty as Augustus (Claudius) and still another of a man who was Augustus' son-in-law and prospective heir (Marcellus); additional Latin names are mentioned, referring to Roman figures, both historical (Seneca, Plautus, Roscius, Nero) and legendary (Hercules, Juno, Mars, Mercury); there is also, of course, the long set-piece recited by the Player of the Fall of Troy derived from Virgil's great Augustan imperial epic. Salvational history also spans the play: at the start the Incarnation is invoked to dispel the fear of the risen dead, and Doomsday looms over the remains of the dead at the end. History of empire, ancient history, history of the Four Rules, salvational history all impinge upon the play's contemporaneity, saturating it with the past, in preparation for another imperial fall.

At the opening of *Hamlet*, the Ghost appears at exactly the same time it had appeared twice before (and will appear again), and at the very instant when that time is being described:

> Last night of all,
> When yond same star that's westward from the pole
> Had made his course t'illume that part of heaven
> Where now it burns, Marcellus and myself,
> The bell then beating one –
> [*Enter* GHOST] (1.1.38–42)

The periphrastic sentence is broken off by the sudden arrival of precisely what it was winding up to name. "*Enter* GHOST". It appears just as "yond same star" once again completes its trajectory and the bell once again tolls one, to complete with its spectral presence the suspended syntax. The Ghost's visitation coincides, too, with the change of the watch at "the dead waste and middle of the night" (1.2.198): one sentry has just been relieved by another ("You come most carefully upon your hour"; "For this relief much thanks," 1.1.6, 8). Like its arrival "Jump at this dead hour" (1.1.68), the Ghost's departure is also punctual. The watch ends ("Break we our watch up," 1.1.173), and day breaks, heralded by a rush of sensations: the crowing of the cock, the scent of morning air, the rising sun. The Ghost's visit, then, is pinpointed by multiple time-telling intervals – planetary, mechanical, martial, diurnal. Each of them might be highlighted in performance through gesture and movement: Barnardo traces the star's arc in the air, a bell sounds one, one guard replaces another, and Horatio points to the reddening horizon (as the sentries turn): "But look, the morn . . . o'er . . . yon high eastward hill" (1.1.171–2). The duration of the Ghost's stay is also clocked: it lasts as long as the watch and is equated with a number of other temporal units: "hour" (1.4.3), "while one with moderate haste might tell a hundred" (1.2.237), a "season" (1.4.5), "a certain term" (1.5.10). In both scenes in which the Ghost appears to the watch, the multiple repetitions of "watch" (thirteen in all) release the pun on the small time-piece that mechanically and more minutely measures out the day.

The time of the Ghost's arrival is momentous, indeed epochal. Signaled by multiple time schemes, it marks the imminent end of Denmark's supremacy – the period which began thirty years earlier, as we learn in Act 5, with the victory of Hamlet I. The play dramatizes the decadent stretch leading to that upcoming end. It is a period of indolence referred to as "the fatness of these pursy times" (3.4.155). Though Elsinore was in the sixteenth century renowned for its impregnability, a fortress palace encircled by ordnances (the famed guns of Elsinore),[87] it is at the play's start altogether unprepared to defend its borders. Its forces are frantically working around the clock, importing artillery and casting cannons, with no regard for sleep or the sabbath (making "the night joint-labourer with the day," not dividing "Sunday from the week," 1.1.79, 81). Like the king napping in his garden after lunch, the country is caught off guard. At the play's start, Denmark has attempted to step up security, but the Danish cannons only fire in celebration of the King's wassail. It is the enemy Norwegian cannons which make the "warlike volley" (5.2.357).

In his history, Samuel Daniel asks how "so great a Kingdome as *England* then was, could with one blow be subdued by so small a Province as

Normandy."[88] He attributes the defeat to its neglect of arms. Enjoying too much security during the fifty years when no longer warring with Denmark, England had "growne neglective of Armes, and generally debaushed with luxurie, and idlenesse."[89] Sir John Smythe in *Certain Discourses Military* considered such neglect the first cause of "utter ruin to empires, kingdoms, and commonwealths"; the Britons were conquered by the Saxons, Danes, and Normans "by reason that they found them altogether without any orders and exercises military – wholly given to idleness, viciousness, and delights[.]"[90] Among both ancients, like Tacitus, and moderns, like Machiavelli, the neglect of arms was considered the most common cause of a kingdom's decline.[91] Luxuriating in peace, states leave themselves open to aggression from abroad. The Earl of Essex opposed the treaty with Spain, predicting that the English would grow unwarlike and in love with peace. James concurred, "Our Peace hath bred wealth: And Peace and wealth hath brought foorth a generall sluggishnesse, which makes us wallow in all sorts of idle delights, soft delicacies, the first seeds of the subversion of all great Monarchies."[92] Bacon in writing "Of the true Greatnesse of Kingdomes and Estates" also stressed the great lesson of history, "a most certain oracle of time," that empire depends on strength of arms.

The Persians and Macedonians had it for a flash. The Gauls, Germans, Goths, Saxons, Normans, and others, had it for a time. The Turks have it at this day, though in great declination. Of Christian Europe, they that have it are in effect only the Spaniards . . . no nation which doth not directly profess arms may look to have greatness fall into their mouths. And, on the other side, it is a most certain oracle of time, that those states that continue long in that profession (as the Romans and Turks principally have done) do wonders.[93]

The play associates imperial ambition with the young Norwegian prince named for his strength in arms. Fortinbras, "with divine ambition puff'd" (4.4.49), returns triumphant from Poland, his entry into foreign territory heralded with cannon shot, and his takeover of Denmark announced by his command at the play's close, "Go, bid the soldiers shoot" (5.2.408). In the past, however, it was the Danish king who was hailed throughout the Western hemisphere (on "this side of our known world," 1.1.88) as "valiant Hamlet" (87). Denmark's glory days were commemorated by the armor in which the Ghost of King Hamlet is encased, "cap-à-pie" (1.2.200), as he marches across the battlements. His exploits included the subduing of Norway in single combat, the smiting of Polacks on the ice, the pummeling of the English, and campaigns against the French. But when the throne passed from one brother to the other, a "falling off" (1.5.47) occurred. In foreign and domestic affairs, King Claudius consistently avoids combat. While King Hamlet took military measures, his brother resorts to diplomacy. Claudius handles the threat at the borders by treaties and agreements, he rids himself of Hamlet by arranging for another king to execute him, and he quells the civil "rebellion" (4.5.121) at the palace gates through deft rhetoric, "o'erul[ing its leader] to a peace" (4.7.59). While King Hamlet was once recognized throughout half the world for his valor, King Claudius is now taxed east and west for his revelry; his debauchery is "traduc'd and tax'd of other nations" (1.4.18). The guns of Elsinore are now fired to celebrate not military supremacy but the King's carousing; they are shot off twice during Claudius' reign, each time to broadcast his "heavy-headed revel" (Q2, 1.4.17). It is this world-wide ("east and west," 1.4.17) advertising of the King's sensuality that Hamlet finds so damaging "a soil" (1.4.20) to Denmark's reputation.

Yet Hamlet is hardly more inclined to take up arms. The Ghost holds that if Hamlet were to remain unstirred after learning of his father's poisoning, he would prove himself "duller . . . than the fat weed / That roots itself in ease on Lethe wharf" (1.5.32–3). And Hamlet *is* like the "fat weed." His failure to stir is signaled by the Ghost's return to rebuke his "tardy son . . . laps'd in time and passion" (3.4.107–8) and "to whet [his] almost blunted purpose" (3.4.111). Hamlet twice berates himself for inertia – before the Ghost's return, when he calls himself "a dull and muddy-mettled rascal . . . Like John-a-dreams" (2.2.562–3) and after, when wondering that nothing can "spur my dull revenge" (4.4.33). He describes himself as sedated, oblivious and listless, his energies sapped as if by a Circean cup of opium or asphodel. His antics add another dimension to his inactivity; "I must be idle" (3.2.90), he says, and proceeds to speak "with an idle tongue" (3.4.10). Though Ophelia eulogizes an earlier Hamlet as soldier as well as courtier and scholar, he retains little trace of his military promise. "I have of late . . . forgone all custom of exercise" (2.2.295–7), he admits, though later before dueling with Laertes he claims to have been in "continual practice" (5.2.207), like Denmark itself making last-minute preparations in anticipation of attack. He writes rather than fights himself out of danger: after he discovers the command for his execution, it is his penmanship that does him a "yeoman's service" (5.2.36). Unlike his swashbuckling counterpart in Saxo and Belleforest, he relies on bribery rather than swordplay to escape the pirates. Most telling of all, he returns from England "naked" (4.7.42), that is, unarmed and without an army, unlike Laertes who arrives from France empowered by a violent "rabble" (4.5.102). Claudius asks, "naked?", as if incredulous that Hamlet would return without military backing. As heir-apparent, "love[d by] the general gender" (4.7.18), Hamlet surely could have mustered up support from the rabble as easily as Laertes, and in protest of the same violation of the principle of succession: the shadowy death of the father in both cases, as we shall see in the next chapter, puts the son's inheritance at risk. Despite his recent "continual practice," Hamlet must be given odds in order to even out the match with Laertes. His mother's observation during the duel – "He's fat and scant of breath" (5.2.290) – allows for the possibility that he is indeed like the "fat weed" incapable of being stirred to action. His unfitness is staged when his mother offers him her handkerchief to wipe his brow, "Here, Hamlet, take my napkin, rub thy brows" (5.2.291). These details suggest that Hamlet is slow to take up arms not only against a metaphoric "sea of troubles" (3.1.59), but also against his father's murderer, not to mention Denmark's inveterate enemy.

After Hamlet's death, Fortinbras does his best to identify the casualties of court intrigue with heroic death in battle. He commands that Hamlet be given military honors, "Bear Hamlet like a soldier to the stage" (5.2.401) to "soldier's music," and the "rite of war" (5.2.404) which culminates in the firing of ordnances. It may be generosity for his defeated counterpart that prompts Fortinbras' solicitude. Or it may be his political cunning that would enhance his own glory by remembering his defeated rival as a war hero. Either way, it is a pointedly ironic way to commemorate a man who draws his sword only to enjoin an oath, falls short of using it on himself or his enemy, returns naked or unarmed to avenge himself, and needs an advantage in a court fencing match.

It is not too much of a stretch, perhaps, to relate Hamlet's lethargy to both his father's inertia in his final days and Denmark's state of unreadiness on the eve of anticipated attack. The Ghost twice specifies that he was "sleeping" within his orchard (1.5.59, 74), and in the Mousetrap play we see his double slumbering both in the dumbshow – "He lies him down upon a bank of flowers" – and in the play proper: "My spirits grow dull, and fain I would beguile / The tedious day with sleep" (3.2.221–2). The queen lulls him to his rest, "Sleep rock thy brain" (3.2.222), to create a tableau of a superannuated Mars collapsed in the lap of Venus. The nap is his "custom" (1.5.60), and so too, we must presume, is the rich meal that leaves him "full of bread" (3.3.80) (in Belleforest, he is killed after a banquet). Stuffed and drowsy, the king in his last days seems to embody the very life his son reproaches himself for leading, "What is a man / If his chief good and market of his time / Be but to sleep and feed?" (4.4.33–5). It is also the life-style of his brother; he is the "bloat King" (3.4.184) distended by drink and sex, carousing at the slightest pretext. All three royal Danish males, then, are representative of what Hamlet terms "the fatness of these pursy times" (3.4.155).[94] He also calls it the "drossy" age (5.2.186), after the dross or scum which rises to the top, the waste matter excreted by the flesh that signals the festering of the body after it goes to seed and rots. Like the body politic itself, "Things rank and gross in nature / Possess it merely" (1.2.136–7).

The pursiness and drossiness that characterize the age return us to "the fat weed / That roots itself in ease on Lethe wharf" (1.5.32–3). The Folio's *rots* is as appropriate as the Quartos' *roots* when decay results from lack of motion. As in the many instances noted in Chapter 1, earth and flesh are interchangeable: growths on the surface of the wharf have their counterpart on the skin in what Hamlet calls "th'impostume of much wealth and peace" (4.4.27), abscesses which like bed sores are the result of too sedentary a life. The "impostume" or "imposthume" (Q2) metaphor is applied to Norway's shocking willingness to spend twenty thousand ducats and two thousand men not in exchange "for the main of Poland" or "for some frontier" (4.4.15–16) but for an unarable "little patch of ground" (18), too small to bury those who will die fighting for it. In this instance, territory is not the cause of conflict. The battle is fought for "an eggshell" (4.4.53) or "a straw" (55) or even "that a fantasy and trick of fame" (61) called "honour" (56). But if military action is the only cure, it is worth the cost. Greville diagnoses similar tumors on the body politic from the neglect of arms:

> By this we plainly view the two *imposthumes*
> That choke a kingdoms welfare; Ease and Wantoness,
> And as we see a foul horizon made fair:
> So doth the warr, and her impietie
> Purge the imposthum'd humors of a peace;
> Which ofte els make good governemente decrease.[95]

As a boil is lanced, so the nation must be bled of soldiers. In Norway as well as Denmark, it appears, these are "pursy times," but Norway purges itself back to health. At the play's end, the Norwegian strongman stands triumphant atop the "quarry" of Danish princes (5.2.369).

Fortinbras, eager for battle, even if the stakes are negligible, gives his army the military exercise necessary to make the state wholesome. Norway, with its population of marauders, those hawkish "lawless" (Q2) or "Landlesse" (F) "resolutes" (1.1.101), is a hungry rather than a sated kingdom. Having levied an army "of such mass and charge" (4.4.47), Fortinbras intends to recover the territories his father lost to Denmark. Dissuaded by his uncle of his intention "to give th'assay of arms" (2.2.71) against Denmark, he redirects his ambitions eastward. "With conquest come from Poland" (5.2.355), Fortinbras' armed forces are heralded at Elsinore by "warlike noise" (354) and "warlike volley" (357). With his dying breath, Hamlet – *de facto* king in the short interval between Claudius' death and his own – casts his vote for Fortinbras as the next king of Denmark, "he has my dying voice" (5.2.361).[96] By a mere transposition of two letters, Q2 and F differ on the strength of that voice. For F, Hamlet's "voice will draw *on* more" (5.2.397); it will be ratified by the parliamentary votes required by an elective monarchy. For Q2, however, the "voice will drawe *no* more"; it ends with Hamlet's breath. From Fortinbras' position, however, the point is moot. He has no need for constitutional backing from Denmark when he has his own ancient claim to the throne: "I have some rights [F Rites] of memory in this kingdom / Which now to claim my vantage doth invite me" (394–5). His present "vantage" is obvious. In Q2 the audience has been treated to the spectacle of his army marching across the stage (*Fortinbrasse with his Army ouer the stage*) when headed toward Poland; while no such procession is seen on the army's triumphant return, it certainly can be heard: "What warlike noise is this?" (354) asks Hamlet. With the double advantage of an ancestral claim and military might, Fortinbras enters Denmark with the same winning combination he had brandished when threatening to attack: "strong hand / And terms compulsatory" (1.1.105–6). Then it was in violation of the "seal'd compact / Well ratified by law and heraldry" (1.1.89–90) between the two states; now, however, there is no Danish dynasty to contest the Norwegian "right/rite of memory." Thus the play ends with the foreign conqueror in command, who with his final words gives an order – "Go, bid the soldiers shoot" (5.2.408) – that we hear instantly performed in the resonating sound with which the play ends: "*a Peale of Ordnance are shot off.*" A salvo to the passing of a prince, perhaps, but also the heralding of a new power on the throne.

Horatio was right in inferring that the Ghost's visitation portended "some strange eruption to the state." As it turns out, the "strange eruption" is not caused by *strangers*, the Norwegian foreigners who threatened attack from the border. The "eruption" arises from elsewhere – from "th'imposthume of much wealth and peace." Denmark's history comes full circle: the era which began thirty years ago in territorial and dynastic expansion ends in collapse, as the result not of outward conquest but of inner degeneracy. It is this epochal structure that has been lost to the tradition of Hamlet criticism. When the play loses its historical context, the Ghost performs no "precursive" or proleptic function. It sets the revenge plot into motion. Nor does the threat of attack signify, except as a cover or decoy for the "real danger" that exists to Hamlet's psyche; it is there that penetration and contamination are feared.[97] The play's multiple allusions to the large sweep of imperial history remain inert. The sluggishness of the state and its princes goes unremarked. Or rather, it is remarked only in respect to Prince Hamlet, and interpreted, as we shall see in the Chapter 6, in terms of some form of psychological difficulty.

As we have seen, the play situates the fall of the Danish empire in a context of imperial rises and falls that includes Priam's Troy, Alexander's Greece, Dido's Carthage, Caesar's Rome, and the notional Duke of Urbino's Vienna. It also signals the two great modern threats to Christendom: the standoff between Luther and Charles V that split Christendom in two and the hovering threat of the Turks who in the sixteenth century had made their way to the very gates of Vienna, the seat of the Holy Roman Emperor. And England is included in this imperial panorama, obliquely, by turning back the clock five centuries to the time when it was itself a subjugated colony between the Danish and Norman Rules. England is not in the dominant role of a nascent imperial kingdom, as we might expect, but in the submissive colonial one of paying taxes and obeying foreign commands.

In the context of this imperial vicissitude, two notorious variants from Q1, both consistently rejected by editors, seem less far-fetched. In Q2 and F, Hamlet announces that the Mousetrap play represents "a murder done in *Vienna*" (3.2.233); in Q1, however, the murder is done in "*guyana.*"[98] The imagined seat of the Inca Empire slips into the place of the capital of the Holy Roman Empire. In F, Hamlet derides players who in their excessive histrionics resemble no human species: neither "Christian, Pagan, or Norman" [Q2 nor man]. In Q1, humanity is divided into a more comprehensive triad of Christian, pre-Christian, and non-Christian: "Christian, Pagan, / Nor Turke" (F2r). The "Turke," the prospective conqueror of Europe, slips into the place of the Norman, the last conqueror of Britain, as if one outlandish conquering stranger were as good as another. It is as if moveable type were conforming to the same principle of imperial interchangeability as history itself.

CHAPTER 4

Generation and degeneracy

Men forget more quickly the death of their father than the loss of their patrimony.

Machiavelli

In the graveyard, Hamlet incognito makes small talk with the sexton, Goodman Delver, "How long hast thou been grave-maker?" (5.1.138). When Delver answers, Hamlet feigns ignorance of what "every fool can tell" (142), at least every fool in Denmark: when it was that "our last King Hamlet o'ercame Fortinbras" (140). That day, it can be assumed from the sexton's response, featured an event of such national import that time could be popularly measured from its occurrence. Only an ignoramus or an outsider would require a gloss. But for the sake of the audience, at the very start of the play, one has been introduced. To explain Denmark's sudden military preparations, Horatio dredges up past history: Norway is threatening attack in order to recover lands King Fortinbras lost in combat with King Hamlet (1.1.105–7). Another crisis also seems at this early point to relate back to that event. The ghost of the man who "was and is the question of these wars" (114) appears, wearing "the very armour he had on, / When he th'ambitious Norway combated" (63–4), as if ready to fight once again for those same lands.

In the graveyard, when Hamlet, playing the fool or foreigner, professes not to know how long ago this epochal event occurred, Delver gives him another benchmark: "It was that very day that young Hamlet was born" (5.1.142–3). The coincidence could not have been more auspicious. The annexing of land and the birth of a prince are a dynastic dream-come-true. One event complements the other. Indeed the legal instruments drawn up at the time of the combat seem designed to assure that the territorial gain will be passed on to the victor's descendants. They stipulate that the forfeit of the lands be absolute: the loser "by a seal'd compact / Well ratified by law and heraldry / Did forfeit with his life all those his lands" (1.1.89–91). In addition, like any *feudum*, the forfeited lands are descendible: "by the same cov'nant / And carriage of the article" (96–7), the victor would receive the lands "[t]o the inheritance" (94). On the very day that Denmark won these inheritable lands, a prince to inherit them was born. Like a happy astrological convergence, the coincidence seems prophetic: Hamlet was born to rule.

Still another event occurred on that day. Goodman Delver began his job: "I have been sexton here, man and boy, thirty years" (5.1.156–7). When Denmark was at the height of its powers, its rule extended spatially through land and temporally through an heir, Delver started digging graves. Like the Ghost and the Norman horseman discussed in Chapter 3, the grave-maker belongs to the mystical world of Last Things, the world that makes itself felt through premonitions, like the "gaingiving" (5.2.211) that troubles Hamlet before his fatal duel: "Thou wouldst not think how ill all's here about my heart" (5.2.208–9). The grave-maker also serves as a reminder of the end that is both imminent (about to come) and imma-nent (present at every moment). As with the empires of the Four Mon-archies, so with Denmark: even at its inaugural triumph, its end is ominously at hand. That the rise of Denmark belongs to the same design as its fall is indicated by their chiasmic relation. What began long ago, in the defeat of Norway and the birth of the Danish prince, ends in the triumph of Norway and the death of the Danish prince. At the play's start, the time looked good for invading Denmark: after the sudden death of King Hamlet, the state appeared "disjoint and out of frame" (1.2.20). At the play's end, the time looks better still: the royal family has been wiped out; Denmark has collapsed. Nothing remains of the royal house of Denmark but a "quarry" (5.2.369). During that thirty-year stretch, Denmark was maintaining its supremacy, Hamlet preparing to come into his own, and the grave-maker numbering the days of both kingdom and prince. At its end, Denmark has fallen, Hamlet is dead; and Delver carries on with his unending work. Unlike dynastic houses, "[t]he houses he makes lasts till doomsday" (5.1.59). "One generation passeth away, and another generation cometh; but the earth abideth for ever" (Eccles. 1:4).

Only one of these three concurrent events has attracted critical attention: Hamlet's birth. Indeed the exchange in 5.1 that draws them together has been thought to have been "expressly inserted in order to fix Hamlet's age."[1] The disclosure has not always been appreciated. Critics from the eighteenth century on complained of its inconsistency with the repeated references to "young Hamlet" as well as with his status as a student intent on returning to Wittenberg. Most commentators have rejected the number, deeming a younger age in the range of seventeen to twenty-three more appropriate. Various grounds for dismissing it have been proposed: Shakespeare was often vague with numbers; he purposefully made the illiterate sexton misremember the date; the age applied not to the character Hamlet but to the first actor to play the character, Richard Burbage; the number was intended as a variable to be determined by whatever actor played the role; "thirty" was a printing-house slip for "twenty."[2]

Yet the "thirty"-year figure has also had its share of defenders. Lewis Theobald, the first editor to comment on the discrepancy, argued that Hamlet was indeed thirty, but only in the final act of the play. Shakespeare, he conjectured, when following his Latin source in which the hero is a boy at the time of his father's murder and an adult when he finally avenges it, neglected to make the necessary adjustment in his compressed dramatization of the plot.[3] What Theobald ascribed to carelessness, later critics attributed to the workings of Shakespeare's imaginative process. His attention was so absorbed by Hamlet that he developed his character without making correspondent adjustments to the plot. Thus the character ages over a ten-year period while the plot covers no more than a few months. The character returns from his sea voyage with a new maturity, but the plot neglects to indicate the many years necessary in order for him to have acquired it. From 1800 on, after Goethe had prominently featured *Hamlet* in his widely influential *Wilhelm Meister*, the question of Hamlet's age tends to be seen in the context of "coming-of-age" narratives.[4] Even in the late twentieth century, *Hamlet* has been associated with the *Bildungsroman* or novel of development; indeed it has been considered the precursor of the German Romantic form, "the first great story in Europe of a young man growing up."[5] Critics like Dowden and Bradley extend the time line as far back as his childhood in order to extend the developmental trajectory of his biography. Dowden suggests that Hamlet's life, under the rule of a "strong-willed" father, has been spent in years of study and contemplation, without ever, until the Ghost's injunction, requiring him to execute a deed.[6] Bradley imagines that the thirty years before the Ghost's shattering disclosure were spent in perfecting the princely skills of soldier, courtier, scholar, lover.[7] Annabel Patterson considers his "superannuation" as a student at Wittenberg a reflection of the shortage of positions for university graduates in England at the end of the sixteenth century.[8] Barbara Everett believes sixteen to twenty-three a more likely figure, for Hamlet is above all "a young man growing up," though he never attains the maturity or mastery of the *Bildungs*-hero, except perhaps in death: "For Young Hamlet grows up and grows dead in the same instant."[9]

Treating "thirty years" as if it were an indicator of his age, criticism has neglected the three-way coincidence of Hamlet's birthday, Denmark's victory, and the beginning of the sexton's occupation. The critical question raised by the number pertains exclusively to Hamlet: what accounts for his advanced age? Yet the information provided by the sexton insists on three coordinate and coterminous time spans: biographical, historical, and eschatological. Indeed the temporal quantity of "thirty" might be better understood as an indefinite verbal unit, like *era* or *epoch*, rather than a precise numerical one. In Shakespeare's time, it was used interchangeably with *generation* to stand for the interval of time between parents and their offspring.[10]

In both classical and biblical sources, the generation was a standard unit of temporal measurement. Polybius, the Greek historian of the Roman Empire, based his model of historical change on the recurrent cycles of government. The three constitutional forms – monarchy, aristocracy, democracy – and their three negative counterparts – tyranny, oligarchy, and mob rule – tended to change at generational divides.[11] Machiavelli, following Polybius, also identified changes in governments with generational turnover: the younger generation tended to dismantle the institutions of the older, so that the monarchy of the father might be superseded by the tyranny of the son before passing to the aristocracy of the grandson, and so on until the full cycle was completed and a new one commenced.[12]

Scripture also used generational units in its organization of the past. As if in response to the command, "Be fruitful, and multiply," the columns of both the Old Testament and the New are filled with long genealogical lists.[13] In scripture, too, it is frequently the case that the younger generation subverts the efforts of the older, often by breaking the older's covenant with God, so that cycles of obedience and disobedience follow generational turns. In Judges 2:8–23, for example, after Joshua's death and that of all his generation, "there arose another generation after them . . . which knew not the Lord . . . And they forsook the Lord of their fathers which brought them out of the land of Egypt" so that the Lord gives them up to their spoilers, until he releases them from captivity, before the next generation backslides again, turning "quickly out of the way in which their fathers walked."[14] For 600 years, the Israelites follow this generational pattern of alternating apostasy and obedience in cycles of defection, oppression, prayer, and deliverance. Of course, the length of a generation in both ancient and scriptural history was as variable as the interval between parents and offspring. Classical scholars long debated the length of Herodotus' generations, before conceding that they were variable, sometimes lasting thirty-three years (a hundred divided by three) but at other times equivalent to twenty-three, twenty-six, thirty-one, thirty-four, thirty-nine, and forty years.[15] The length of a generation in scripture is still more difficult to fix, especially in the antedeluvian ages when the need to populate cities and make up armies required both longevity and prolonged reproductive cycles.

Unlike other temporal units – decades or centuries – generations bear a relation to the human life cycle. Particularly in a patrilineal system, climacteric events tend to occur at the generational turning-point. Shakespeare often poises his plays at this divide, when an important death or marriage threatens to destabilize persons, families, and states.[16] Measured from the time of the historic day when Denmark overcame Norway, as described by Horatio and dated by the sexton, the play's narrative spans a thirty-year time period. Its action, however, is limited to the last months of that generational span. At this point, three father-son units hover over the climacteric divide.[17] For all three, the event Claudius terms the "common theme" (1.2.103) – the death of fathers – has occurred or is about to occur. In both family and kingdom, the generational shift constitutes the weak point in the genealogical chain; it is there that continuity tends to falter and conflict to loom. In monarchy, the theory of the king's two bodies, one mortal and the other transtemporal, works to smooth over the rift, so that the announcement "The King is dead" could be followed with the ostensibly contradictory "Long live the King." A nobleman's funeral obsequies are intended to demonstrate and affirm the same uninterrupted succession.[18] Ideally, the system of primogeniture brings about what the funeral rite symbolizes. If the generations are on course, the firstborn son steps into the place of the father; the closer the resemblance between them, the smoother the transition, and the less the social order is disturbed. Even in an elective monarchy, like that of Denmark up until 1660/1, succession tended to pass from father to son. In 1632 the English ambassador to Denmark reported, "Though that Crown be purely elective, yet for these three last Kings, they wrought so with the people, that they got their familiar sons chosen, and declared before their death."[19] It was, however, perfectly legal for succession to fall on anyone of blood royal, as long as he had, as does Claudius, the support of the electoral body.

While *Hamlet* begins shortly after the sudden death of a king and father, no generational turn takes place: Hamlet II does not succeed Hamlet I.

The play's earliest audiences might well have been surprised to find that kingship had passed to the king's brother rather than his son and name-sake. It is the brother who sits triumphantly on the throne in sumptuous regalia while the son lurks on the periphery in sullen black. It is time for Hamlet to rule but it is Claudius who is made king. It is time for Hamlet to marry, in consultation with "the voice and yielding of that body/ Whereof he is the head" (1.3.23–4), but it is Claudius who weds with the approval of the "better wisdoms" of the Council, "For all, our thanks" (1.2.16). Elevated to the throne by the electorate and fastened to it by his marriage to the Queen, Claudius has preempted the heir-presumptive. That he has, in the eyes of the court and state, done so legally in no way lessens the blow, for Hamlet had every reason to expect to succeed his father. His possession of the patronymic would have kept the prospect perennially in view; so, too, might have the propitious coincidence of his birth with imperial victory.

In private, the Polonius family mentions Hamlet's status as heir-apparent. Laertes warns Ophelia of the risks of seduction by a man who will one day be sovereign: "For he himself is subject to his birth" (1.3.18) and Polonius reports of having done the same, "'Lord Hamlet is a prince out of thy star'" (2.2.141). Ophelia, shattered after witnessing the first bout of Hamlet's madness, bemoans in an aside the decline of "Th'expectancy and rose of the fair state" (3.1.154). In public, however, nothing is said of this expectation, at least not openly. At court, Hamlet's inappropriate black garb at his mother's marriage is taken to signify his continuing grief for his father's death. The King attempts to reason him out of his "obstinate condolement" (1.2.93) by stressing the inevitability of the loss – "But you must know your father lost a father, / That father lost, lost his" (1.2.89–90) – and then by offering himself as surrogate.

> [T]hink of us
> As of a father, for let the world take note
> You are the most immediate to our throne,
> And with no less nobility of love
> Than that which dearest father bears his son
> Do I impart toward you.
>   (1.2.107–12)

Yet Hamlet's expectation renders Claudius' attempt to cheer him sharply ironic. Offered as consolation, the proclamation can only gall. The last thing Hamlet would want is another father, an imposition that would force him back to the position of son. In his first words to Hamlet, the King celebrates the closer kinship brought about by his marriage. By making his "sometime sister, now [his] queen" (8), he has also made his sometime nephew now his son, as he emphasizes when he first addresses him: "But now, my cousin Hamlet, and my son" (64). The King's deployment of the infantilizing epithet is particularly noticeable in Q1: "And now princely Sonne Hamlet," "dearest Sonne," "Sonne Hamlet," "Spoke like a most louing Sonne." While Claudius seems to relish calling Hamlet *son*, Hamlet never in Q2 and F (and only once in Q1) indulges Claudius by addressing him as father. "Farewell, dear mother," he says to the King and is corrected, "Thy loving father, Hamlet" (4.3.52–3). "Hamlet, thou hast thy father much offended," says the Queen, and is corrected, "Mother, *you* have *my* father much offended" (3.4.8–9, emphasis added). Claudius' attempts to be paternal are countered by Hamlet's refusal to be filial. As Hamlet caustically rejoins, "I am too much in the sun" (1.2.67). The "sonne" [Q1, Q2] / "Sun" [F] homonym is doubly expressive of Hamlet's resentment. Hamlet is too much in the blistering presence of Claudius' sovereign *sun* but he is also too much, and for the second time, in the subordinate position of a *son*; Claudius' coronation has pushed Hamlet back in the successional line-up. Claudius names him his successor, but as Hamlet intimates when Rosencrantz reminds him of the King's pronouncement, he doubts he will survive the interim (3.2.332–5).

Hamlet has reason to grieve inordinately, for he has lost more than a father.[20] "Thou know'st 'tis common," the Queen intones, and Hamlet concurs, "Ay, madam, it is common" (1.2.72, 74). While it is common for sons to suffer the death of fathers, it is decidedly *un*common for an only son to inherit nothing of his deceased father's estate.[21] Common law, or *lex terrae*, protected the right of the firstborn son to inherit his father's property.[22] The *ius coronae* or law of succession depended upon the same principle of lineal descent, so that the kingdom was to descend to the issue of the king, male over female, by primogeniture. Jurists noted the correspondence between how the throne and estates devolved from one generation to the next.[23] By all legal expectation, Hamlet II, of age and fit to rule, stood to inherit Hamlet I's kingdom. And yet in the constitutional form the play specifically assigns to Denmark, it is perfectly legal for the kingdom to pass to a collateral relation rather than the lineal. In an elective monarchy, the electoral body would have had the power to pass over the heir-apparent. In the play's first scene at court, Claudius apparently addresses such a parliamentary body when he acknowledges their support of his marriage, and perhaps by extension, his coronation: "Nor have we herein barr'd / Your better wisdoms, which have freely gone / With this affair along. For all, our thanks" (1.2.14–16). In Q2, the stage direction introducing the scene calls for the entry of such an advisory body – *Enter Claudius, King of Denmarke, Gertradt he Queene* [sic], *Counsaile* – and distinguishes its members from other court attendants, *Cum Alijs*. With parliament's vote behind him, Claudius is the legitimate king; as far as is known at court, he has committed no legal offense in ascending to the throne. The great historian of the common law, William Blackstone, was the first to insist that Claudius obtained the kingship by due process. Hamlet, he maintains, charges Claudius of being many things during the course of the play, "drunkard, murderer, and villain, one who has carried the election by low and mean practices . . . but never hints at his being an *usurper*."[24]

Only if Denmark had been an hereditary rather than an elective monarchy would Claudius have been a usurper. In an hereditary monarchy the throne would only pass to a king's brother in the absence of lineal descendants to the deceased king. To have been crowned, Claudius would have had to have resorted to Richard of Gloucester's tactic of eliminating his elder brother and his issue. And the heir-apparent would have survived only by fleeing to exile, as did the two princes after Duncan's death in *Macbeth*. At the very least, he would have been imprisoned, as was Henry IV's royal cousin. Yet the overwhelming critical consensus still holds that Claudius has usurped the throne that should have passed to Hamlet. Even when the presence of the elective monarchy is acknowledged, its relevance to Shakespeare's play is denied or rendered moot.[25] Its awkward presence is assumed to be the result of Shakespeare's close following of his sources (both Saxo and Belleforest refer to the elective process[26]), or of his even more uncharacteristic fidelity to historical fact (Denmark's monarchy was elective until 1660/1).[27] In the rare instances when the politics of the play are taken seriously, they are translated into the more familiar terms of England's own hereditary monarchy. As John Dover Wilson confidently proclaims, "Hamlet is an English prince, the court of Elsinore is modeled upon the English court, and the Danish constitution that of England under the Virgin Queen."[28] Even new-historicist readings which relate the succession process in the play to the succession crisis in the final years of Elizabeth's reign proceed as if Denmark's monarchy were just like England's, as if relevance depended on correspondent constitutional forms.[29]

Yet Denmark's electoral constitution is crucial to the play's dramatic set-up. It allows for a situation impossible in a primogenitary monarchy: the Prince remains at court in company of the King who was preferred over him. This is not a comfortable situation for either Prince or King, and for that very reason it provides a tensely dramatic one for the audience. Even before King Claudius discovers the risks of letting the Prince's "madness range" (3.3.2) and resolves to "fetters put about this fear/ Which now goes too free-footed" (26–7), Hamlet experiences life at court as incarceration, "Denmark's a prison" (2.2.243).[30] The King suspects "Hamlet's transformation" (2.2.5) from the start, fearing that he is "mad in craft" (3.4.190) rather than genuinely so. He dismisses the various diagnoses of his madness, convinced that there is something more dangerous behind his "lunacy" (3.1.4) than his father's death, his mother's remarriage, or Ophelia's love:

> There's something in his soul
> O'er which his melancholy sits on brood,
> And I do doubt the hatch and the disclose
> Will be some danger.   (3.1.166–9)

This is why he wants Hamlet first at court under constant surveillance and then, when danger escalates and he fears for his own life, extradited and executed. When the time comes for that "something in [Hamlet's] soul" to finally "hatch" and "disclose," the horrified onlookers have a name for it. As Hamlet stabs the King, they cry, "Treason! treason!" (5.2.328).[31]

In this context, the grand precipitate of all psychological readings of Hamlet looks considerably less mysterious: "I have that within which passes show" (1.2.85). The Prince cannot utter his expectation of succession during the reign of the King who preempted him, not because the disappointment is beyond the reaches of language or the ken of his auditors. On the contrary, for the play's early audiences, at least, what Hamlet keeps within himself may well have gone without saying; it is what Sir Edward Coke, the great jurist and legal historian of the period, identified as the "secret in the heart," known to God alone.[32] In the current political regime in which the King legally occupies the throne, to utter such an expectation (even to "compass or imagine" it) would be High Treason.[33] The court scene ends with Hamlet reiterating the need to keep silent, "But break, my heart,/ For I must hold my tongue" (1.2.159). However, by the end of the act, after the Ghost's disclosure, he discovers how to let his tongue loose. The persona he assumes licenses him to express his resentment, not openly but in the "wild and whirling words" (1.5.139) of the Antic, the madman who even in a court of law is not held accountable for the meaning of his words.[34]

When the King asks how he "fares," Hamlet informs him how well he dines: "Excellent, i'faith, of the chameleon's dish. I eat the air, promise-crammed" (3.2.93–4). Hamlet pretends to flourish on the proverbial diet of the chameleon: like it, he appears to survive on "air," or the breath of the present king which has named him *heir*. But in fact he is like the capon which cannot be fattened with mere promises: "You cannot feed capons so" (94). Gelded by the "cutpurse of the empire" (3.4.99), Hamlet is like a castrated cock. He has lost the dynastic "purse," a figure for the *testes* which in turn stands for both his testicular and testamentary rights as his father's biological issue and legal heir.[35] Asked by Rosencrantz for the "cause of [his] distemper" (3.2.328), Hamlet replies candidly, "I lack advancement" (331). When Rosencrantz naively asks, "How can that be, when you have the voice of the King himself for your succession in Denmark?" (332–3), Hamlet counters with the proverb, "While the grass grows, the horse starves."[36] The horse cannot graze on the mere prospect of pasture any more than the capon can be fattened with air or Hamlet can live on the "voice of the King." That Hamlet expresses his resentment in riddles, puns, and proverbs should not surprise: ambiguity, as Steven Mullaney has demonstrated, is the natural idiom of suppressed political discontent.[37]

That the kingdom passed from king to brother would certainly disappoint the expectant son. As he puts it bitterly to Horatio, his only confidant, Claudius "[p]opp'd in between th'election and my hopes" (5.2.65). From the standpoint of the state, however, the upset is by no means undesirable, for the brother brings stronger continuity than the son could have. He occupies the same throne and the same bed with the same wife and queen. Only in Hamlet's eyes, it seems, is there a wild disparity between the two brothers. Despite Hamlet's attempts to convince her otherwise, the Queen seems perfectly happy with the substitution; the Council approves her choice, and the "general gender" (4.7.18) readily shift their loyalty from one brother to another, paying as much as "a hundred ducats apiece for his picture in little" (2.2.361–2). What is more, both kings have the same heir.

Or do they? By repeatedly proclaiming Hamlet his heir, Claudius underscores his predecessor's apparent failure to do so. In this respect, Claudius is, at least in show, the better father. "Think of us as of a father," he enjoins (1.2.107–8), and in the next line gives Hamlet good reason to do so by appointing him his successor. He names him his heir publicly and officially, before the court and counselors, and imagines it proclaimed throughout the realm to the sound of drums and trumpet that "bray out / The triumph of his pledge" (1.4.12). We know word has gotten around when Rosencrantz reminds Hamlet of it (3.4.332–3). Before the duel, Claudius proclaims his support again when he ceremoniously tosses into Hamlet's cup a "union" or pearl, symbolic of the union that is the monarchy and claims that it is "[r]icher than that which four successive kings / In Denmark's crown have worn" (5.2.269–71); the pledge is brayed out again to drum rolls and fanfare (269–75). Hamlet's uncle thus ostentatiously performs what his father apparently neglected to do. His father made no provision to secure the succession of his son against any contending claims that might legitimately arise in an elective monarchy.[38] This is no small oversight. Even Hamlet, during the brief interval between Claudius' death and his own when he is *de facto* king, manages with his dying words to nominate his successor: "But I do prophesy th'election lights / On Fortinbras. He has my dying voice" (360–1).

In the rival empire of Norway, the king's brother instead of his son has also ascended to the throne, but without generational upset. Thirty years ago, the death of Fortinbras I apparently put his brother on the throne, Fortinbras II being then still in his minority. A generation later, the heir-apparent is ready to assume the throne, just at the point when his uncle's powers are waning. Suffering from "sickness, age, and impotence" (2.2.66), old Norway is alerted to what is happening in his own kingdom only when informed by a dispatch from another nation (1.2.27–33). His decline is timely, for the next in line is eager to step up. Behind his uncle's back, Fortinbras II has mustered a rag-tag army of "landless / lawless resolutes" and convinced his uncle that their target is Poland, not Denmark (2.2.62–4). Once apprised of his nephew's real intent, his uncle reins him in and redirects his aggressive energies. It can be only a matter of time, however, before Fortinbras, "with divine ambition puff'd" (4.4.49, Q2) will lash out on his own.

Monarchy in the Mousetrap play also seems to be on a generational timetable. The play opens by marking the passage of thirty years, and with unusual emphasis in terms of both solar and lunar cyclical movement:[39]

> *Full thirty times* hath Phoebus' cart gone round
> Neptune's salt wash and Tellus' orbed ground
> And *thirty dozen moons* with borrow'd sheen
> About the world have *times twelve thirties* been[.]
> (3.2.150–3, emphases added)

The old ruler, like old Norway, is on the verge of death, as he allows in his dialogue with the queen. She notes his decline, "You are so sick of

late, / So far from cheer and from your former state" (3.2.158–9), and he
admits it, "Faith, I must leave thee, love, and shortly too: / My operant
powers their functions leave to do" (3.2.168–9). His "operant powers" are
shown to fail when he gives in to midday drowsiness, "My spirits grow
dull," and drops off, "fain I would beguile / The tedious day with sleep"
(221–2). The king is failing, but not fast enough for his young nephew
who with poison hurries along the natural process. Hamlet's running
commentary makes the nephew's motives clear, "A poisons him
i'th'garden for his estate" (3.2.255). Like the play's other two nephews,
Hamlet II and Fortinbras II, Lucianus grows impatient while awaiting his
turn at the top.

In Polonius' family, too, the son seems keen to slip out from parental
control. As Fortinbras, unbeknownst to his uncle, plans to attack
Denmark, as Hamlet wishes to return to Wittenberg, a wish "most retrograde" (1.2.114) to his stepfather's and mother's desire, so Laertes determines to go to Paris, despite his father's objections. After his son's
"laboursome petition," Polonius yields his "hard consent" (1.2.59–60),
though not without strings attached – the purses, letters, and spy he
dispatches after him (2.1.1–73). Yet Polonius' rhetorical lapses ("What
was I about to say? . . . I was about to say something. Where did
I leave?" 2.1.50–2), long-winded preambles ("to expostulate . . . Why
day is day, night night, and time is time," 2.2.86, 88), and tautological
repetitions ("And now remains . . . Thus it remains; and the remainder
thus," 2.2.100, 104) suggest that he, too, is in decline. He provides an
illustration for Hamlet's unidentified satirical book which maintains "that
old men have gray beards, that their faces are wrinkled, their eyes purging
thick amber and plum-tree gum, and that they have a plentiful lack of
wit, together with most weak hams" (2.2.196–200). To Hamlet's mind,
Polonius is so far gone on the generational cycle that he has come around
again for a second childhood as a "great baby" (378): "an old man is twice
a child" (2.2.381).

As the powers of Polonius are waning, those of his son are on the rise.
The namesake of a famous Greek father, Laertes seems on course to
replace his own. The precepts his father bids him "character" (1.3.59) in
his memory before departing for Paris have no doubt been inscribed there
countless times before. After a lifetime of programming, he both speaks in
precepts and responds to them. Like his father, Laertes gives Ophelia
advice, more winningly and delicately, to be sure, but with the same
import: Guard your chastity, Beware Hamlet. And his warnings take the
same sententious form as the father's. Laertes admonishes Ophelia, "The

chariest maid is prodigal Enough / If she unmask her beauty to the moon" (1.3.36–7) and his father bluntly warns, "Tender yourself more dearly / Or . . .you'll tender me a fool" (1.3.107–9). Both males share the same double standard. Laertes, as Ophelia fears, "recks not his own rede" (1.3.51). While instructing Ophelia to follow "the steep and thorny way to heaven," he will opt for "the primrose path of dalliance" (1.3.48, 50). So, too, his father is content to have his son swearing, gambling, even drabbing in Paris, while he keeps his daughter in chaste and solitary confinement. Unlike Hamlet, though, Laertes after his father's death shows a certain proclivity to be son again. No sooner does he lose his own father than he falls under the spell of the very father figure Hamlet has rejected. Claudius pacifies Laertes by pulling on his filial heart strings ("Was your father dear to you?" 4.7.106) and prodding him to revenge with paternalistic precepts urging immediate action: "Time qualifies the spark and fire of [love]," "And nothing is at a like goodness still," "We should do when we would," etc. (110–22). Earlier Claudius had commended Laertes – "Why now you speak / Like a good child" (4.5.147–8) – for his filial piety, but also, perhaps, for the commonplace he uses to express his instincts: "the kind life-rend'ring pelican" (4.5.146) who feeds its offspring with its own blood, an emblem for the self-sacrificial parent (as well as the parricidal child).

The great display of Laertes' patrilineal allegiance occurs after he learns of his father's suspicious burial. He dashes back from Paris, gathers a mob behind him, and storms the palace portal demanding, "Give me my father" (4.5.116). The imperative encapsulates all the precepts his father had him character in his memory, for they are all reducible to the fifth commandment, or rather the first part of it: "Honour thy father." The avenging of a father's murder is the ultimate proof that the foundational injunction has been obeyed. As Laertes reasons, revenge puts the legitimacy of a son to the test. Any reluctance to avenge a father's murder disgraces the entire family triangle, proving the son a bastard, the mother an adulteress, the father a cuckold.

> That drop of blood that's calm proclaims me bastard,
> Cries cuckold to my father, brands the harlot
> Even here between the chaste unsmirched brow
> Of my true mother.   (4.5.117–20)

The link between revenge and lineal honor is foregrounded in the account of Pyrrhus' avenging of his father Achilles, as recited by the Player. The description of the ancient Greek avenger stalking his victim is anachronistically shot through with the medieval Norman-French technical vocabulary of heraldry.[40] As Pyrrhus wends his way through the burning streets of Troy, the splattering blood of his enemies emblazons his "sable arms" (2.2.448) so that they are "smear'd with heraldry more dismal" than solid black or "sable" (451–2).

> Head to foot
> Now is he total *gules*, horridly *trick'd*
> With blood of fathers, mothers, daughters, sons,
> Bak'd and impasted with the parching streets
> . . . .
> . . . Roasted in wrath and fire
> And thus o'ersized with coagulate *gore*,
> With eyes like *carbuncles*[.]
> (452–9, emphases added)

As editors routinely note, *sable*, *trick'd*, and *gules* are derived from heraldry, but as can be gleaned from John Guillum's *A Display of Heraldrie* (1611) so, too, are *gore* and *carbuncles*. *Sable* (one of the five heraldic tinctures) makes up the black field which is *trick'd* or marked with *gules* (another heraldic tincture), drops of red blood called *Gutte de Sang*[41] (Illustration 4a). The searing heat from burning Troy bakes the *goutty gules* into an embossed surface of "coagulate *gore*." As Guillum explains, in heraldry, a *gore* is a charge consisting of two arched lines meeting in the centre of the shield (Illustration 4b). Topping the heraldic shield of Pyrrhus' blood-stained body are the two gleaming *carbuncles* of his eyes; reflecting the flames of burning Troy, they resemble the lustrous gems which, according to Guillum, sparkle like fire: "the *Escarbuncle* is of most use in Armes"[42] (Illustration 4c).

The armorial assignment – the result of enemy bloodshed rather than his own noble blood – transforms the avenger into a stalking escutcheon. As if in recognition of his cold-blooded savagery, he achieves a coat of arms intended as the insignia of chivalry. Laertes displays a similarly fierce pedigree in avenging his father's honor, "To hell, allegiance ! Vows to the blackest devil! . . . I dare damnation" (4.5.131, 133). When the King asks him, "what would you undertake, / To show your self in deed your father's son / More than in words?", he responds that he would be willing "To cut his throat i'th'church" (4.7.122–5), preferring to commit sacrilege in the asylum of the church than to scant his filial duty, respecting the fifth commandment at the expense of the first.[43]

And yet the loss of honor inciting Laertes cannot be separated from the interception of its material counterpart. When after news of his father's

(a)

Gore sinister

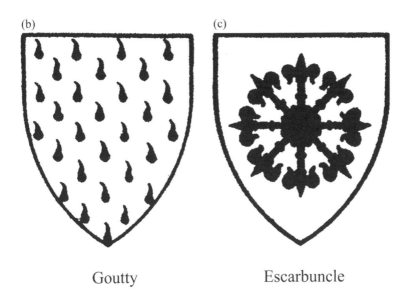

Goutty   Escarbuncle

Illustration 4. Heraldry: (a) *gore*, (b) *goutty gules*, (c) *carbuncle*, from John Guillim, *A Display of Heraldrie* (1611).

suspicious death he storms into the palace demanding, "Give me my father" (4.5.116), he is not asking that his father be handed over, dead or alive. "Father" here also stands for what should remain to the son of his father: his patrimony. The absence of ceremony and honors at a nobleman's burial signifies a disgraceful death. Official instructions for the burial of the great specified that the survival of a nobleman's honor beyond death depended on the ceremonial transfer of his ancestral arms.

[T]o the intent that the defunct may be known to all men to have died honourably in the Kings allegiance, without spot or infamy, or other disworship to his name, blood & family: and that this heir, if he have any, or next of whole blood, or someone for him . . . may publicly receive in the presence of all the mourners, the coat, armour, helm, crest, and other achievements of honour belonging to the defunct.[44]

That Polonius was buried with "no trophy, sword, no hatchment o'er his bones, / No noble rite, nor formal ostentation" (4.6.211–12) signals that he has not "died honourably," that his death has caused the taint to his family honor, the "disworship to his name," he feared would result from his daughter's seduction (1.3.95–7) or his son's profligacy (2.1.30). Like honor, dishonor runs in the family: corruption of the blood lies in the bloodline, and is passed on to the nobleman's issue. The father's infamy thus descends upon his issue, just as his honor would have, for the aristocratic birthright works for better or worse. If honor does not descend from father to son, title and estate cannot either. After the attaint of "hugger-mugger" burial (4.5.84), the family name needs to be formally cleared. This is what Laertes demands in his complex response to Hamlet's public apology before the duel. He will accept his apology only "in nature,"

> but in my terms of honour
> I stand aloof, and will no reconcilement
> Till by some elder masters of known honour
> I have a voice and precedent of peace
> To keep my name ungor'd.   (5.2.242–6)

Heraldic vocabulary is more pervasive here than editors have allowed. Laertes' "reconcilement" depends on the formal restitution of the family name by the pronouncement (according to "precedent") of some official body ("elder masters of known honour"), like the College of Arms.[45] The impaneling of such a body is required to clear Laertes' good name: to keep it unwounded or "ungor'd." *Gore*, as we have seen, is an heraldic term, and signifies "a diminution or blemish or defacing" on an escutcheon and is counted "among those marks denoting ungentlemanliness."[46] Thus "gore" names not only blood, the basis of lineage, but also the heraldic charge signifying its staining.[47] In addition, it refers to a wedge-shaped tract of land, thereby encapsulating another genealogical mainstay.[48]

Thirty years marks not a point in Hamlet's lifetime, after twenty-nine and before thirty-one, but rather the endpoint of a generational cycle. The play is structured to dramatize the devolution from one generation to the next. Three father–son units are poised at the generational brink, each son scheduled to supersede his father. The older generation is clearly failing: the king in the Mousetrap is on his last legs; Norway is reported bedrid; Polonius shows signs of incipient senility. Even the play's incidentals mark volatility at the generational divide. When the touring company arrives in Elsinore, Hamlet notes how both tiers of Players are about to move up a notch. Hamlet's "old friend" (2.2.419), now bearded, will soon graduate from adult to old men's parts; the boy, now taller and his voice about to crack, will shortly outgrow ladies' parts. The Players have been ousted from the city, to the detriment of both their reputation and profit, by a rival acting company of boys, an "eyrie of children, little eyases"; "What are they children?" (2.2.337, 43, F). Yet, as Hamlet notes, while at present "the boys carry it away," in time they will grow into the adults they now outface: "their writers do them wrong, to make them exclaim against their own succession" (2.2.348–9).[49]

The same kind of generational conflict resurfaces during the showdown at Ophelia's burial: both Laertes and Hamlet invoke the battle between the gods and their progeny, the giants who attempted to scale Olympus, home of their elders, by stacking one mountain atop another, heaping Ossa upon Pelion (5.1.246–7).[50] The antagonism moves in the opposite direction in Hamlet's allusion to the biblical tyrant who, upon hearing the prophecy that his successor was about to be born, ordered the massacre of all newborn males. It was this news that drove Herod literally to run mad in the medieval mysteries. "And now run I wod," he announces, and the stage directions specify that the actor is to run off the stage into the space of the audience.[51] In his advice to the Players, Herod is an example of over-acting – "It out-Herods Herod" (3.2.14) – but Herod is also one of Hamlet's theatrical precedents, for he too, as we saw in Chapter 1, was remembered for his "running mad" stunt.[52] In all these peripheral examples, the conflict between old and young concerns material stakes: the London stage, Mount Olympus, the kingdom of Judaea. Likewise, with the play's three sons, domain is at issue. The inheritance of all three has been diverted: the Crown lands Fortinbras stood to inherit were wagered away by his father; the realm Hamlet was born to rule passed to his uncle; the estate Laertes would have inherited is forfeited by the tainting circumstances of his father's death.

In view of these multiple failures in lineal succession, it may be worth mentioning the relation of Hamlet's name not only to Shakespeare's only son, Hamnet (a variant of Hamlet), who died at the age of eleven in 1596, but also, if we do not press the analogy too far, to Noah's son Ham. For Ham's atrocious act of filial disrespect – the viewing and mocking of his father's drunken nakedness, as illustrated in Gyles Godet's *A briefe Abstract of the Genealogy of All the Kinges of England* (c. 1562) (Illustration 5) – Noah cursed Ham's offspring to a level below subservience, "a servant of servants shall he be unto his brethren" (Gen. 9:25).[53] According to Sir Walter Raleigh's rendering of the account, Ham for deriding his father "was disinherited, and lost his preheminencie of his birth."[54] Hamlet, too, could be said to have received a curse in place of an inheritance. His father's legacy to him, the bequest by which he would be remembered – "Remember me" (1.5.91) – is the charge to avenge his murder (1.5.25). The father's "will" makes itself known through a lethal imperative (one that requires the son's sacrifice) rather than a sustaining and perpetuating legacy. Hamlet is left not with the patrimony promised by the patronymic, but with a suicidal paternal command to redress the injustice, sufficient basis, perhaps, for cursing the day he was born, "O cursed spite / That ever I was born to set it right" (1.5.196–7).

In Q1, Denmark's imperial banner day occurred not thirty years ago, but only twelve. According to the grave-digger in that text, a "dozen yeare" have passed since "our last king *Hamlet* / Slew *Fortenbrasse* in combat" (Iv). In Q1, as in the other two texts, the great victory is shadowed by mortality, "heres a scull hath bin here this dozen yeare." A "dozen yeare" is generally discredited as an absurdly low fixing of Hamlet's age. But if equated with a generational span rather than Hamlet's age, and if that generational age is the interval between mother and daughter rather than father and son, then twelve is not an implausible alternative for thirty. It is the approximate age when a woman is capable of generation. Juliet is thirteen, and at that age her mother had married and given birth; Marina and Miranda, at fourteen and fifteen respectively, are also at the onset of their childbearing capacity, and therefore ripe for marriage. As twelve years marks the beginning of puberty, so thirty years covers the full generational span, from the coming of the menses to their cessation.[55] Both of these generational numbers, then, reference the mensural unit of the woman's reproductive capacity.

Illustration 5. *Noah derided by Ham*, in Gyles Godet, *A briefe Abstract of the Genealogy of All the Kinges of England* (1562), fol. 2v.

In addition, both durations are coordinated with the lunar cycle for which the *menses* and its cognates (menstruation, menarche, menopause) are named: the thirty days between one new moon and another and the twelve courses of that cycle making up a year. In *Hamlet*, the two women are placed at the extremes of the childbearing continuum: Ophelia has just entered the female generational span and Gertrude is on her way out. Here, too, there is a generational upset, for it is the matron and not the maiden who has just married.

In his first soliloquy, Hamlet is scandalized by the marriage: "Let me not think on't" (1.2.146). What exactly is it he cannot bear to think on? It is not only his mother's sensuality, for that was apparent to him during her marriage to his father: "Why, she would hang on him / As if increase of appetite had grown / By what it fed on" (1.2.143–5). Nor is it her promiscuity, as it was in both Saxo and Belleforest where her son accuses her of copulating indiscriminately like a mare.[56] Rather it is the haste with which she went from one husband to another. "O most wicked speed! To post / With such dexterity to incestuous sheets" (156–7). Like a beast driven solely by appetite, she could not wait: "O God, a beast that wants discourse of reason / Would have mourn'd longer" (150–1). Custom requires a decent interval between the loss of one husband and the taking of another. By English civil law, a widow was typically expected to wait at least a year after her late husband's death before remarrying; a two-year interval appears to have been observed customarily.[57] But Hamlet measures his mother's mourning in contracting units of months. "But two months dead – nay, not so much, not two . . . Within a month . . . A little month . . . Within a month" (1.2.138–53). The *doleful month, month's mind*, or *month's mourning* was the *trigintal* period when the coffin or grave was draped as were the rooms in which mourners were confined; the period coincided with the thirty days after burial in which the soul was believed to linger near the body. The number thirty was also associated with the *trental* or "month's mind," a sequence of thirty requiem masses often said once a day over a thirty-day period, the most popular unit of prayer for the dead before the Reformation.[58] In the context of his mother's sexuality, another thirty-day period might well reverberate: the "terms" or "courses" or "months" of the regular discharge of the *catamenia* or *menses*, the Greek and Latin words for "month."[59] Like tides, the monthly efflux was thought to wax and wane in sympathy with the lunar cycle.

Two other less conventional measurements of the duration are given, both strengthening the gynecological connotation of *month*. The brief

interval between the two husbands is shorter than the time it takes for a
pair of women's shoes to wear out: "ere those shoes were old / With which
she follow'd my poor father's body" (1.2.147–8). Gertrude's wearing of the
same shoes through both ceremonies may look like another measure of
the court's thriftiness: "The funeral bak'd meats / Did coldly furnish forth
the marriage tables" (1.2.180–1). But like *meats*, *shoes* carry a carnal sense.
Typically gendered female in the period, especially when marred by a hole
in the sole, *shoes* are "rings" or "cases" into which the phallic foot is
inserted.[60] Hamlet's second measure of the interval introduces another
kind of obscene "rings":

> Ere yet the salt of most unrighteous tears
> Had left the flushing in her galled eyes,
> She married.   (1.2.154–6)

A scattering of sexualized terms encourages an analogue between the
widow's bloodshot eyes and the menstrual genital ring. *Salt* was considered a stimulus to both lust and fertility. *Eyes* were a familiar euphemism for the female genitalia, women like horses were "galled" or chafed
from excessive mounting, and "flushing" describes the cleansing of both
the bloodshot eyes with tears and the polluted uterus with blood. While
both ocular and vaginal rings are still bloodshot, Gertrude takes a second
husband. So rampant is her appetite that she cannot wait out the period of
either efflux before going to bed with her new husband. While the former
is a breach of custom, the latter violates the Levitical taboo forbidding
coition during the menses.[61]

Gertrude's "wicked speed" runs still another time limit. In the closet scene,
Hamlet makes it quite clear that his mother's age compounds her offense.

> Rebellious hell,
> If thou canst mutine in a matron's bones,
> To flaming youth let virtue be as wax
> And melt in her own fire.   (3.4.82–5)

If there is "mutine in a matron's bones" how can "flaming youth" be
expected to control its "compulsive ardour" (3.4.86)? The generational
opposition is more emphatic in Q1: "Whode chide hote blood within a
Virgins heart / When lust shall dwell within a *matrons* breast?" (G2v,
emphasis added). Gertrude's rampant appetite is out of sync with her
advanced age: "for at your age / The heyday in the blood is tame"
(3.4.68–9). The "heyday" or highpoint of female sexual desire should
correspond with the period of fertility. Q1 is again more explicit, in urging

that appetite should diminish as the efflux begins to ebb: "Why appetite with you is in the waine, / Your blood runnes backeward now from whence it came."

Hamlet repeatedly associates his aging mother with the overblown garden of Denmark. His first assault on her sexuality is preceded by a generalized complaint about the state of the realm: "'Tis an unweeded garden / That grows to seed; things rank and gross in nature / Possess it merely" (1.2.135–7). The diatribe slips into a consideration of his mother: like that garden, her fallow womb has gone to seed.[62] Neither place is capable of bearing flower or fruit. Rankness characterizes both its growth and her appetite: profuse and luxuriant, both continue beyond maturity. What was fertile is now fallow, what once flowered and fructified is now teeming with unwanted growth. The two sites of productivity, the garden and the womb, are both wastelands: "an unweeded garden" and an "ulcerous place" (3.4.149) respectively. To persist in unclean love-making, Hamlet warns his mother, would be like fertilizing or manuring what is already rotten: "And do not spread the compost on the weeds / To make them ranker" (153–4). Claudius' resemblance to "a mildew'd ear" (64), a diseased kernel of wheat or corn, indicates that his seed, too, is sterile, his kisses "reechy" (3.4.186). The seminal fluids exchanged "[i]n the rank sweat of an enseamed bed" (3.4.92) are greasy waste-matter – *seam* rather than *semen*, secreting fat rather than germinating seed. The marital bed, traditionally overspread with flowers on the wedding night, its wooden frame often engraved with flowers and fruit, is instead covered with moldy refuse, "compost" (3.4.153) and "garbage" (1.5.57), as if a cornucopia had spilled out there and rotted. Instead of a garden, it is a pigpen or "nasty sty" (3.4.94).

Hamlet's fixation on his mother's "ulcerous place" continues in her closet, a woman's most intimate and private retreat, customarily re-served for the entertainment of her husband or lover.[63] The meeting has been set up so that Gertrude could berate her son ("Look you lay home to him," 3.4.1), but ends up with Hamlet shaming his mother. When Gertrude upbraids him for having offended his stepfather – "thou hast thy father much offended" (3.4.8) – Hamlet turns the tables: "you have *my* father much offended" (9, emphasis added). And the tables remain turned: in a scene of shocking indecorum, the son instructs the mother, and about matters of the utmost intimacy: her sexual activity. Before entering, Hamlet resolves not to follow the matricidal example of Nero.

> Let not ever
> The soul of Nero enter this firm bosom;
> Let me be cruel, not unnatural.
> I will speak daggers to her, but use none.
>
> (3.2.384–7)

His disclaiming of the precedent only serves to foreground it. The mention of daggers in the context of Nero and his mother recalls accounts in which the emperor, whose stepfather was also named Claudius, after committing incest with his mother, had her killed and her body opened so that he might see the womb that bore him.[64] In the Folio, Hamlet announces his arrival in his mother's enclosed space by punning on "mother" and the Latin *mater*, a common synonym for the matrix or womb.[65] The stage directions in F call for shouts from "*within*" of "Mother, mother, mother" (F 2381) before Hamlet appears to ask the loaded question twice in succession, "Now mother, what's the matter?" (3.4.7); "What's the matter now?" (12). The answer lies in the question: as for Nero, it is the matrix itself, the spotted "inmost part" and "ulcerous place" from which he originated. Hamlet's words enter his mother "like daggers," just as he had planned ("I will speak daggers to her," 3.3.387). Michael Neill's comparison of Hamlet's words to "a surgeon's knife" are apt, but the reference to Nero as well as the invocations of maternal matter suggest an anatomical part more specifically gendered than the "heart."[66] It is her own diseased womb which Hamlet's words are referencing, as if like an écorché in a Vesalian engraving she could access that part for self-examination.[67] Indeed the title-page of Vesalius' *De humani corporis fabrica* (1543) shows the anatomist, surrounded by a large male audience, in the act of dissecting the uterus from a naked female corpse; Katharine Park has noted that the engraving references Nero's notorious desire to see his mother Agrippina's womb.[68] As Gail Kern Paster has demonstrated, among the body's many embarrassments in this period, none ranks higher than that of the female reproductive apparatus. The female nude illustrating anatomical treatises typically strikes the pose of the *Venus pudendum*, her right hand covering the area named for the shame it gives. In anatomical drawings, even the fetus covers its eyes before the shame of its encasing uterus.[69] Hamlet repeatedly remarks on his mother's lack of shame: her act has blurred the "blush of modesty" (3.4.41), "Heaven's face does glow" (48) in outrage: "O shame, where is thy blush?" (81). Finally his mother can bear no more, and admits her shame.

> O Hamlet, speak no more.
> Thou turn'st my eyes into my very soul,
> And there I see such black and grained spots
> As will not leave their tinct.   (3.4.88–91)

Gertrude's moral condition, her very soul, is shown through Hamlet's probing of her maculated womb, which will, according to him, become only more spotted and engrimed if she returns to the "nasty sty" of Claudius' bed.

There is one healthy garden, however: the "bank of flowers" specified by the stage direction to the dumbshow and perhaps also remaining on stage for the spoken version. Henslowe's Diary lists several such props for garden settings.[70] In the dumbshow, the king rests first on the queen ("declines his head upon her neck") and then "[l]ayes him down upon a bank of flowers," as if her body and the bank formed one continuous slope. In the spoken version, the king drowsily leans on the queen until he bids her depart, "Sweet, leave me here awhile . . . fain I would beguile the tedious day with sleep" (3.2.220–2), at which point she might ease him onto the flowery bank while cradling him to rest with an ominous lullaby: "Sleep rock thy brain" (223). The king's position mirrors the one Hamlet has conspicuously assumed while watching the entertainment: "Lady, shall I lie in your lap?" (3.2.110–11) he asks Ophelia.[71] Ophelia's lap is another version of the flowery bank, a fertile plot. Her abrupt refusal ("No, my lord," 112) shows that she has heard the innuendo Hamlet denies intending, "Do you think I meant country matters?" (115). In his exchanges with Ophelia, Hamlet hardly ever means anything else. As with country folk who make their living by raising and tending livestock, copulation and breeding are never far from his mind, at least in Ophelia's presence.

In the Mousetrap play, the flowery bank represents the coveted flourishing realm which incites the nephew to poison the king.[72] The Mousetrap plot turns on the desire for this cultivated plot, as is clear from Hamlet's one-line synopsis, "A poisons him i'th'garden for his estate" (3.2.255). The garden, three times represented – in the Ghost's narrative and in both the silent and spoken versions of the *Murder of Gonzago* – is the scene of the crime, but it is also its motive. In the narrative, the presence of a "serpent" suffices to connect the garden with Eden. Yet it is not original sin but rather the first crime which is reenacted there. The play three times makes occasion to reference Cain's slaying of his brother Abel: Claudius ironically derives his long succession of fathers who died natural deaths from Cain's violently murdered victim, "the first corse" (1.2.105). At prayer, he admits that his fratricide has the "primal eldest curse upon't" (3.3.37). Finally Hamlet wonders in the graveyard if the skull he disinters might not be "Cain's jawbone, that did the first murder" (5.1.76). In Genesis, as in *Hamlet*, sibling rivalry motivates fratricide, over God's favor in the former, over the garden estate in the latter.

The unusual title by which Claudius addresses Gertrude in his inaugural speech, "[t]h' imperial jointress" (1.2.9), identifies her as what joins him to the empire, and the empire to him. But it also suggests a legal *jointure*, an estate settled on a wife which reverts back to her in the event of her husband's death.[73] Had the kingdom settled on Gertrude at her father's death, as it does in both the Latin and French sources, it would have reverted to her at her first husband's death to be passed to her second husband upon marriage.[74] In the absence of any directive from Hamlet I, Gertrude's status as imperial jointress may be a critical factor in the election. In the English translation of Belleforest, one of Gertrude's prototypes is well aware of the inextricability of her erotic and political power.

[A]nd I am not only a queene, but such a one as that, receiving whom I will for my companion in bed, can make him beare the title of a king, and with my body give him possession of a great kingdome, and goodly province.[75]

What man the "imperial jointress" chooses to conjoin with, then, would be of paramount concern to the empire: whether she links herself to an angel or "prey[s] on garbage" (1.5.55, 57), whether she feeds on a "fair mountain" or battens on a sodden "moor" (3.4.66–7), whether she "hangs on" Hamlet I or is "conjunctive" to Claudius (1.2.143, 4.7.14). Union to her in marriage would settle the realm on her husband. This might explain why the play does not distinguish between the two occasions of the coronation and the nuptials. In the opening court ceremony, when the King gives thanks to his Council – "For all, our thanks" (1.2.16) – it is unclear whether the acknowledgment is for its support of his marriage or of his coronation. Laertes arrives from Paris around the same time that Horatio arrives from Wittenberg, the former "to show [his] duty in [the King's] coronation" (1.2.53), the latter, suspects Hamlet, to attend his mother's wedding (1.2.176). As Hamlet repeatedly complains, only a short interval separates his mother's remarriage from his father's funeral. An even shorter one, it would seem, separates his mother's remarriage from his uncle's coronation.

Repeatedly the play conjoins Claudius' kingship with his courtship of Gertrude. His takeover of the realm depends on both the killing of the King and the wooing of the Queen. The Ghost describes how Claudius first poisoned the King and then "won to his shameful lust / The will of [his] most seeming-virtuous Queen" (1.5.45–6). The dumbshow drama-tizes the same two-step procedure: the poisoner both kisses the crown and woos the queen. And Hamlet suffers a double loss, as he twice maintains: his uncle has both "kill'd [the] king and whor'd [his] mother" (5.2.64); as a result, he is left with "a father killed, and a mother stain'd" (4.4.57).

Had the "queen-mother" preferred her son to her brother-in-law, the empire might well have settled on Hamlet. By securing the throne for Claudius, Gertrude's "o'erhasty marriage" (2.2.57) pushes Hamlet back to the loathed secondary position of son. Conjugal union with the imperial-jointress fastens Claudius to both Gertrude and Denmark; her "conjunct-ive" status makes her most precious to him (4.7.14). But by marrying him, she has alienated her son from what even in an elective monarchy would have been considered his birthright. Hamlet despises the union up to the bitter end, hence the irony of the pun with which he finally dispatches Claudius: "Drink off this potion. Is thy union here?" (5.2.331). In this instance, the *union* is specifically the pearl dropped by Claudius in the poisoned cup, a jewel richer than that worn in the Crown of four successive Danish kings (5.2.269–71), and intended for Hamlet, ostensibly as a pledge of the kingdom or *union* he has promised him. With the forcing of poison down Claudius' throat, the multiple senses of *union* coalesce: the unique pearl, the monarchy, and the conjugal bond that makes man and wife one flesh, by Hamlet's imprecation, even after death do them part: "Is thy union here? / Follow my mother" (5.2.331–2).

That second marriages pose a threat to the issue of the first was a commonplace in the period.[76] Indeed a warning about it might have appeared among Polonius' precepts to his son, as it did in Sir Walter Raleigh's little book, *Instructions to His Son* (c. 1610). The son is instructed to take precautions against his death lest his wife's second marriage divert his estate from his own flesh and blood. His widow should be left no more than subsistence, and that only for the duration of her widowhood.

[F]or if she love again, let her not enjoy her second love in the same bed wherein she loved thee . . . but leave thy estate to thy house and children . . . To conclude, wives were ordained to continue the generations of men, not to transfer them and diminish them either in continuance or ability; and therefore thy house and estate, which liveth in thy son and not in thy wife, is to be preferred.[77]

In an important essay on *Hamlet* emphasizing Hamlet's alienation from his inheritance by his mother's remarriage, Lisa Jardine has drawn attention to the official tables of "Kindred and Affinity" posted on church walls which prescribed what relations in marriage are forbidden by scripture and law.[78] By their light, the Danish royal union is incestuous: "A man may not marry his . . . Brother's Wife . . . A woman may not marry with her . . . Husband's Brother." The royal bed is thus technically a "couch for incest," its sheets "incestuous." But in his inaugural address, no sooner does Claudius openly, even proudly proclaim his transgression – he has taken to wife "our sometime sister, now our queen" (1.2.8) – than he celebrates its legitimization by the "better wisdoms" of his Council: "Nor have we herein barr'd / Your better wisdoms, which have freely gone / With this affair along" (1.2.14–16). He thanks his supporters – "For all, our thanks" (16) – and some sign from them (applause? assenting nods?) would confirm their approval.

This conjugal union celebrated at the play's opening consolidates Claudius' position. In an elective monarchy, both the brother and the son of the deceased king would have consanguineous claims to the throne. What decides the contest in the brother's favor is his conjugal (and coital) union with the "imperial jointress" (1.2.9). "Man and wife," as Hamlet points out, "is one flesh" (4.3.55), and their union is both sacramental and legal. The prior tie between "man and mother," however, proves less binding. By becoming her "husband's brother's wife" (3.4.14), she obliterates the claim of her first husband's son, and the electorate legitimizes the result. In the absence of any directive from the will of the deceased father, succession is guided by the will of the mother. Carnal desire prevails over the maternal bond. "Let her not enjoy her second love in the same bed wherein she loved thee," Raleigh warned his son. The spectral King Hamlet also warns his son against the same enjoyment: "Let not the royal bed of Denmark be / A couch for luxury" (1.5.82–3). In another of the play's many generational inversions, it falls upon the son rather than the husband to play the part of the cuckold: "[G]o not to my uncle's bed" (3.4.161); "Let [not] the bloat King tempt you again to bed" (184). Hamlet's complaint that his uncle has "popp'd in between th'election and my hopes" (5.2.65) suggests a breach that is both electoral and sexual.[79] That a son's feelings for his mother should be sexual may have seemed less transgressive than prudent at a time when endogamous unions were used to keep dynastic power and property intact.[80] Had Gertrude elected to commit incest with her son rather than her brother-in-law, Hamlet would have stood in better stead to succeed his father.

That Hamlet's feelings for his mother are intense has never been denied. When his mother's political prominence slips from view, however, it becomes difficult to account for this intensity, particularly its sexual charge. No one has been more sensitive to its excess than T. S. Eliot who pronounced the play an aesthetic failure precisely because it failed to "drag to light" "the essential emotion of the play": Hamlet's "disgust" for his mother.[81] According to Eliot, in order for such emotion to be expressible in art, some observable phenomena – "external facts" or "objective correlative" – must be provided to account for that emotion. Because Gertrude, a "negative and insignificant" character, is incommensurate with the "disgust" she occasions, the play's emotional center remains obscure, "inexpressible, because in *excess* of the facts as they appear." But *does* Eliot have all the facts? What if it were admitted, as fact, that Gertrude's sexual desire, legitimized by her "o'erhasty marriage" (2.2.57), has alienated Hamlet from the succession? Would not that fact tilt the balance closer toward satisfying Eliot's exacting aesthetic criterion of "complete adequacy of the external to the emotion"?

It is tempting to read Eliot's 1919 essay in light of a theory, then recently advanced, which was content to discover what might be termed a *subjective* correlative for Hamlet's emotion.[82] In 1910, Freud's disciple Ernest Jones published an essay elaborating on Freud's footnote in *The Interpretation of Dreams* (1900), the first intimation in print of what was to become his Oedipal complex.[83] In Jones' essay, Hamlet's vehemence toward his mother has a "correlative," however obscure, not in Eliot's "externals" or "facts" but in Hamlet's deeply buried unconscious guilt. The disgust Hamlet feels for his mother is a displacement of his own self-loathing, produced by his repressed incestuous desire, recently activated by his father's murder and his mother's remarriage. Incestuous desire, one imagines, would by any system of equivalencies correlate with excessive feeling; and yet, as Jones points out in addressing Eliot's critique, such feelings are not only "inexpressible" but ineffable, even in soliloquy: "there are thoughts and wishes that no one dares to express even to himself."

But in Denmark's political climate, another inhibition restrains Hamlet's tongue. If desiring the Queen is tantamount to desiring the realm, only the King can entertain the desire. The son must keep the guilty secret to himself, less because it is taboo than because it is tantamount to the highest crime in the land.

Ophelia's virginity, like Gertrude's sensuality, is a preoccupation from the start. As Gertrude is associated with nature gone to seed, so Ophelia figures as the prospect of fecundity. Of utmost concern to her father and brother is that she not be despoiled. Like an unopened bud or "button" (French, *bouton*, "bud"),[84] she is fragile and at risk.

> The canker galls the infants of the spring
> Too oft before their buttons be disclos'd,
> And in the morn and liquid dew of youth
> Contagious blastments are most imminent.
> (1.3.39–42)

To protect the "button" from canker and blight, her brother and father provide her with safeguarding precepts. That she has taken Hamlet's professions of love at face value proves her incapable of looking out for herself. Her father accuses her of speaking like an immature "green girl" (101) who has not yet flowered into womanhood.[85] "Unsifted in such circumstance" (102), she needs to be informed by edifying precepts. Of course, had she been "sifted" by experience, she might well have lost the virginity the precepts are designed to protect. How can she learn first hand that men are false without herself undergoing betrayal? Both brother and father fortify her against seduction with admonitory precepts. Their advice takes the conventional form of *sententiae*: wise sayings or commonplaces fashioned to be remembered. Laertes offers the two quoted above warning against canker and blight in a list that includes five alternatives, all urging her to avoid temptation.

* And keep you in the rear of your affection
  Out of the shot and danger of desire. (34–5)
* The chariest maid is prodigal enough
  If she unmask her beauty to the moon. (36–7)
* Virtue itself scapes not calumnious strokes. (38)
* Be wary then: best safety lies in fear. (43)
* Youth to itself rebels, though none else near. (44)

Polonius' blunter advice is aimed to shatter Ophelia's belief that Hamlet "hath importun'd me with love / In honourable fashion" (110–11). Her father counters with a battery of commonplaces on the treachery of a lover's words. He likens the vows of a burning lover to:

* springes to catch woodcocks (115)
* blazes . . . / Giving more light than heat (117–18)
* brokers / Not of that dye which their investments show (127–8)
* mere implorators of unholy suits (129)
* sanctified and pious bawds (130)

"In few, Ophelia, / Do not believe his vows" (126–7). Lovers' promises enter the "too credent ear" (30) to prepare the way for sexual entry by "canker" worm and penetrating "blastments." The result is deflowering,

Illustration 6. *Nude Woman with Gestating Child*, in Adrianus Spigelius, *De Formato Foetu* (1626), fol. 35, Tab. III.

the birth of a bastard, and the despoiling of family honor, rather than the auspiciously blossoming womb and fetal flower, as gorgeously illustrated in Spigelius' *De Formato Foetu* (Illustration 6).

The early quartos assign special significance to these sententious passages by printing quote marks in the margin. In Q2, three such marks appear before Laertes' maxims to Ophelia (Illustration 7). The " mark is the typographic equivalent of the pointing finger drawn in margins of books and manuscripts to signal axiomatic passages to be committed to memory or to its material adjunct, the tablebook.[86] As her brother takes his leave, Ophelia promises him that his advice will be kept in mind: "'Tis in my memory lock'd, / And you yourself shall keep the key of it" (1.3.85–5). For safekeeping, she has locked up his advice in her memory chest, an assurance that her "chaste treasure" (31) will be

" The charieſt maide is prodigall inough
If ſhe vnmaske her butie to the Moone
" Vertue it ſelfe ſcapes not calumnious ſtrokes
⁂ The canker gaules the infants of the ſpring
Too oſt before their buttons be diſcloſ'd,

Illustration 7. Laertes' *sententiae*, *The Tragicall Historie of Hamlet* (London, 1603), C2v.

similarly kept under lock and key. Her father insists on more. To protect her chastity, to behave as "it behoves my daughter and your honour" (1.3.97), she must shut herself up under lock and key, literally. And so she does, as her father proudly reports:

> And then I prescripts gave her,
> That she should lock herself from his resort,
> Admit no messengers, receive no tokens.
> (2.2.142–4)

The language of locks and keys in the context of protecting Ophelia's "chaste treasure" summons up images of the mechanical device designed for the purpose. The chain of prophylactic precepts form a chastity belt to defend the forfended area beneath her waist. And it does its work straight away. "She took the fruits of my advice" (2.2.145), and retires to her closet, returns old gifts and letters and refuses new ones, surrendering them to her father, as required, "in obedience": "as you did command, I did repel his letters and denied / His access to me" (2.1.108–10). Hamlet subsequently obtains private access to her only twice: when he barges in on her in her closet and when he encounters her under the concealed surveillance of her father and the King.

More famously and ceremoniously Polonius gives advice to his son, "And these few precepts in thy memory / Look thou character" (1.3.59–60), and in Q1 their gnomic status is indicated by eleven quote marks (Illustration 8). Precepts to both son and daughter are designed to maintain family honor (his reputation and her chastity), but through opposite strategies. Ophelia's maxims are intended to remove her from the world, while Laertes' enable him to negotiate it. His precepts instruct him on how to present and comport himself publicly: how to speak, dress, interact, manage money. Polonius' master precept – "This above all: To thine own self be true" (1.3.78) – is often seen to be ironic when so many of his sayings instruct Laertes if not to falsify, at least to keep his cogitations to himself: "Give thy thoughts no tongue" (59); "Give every man thy ear, but few thy voice" (68); "Take each man's censure, but reserve thy

Cor. Yet here *Leartes?* aboord, aboord, for fhame,
The winde fits in the fhoulder of your faile,
And you are ftaid for, there my bleffing with thee — *Laynig his Hand*
And thefe few precepts in thy memory.   *m Sheakes Head*
" Be thou familiar, but by no meanes vulgare;
" Thofe friends thou haft, and their adoptions tried,
'· Graple them to thee with a hoope of fteele,
" But do not dull the palme with entertaine,
'· Of euery new vnfleg'd courage,
" Beware of entrance into a quarrell; but being in,
" Beare it that the oppofed may beware of thee,
" Coftly thy apparrell, as thy purfe can buy.
" But not expreft in fafhion,
" For the apparell oft proclaimes the man.
And they of *France* of the chiefe rancke and ftation
Are of a moft feleƈt and generall chiefe in that:
" This aboue all, to thy owne felfe be true,
And it muft follow as the night the day,
                                C 2   Thou

Illustration 8. Polonius' *sententiae, The Tragicall Historie of Hamlet* (1604/5), C3v.

judgment" (69). But underlying Polonius' advice is the assumption that there is some fixed core faculty in Laertes – call it "thought," "voice," or "judgment" – that will remain unswayed by worldly trafficking. His advice to him, therefore, can take the form of flexible guidelines, to be applied at his son's discretion: it is left to him to judge the line between "familiar" and "vulgar" (61), "rich" and "gaudy" (71), proportionate and "unpropor-tion'd" (60). As long as this executive faculty remains intact, Laertes' reputation can survive considerable assault, including charges of swearing, drinking, even whoring, as long as they are not "so rank / As may dishonor him" (2.1.20–1). It is because no such faculty is assumed in the daughter that her prescripts are issued as specific commands regarding Hamlet rather than general maxims for conduct in the world. "Do not believe his vows" (1.3.127); "I would not . . . have you . . . give words or talk with the Lord Hamlet" (132–4); "Look to't, I charge you" (135). "I shall obey" (136), she promises, and behaves accordingly, "as you did command" (2.1.108), by reclusing herself.

The play allows Ophelia no mind of her own; instead it has her minding her father's precepts. His warnings take the place of thought. Perhaps this is why she seems to draw a blank when called upon to think.

When Polonius asks her about Hamlet's professions of love, she responds, "I do not know, my Lord, what I should think" (1.3.104). And her father tells her what to think: "Marry, I will teach you. Think yourself a baby" (105). Her brother also tells her. Hamlet's affection, he warns, is short-lived: "The perfume and suppliance of a minute, / No more" (1.3.9–10). "No more but so?" she queries. "Think it no more," he replies (10). That precepts may indeed be doing the work of thought is also suggested when Hamlet, preparing to settle in for the Mousetrap play, asks if he can lie in her lap. "No, my lord" (3.2.112), she snaps, as if he had just implored "unholy suits" (1.3.129). He clarifies his meaning, "I mean, my head upon your lap" (3.2.113), and asks her to clarify hers, "Do you think I meant country matters?" (115). "I think nothing" (116) she demurs, literally disclaiming thought of any stripe. But Hamlet obscenely fleshes out her thoughtless "nothing" to make it synonymous with "country matters," indeed *the* prime "country matter," audible in both "country" (cunt) and "matter" (*mater*, womb): "That's a fair thought to lie between maids' legs" (3.2.117). His quip lowers the region of her thought from head to lap, from her head to her maidenhead, so that one place of conception is superimposed upon the other.

Ophelia's madness has the entire court guessing at what is going on in her mind. Before her first mad entrance, signaled in F with the direction *Enter Ophelia distracted*, an account is given of how "hearers" struggle to bring her speech into alignment with their own thoughts, not hers:

> Her speech is nothing,
> yet the unshaped use of it doth move
> The hearers to collection. They aim at it,
> And botch the words up fit to their own thoughts[.]
> (4.5.7–10)

Indeed there is some question as to whether she intends anything by her speech. Her ostensibly knowing "winks and nods and gestures . . . would make one think there might be thought, / Though nothing sure" (11–13). After she departs, the King sympathetically comments, "poor Ophelia / Divided from herself and her fair judgment / Without the which we are pictures, or mere beasts" (84–6). Ophelia has lost her mind: the faculty that distinguishes human beings from both superficial pictures and irrational beasts. One thing is clear to her auditors, however: whatever she is saying, it relates to her father: "She speaks much of her father" (4.5.4); "Conceit upon her father" (4.5.45); "it springs / All from her father's death" (4.5.75–6). When Laertes first sees her in this state, he, too, makes the connection, "O Rose of May" (she is now an open blossom rather than a tight bud or "button"), "is't possible a young maid's wits should be as mortal as an old man's life?" (4.5.157–60). Her sanity has lasted only as long as her father's life. In Q1's rendition of the line, Laertes makes a different connection: "I'st possible a yong maides life, / Should be as mortall as an olde mans sawe?" (H1v). Her life has lasted only as long as her father's sayings.

On the surface, the Q1 correlation is nonsense. The whole purpose of *sententiae* is that they survive their source, passing down from generation to generation and conveying the same moral, ethical, and literary value. Often they pass from father to son in the material form of the tablebook, a portable booklet designed to record memorable lines from what one has read or heard.[87] Numerous tablebooks have survived from the sixteenth century, though very rarely in the hands of sixteenth-century women.[88] Hamlet famously writes in his "tables" after hearing his father's "commandment" (1.5.107, 102); Laertes might similarly "character" his father's dictates in a tablebook (1.3.59). Though Polonius in Q2 calls the maxims he gives Ophelia "prescripts" ("precepts" in F), there is no suggestion that she writes them down. After his death, she keeps them alive orally, though in strangely altered form. They are just recognizable in Horatio's account.

> She speaks much of her father, says she hears
> There's tricks i'th'world, and hems, and beats her heart,
> Spurns enviously at straws[.]   (4.5.4–6)

Once speaking "like a green girl" (1.3.101), Ophelia now sounds quite jaded. Accused at first of being "unsifted in such perilous circumstance" (102), she now finds peril everywhere. She warns against "tricks i'th'world" (4.5.5), ruses devised by men to seduce maidens. At court, the "straws" she "spurns" (6) would stand for the tokens or trifles her father has ordered her to refuse and return; in the country or barnyard, however, "straws" are an apt metonymy for strawmen: the hollow stalks or reeds which have spilled their grains or seed. When she enters, she continues to speak much of her father, or of what her father used to speak, though in a notably vulgarized idiom. She sings a ballad of a maiden who did just what the paternal precepts warned against: she gave too "credent ear" (1.3.30) to her lover's vows – "*you promis'd me to wed*" (4.5.63) – when she should have forbidden him, as her father instructed her to do, all "words or talk" (1.3.134). Rather than locking herself from his resort, she appeared at his window, ended up "*tumbled*" in his bed (4.5.62), and thereby spoiled of all prospects of marriage. Ophelia mentions two other maidens who came to bad ends: "They say the owl was a baker's daughter" (4.5.42–3) and "It is the false steward that stole his master's daughter" (4.5.170–1). However brief and vague, both allusions suggest a father who exposed his daughter to the kind of "perilous circumstance" Polonius warned his daughter against, the "tricks i'th'world" she comes to suspect everywhere after his death. The yeast that causes the baker's dough to rise also makes his daughter's belly prone to swelling.[89] Her transformation to an owl recalls the metamorphosis of the ravaged Philomela into a nightingale, and perhaps that of her sister Procne who before turning into a swallow baked the ravager's child into a pie.[90] Risk of conception was also increased in the case of "the master's daughter" whose father entrusted her, like a household good, to his "false steward." Ophelia's refrain or "wheel" – "A-down a-down" (4.5.169–70) – applies not only to the lowering of her father into the ground, but also to the tumbling in bed of all three legendary maidens.

Eighteenth-century critics, sensitive to questions of decorum, found offense in Ophelia's mad utterances. Her obscene songs of sexual betrayal and seduction ("*young men will do't if they come to't* – / *By Cock, they are to blame*" [4.5.60–1]) were deemed inappropriate for the virgin daughter of the court's highest official. Hamlet provides a gloss on this indecorum when, in promising a warm reception to the Players, he grants a special prerogative to the youth performing women's parts: "the lady shall say her mind freely – or the blank verse shall halt for't" (2.2.323–4). Modern editors have had difficulty explaining this line, perhaps because of a reluctance to identify any kind of speaking freely or free speech with obscenities; the play, however, unequivocally conjoins license and licentiousness. In her description of Ophelia's drowning, Gertrude calls shepherds "liberal" because of their licentious nomenclature: they use a "grosser name" for the penile wildflowers she calls "long purples" and chaste maidens call "dead men's fingers" (4.7.168–70).[91] Whatever Gertrude has in mind, she decorously avoids pronouncing that "grosser name," though her lingering over this particular flower might suggest a certain fascination. Ophelia, however, comes much closer to speaking "her mind freely," and her blank verse does come to a halt, as if too refined to bear so lewd a burden. The graceful iambic feet of her earlier utterances give way to the cloddish clip of the ballad or the stumbling prose of dialogic bits and pieces. Even before her madness, however, Hamlet suspects her of having "country matters" on her mind, like "liberal shepherds." He accuses her of disguising them with the faux-innocence of baby-talk, "you lisp, you nickname God's creatures"

(3.1.146–7). But he gives the boy actor license to let out the stops when impersonating a lady, extending to him what he forbids "those that play your clowns" (3.2.38–9): the freedom to "speak more than is set down" (3.2.39), to depart from the restrictions of the scripted playtext (in blank verse) into free-wheeling open improvisation. Such a dispensation would give playgoers what dramatic decorum withholds: an aristocratic lady mouthing vulgarities. While the Queen recoils from the "liberal" Ophelia ("I will not speak with her" [4.5.1]), and Laertes would sear his eyeballs and parch his brains to be spared the sight (4.5.154–5), the audience, or some part of it, appears to have taken pleasure in the impersonation (by a male) of a noble lady of Ophelia's station speaking or singing "her mind freely," like a country wench (*"Hey non nony, nony, hey nony"*)[92] at a rustic festival.

A similar abandon is reflected in Ophelia's appearance, particularly in Q1's two stage directions, *"Enter Ofelia playing on a Lute, and her haire downe singing"* (G4v) and *"Enter Ofelia as before"* (Hv). The resemblance of the lute, pear-shaped and with a bent neck, to the womb was commonplace; that it rested on the lap when played heightened the association. On stage and in narrative, unbound and disheveled hair gave sign of deep distress caused by loss, sometimes of a loved one (especially an homonymic *heir*), sometimes of virginity or chastity.[93] Ophelia's movements, too, would be out of control: her gestures, winks, and nods appear involuntary, the result of loss of muscle control, like spasms or tics. So does the pounding on her heart (4.5.5), a reflex, perhaps, to the upward surging symptomatic of the gynecological disorder known as "mother fits" or *Hysterica passio*.[94] Others must constrain her movements: she is initially denied admission to the Queen, then bursts in but shortly darts out, with attendants trailing, "Follow her close" (4.5.74). Laertes calls her "a document in madness" (176), but her appearance, language, gestures, and movements also indicate the ruination of what the play constantly substitutes for her mind. So, too, does the undoing of her bunch of flowers.

"I a bin gathering of floures," Ophelia announces in Q1 (Hv), and in all three texts she proceeds to pull her nosegay apart for distribution. Because fruitful and decorative, literary or rhetorical passages were often called *flowers*. Titles like George Gascoigne's *An Hundred Sundrie Flowers* (1572) or Nicholas Udall's *Floures . . . gathered out of Terence* (1533) classify their content as literal *anthologies* or *florilegia*: bindings (*legein*) of Greek *anthos* or Latin *flora*. The same ambiguity is captured by the English *posy*, a gathering of either horticultural or literary flowers.[95] Isabella Whitney collects *A Sweet Nosgay* (1573) of "a hundred and ten Phylosophicall we call the diuine intelligences or good Angels (*Demones*) they were the firſt that inſtituted ſacrifices of placation , with inuocations and worſhip to them, as to Gods: and inuented and ſtabliſhed all the reſt of the obſeruances and ceremonies of religion, and ſo were the firſt Prieſts and miniſters of the holy miſteries. And becauſe for the better execution of that high charge and function, it behoued them to liue chaſt, and in all holines of life, and in continuall ſtudie and contemplation: they came by inſtinct diuine, and by deepe meditation, and much abſtinence (the ſame aſſubtiling and refining their ſpirits) to be made apt to receaue viſions, both waking and ſleeping, which made them vtter propheſies, and foretell things to come. So alſo were they the firſt Prophetes or ſeears, *Videntes*, for ſo the Scripture tearmeth them in Latine after the

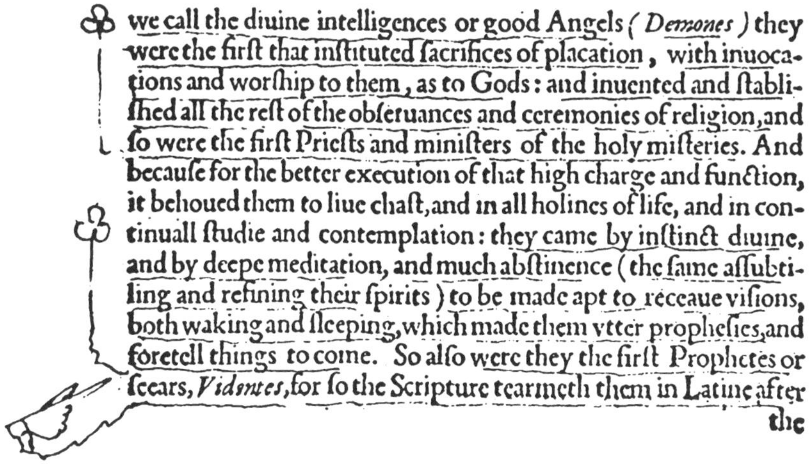

Illustration 9. Marginal flowers in Ben Jonson's copy of George Puttenham, *The Arte of English Poesie* (1589), p. 4.

Flowers" culled from Hugh Plat's *Floures of Philosophie* (1572), "*Plat* his Plot," and specifically recommends their odor to ward off pollution: "yet ordaine to smell to these, and when you come into a pestilent aire that might infect your sound minde: yet sauour to these SLIPS in which I trust you shall find safety."[96] In reading such texts, readers like Ben Jonson often highlighted passages by penning flowers in the margins (Illustration 9), a practice that made reading like gathering flowers and writing like setting them in new floral beds or arrangements.

Ophelia has been given enough prescripts – flowers on protecting her unopened flower – to comprise such a posy. As Hamlet wipes his tables clean when he wants to forget what he has learned, so Ophelia disperses her nosegay. Some of her flowers are named after thoughts ("And there is pansies, that's for thoughts," pansies for *pensées*, 4.5.174–5),[97] others are said to strengthen memory ("rosemary, that's for remembrance," 173), others betoken regret ("There's *rue* for you. And here's some for me," 178–9). Thoughts, memories, and remorse are in the same gathering as flowers which stand for the vices of the seducer: *daisies* (181) for dissembling, *fennel* (178) for flattery, and *columbine* (178) for infidelity.[98] With the help of syntax, her flowers carry the same lesson as the precepts, ballad, and tales: beware male treachery.

What are we to think before so many signs of undoing? If the *anthology* was compiled to protect Ophelia's virginity, what does it signify when that anthology is taken apart, *undone*? (Whitney instructs against such recklessness, "spoil them not, nor do in pieces tear them."[99]) Has Ophelia lost her mind or that part for which *mind* functioned as both euphemism and synonym? Has she had a breakdown or has she been deflowered? Laertes curses Hamlet for having "[d]epriv'd" his sister of her "most ingenious sense" (5.1.241–2); has something else been taken as well? The ambiguity carries over to her burial. The sexton tries to convince his mate that Ophelia was *compos mentis* at her drowning and therefore as a suicide unfit for burial in consecrated ground: "she drowned herself wittingly" (5.1.1–13). Yet the debate at her interment between the priest and her brother seems to be as much about her virginity as her sanity. Though Laertes passionately insists on her purity, "her fair and unpolluted flesh" (5.1.232), the Church grants "her virgin crants, / Her maiden strewments" (225–6) only begrudgingly.

Like his sister, Laertes has a hard time minding his father's precepts after his ignominious death; and like her, too, he falls apart. He and his sister divide between them the two dramatic strains of *madness*. Ophelia is insane, Laertes enraged. In 4.5, their reactions at his death are quite closely parallel. Their entrances are both announced by messengers: first a description of Ophelia's psychic breakdown, then of Laertes' anarchic rebellion. Both messengers are rhetorically challenged by the need to describe something beyond the pale of language and reason. The ocean serves as analogy for both: Ophelia is "as raging as the sea" (Q1) and Laertes with his rebellion is like the ocean overwhelming its lists. Ophelia, bereft of her wits, is reduced to ambiguous "winks, nods, and gestures," and speaks things in doubt that carry but half sense but which may "strew / Dangerous conjectures in ill-breeding mind" (4.5.11, 14–15). The rabble or "riotous head" (4.5.101) backing Laertes is also inarticulate, expressing themselves with "caps, hands, and tongues" (107) and clamoring for something that also carries "but half sense" and might well "strew / Dangerous conjectures": a monarchy not by succession or parliamentary election, but by popular demand: "They cry, 'Choose we! Laertes shall be king'" (106). In Act 4, consternation precedes the entrance of both. Ophelia, we are told, is "importunate" (1); she appears to be restrained from entering until Gertrude consents to her admission ("Let her come in," 16). Before her second entrance, she is definitely making a racket, "*A noise within*" (4.5.152). The same stage direction (F) precedes Laertes' entrance as the rabble overcomes the palace guards and breaks down the doors, *"Noise within"* (F 2851). In Q1, Ophelia enters playing discordantly on a lute, her hair in disarray. Laertes enters with his arms drawn against the King, a "riotous head" behind him. The siblings are grieved by more than their father's death. They are maddened by his "hugger-mugger" (4.5.84) burial. Both are distraught by the lack of ceremony. Ophelia laments that he was slipped into an unmarked grave, "bewept . . . not" (39). Laertes is furious that he was buried without heraldic rites. The father's death appears to lead to the dishonoring of both children: the daughter's distraction suggests her ravishment; the son's desperate rage signals his disentitlement.

Ophelia's final gesture is a grotesque valedictory tribute to that spoiled family honor. At its center is a willow tree, the fruitless emblem of sterility, the bleak inverse of the genealogical oak. Instead of fruitful boughs, the willow branches are barren, made up of "hoary leaves" (4.7.166), their hoariness suggesting not only desiccation but also whore-like adulteration. The "fantastic garlands," "crownet," and "trophies" (167, 171, 173) that she attempts to hang on the willow's drooping limbs mimic heraldic achievements. Genealogical trees are commonly festooned with armorial shields as well as flowers, as in the engraving of King James' ancestral tree (Illustration 10) as well as the illuminated pedigree roll of the Heveningham family (Illustration 11). Often the heraldic coats of arms hanging on those trees are themselves emblazoned with trees or their metonymic equivalents: flowers, fruits, and leaves. Ophelia's garlands, however, are made up not of cultivated flowers like roses but of wild flowers and weeds, among them sinister and obscene stinging nettles and "long purples." Gertrude calls Ophelia's decorations "weedy trophies" and "crownet weeds" as if they aspired to achieve the chivalric ostentation omitted at her father's burial: "no trophy, sword, nor hatchment" (4.5.211). Like Polonius' spare grave consisting of "turf" and "stone" (4.5.31–2), the fruitless, weed-strewn tree blazons dishonor. The genealogical stock has been ruined by "things rank and gross in nature" (1.2.136). Ophelia leaves behind an emblem of spoiled genealogy, an image of blasted dynastic promise, a pitiful farewell to arms and the man.

Then there is Ophelia's fatal drop from the grisly tree. Ophelia, mindless of the danger she is in, "incapable of her own distress" (4.7.177) (just as at the play's start she was "unsifted in such perilous circumstance," 1.3.102), is momentarily buoyed up by her wide-spreading clothes and chants "old lauds" or "melodious lays" (4.7.176, 181) perhaps the same ones she sang at court of downfallen maids. The wide expanse of her skirt – "her clothes spread wide" (174) – itself suggests the opening of

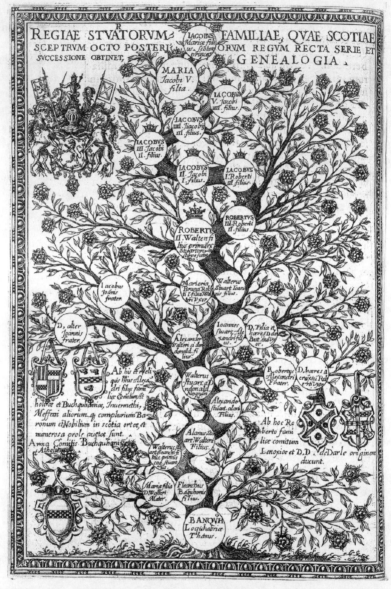

Illustration 10. *Genealogical Tree Festooned with Flowers and Arms*, in John Leslie, *De origine, moribus & rebus gestis Scotorum libri decem* (1578).

Illustration 11. *Pedigree Roll of the Heveningham Family* (1597).

Illustration 12. *"There's rue for you": Mrs. Lessingham in the Character of Ophelia* (1772).
Burney V, no. 250.

what virgins should keep *closed*: the chest of the "chaste treasure" (1.3.31) whose pilfering was so dreaded by her brother and father.[100] Her skirt billows out to keep her afloat like an aquatic tail: "And mermaid-like awhile they bore her up" (4.7.175). It is in clambering to hang "her crownet weeds" that "down her weedy trophies and herself / Fell in the weeping brook" (173–4). Flowers may have decorated her person even before her death. In the earliest illustration of Ophelia on record, based on a production in 1772, sprigs of flowers are fastened to her gown (Illustration 12).[101] In both life and death, her flower-strewn body

Illustration 13. *Flora Inseminated by Zephyrus*, in Vincenzo Cartari, *Imagini de i dei de gli antichi* (1571).

travestied the image of Flora, the goddess of fertility. Once inseminated by the winds or "blastments" of Zephyrus (1.3.43), which like lovers' vows enter via the ear, Flora became fecund with all the flowers of the spring. The myth, recounted in Ovid's *Fasti*, was frequently illustrated on the Continent, most famously in Botticelli's painting of the *Primavera*, but also in engravings like that featured in Vincenzo Cartari's *Imagini de i dei de gli antichi* (1571) (Illustration 13).[102] Closer to home, however, is Jacques Le Moyne's water-color painting *A Young Daughter of the Picts*, purchased by Theodore de Bry in London, who then copied it and published it under the same title in his *America I* (1590) (Illustration 14).[103] In the

Illustration 14. *A Young Daughter of the Picts,* Jacques Le Moyne de Morgues (1585–8).

painting, the young Pict daughter is covered with a splendid profusion of flowers. According to John Speed, who reproduced the damasked maiden in his *Historie of Great Britain,* all Pict virgins were so decorated: "thir whole body was garnished over with the shapes of all the fairest kinds of flowers and herbs." The painting places at the root of British civilization (the root, too, is part of de Bry's picture, as it is of Spigelius' blossoming woman in Illustration 6, just visible in the lower left corner) a rendering of the dynastic dream: a floriated woman in a flourishing landscape, with a thriving manor nestled in the fold of undulating hills.

At the announcement of his sister's drowning, Laertes breaks into tears.

> It is our trick; nature her custom holds,
> Let shame say what it will. When these are gone
> The woman will be out.   (4.7.186–8)

The sight of Ophelia's flower-strewn corpse throws Hamlet into similar hysterics, as his mother's use of a gestational metaphor to describe his passion suggests: "And thus awhile the fit will work on him. / Anon as patient as the female dove / When that her gold couplets are disclos'd" (5.1.280–2).

One might ask, "What's Ophelia to them or them to her that they should weep for her?" The Player wept for Hecuba whose "lank and all-o'erteemed loins" (2.2.504) were incapable of producing any more sons to replace those slain in war.[104] Their "grandsire" (2.2.460) has been hacked to bits and their dam's "teeming date" dried up. A civilization was felled at its wellspring. As we shall see in Chapter 5, it is before the florid body that both Hamlet and Laertes reach their hysterical pitch, as if to keep alive the prospect of continuing lineage.

The play introduces by way of allusion three women from antiquity who suffer similar hysterics. Besides Hecuba, there is Niobe, to whom Hamlet compares Gertrude in mourning, "Like Niobe, all tears" (1.2.149). Like Hecuba, Niobe was famed for her fertility, having given birth to seven sons and seven daughters. According to Ovid, Niobe took such pride in her "huge and populous race" that she attempted to supplant the goddess Latona, who having given birth only to the twins Apollo and Artemis had only "the seventh part of the issue borne" by Niobe.[105] To punish her subversive pride, Latona's two children shot dead Niobe's fourteen, first the sons then the daughters, leaving her bereft (her husband killed himself after the slaughter of the sons) and weeping, even after having been turned to stone: "And into stone hir verie wombe and bowels also bind. / But yet she wept . . . She weepeth still in stone."[106] In Judges (11:30–40), Jepthah's daughter is also remembered for her weeping. Knowing that her father would break his vow to God unless he sacrificed her, she pleaded for a two-month respite in which to bewail her virginity, "Let this thing be done for me: let me alone two months, that I may go up and down upon the mountains, and bewail my virginity, I and my fellows." Like Hecuba and Niobe weeping for lost children, Jepthah's nameless daughter weeps inconsolably for children she will never have. Faced with the reality of no progeny, all three weep inconsolably.

Through the bereavement of mythical Niobe, ancient Hecuba, and biblical Jepthah's daughter, the play instances what may be the bleakest moment of a civilization: the extinction of a bloodline, that of a family, dynasty, or race. In the "unweeded garden" and "sterile promontory" that is Denmark, there is copulation but no generation. There is, however, Laertes' parting wish that life issue from Ophelia's body:

> Lay her i'th'earth,
> And from her fair and unpolluted flesh
> May violets spring.   (5.1.232–3)

No sooner is she interred ("Lay her i'th'earth") than her brother imagines her corpse as fertile earth from which flowers could sprout (as they appear to have sprouted on the body of the Pict virgin) – and of all flowers, *violets*, the very flower that perished in sympathy with her father: "I would give you some violets, but they withered all when my father died" (4.5.181–3). Nor does the prospect end here. Gertrude tosses flowers atop her corpse, to produce another phantasmagoric projection of a flourishing estate. As we shall see in the next chapter, the prospect of estate sets up the third conflict between two peers over land and its female surrogate. The first occurred thirty years ago when Norway and Denmark fought over land; the conflict was repeated when one brother killed another for his realm and queen; finally Hamlet and Laertes grapple in Ophelia's grave, literally over her dead body. As Hamlet acknowledges, Laertes' situation is close to his own: "By the image of my cause I see / The portraiture of his" (5.2.77–8). Both sons have been dishonored and disentitled by the sudden and violent death of their father. Ophelia's corpse festooned with flowers stands for the estate and progeny denied them both.

In this play, women as well as men are generationally disposed. A generation – whether it be termed "forty years," "thirty years," "three and twenty years," or "a dozen yeare" – has come full circle since the time of that momentous day in Denmark's imperial history. The young, both male and female, are positioned to take over from their elders. Ophelia comes of age, but no sooner does the bud open – "O rose of May" (4.5.157) – than it is blasted. Laertes, on the brink of coming into his own, is disentitled by his father's dishonorable death. The young fail to advance in the place of the old. Instead, Denmark's ruling dynasty is extinguished. This is what it means that weeds rather than flowers are growing in the garden of Denmark. The flowery bank is the fantasy representation of the state. The reality is less wholesome. An "unweeded garden" (1.2.135) or "sterile promontory" (2.2.299), Denmark more closely resembles another bank, the "Lethe wharfe" where "the fat weed" (1.5.32–3) "roots"(Q1, Q2) and "rots" (F). "The Poisoner" in the Mousetrap play culls a "mixture rank, of midnight weeds" (3.2.251) from such a lethal bank, and from that gathering is extracted the "juice of cursed hebenon" (1.5.62), the equivalent of the "leperous distilment" (1.5.64) poured by Claudius into his brother's ear. The source for the fatal unction Laertes contributes to Claudius' scheme derives from both *mound* and *bank*, the "mountebank" (4.7.140) who provides a weedy "mixture" so deadly that there is no antidote for even the slightest dram:

> no cataplasm so rare,
> Collected from all simples that have virtue
> Under the moon, can save the thing from death
> That is but scratch'd withal. (142–5)

With this "unction" (4.6.140), the sword is anointed and the cup laced. Distillations of the fatal weeds turn out to be the bane of Denmark. They poison King Hamlet (in narrative and then in its two dramatic reenactments), the Queen ("The drink, the drink / I am poison'd," 5.2.316), Claudius ("The point envenom'd too! Then, venom, to thy work"; "Drink of this potion," 327, 331), Laertes ("I am justly kill'd with mine own treachery," 313), and finally Hamlet is wounded fatally with the "[u]nbated and envenom'd" sword (323); "No medicine in the world can do thee good" (320).

Not even the flower girl Ophelia is spared. She falls trying to hang her garlands of weeds and falls deeper still when pulled to her "muddy death" (4.7.182) by the weight of her sodden garments – her weed-strewn weeds. Through the play's surrealistic semantics, at her moment of death, she turns into a mudbank covered by noxious weeds. Like the body of the state, "things rank and gross in nature possess it merely" (1.2.136–7). If the floriated Pict virgin heralds the beginning of a civilization, the weed-strewn Ophelia marks the end.

When Coleridge imagines the scene of Ophelia's drowning 200 years after its writing, Ophelia is still a flowering piece of earth. In the marginalia to his copy of the play, he visualizes her as "a little projection of land into a lake or stream, covered with spray-flowers quietly reflected in the quiet waters, but at length is undermined or loosened, and becomes a fairy isle, and after a brief vagrancy sinks almost without an eddy." A half-century later Sir John Everett Millais, a great admirer of Coleridge, painted Ophelia as just that: a flowering diaphanous "fairy isle"

Illustration 15. *Ophelia,* Sir John Everett Millais (1851–2).

(Illustration 15). In what holds claim to being England's favorite painting, Ophelia's death is poignantly beautified. The wildflowers, meticulously rendered from nature, carry no genealogical promise. Nor does her eroticized pre-Raphaelite corpse.

CHAPTER 5

Doomsday and domain

No man's Heart can wholly stand up against Property.

Coleridge

From beginning to end, the Graveyard scene centers on the grave. Upon entering, all characters gravitate there: the sexton appears with spade in hand and proceeds to dig the grave; Hamlet and Horatio linger there contemplating its exhumations; and the royal funeral procession clusters around it for the burial service. As space is organized around the clay pit, so too is time. The scene lasts as long as it takes to prepare a grave ("make her grave straight," 5.1.3), commit a body ("Lay her i'th'earth," 231), and perform an abridged burial service ("the bringing home / Of bell and burial," 226–7).[1] Just before its completion, the graveside service is disrupted and action drops from the edge of the grave to inside it. As earth is about to be shoveled over Ophelia's floriated corpse, Laertes bids the sexton, "Hold off the earth awhile" (242). As the mourners look on, he leaps into the grave and Hamlet follows. They grapple there, are pulled asunder, and must either scramble out or be yanked up in order to be free to exit at the scene's end. Everything in 5.1 is focused on that little patch of recessed ground that at the Globe would have been indicated by the open trap, the $5' \times 2'$ rectangle at the center rear of the stage floor.

The graveyard, the resting place between this world and the next, is certainly an appropriate setting for Hamlet's meditation on death and Last Things before his own imminent end. *Memento mori* are in evidence: skulls, bones, and the loose earth into which these remains will eventually dissolve. In contemplating them, Hamlet achieves the desired renunciation. His contempt for the world climaxes viscerally when handling a skull whose lips he once kissed: "And smelt so? Pah!" (194).

Modern criticism has taken the graveyard meditation to mark a profound change in Hamlet. It is assumed that his garments have been altered to indicate the change, from the madman's dishabille to a traveler's sea-cloak.

From then on, he seems to be waiting for some higher power to take over, be it providence, fate, chance. Bradley calls this mood "sad or indifferent self-abandonment" – a general "letting go" in the conviction that "*nothing matters.*"[2] After the sea voyage, he appears altogether calm, tranquil, and resigned to whatever happens, above all, to death.

But this tradition has strangely ignored the sensational outbreak that follows the meditation: the fight between Hamlet and Laertes in the grave and over the grave. The grave here turns from the object of quiet meditation to the site and cause of an outrageous skirmish. Hamlet's contemplation of death culminates not in calm renunciation but rather in a wild display of his attachment to the world. Why should such a crazed rivalry erupt in the shadow of Last Things? Why should a solemn scene centered on a grave conclude with a struggle over it?

At the opening of Act 5, the sexton is bothered by the coroner's decision to bury the young woman's body in the consecrated grounds of the churchyard. He begins by questioning the verdict, "Is she to be buried in Christian burial?" (5.1.1) and in Q1 downright opposes it, "I say no, she ought not to be buried / In christian buriall."[3] His companion defends the decision, but the sexton gives two garbled legal arguments to prove the death a *felon da se*. She died not defending herself but offending herself: *se offendendo*.[4] The legality of the ruling is moot, however, for as both the sexton and his companion end up agreeing, the decision was based on the rank of the deceased rather than her mental state. "Will you ha' the truth an't? If this had not been a gentlewoman, she should have been buried out o'Christian burial," says the one (5.1.23–5). And the other responds, "The more the pity that great folk should have countenance in this world to drown or hang themselves more than their even-Christen" (5.1.26–9). The entitlements of the "great" extend beyond this world and into the next. Their possession of estate gives them privileged access to the consecrated land of the churchyard which in turn holds out better prospects for a place in the kingdom to come.

The graveyard would seem an odd setting for the voicing of class antagonism. Death is, after all, the Great Leveler, felling high and low alike with its scythe, eliminating social inequalities among "even-Christen." This was the lesson abundantly illustrated in the borders of Queen Elizabeth's Prayer Book (1569) by a series of hierarchically arranged engravings in which Death levels men and women of estates, from Emperor and King to Beggar and Rogue, from Empress Queen to Poor Woman.[5] Even more affecting, perhaps, were the paintings of the Dance of Death schema on church walls, like the one in the cloisters of St. Paul's which was copied in the nave of the Guild Chapel in Stratford.[6] In these frescos, figures of all ranks are being pulled toward the west, in the direction of the setting sun (in the opposite direction from the chancel arch depicting the resurrection) and finally toward the grave where lies a dead king eaten by worms. Yet as Vanessa Harding emphasizes in her account of burial arrangements in early modern London, class distinctions hardly vanished at death: "There was a broad correlation between burial location and social importance."[7] Both within the church and in the churchyards, the disposition of graves tended to reproduce the social order. As Harding points out, those who had held lands in both the city and the country were invariably buried in the church. There they retained both their titles and their private plots, often in the company of their ancestors; their names were inscribed on tombs or slabs, and their bodies tended to remain in place undisturbed. Even after the Reformation, the plots within the church closest to the altar or chancel were regarded as the most hallowed and most prestigious, and the elite were interred there.[8] Those of middling to lower ranks, however, were buried in the undifferentiated space of the churchyard.[9] There they tended to lose both name and plot, for their graves were unmarked, and regularly cleared out to make room for new corpses. While "[n]o burial was secure against future disturbance," the elite certainly rested more securely within the stone confines of the church and under the surveillance of their descendants.[10]

It was not only that certain burial spaces were more desirable than others; all consecrated space seems to have been at a premium in early modern London. As the population of the city multiplied, so too did the death rate, particularly in time of plague. And yet consecrated burial space was limited to what was circumscribed within the church walls and the churchyard. Indeed it might be said that as the death rate mounted, the acreage for burying the dead decreased. Private tombs increasingly encroached upon what was once the open communal space of the church. And the churchyard, too, was losing ground, sometimes to the church itself when it needed more room for worship, storage, or its ministry. To accommodate the overflow, new grounds were consecrated in the less desirable land outside the city's center. But the main expedient was to use the same grave pit for multiple corpses and periodically exhume the miscellaneous remains for deposit in charnel houses. During plague years, the city had to resort to both expedients: huge pits were dug in the peripheries to contain the infected bodies. In his plague pamphlets of 1603, Thomas Dekker wrote of mass graves that received as many as fifty bodies per day.[11] In short, there were more Christian dead than consecrated ground for their committal. As Harding notes, the scarcity of space led to something of a land market for burial ground. Prices were set not only on tombs, but on plots of ground in the church, and eventually in the churchyard as well. Parishioners vied for the choice spots, and their disposal was carefully monitored by the vestrymen and officers of the church.[12] Choice burial ground gave an advantage in both this world and the next. Tombs in the church, perpetually in view of the parishioners, preserved the memory of the deceased.[13] In addition, despite Protestant protest, burial within the most hallowed regions of the church was imagined to strengthen the chance of salvation. As Philip Ariès has maintained, "the commemoration of the living person was not separated from the salvation of the soul."[14]

In More's *Utopia*, there is no private property. Inhabitants rotate periodically from city to country, from one abode to another, to prevent identification with any one location. At death, only the despairing and guilty are committed to earth. All other Utopians are cremated. In the regime that inverted the priorities of sixteenth-century England's land-based social order, the attachment of persons to land – in death as in life – can only be vitiating.

The same inequities organizing the land of the living were reproduced in the land of the dead. In the context of early modern burial practices, the graveyard may well have been an appropriate place to stage a protest against the privileges of "great folk" (5.1.27). The sexton and his companion are certainly the right ones to voice it.[15] In both stage directions and speech prefixes, they are called *Clowns*. The use of the word to designate comical stage figures was quite recent, and certainly not independent of the older and still prevalent use of the word for a person of rural origins. By a spurious etymology cited by Holinshed, *clown* was derived from the Latin *colonus*, "a tiller of the soil."[16] Like its synonym *rustic*, from the Latin *rus*, and *peasant*, from the French *païs*, the name linked a man to the land which was his subsistence. To sophisticated city audiences and readers, country folk – caricatured as naive, gullible, and slow-witted – were comical. Richard Tarlton introduced the stage tradition of rusticated clowning, his russet suit ("vile russetings" according to one satirical account), buttoned cap, tabor, and pipe proclaiming his country origins.[17]

The Clowns who appear in the graveyard activate both meanings of their speech prefix. There is ample opportunity to be comical in their attempt to understand the coroner's verdict and in the various slapstick routines afforded by grave-digging. Yet they are also clowns in the older sense, representing the lowest stratum of society. Goodman Delver, termed a "peasant" (5.1.136) by Hamlet, follows his mate's complaint against "great folk" with a claim to the greatness of his own laboring kind. His first assertion comes in answer to his riddle, "Who builds stronger than a mason, a shipwright, or a carpenter?" (5.1.50–1). "A grave-maker," he responds, "[t]he houses he makes lasts till doomsday" (58–9). His mortuary houses attain the ultimate dream of the great dynastic houses: endurance through the ages until the end of time. The last to perish, his house was also the earliest to begin. Delver's ancestor Adam was the "first gentleman" and he is among his direct descendants: "There is no ancient gentlemen but gardeners, ditchers, and gravemakers" (29–31). In his social order, it is the workers of the land rather than its owners who make up the gentry. The sexton's patronymic, Delver, affiliates him with that ancestor whose Hebrew name (*adamah*, clay) similarly associated him with the earth he was expelled from Eden to work. A line of work, "Adam's profession" (31) substitutes for a bloodline.

Also descending from Adam is a coat of arms, for Adam was "the first that ever bore arms" (33). "Scripture says Adam digged. Could he dig without arms?" (36–7).[18] The "arms" Adam used to delve are, of course, the upper limbs of his body. The spade extends the arms; at its extremity, an iron palm substitutes for the hand. The same prosthetic arm Adam used to cultivate could also be used to destroy, as if in compliance with God's injunction to "Beat your plowshares into swords, and your pruning hooks into spears" (Joel 3:10).[19] Spades were the peasant equivalent of military weapons, the kind of arms in which Fortinbras is strong. His arms are used not to work the land but to enlarge it. Backing him are enough other arms to be called an *army*, the "army of such mass and charge" (4.4.47) which Q2 numbers at "two thousand"; the stage directions of all three texts require that a number of them accompany their leader upon his first entrance. The peasant's aggressive wielding of his arms is also land-driven. As Fortinbras' army increases his land, so the peasant deploys his arms in order to secure his use of it. In early modern London, shovels might well have recalled the protests against the enclosure of common lands; they were famously used in the reign of Henry VIII to hack down the hedges and fill in the ditches that marked off exclusive property. In his *Survey of London* (1603), John Stow repeats Edward Hall's account of how a group of Londoners assembled behind "a Turner in a fooles coate . . . crying through the Citty, shouelles and spades, shouelles and spades."[20] In the early seventeenth century, a radical group called the Diggers emerged in Shakespeare's birthplace and country

Illustration 16. *Robert Scarlett* (1747, based on painting of 1665), Peterborough Cathedral.

residence. They publicized themselves in a pamphlet entitled "The Diggers of Warwickshire to All Other Diggers" (1607) and clamored against their exclusion from the common lands, not by claiming gentility but by denying all claims to private property.

The spade's association with land was furthered by the resemblance of its shape to the heraldic shield or escutcheon on which armorial bearings were emblazoned. The interplay between the two shapes can be seen in an oil painting copied in 1747 from a portrait from 1665, based on a mural from c. 1600 (Illustration 16).[21] It is a portrait of Robert Scarlett (1496–1594), sexton of Peterborough Cathedral, celebrated for having interred two queens (Catherine of Aragon in 1536 and Mary Queen of

Scots in 1587) as well as two generations of Peterborough householders before dying at the age of 98.[22] Hanging directly over his spade (and his arm) is a coat of arms, belonging not to him, of course, but to the Cathedral. The royal arms themselves took such a form, and may on stage have appeared on "a cloth of estate" draped over the King's throne.[23] In books of heraldry, Adam's spade, his identifying implement in the medieval mystery plays, is sometimes given as the most ancient form of escutcheon.[24] Thus Delver's self-appointed Adamic "arms" declare both his armigerous nobility and his military might – preserving the link between title-bearing and arms-bearing originating in the feudal pledge of military service in return for land and title.

Delver's self-entitling boast prepares him for his confrontation with the disentitled Hamlet. The puffed-up peasant encounters the stripped-down prince. This is the conventional encounter between royal-in-disguise and unsuspecting commoner, popular from ballads as well as stage representations. The divide is signaled by the positioning of the two men, Hamlet standing high above the sexton who is stooped over by his labor in the trap a few feet beneath him. The friction between them begins when Hamlet finds offense in the way the sexton performs his job: "Hath this fellow no feeling of his business a sings in grave-making?" (5.1.65–6). Q1 suggests that it is Hamlet's sense of decorum which is offended; he objects to the sexton's being "thus *merry* in making of a *graue*" [italics added], a formulation that simultaneously hints at the scene's own indecorous mixture of grave matters and clowning, prince and pauper.[25] Horatio answers Hamlet's question with a proverb, "Custom hath made it in him a property of easiness" (67).[26] The routine repetition of the task has hardened him to its morbidity. Hamlet's paraphrase gives a social edge to the proverb, "'Tis e'en so, the hand of little employment hath the daintier sense" (68–9). The calloused hand of the manual laborer is insensitive to the discriminations felt by the smooth hand of the pampered gentleman. The context renders Hamlet's affirmational "'Tis e'en so" ironic by stressing the opposite relation: the *un*evenness between the idle rich and the laboring poor, hardly "even-Cristen" all.

There may be more to offend Hamlet's "daintier sense" in the sexton's generic mixing of what Sidney with like-minded aesthetic sensibility termed "hornpipes and funerals."[27] As Sidney also knew, generic mongrelization broke down class division through its "mingling kings and clowns."[28] The "judicious" in the audience might have noted that Delver's song has a rather posh provenance. Its three stanzas closely match up with a well-known courtly lyric first printed in 1557 under the title "The aged louer renounceth love" in the anthology *Songes and Sonettes, written by the right honorable Lorde Henry Haward late Earle of Surrey,* now known as *Tottel's Miscellany.*[29] As the ascription makes clear, the "aged louer," accustomed to holding dainty pen rather than dirty shovel, belongs to the privileged class of "little employment."

> My muse dothe not delight
> Me as she did before:
> My hand and pen are not in plight,
> As they have bene of yore.

The incongruity between rustic singer and courtly song might be emphasized by the Clown's pitching his voice into a high falsetto in imitation of court madrigals. The asyntactical "O" and "a's" included in all three texts have been generally taken as cues for boorish grunting given out during the exertion of digging. It is just as plausible, however, that the vowels substitute for a musical notation, indicating that the singer should draw out the notes of his vowels, perhaps to attain a warbling or trilling effect. A rustic singing a court lyric would be as incongruous as an aristocratic maiden like Ophelia singing an indecent ballad like "St. Valentine's Day." Courtly lyrics are as out of place in the country as "country matters" are at court.

Possessing title, arms, genealogy, and cultural capital, the debonair peasant also entitles himself to property. When Hamlet asks, "Whose grave's this?" (5.1.115–16), Delver gives a proprietary answer, "Mine, sir" (117). He exercises a landlord's privilege by disposing of the land at will, blithely admitting and evicting "tenants" from the "houses" of his mortuary manor, casting out old occupants to make room for new.[30] Though his "houses" (59) may well last till the end of time, residency takes the form of short-term arrangements: lodgers and "tenants" (44) are tossed out like unwanted guests. The graves he builds are more like charnel houses than dynastic houses, muddling identity rather than preserving it. No markers or locations differentiate the remains of the dead; no inscription, armorial crest, or effigy individuates the interred. While estate houses were intended to perpetuate lineage, this bone house reduces distinction to a powder of dust and bones. The sexton sings in the person of someone whose human form has already disappeared in earth: "Age . . . hath shipp'd me intil the land / As if I had never been such" (5.1.70–3). Hamlet indiscriminately dubs the remains of the dead with the same indeterminate pronoun, "Lord Such-a-one, that praised my Lord Such-a-one's horse" (5.1.83–4).

It is the very anonymity of the remains which frees Hamlet to flesh them out. He chooses to make them all quite grand. Lords and ladies, courtiers, politicians, lawyers, landlords: they are all, like Ophelia, "of some estate" (214). Indeed one might have expected them to have been buried in the church. All appear to have come by land through inheritance, purchase, or legal devices. As a consequence, Delver appears to be tossing about not just any remains but those of his landed betters. In his humble office as sexton, he "o'eroffices" (78) his dead superiors. He seems to take particular relish in injuring their heads, as if "his action of battery" (100–1) were aimed at the top of the top: "See how the slave joles their heads against the earth" (Q1), knocking them upon their "mazard[s]" (88) and sconces "with a dirty shovel" (100). There may be a context, then, for Q1's stage direction to the sexton, just as Hamlet approaches: "*he throwes up a shouel*" (H4r). In the Folio version of his most famous soliloquy, Hamlet lists among his grievances "the poor man's contumely," though modern editors prefer the less socially charged "proud man's contumely" (3.1.71). In the Q1 version, the resentment is quite explicit: the poor are "scorned by the right rich" so that the rich in turn are "cursed of the poore." The peasant, by banging the skulls of his social betters, plays out the same conflict in the name of those who "grunt and sweat under a weary life" (3.1.77).[31]

The peasant might take particular pleasure in bashing the one skull he identifies by name, "Yorick's skull" (5.1.175). He has good reason to remember him, for he bears him a longstanding grudge: the "madde rogue" (173) poured a flagon of Rhenish on his head.[32] The court jester made a laughing stock of the rustic Clown (it is the kind of gibe that would have "set the table on a roar," 185), and it is now the Clown's turn to retaliate. Not that the Clown himself does not pull rank. After all, as the Q1 speech prefix specifies, his assistant is only number "2" (H3v). He browbeats his subordinate with his riddle, and then bids him "cudgel thy brains" (56) no longer, for like a "dull ass" (56–7) a beating will not make him go any faster.

In the face of such antagonism from below, Hamlet identifies with his own highborn kind. He experiences Delver's manhandling of the remains as disrespect not for the dead but for those on top. As the peasant flings the bones to the ground, Hamlet marks the turn of events, the "fine revolution" (89) that reduces high-bred bones to country game-pieces. Aristocratic legbones end up as rustic "leggits": "Did these bones cost no more the breeding but to play at loggets with 'em?" (90–1). There is no mistaking where Hamlet's sympathies lie. His well-bred bones give him away: "Mine ache to think on't" (91).

Hamlet from the graveside speaks down to the sexton, addressing him as "sirrah" (116) and referring to him as "fellow" (65), "mad knave" (99), "ass"

(77), "peasant" (136), and "slaue" (Q1, H4r). He takes the upper hand in their conversation, as is the prerogative of rank, by asking questions. But Delver, while deferentially addressing him as "sir" (117, 124, etc), hardly stays in place. The Prince begins by asking, "Whose grave's this, sirrah?" (115–16) and three times rephrases the question – "What man dost thou dig it for?" (126), "What woman then?" (128), "Who is to be buried in't?" (130) – yet receives no answer. When he asks "How long hast thou been grave-maker?" (138), he must wait some twenty lines for a straight reply. Similarly, when he asks how Hamlet became mad, he is given a circular response: "with losing his wits" (154). Delver's evasive responses hedge rather than answer his superior's requests for information. "How absolute the knave is" (133), marvels Hamlet, and his choice of words reveals the source of his wonder: a lowly *knave* or manservant should be dependent, not *absolute*, and yet the knave responds not to satisfy the Prince's requests for information but rather to please himself (and provoke the audience's laughter).[33] To defend against the Clown's quibbling, Hamlet recommends holding fast to the topic at hand (he keeps rephrasing his questions), as a mariner sticks to his navigational course or shipman's card: "We must speak by the card, or equivocation will undo us" (133–4). That this verbal contest reflects class antagonism is made clear by Hamlet's observations: "The toe of the peasant comes so near the heel of the courtier he galls his kibe" (136–8). Hamlet's metaphor itself reveals an unsettling of the status quo. The social formation is imagined not as a vertical hierarchy, a standing body with highborn as head and lowborn as feet, but rather as a horizontal foot race in which the peasant is a small measure away – a mere pedestrian foot – from the discomfited courtier.

When in dialogue with the Clown, Hamlet is on the receiving end of the "antic disposition." Until then, it has been *his* equivocation which threatened to undo his interlocutors. When asked how he "fares" (3.2.92), he responds by expressing dissatisfaction with his diet. When asked the subject of the book he is reading ("What is the matter?" 2.2.193), he responds as if he had been asked what the trouble was. Upon learning that the King after the Mousetrap production is "marvelous distempered," he asks, "With drink, sir?" (3.2.293–4). When Ophelia says she thinks "nothing," Hamlet has her thinking "country matters" (115–16). These are all instances of the impertinence he warns clowns against in his advice to the Players: the introduction of extraneous matter that derails the subject at hand.[34] His antic diversion drives Guildenstern to beg that he put his "discourse into some frame, and [start] not so wildly" from the matter (3.2.300–1). This scattering of dialogue in ambiguity is the Clown's prerogative. If his straight-talking interlocutor gets lost in the Clown's quibbling detours, he is "undone." The dialogic contest illustrates the ambiguity in the word *equivocation* itself; like Hamlet's "e'en so," in this context, it hints at disparity rather than equity – the volatile unevenness of vocations.[35]

It is from the professional clown, too, that Hamlet has picked up the habit of insulting those to whom he should be deferential, including the Ghost of his father ("old mole," 1.5.170), the King ("Farewell dear Mother," 4.3.52), his mother (accusing her of "making love / Over the nasty sty," 3.4.93–4), the old counselor ("You are a fishmonger," 2.2.174). He also shares the clown's penchant for obscenity, a trace of his rusticity which puts him in close proximity to breeding animals. In the presence of women, whether his mother or Ophelia, he tends to speak of "country matters," in the manner of "liberal shepherds" (4.7.169) who find grosser names for the copulative parts and acts, and whatever happens to resemble them. But the kinship runs deeper still. By convention, the stage clown speaks out of need, making jokes in order to make a living. Typically he complains about the bad terms of his service. In Q1, in extending his advice to the Players, Hamlet himself gives voice to the clown's privation. When criticizing their routine deviation from the script, he rattles off the punch lines to four stock jokes, each of which is grounded in complaint. The Clown's jokes all give vent to the unsatisfactory conditions of his employment. He grumbles that he hasn't time to eat his porridge, his wages are in arrears, he is unliveried, and his beer is fermented.

> Cannot you stay till I eate my porrige? And, you owe me
> A quarters wages: and, my coate wants a cullison:
> And, your beere is sowre. (F2v)

Hamlet also expresses his own discontent, sometimes mysteriously, "I have of late, but wherefore I know not, lost all my mirth" (2.2.295–6), sometimes head-on, "I lack advancement" (3.2.331). In sum, "th'expectancy" of the state (3.1.154) does not have what he expected. He repeatedly classifies himself among the "discontented" (Q1), referring to himself as "[b]eggar" (2.2.272), "so poor a man" (1.5.192), "dreadfully attended" (2.2.269), an unfed capon, a starving horse, "a rogue and peasant slave" (2.2.543).

The graveyard forms the backdrop to a showdown between peasant and Prince in which the former gets the better of the latter in a display of the "poor man's contumely." The change so often noted in Hamlet's mood in Act 5 might more precisely be described as a shift in social position after his stint in the *dis*-position of the antic. Confronted with the uppity peasant, he reverts back to his proper princely station. He becomes the superior "sir" to the sexton's inferior "sirrah." And yet he loses ground, for the rustic lords it over not only the terrain ("mine, sir"), but also the language ("equivocation will undo us"). He brow-beats Hamlet as he cudgels the brains of his assistant and knocks the pates of the exhumed elite. It is Hamlet who is baffled by the peasant's equivocation, and who must laugh off his insults. "Cannot you tell that?" asks the Clown, incredulous that anyone should not know when the Prince was born: "Every fool can tell that" (5.1.142).

The graveyard scene's abundant *mementoes mori* direct thought to the next world. So, too, does Ophelia's consignment to her resting place until the sounding of the "last trumpet" (5.1.223) when the dead will take leave of their mortuary "lodgings" and rise to receive their eternal place of rest or torment. And yet in 1600 the eschatological setting might have brought to mind more immediate issues of allocation. Last Things were at the heart of a long tradition of radical protest. From the fourteenth century through the seventeenth, populist protest was grounded on the conviction that Christ's Second Coming would usher in a messianic kingdom on earth in which all land would be held in common.[36] "Mine and Thine would disappear."[37] Such movements looked forward at the end of time to the egalitarianism that had existed at its beginning, when "all men were alike; there was no principality, there was no bondage, or villeinage; that grew afterwards by violence and cruelty."[38] Populist uprisings projected a return to the Edenic state summarized in the proverbial couplet, quoted by Holinshed in his account of the Peasants' Revolt of 1381, "When Adam delu'd, and Eue span, / Who was then a gentleman?"[39] Land existed to be cultivated and sheep to be sheared, but there was no estate and no chattel; nor without private property were there titles. Delver's grumblings and set-to with the Prince as well as the references to Eden and Doomsday might well signal this tradition, though the upheaval he envisions is not quite that of the millenarian sects, for in his Eden property and privilege are not abolished, but transferred, from those who hold the land to those who work it: "gardeners, ditchers, and grave-makers" (5.1.30–1).

For an English audience, when the lay of the land was at issue, Doomsday had another resonance. *Doomsday* or *Domesday* was the name of the great survey taken by William the Conqueror to record the reallotment of land after the Norman Conquest. Completed in 1086, the Domesday Book recorded the extent, value, ownership, and occupancy of all the land of England, specifying the quantity of meadow, pasture,

wood, and arable land of the various estates. Considered a legal record of
ancient rights and tenure, the Book, located in the royal treasury of the
Exchequer, continued well into the early modern period to be consulted
in disputes over land and collateral property.[40] It registered surnames
associating owners with lands, buildings, estates, and livestock awarded by
the new king in exchange for military service.[41] Accounts of Domesday
typically appear in Tudor histories and legal treatises. In *The Collection of
the Historie of England* (1618), for example, Samuel Daniel describes
William's commissioning of the "general suruey of the Kingdome":

> to take the particulars both of his owne possessions, and euery mans else in the
> Kingdome, the Nature and the quality of their Lands, their estates, and abilities;
> besides the descriptions, bounds, and divisions of Shieres and Hundreds, and this
> was drawne into one booke[.][42]

The Book, according to Daniel, provided "a deed to all land of the kingdom," primarily, it appears, for purposes of land taxation. Its famous
precedent was the Danish geld-book that kept account of the tribute England
paid to the Danes before the Norman Conquest. The play references the land
tax when Claudius determines to send Hamlet to England "[f]or the demand
of our neglected tribute" (3.1.172).[43] Its payment demonstrates England's
tributary status; the conquered must pay ground-rent, as it were, to the
conquering landlord, or suffer further marauding. With wounds still "raw
and red" (4.3.63) from the conqueror's sword, England will not balk at
Denmark's command to execute the Prince.

   In a land-based society, the Book's name contained one of the most
basic puns in the language: *Doom* as judgment and *dom* as domain
(king*dom*, earl*dom*, duke*dom*). A close connection between land and law
prevailed when the common law, according to John Pocock, was "above
all a law regulating the tenure of land."[44] The law principally functioned
to obtain, retain, or transfer land. At several points, the early *Hamlet* texts
demonstrate the close semantic kinship between *law* and *land*. Fortinbras
at the start of the play intends to attack Denmark with an army of
resolutes who are *landless* in Q and *lawless* in F (1.1.101). Editors cannot
go wrong here, for either form of lack would motivate aggression. *Land*
and *law* also coalesce in the graveyard where it is unclear whether the
*law*yer with all of his arguments and instruments is the same as the "great
buyer of land," with "his recognizances, his fines, his double vouchers, his
recoveries" (5.1.101–4). Is Hamlet supposed to handle one skull (the
lawyer/landlord's) or two (the lawyer's and the landlord's)? Sir Thomas
Littleton's *Tenures*, the standard introduction to the law of property in the

sixteenth century, warns that oppression results from the collusion between proud landlords and crafty lawyers; in the *Life and Death of Jack Straw* (1593), John Ball complains that the poor man's substance is spent giving "[t]he landlord his rent, the lawyer his fees."[45]

The survey's eschatological title often received a gloss, "This book is metaphorically called by the native English Domesday, that is, the Day of Judgment. For as the sentence of that strict and terrible last account cannot be evaded by any subterfuge, so when this book is appealed to on those matters which it contains, its sentence cannot be quashed or set aside with impunity."[46] When territorial disputes arose, its arbitrations were thought to possess the finality and irrevocability of the Last Judgment. The name established the authority and permanence of land tenure itself. Some believed that its tenures predated the Conquest and had existed, like the common law itself, from time immemorial.[47] According to legal historians, peasants turned to the Domesday Book during numerous peasant uprisings and protests of the fourteenth and fifteenth centuries in order to trace their claims back to "ancient demesne" or immemorial custom, and by obtaining, at their own cost, an "exemplification" from the Book.[48] Although generally unsuccessful (their claims were either not in the Book or else not honored by the Commons and landlords), peasants continued to appeal to the Book, according it "an almost talismanic symbol of liberation from servitude and oppression."[49] Doomsday was, after all, the Day of Judgment when the rich would be humbled and the oppressed would be freed.[50]

Like the tradition of chiliastic protest and the institution of the Domesdsay, the graveyard scene conjoins concern about Last Things with issues of entitlement. Ophelia's burial raises questions of salvation as well as privilege. The location of the ground in which her body is laid to rest will have a bearing on her soul's ultimate destination. At a time when people could still remember how land, by some estimates as much as one-third of the realm, had been bequeathed over time to the Church in exchange for lasting spiritual benefits, the relation of *soul* to *soil* may have been more than phonetic. The two signifieds were also linked by the formulaic wording of last wills and testaments, commending the soul to God and disposing "all lands, tenements and heriditaments whatsoever."[51] That King Hamlet's soul is unprepared for death is clear. Caught in his garden unawares, he was "cut off even in the blossoms of my sin" (1.5.76), his crimes "broad blown, as flush as May" (3.3.81), with no opportunity for absolving last rites (1.5.77). To the Ghost, what is "horrible, O horrible! Most horrible" (80) is not that he was murdered but that he was given no time to repent before death: "No reck'ning made, but sent to my account / With all my imperfections on my head" (78–9). Only with incomparably long and hard suffering in the next life would the "foul crimes" not repented in this be "burnt and purg'd away" (1.5.12–13).[52]

It was not only King Hamlet's soul, however, which was unprepared for death. His estate seems to have been similarly unsettled, as if he had died not only "[u]nhousel'd, disappointed, unanel'd" but also intestate (1.5.77). While his uncle publicly proclaims Hamlet his successor (1.2.109) and grandiosely bestows upon him the symbolic gift of a "union" [F] pearl – "Hamlet this pearl is thine" (5.2.284) – there is no sign that his father ever made such a provision. As we have seen in Chapter 3, crown, throne, and matrimonial bed all pass to his brother rather than his son. Nothing remains to distinguish the firstborn son except the patronymic, a merely nominal connection between the deceased father and his "sole son" (3.3.77), the only vestige of the birthright that once designated him "[t]h'expectancy and rose of the fair state" (3.1.154). During his sea journey, he does, it is true, have in his possession his "father's signet" (5.2.49), "the model of that Danish seal" (5.2.50), but not by his father's bequest: "Why, even in that was heaven ordinant" (48), Hamlet allows, or as Horatio explains to Gertrude in Q1, "by great chance he had his fathers Seale" (H2v).[53]

The Ghost's appearance clad in the most significant ancestral token seems to flaunt this failure of transmission. It is unusual attire for stage ghosts, who conventionally appear in drapery resembling winding sheets, like those worn by the "sheeted dead" who gibbered in the Roman streets (1.1.118, Q2 only). The dialogue repeatedly emphasizes the anomaly; both before and after the Ghost's appearance, we learn that it is in "the very armour" (1.1.63), "armed at point exactly," "cap-a-pie" (1.2.200), "[a]rm'd . . . from head to foot" (1.2.226–7), "in arms" (1.2.255). In a play so attentive to arms, military and heraldic, their retention by the dead father may indicate a larger withholding. As Jones and Stallybrass note in their discussion of the Ghost, "it is exactly such suits of armor that were transmitted as the markers, and indeed, creators of genealogy."[54] The transmission was an important symbolic moment in the funeral ceremony, marking the transfer of the father's identity to the son and heir: "The rite of mourning was itself a ritual transmission of the father's armor to the son." Hamlet receives neither the father's armor nor his estate. He is left empty-handed. He has King Claudius' promise of the succession, as the play reiterates, but as Hamlet intimates through puns and proverbs, he needs something more substantial than breath.

The surreptitious death of Polonius may well have left his son similarly destitute. Like Hamlet, he does not receive the symbolic trappings of lineage. Laertes more readily accepts his father's murder than the disgrace of his burial. The lack of "formal ostentation" (4.5.212) would have implied that his father died in disgrace. The image of his denuded grave similarly haunts Ophelia, his burial in the "cold ground" (4.5.70) marked by a stone placed at his heels rather than an inscribed tomb at his head suggesting various inauspicious inversions.[55]

The future of both Hamlet and Laertes has been despoiled by their fathers' sudden and shady passing. One departs intestate, the other in "hugger-mugger" fashion (4.5.84). The devolution from one generation to the next requires that the spiritual and material affairs of the deceased be in order. But in both families, the father's irregular death blocks the son's birthright and drives him to extremes. One dispropertied son turns antic ("my wit's diseased," 3.2.313), the other stirs up a "riotous head" (4.5.101) or rebellion. Cut off from their birthright and the continuity it guaranteed, both sons behave insanely at Ophelia's funeral. Their severance from patrilineality is staged in the renunciation of the collected axioms of their tablebooks, instructing sons on the maintenance of family honor and estate. In the wake of the father's death, neither son can hold to those axioms. In order to make way for his father's command, Hamlet effaces all previous inscriptions:[56]

> Yea, from the table of my memory
> I'll wipe away all trivial fond records,
> All saws of books, all forms, all pressures past
> That youth and observation copied there.
> (1.5.98–101)

So, too, Laertes, whose memory is similarly charactered with paternal precepts, tosses all ethical guidelines to the winds.

> To hell, allegiance! Vows to the blackest devil!
> Conscience and grace, to the profoundest pit!
> I dare damnation. (4.5.131–3)

The "riotous head" he leads into the royal palace gives form to his own derangement. With "caps, hands, and tongues" (4.5.107), the rabble shouts constitutional nonsense, as if anarchy, democracy, and monarchy were compatible forms, "Choose we! Laertes shall be king" (4.5.106). A messenger compares his rebellion to the return of primordial chaos, "as the world were now but to begin,/ Antiquity forgot" (4.5.103–4). The rabble is powerful enough to overbear the King's officers, overwhelm his Swiss mercenaries, crash through the palace gates ("The doors are broke,"

4.5.111), and threaten insurrection ("giant-like" rebellion, 121), but once confronted by Claudius' assured majesty, it does no more than "peep to what it would" (4.5.124). Pacified by Claudius, Laertes consents to a rigged duel, a more strategic but even less honorable way of redressing his father's death.

At the grave, the madness of both sons flares up: Laertes' rebellious rage triggers Hamlet's "lawless fit" (4.1.8). Tablebooks wiped clean, custom and tradition forgotten, allegiances thrown to hell, both young men act without the restraints of manners and the law. They are unhinged, literally cut off from the stabilizing ties of lineage and tradition. As Hamlet later notes, their common sorrow makes them mirror images of one another: "For by the image of my cause I see / The portraiture of his" (5.2.77–8). The death of their respective fathers has left each son without prospects. Their common plight leads to rivalry rather than sympathy, and a wild territorial battle ensues over a flower-strewn plot of earth. "The bravery" (5.2.79) of one man's grief puts the other into a "tow'ring passion" (80). The sight of Ophelia's floriated body in the grave plot exacerbates in both men the desire for what they might have had. Ophelia, who has always been a flower ("rose of May," 4.5.157) or bearer of flowers, held out the promise of lineal flourishing. Her pathetic death compounds with patri- monial loss, leaving both brother and lover doubly debarred, from both property and progeny. Both men are pushed over the edge by the blasted image of their patrilineal dream, their outrageous behavior symptomatic of a society deeply invested in land.

Hamlet, returning from his voyage at sea and still wearing his "sea-gown" (5.2.13) ends up joining the sexton on the terra firma of the burial ground. The graveyard setting prompts what has always been recognized as a meditation on the vanity of all earthly things. What has not been noted, however, is the extent to which Hamlet's renunciation of earthly things concentrates on earth itself. Unlike the vanitas paintings that feature a full array of vanities – paintings, musical instruments, coins, jewelry, goblets, books – this *contemptus mundi* is limited to the desire for dominion, what would have been symbolized by the globe or map. The worldly figures held in contempt are not only great world conquerors like Alexander and Caesar but lesser landlords, those of "some estate" (5.1.214) now residing in the churchyard. Hamlet imagines that the exhumed skulls belonged to lords and ladies like "Lord Such-a-one" (83) and "Lady Worm" (87). He considers one wellborn skull after another until he comes upon one that might have belonged to a lawyer, once containing the arguments, instruments, and suits to defend the acquisition and holding of property. His speculation slips seamlessly from the lawyer to a landlord, "a great buyer of land" (102). Perhaps the lawyer has become a landlord through his manipulation of legal mechanisms and loopholes; "his statutes, his recognizances, his fines, his double vouchers, his recoveries" (102–4) work in place of family ancestry to make him "th'inheritor" (110). In the end, all that is left of his land is the dust in his cranium, a "fine pate full of fine dirt" (105–6), and the small stretch of land covered by his shrinking body, no bigger than the box filled by the disintegrating "conveyances" (5.1.108–9) by which land was transferred: "the length and breadth of a pair of indentures" (107–8). That the body at death should cover the same acreage as a legal document is apt. Parchment, as Hamlet finds cause to remark, is made of "sheepskins" and "calveskins" (112–13). Human skin, as the grave-digger implies, when tanned will turn into water-resistant leather, like any animal skin. The tanner's "hide" invokes another overlap between flesh and earth. A "hide" is an Anglo-Saxon land measurement, often equated with the amount of land needed to support a peasant family, used well into the seventeenth century for taxation purposes and the most frequently recorded areal unit of the Domesday Book.[57] In discussing the Conqueror's survey, Holinshed notes that "an hide of land conteineth an hundred acres . . . Those therefore are deceiued, that take an hide of land to contein twentie acres."[58] Polydore Vergil traced the origin of the measurement to the oxen's hide from which Dido had a long cord made to mark off the boundaries of Carthage.[59]

   Hamlet's meditation enlarges from real estate to global dominion when he considers those who obtained land not through the right of the law but through the might of conquest. Emperors who were in life as grand as the extent of their empires are in death reduced to infinitesimal particles of the continents they once owned. Alexander whose empire extended across three continents amounts to no more than "noble dust" (197–8). Caesar, "that earth which kept the world in awe" (208), shrinks to a piece of loam with which to mend a wall, a particularly humble end for a ruler reputed to have built the tower of London. Whether ancient emperors or modern landlords, men enlarge themselves with land in life only in death to dwindle to earthy bits and pieces. Tenants who once held land are now held by the land, "claw'd" (Q2) or "caught" (F) in death's "clutch" (71), snatched by the grave represented on stage by the trap.

   In his appearances before and after the graveyard scene, Hamlet is similarly preoccupied with examples of territorial transfer, one by conquest and the other by purchase. As he leaves Denmark for England at the

end of Act 4, he crosses paths with the Norwegian troops en route to
Poland. The army is led by the same prince who at the start of the play
threatened to invade Denmark in order to recover lands lost by his father
long ago. He now enters not to conquer Danish land but to pass through
it, having requested and received permission to march peacefully through
Danish "dominions" (2.2.78, 4.4.1–4). His army is headed for Poland to
fight not for "the main" or mainland (4.4.15), nor for its "frontier" (16),
but rather for "a little patch of ground" (18) smaller than the grave plot
that will contain the bodies of those who have fallen fighting for it.

When Hamlet appears after the graveyard scene, he encounters the
courtly counterpart to the imperial Fortinbras. The courtier Osric, a
"Bragart Gentleman" in the stage directions of Q1 (I2r), has enlarged
himself through purchase of "much land and fertile" (5.2.86); he has
grown "spacious in the possession of dirt" (88–9). Indeed his inflated
rhetoric, grandiose gestures, and extensive headgear all express a desire to
expand himself still further.[60] At the same time, his outlandish manner
indicates how recently landed he is. He is a "water-fly" (82–3), belonging
by nature to elements other than earth. Recently landed, he has not
mastered the manners of those who are born to the manor and therefore
makes good sport for Hamlet who was, and for Horatio who was not, but
is content to have "no revenue . . . but [his] good spirits" (3.2.58).

So Hamlet's renunciatory exercise is enclosed by two examples of expansion, Fortinbras' conquest of other lands and Osric's purchase of real estate.
As in the graveyard, Hamlet in these two encounters derides the desire for
land, finding a "fantasy" (4.4.61) in Fortinbras' imperial ambitions and
"bubbles" (5.2.190) in Osric's courtly pretensions. The *contemptus mundi* of
the graveyard is thus framed by additional disavowals of dominion and
domain. Men make themselves great in life through acquisitions of land by
birth, law, purchase, and arms. But this desire for self-aggrandizement
repeatedly finds its end in dust, reduced either to the small stretch of burial
ground coterminous with the dead body or to the infinitesimal particles of
that very element that in varying increments was once the primary object
of desire. The outcome hearkens back to Genesis where the first man is
named after clay, fashioned from earth, and sent forth to till it before
dissolving back into it. The *human/humus* connection has particular relevance to a system in which property and proper names are synonymous:
Denmark names both king and kingdom; *house* indicates both estate and
family line; the *manor/manner* homonym conjoins estate and breeding;
court names both royal residence and its attendants; *groundlings* are
theater-goers who stand on the ground, for a penny and temporarily.

The funeral procession cuts off Hamlet's *contemptus mundi* exercise. He has just finished reducing the conquerors Alexander and Caesar to bits of loam and plaster when he spots the royal cortège. At Ophelia's grave, after having so studiously abstracted himself from contemptible earth, Hamlet ends up engrossed in it, quite literally when he leaps into the freshly dug grave. After downsizing empires and estates and plots, he projects a cosmic land mound, "Singeing his pate against the burning zone" (5.1.277). It is as if the desire he has just renounced, the desire to make oneself great through land, has returned, like the nagging bad dreams that he earlier admitted were keeping him from being contented within the empty confines of a nutshell (2.2.254–6). The return of the bad dreams is prompted by the lowering of Ophelia's corpse into the grave. Gertrude sets off the fantasy when she scatters over the grave flowers that were intended, she says, for Ophelia's and Hamlet's bridal bed.

> [*scattering flowers*] Sweets to the sweet. Farewell.
> I hop'd thou shouldst have been my Hamlet's wife:
> I thought thy bride-bed to have deck'd, sweet maid,
> And not have strew'd thy grave.   (5.1.236–9)

The prospect of Hamlet and Ophelia in the marriage bed launches Laertes into the grave to catch the bride "once more in [his] arms" (5.1.243).[61] The union of Hamlet and Ophelia, after all, is what Laertes has feared from the very start, when before leaving for France, he warned Ophelia not to open her "chaste treasure . . . / To [Hamlet's] unmaster'd importunity" (1.3.31–2). Now as the sexton is about to shovel earth over her corpse, he leaps into the pit, proclaims his wish to be buried alive with her, and calls down over them a mountain of dust higher than Olympus.

> Now pile your dust upon the quick and dead,
> Till of this flat a mountain you have made
> T' o'ertop old Pelion or the skyish head
> Of blue Olympus.   (5.1.244–7)

Unaware of Hamlet's presence, Laertes has Ophelia to himself in a grave that is both a nuptial bed and a family house, with a brother and sister in residence, as if lord and lady of the manor, sealed off from outsiders, with a massive estate accumulating outside the front door.

Challenged by Laertes' outburst, Hamlet, thought dead or in England, imperiously announces himself, "This is I, / Hamlet the Dane" (250–1). With surprising uniformity, editors note that Hamlet, by identifying himself with the royal epithet, "the Dane," for the first time "assumes his title" as "the ruler of Denmark."[62] They do not comment, however, on

the indecorum of such a proclamation at a funeral, or on its advisability
before the duly elected King and his followers. In all events, it is the grave
plot and not the realm over which Hamlet asserts his authority. The
declaration of his peerless identity initiates a competition over who loved
the dead woman more: the brother or the man who loved her "[f]orty
thousand" times as much as a brother (264), only "twenty" times that
much in Q1 (I2). Provoked by what he takes to be Laertes' attempt to
"outface" him (273), Hamlet determines to outdo Laertes' extremes:
"What wilt thou do for her? . . . show me what thou't do . . . I'll do't"
(266–72). Their rivalry turns into an hysterical wooing match, tagged as
such by Hamlet's idiotic auxiliaries: "*Woo*'t weep, *woo*'t fight, *woo*'t fast,
woo't tear thyself, / *Woo*'t drink up eisel" (5.1.270–1, italics added). Laertes
leaps into the grave, and Hamlet follows him, "Be buried quick with her,
and so will I" (274). Laertes has "prate[d] of mountains" (275), and
Hamlet echoes him, invoking a still bigger mound over the grave, reaching not just to the Olympian summit but to the burning zone of the sun, a
land mass so high it would outscale Laertes' mound, reducing it from a
peak on the surface of the earth to a bump on the surface of the skin, from
a topographical mountain to a dermatological "wart" (278):

> [L]et them throw
> Millions of acres on us, till our ground,
> Singeing his pate against the burning zone,
> Make Ossa like a wart.   (275–8)

True to his word, Hamlet does just what Laertes has done, matching both
his gymnastic feat and his rhetorical tour de force.

   This is the stuff patrilineal dreams are made of: estate and generation
endogamously enclosed. It is the paramount fantasy of exclusive domain,
all the more poignant and ludicrous because both estate and bride have
been lost in the patrilineal foul-up. The fantasy is performed as the
bloodline of both men is on the brink of extinction. Though their grief
is expressed in terms of dust rather than tears, earth rather than water, it
matches in its extremity that of Niobe (1.2.149) and Hecuba (2.2.497–514,
552–3), the two types of extreme grief mentioned in the play. It was after
seeing all her children destroyed that Niobe became "all tears," even after
her transformation to stone. It was after seeing her teeming progeny
wiped out that Hecuba wept so profusely, as did all who heard her story,
including, as Sidney learned from Plutarch, hard-hearted tyrants. Both
women are emblems of insuperable grief in a patrilineal system which can
imagine nothing more tragic than genealogical extinction.

Now two men are in the pit with Ophelia, competing for the same plot and the same female. The triangle is familiar: it is both incestuous (the woman is sister to one of her suitors) and fratricidal (the men are close enough in blood to be termed "brothers," 5.2.239, 249).[63] Hamlet appears to win the contest, to outLaertes Laertes, perhaps with a lustier leap, certainly with the larger high-rise. His "millions of acres" (5.1.276) outsize Laertes' mountain of dust. His triple-decker pile, Ossa atop Pelion atop Olympus, brushes against the sun itself.

What is to be said about the wild graveside manner of these two young noblemen? The scene that began debating the ground in which the dead maiden should be housed while awaiting the apocalyptic "last trumpet" (5.1.223) ends by staging over her grave a violent rivalry in units of acreage. As with burial practices, popular millenarianism, and the Domesday survey, territorial prospects loom in the face of the hereafter.

Although the flare-up at the grave has received scant critical attention, there is evidence that it left an impression on the play's earliest audiences. An anonymous elegy to Richard Burbage, the first actor to play Hamlet, highlights one detail from his performance: "Oft have I seen him leap into the grave."[64] The leap was no doubt spectacular, no ordinary jump but a thrust in mid-air with limbs out-splayed. That the leap should have accompanied Hamlet's claim to kingship makes it all the more startling. For a royal entrance to be stately it must maintain perfect balance. Majesty must give the impression of being firmly "in state," proceeding in an even stride as if never leaving the ground.[65] Leaping is the trick of tumblers and saltinbanks [L. *saltare*]; on the commercial stage, it was part of the clown's repertory, culminating in the capering jig which drew the play to a close. Will Kemp was particularly applauded for his acrobatic skills, and performed such leaps on his legendary progress from London to Norwich; both horse and horseman, he dubbed himself Cavaliero Kemp. Hamlet's own "antic disposition" seems to have been modeled on such acrobatic performances; "leaping" might well have been a variation on the "running mad" stunt contemporary audiences particularly relished in Hamlet (see Chapter 1). Indeed Hamlet's salient leap may have been in imitation of the clown's stock entrance. In Joseph Hall's anti-theatrical satire, the clown enters with a disruptive bound, "Midst the silent rout, / Comes leaping in a self-misformed lout, / And laughs, and grins, and frames his mimic face."[66] What distinguishes the clown's act is his loss of control over bodily movement. Yet what is amusing in a clown is horrifying in a prince. Ophelia reports having been "affrighted" by

Hamlet's antics (2.1.75), likening him to a demon "loosed out of hell": "His knees knocking each other," "thrice his head thus waving up and down," and sighing so deeply, "[a]s it did seem to shatter all his bulk / And end his being" (83, 81, 93, 95–6). The spasmodic movements of the body are like the distorting grimaces of the face ("a look so piteous," 82), the disjointed frame of discourse ("wild and whirling words," 1.5.139), or the disordered state of his attire ("unbrac'd," "ungarter'd," 2.1.78–80) – all signs of his disturbance or "distemper". Hamlet's mighty bound might well have been the high point of his antic act. It is certainly the most flagrant violation of his warning to the Players that even in "gait" they "o'erstep not the modesty of nature" (3.2.32, 19). His outstretched legwork constitutes a literal "overstepping" of the modesty of his own royal person, or at least of the person he once was, as Ophelia remembers him: "The glass of fashion and the mould of form" (3.1.155).

Baffled by Hamlet's leap, modern commentators have gone so far as to deny that Shakespeare intended it.[67] Yet all three early texts support the report of Burbage's elegiast. The stage direction to Q1 is explicit: "*Hamlet leapes in after Leartes*"; and while Q2 provides no stage directions, and F specifies only that Laertes "Leaps in the graue," Hamlet's course of action is implied in both texts by his resolution to copy Laertes' every move, "What wilt thou do for her? . . . 'Swounds, show me what thou't do . . . I'll do it . . . Dost come here . . . To outface me with leaping in her grave? / Be buried quick with her, and so will I" (5.1.266–74). Additional evidence that the leap was performed exists in the eighteenth-century editions. In his 1709 edition, Nicholas Rowe inserted the stage direction *Hamlet leaps into the grave*, not because he was following the authority of Q1 (it was not discovered until the next century), but presumably because it was customary even after the Restoration for Hamlet to perform the leap. Succeeding editors followed suit, so that Pope, Theobald, Hanmer, Capell, and Johnson all insert it.

And yet modern commentators have been skeptical. How does one stage the leaps that land two young men in a grave in position to grapple with one another atop the recently lowered corpse or coffin of Ophelia? It appears to have been increasingly omitted in production after neither Irving nor Booth observed it. Granville-Barker's claim that only Laertes leaps into the grave was much welcomed;[68] it spared Hamlet the undignified leap, relocated the scramble outside the grave, and put an end to what may well have been a 300-year theatrical tradition of having the contest take place "horribly and grotesquely" in the grave.[69] A number of modern editors omit Hamlet's leap. The Cambridge editor admits to finding his leap and scuffle "unthinkable," and directs Hamlet to disclose himself in dignity by nobly "*Advancing*" rather than foolishly leaping, so the two men do their wrestling outside the grave. Laertes' leap, however, is retained, and it lands him less luridly atop F's "coffin" rather than Q2's "corse." Even when Hamlet is permitted his leap, it goes unremarked, while his simultaneous self-entitling claim invariably receives a glorifying gloss, "Hamlet asserts his title to the throne"; "he now assumes his title." The jarring incongruity of Hamlet's proclamation of his royal right and a clown's leap thus fail to register. The voiced claim to sovereignty goes unchallenged by the body's foolish leap.

Hamlet's leap has also posed a problem for critics who find a new tranquility in Hamlet after his sea adventure. How can such abandon be consistent with the self-possession of his meditation? As one influential critic maintained, Hamlet upon his return is "the complete Prince; dignified, cool, reflective."[70] How is his outrageous lack of control to be reconciled with his new-found composure? Earlier commentators, however, were untroubled by this relapse for they assumed that Hamlet, once again in the company of the King and court, had again taken cover in his antic guise. It is clear, for example, that Samuel Johnson accepted Hamlet's wild behavior in this scene as a continuation of his antic disposition. He faulted him not for his "sore distraction" at the grave (the situation required it) but for the excuse he later provides, "Was't Hamlet wrong'd Laertes? Never Hamlet . . . Who does it then? His madness" (5.2.229, 233). How could Hamlet plead to be genuinely *non compos mentis* when he had previously revealed his plan to pretend to be *non compos mentis*? Having revealed his intention to be "mad in craft," his subsequent claim that he was mad indeed was a "falsehood" "unsuitable to the character of a good or a brave man."[71] George Steevens agreed, deeming Hamlet's conduct at the funeral "undefensible" and pronouncing his attempt at self-defense "a dishonest fallacy."[72] All the same, Steevens entertained a defense recently proposed to him by a medical doctor, a Dr. Akenside, that Hamlet's mind was "in some degree impaired." What Johnson had thought a vitiating "falsehood" might in fact be an absolving truth: Hamlet was indeed suffering from a mental disorder. A psychological diagnosis thus appears on the critical scene as a solution to a moral impasse. In order to preserve Hamlet's integrity, his sanity is sacrificed, at least in part.

For the first time, critics begin to suspect that his madness in this instance was not "put on" but genuine. In the next decades, several critics find an explanation for Hamlet's graveside "extravagancies" in some form or degree of insanity. Mackenzie in 1770 allows that, "At the grave of Ophelia, indeed, [Hamlet's behavior] exhibits some temporary marks of a real disorder. His mind . . . is thrown for a while off its poise, and in the paroxysm of the moment breaks forth into that extravagant rhapsody which he utters to Laertes."[73] So, too, Richardson considers Hamlet here to be "[t]rembling on the brink of madness," as is evidenced by the general loss of control which produces "involuntary improprieties."[74] What differentiates Hamlet's madness in this scene from his "antic disposition"? Why is it "real" there and "pretended" elsewhere? Simply because it is more pronounced. Indeed it is compounded: the "act" of madness is played atop a genuine madness. While pretending madness, he is in fact suffering from it, "counterfeiting an insanity which in part exists." The result is wild exaggeration: involuntary "extravagancies which he affected to render still more extravagant."

The "real disorder" diagnosed at the grave is eventually read back into Hamlet's other antic displays, specifically those which critics had found morally offensive, like Hamlet's abuse of Ophelia or his stabbing of Polonius. It is at such points that the play is opened up to a new hermeneutic that locates traces of mental imbalance in Hamlet's "pranks" and "jests." Hamlet's admission to a "sore distraction" (5.2.225) is then deemed clinically accurate, while his claim to be putting on a mad act becomes suspect. The "antic disposition" is not a disguise, exactly, for it covers up a real mental disturbance; by assuming it, Hamlet is pretending to be what he in truth is. Evidence of the nineteenth century's preoccupation with the question of Hamlet's sanity can be found in the 1877 Variorum *Hamlet* which includes a long section of criticism under the rubric, "Insanity, Real or Feigned?" And it continues into the next, for example in J. Dover Wilson's identification of eight instances when Hamlet simulates madness to conceal real derangement, including his giddiness after the Ghost's appearance ("well said, old mole," 1.5.170), his rough treatment of Ophelia, his manhandling of Polonius' body ("I'll lug the guts," 3.4.214), and his abandon after the Mousetrap's success (he dances a jig). On all these occasions, according to Wilson, Hamlet is "conceal[ing] his nervous breakdown behind a mask which would enable him to let himself go when the fit is upon him."[75] Hamlet's shift from sobriety to giddiness reflects not the doffing and donning of his mad disguise, but rather the involuntary oscillation between dejection and exhilaration typical of mental imbalance. The diagnosis of mental instability replaces the earlier criticism of his character: he is psychologically disturbed rather than morally flawed.

And yet, he surely is not insane, as Bradley was quick to insist, for that would have relieved him of the responsibility for his actions and thereby disqualified him as a tragic agent. And it is here that Freud comes to the rescue with the introduction of an area of the psyche for which no man can be responsible: the "unconscious." For that domain of the psyche contains repressed parricidal and incestuous desires that by definition remain inaccessible to consciousness and therefore beyond the subject's control. In Freud's influential interpretation, Hamlet's aberrant behavior is driven by those buried desires recently stirred up by their enactment by another man: his uncle's killing of his father and sleeping with his mother. Confronted by his own illicit desires, he is paralyzed by guilt, though he experiences it quite otherwise, as the inexplicable inability to accomplish his revenge: "I do not know / Why yet I live to say this thing's to do" (4.4.43–4). For Freud, too, the madness Hamlet feigns melds into real neurosis. His internal struggle to repress those desires creates such a conflict within him that he becomes just as imbalanced as he pretends to be. As Ernest Jones states in his elaboration of Freud's comments, Hamlet "is reduced to the deplorable mental state he himself so vividly depicts."[76] Nowhere are his unconscious workings more apparent than in his scurrilities during the nunnery scene and before the Mousetrap play, when his simultaneous attraction to and revulsion for his mother extends to Ophelia. But for Jones, there is one scene in which Hamlet is released from these maddening repressions. At the grave, freed from his inhibitions by "remorse," he can admit an "affection" for Ophelia untrammeled by his Oedipal desire for his mother and thereby purged of animosity. At the burial site, it is not Hamlet's madness that peaks but rather his sanity, for it is there that he achieves "a healthier attitude towards Ophelia," uninfected by the sexual current of his earlier outbursts.[77] The towering priapic mounds projected at the wooing match over the open hole in the ground are curiously passed over.

Freud's disciple Jacques Lacan, however, is fully attentive to the symbolism of the open trap as well as of the phallic fantasizing of the two contenders. In his essay "Desire and the Interpretation of Desire in *Hamlet*," an abridgment of several lectures, Ophelia rather than Gertrude takes center stage. To his ear, her very name is a give-away: *O-phallus.*[78] She is the sought-after phallus, "the bait" (11), "the object whose loss is the cause of his desire" (37). In his "topology of desire," the grave figures as a key landmark. His long excursus on the play keeps circling back to it: "The whole scene is directed toward that furious battle at the bottom of the tomb" (24). Though the desired object is "located outside the realm of what can actually be represented on stage," there is no denying the symbolic significance of that hole. The concave trap marks the site of loss, what he terms "a hole in the real" (37), the "black out" (49) that shapes desire: the primal and inexpiable loss exacted by the dissolution of the Oedipal complex. Hamlet seeks what is lost throughout the drama – "'tis here, 'tis there" – mainly in the veiled phenomena whose very loss is registered in their occluded presence: the Ghost, Polonius behind an arras, and finally and most morbidly, the shrouded Ophelia. Claudius proves something of a decoy, as Hamlet realizes when he passes him up at prayer: "Claudius, as he knelt there before him, wasn't quite what Hamlet was after – he wasn't the right one" (51). Of course, "the right one" is never to be found, as is revealed in Lacan's reading of Hamlet's enigmatic "The body is with the king but the king is not with the body" (4.2.26–7). The substitution of *phallus* for *king* dispels the mystery: while the subject depends on the phallus, the phallus is never to be had: "it always slips through your fingers" (52). The shrouded Ophelia is as close as Hamlet can get to the elusive desideratum.

But why the histrionic hysterics? As Lacan rightly notes, there is no precedent in the *Hamlet* sources. For him, the open grave carries massive symbolic import as the site of loss, "the hole in the real" experienced at death, and all the more acutely when the compensatory rituals of mourning are absent or truncated, as they are in Ophelia's "maimed rites." Signifiers go wild, working over-time ("from the heights of heaven to the depths of hell,") in an attempt to make up for loss: "For it is the system of signifiers in their totality which is impeached by the least instance of mourning" (38). It is this gap or hole in the system that produces the maniacal excess of the two men's outbursts. Their hyped-up rhetoric registers the enormity of their loss. But the display is only a sensationalized version of Hamlet's condition throughout the play, the result of a prior wound dating back to the symbolic castration exacted by the dissolution of the Oedipal complex. The interminable search for its repair is evident in Hamlet's antic idiom: "the ambiguity of metaphor, puns, conceits, mannered speech" (33) as well as his "impudence and insults" (33). It is here, and not in Hamlet's profound monologues, that Lacan locates "the basis of [the play's] psychological dimension" (33). If his clowning were omitted, "more than eighty per cent of the play would disappear" (33), a calculation that seems designed to replace the proverbial "*Hamlet* without the prince" with "*Hamlet* without the clown."

It is Lacan's concentration on Hamlet's loss that alerts him to the import of the scene at Ophelia's grave. And yet that loss is not as generalized or intransitive as his reading implies. Lacan insists that the object of desire is beyond representation, but both the object of desire and its loss *are* represented by two landscapes: the flower bank and the stage trap, the fruitful mound and sterile cavity. Lacan pits the two men in a Hegelian fight-to-the-death between near-doubles in "the fight for pure prestige." Or is it a fight for real estate? In Lacan's reading, as in modern readings generally, the object of desire that sets one man against another tends to vanish. But Cain fells Abel over the blessing, Jacob slays Esau over the birthright, Norway combats Denmark over crown lands, Claudius murders Hamlet I over the kingdom, Gonzago poisons Lucianus for "estate," Norway fights Poland over a small non-arable plot, and finally Laertes and Hamlet grapple over the even smaller and more barren plot that Ophelia has become. Hamlet *is* indeed driven by what he lacks, but the signifiers activated around that loss are quite materially specific. The frenetic signifiers that attempt to fill the void of loss are inordinately concerned with quantities of earth. For the two males, both highborn and "expectant," the loss is absolute: each is at the dead-end of his dynastic line. The grave pit containing the dead body which has been associated from start to finish with child-bearing capacity gives material form to the extinction of all future prospects: the utter spoil of the roseate "expectancy" conferred by noble and royal birth.

Hamlet's antics have been variously classified by the critical tradition. His quirky behavior has been attributed first to blemished character and then to a diseased mind, the former censured by moral standards, the latter analyzed as psychological or psychoanalytic symptom. In both cases, the origin of the antic in stage convention has been forgotten. Yet it provides the idiom through which Hamlet expresses his resentment and hostility. Through insolence, irrationality, and humor, Hamlet follows his role models in flouting authority in all its guises. By abrogating "all forms and pressures past" – the constitutive principles of "the expectancy of the fair state" and the "mould of form" (3.1.155) – he cuts himself off from the patriarchal structures that uphold personal and social identity. Why hold on to mainstays of social order once denied his part and share in them? In the face of death, the desire is exacerbated rather than mortified. Domain looms large in the shadow of Doomsday. Survival in this world asserts itself against the background of salvation in the next. Two desperately disenfranchised men invoke piles over a sexualized pit, clutching at the chimera of estate and lineage, while themselves on the brink of extinction.

When he next encounters his rival, Hamlet asks his pardon, disclaiming responsibility for his outbreak: "Was't Hamlet wrong'd Laertes? Never

Hamlet . . . Who does it then? His madness" (5.2.229, 233). Earlier in the play, Hamlet had defended himself with the same excuse. When asked by Rosencrantz why he cannot give him "a wholesome answer," Hamlet explains, "My wit's diseased" (3.2.306–7, 313). With that adjective, he both describes his condition and names its cause. Until the eighteenth century, *diseased* shared both spelling and pronunciation with *diseized*: to be illegitimately dispossessed of lands. The word crops up earlier in the play, in Horatio's account of the seminal combat of thirty years ago when King Fortinbras, like King Hamlet, staked "all those his lands / Which he stood seiz'd of" (1.1.91–2). While *seiz'd* in this context typically receives an editorial gloss explaining its reference to the legal possession of land, the term goes unheard and unremarked in "My wit's diseas'd." The pun epitomizes not only the relation between human and humus so central to this book, but also a sedimentation in language so deep as to be almost beyond retrieval, at least for modern sensibilities which have turned to less worldly matters to explain Hamlet's unwholesomeness or "insanity."

CHAPTER 6

Hamlet's delay

> Well, Hamlet, in a certain sense, must be considered one of these
> clowns.
>
> Lacan

Why does Hamlet delay? That a single question should be seen from one
generation to the next as *the* question to ask of the play is a unique
phenomenon in the history of criticism.[1]

Great minds have been asking it for some two hundred years now, from
Coleridge and Schlegel around the turn of the eighteenth century, to
Bradley and Freud around the turn of the nineteenth, to Lacan, Lévinas,
and Adorno in the middle of the twentieth and Derrida and Zizek at its
end. So it could be said still to hold the title of "question of questions" or
"problem of problems," as critics continue to frame their criticism around
this riddle, this sphinx, this Mona Lisa of literature. One can understand
the perennial allure of the question. "Why does Hamlet delay?" "Hamlet
delays because of _____." Fill in the blank, and you have the answer to
Hamlet's character. And that answer is also the key to the play – and the
play that is at the heart of Shakespeare's canon. There have been times,
certainly, when critics have given up on the question, dismissing it as passé,
moot, or uninteresting. But it continues to resurface, so that it is hard to
find a reading that does not propose or imply a solution, even among
today's most theoretically sophisticated literary critics. An old and tired
question continues to produce new, even cutting-edge critical responses.

Yet the question appears not to have emerged until the last decades of
the eighteenth century, and then in relation to the climactic moment of
the play. Hamlet, having at last established Claudius' guilt, happens upon
him alone at prayer, unarmed and unguarded. It is the perfect opportunity
to exact revenge. He draws his sword: "Now might I do it pat, now a is
a-praying. / And now I'll do't" (3.3.73–4). Then, reconsidering, he pulls
it back, "No. / Up, sword, and know thou a more horrid hent" (87–8).

Hamlet anti-climactically refrains from performing the act he has until then been gearing up to perform. Why the deferral? Hamlet gives his own explanation. He wants to catch Claudius in some damnable act, "[t]hat has no relish of salvation in't" (92): in a drunken stupor, making incestuous love, swearing while gambling.

> Then trip him, that his heels may kick at heaven
> And that his soul may be as damn'd and black
> As hell, whereto it goes. (93–5)

Eighteenth-century commentators were appalled by Hamlet's intention not only to kill a man but damn him too.[2] As George Stubbes insisted in the first extended essay published on the play (1736), while revenge might require the slaying of the body, no extreme of filial devotion could justify the eternal ruining of the soul:

To desire to destroy a Man's Soul, to make him eternally miserable by cutting him off from all hopes of Repentance; this surely in a Christian Prince, is such a Piece of Revenge as no Tenderness for any parent can justify.[3]

How could this diabolic desire be reconciled with the nobility and decency of Hamlet's character? Unable to come up with an answer, Stubbes could only wish away the lines, "There is something so very Bloody in it, so inhuman, so unworthy of a hero that I wish our Poet had omitted it."

In performance, the three execrable lines could easily be omitted. The Players' Quarto of 1676, the basis for the acting versions performed until the very end of the nineteenth century, ticked the lines with inverted commas to indicate that they were "left out upon the Stage."[4] For over 200 years after that, from Betterton in 1663 to Forbes-Robertson in 1897, they appear to have been cut in performance.[5] David Garrick, in the text he prepared for his own production in 1772, went further and deleted the entire "horrid soliloquy";[6] the editor George Steevens applauded him for omitting Hamlet's "abhominable Reason."[7]

Editors and commentators, however, could allow themselves no such easy solution, with the exception of Thomas Bowdler who expurgated Hamlet's entire monologue from his *The Family Shakspeare: In Which . . . Those Words and Expressions are Omitted Which Cannot with Propriety Be Read in a Family* (1807). In his 1765 edition of the play, Samuel Johnson admitted to the same impulse:

This speech, in which *Hamlet*, represented as a virtuous character, is not content with taking blood for blood, but contrives damnation for the man that he would punish, is *too horrible to be read or to be uttered* [italics added].[8]

His censure, however, only drew attention to the three lines he wished eradicated; critics rallied either in support of his judgment or in defense of the speech, or rather of its speaker. Francis Gentleman found the words inexcusable: they bespoke "a diabolical bent . . . more suitable to an assassin of the basest kind" than to "a virtuous prince and a feeling man."[9] Other critics devised excuses. Joseph Ritson insisted that anything less than the revenge Hamlet desires would have been "an act of injustice and impiety to the *manes* of his murdered parent."[10] Thomas Davies exonerated Hamlet by maintaining that it was poor dramaturgy on Shakespeare's part rather than an atrocity on Hamlet's: the speech was his inept contrivance to delay the play's catastrophe.[11] Edmond Malone, who often blamed what he found reprehensible in Shakespeare on the crude sensibilities of his times, assumed the lines followed stage convention. His 1821 edition, completed by James Boswell the younger, cited four analogues from the seventeenth-century stage in which avengers expressed the same fiendish intention of catching their victims in some godless or damnable state – cursing at tennis, dead drunk, consumed by lechery – before cutting them off. The only trouble was that every one of his examples was published *after* Shakespeare's play.[12] The search for precedents revealed only imitations. Hamlet, it appeared, was not only guilty, but the cause of guilt in others. An imaginary dialogue written in 1782 concludes with the admission that the speech is indefensible. In an underworld encounter between two great heroes, Corneille's Theseus and Shakespeare's Hamlet, the former arraigns the latter for three counts of "cruel and inconsistent conduct": insulting Ophelia, upbraiding his mother, and "with the most diabolical revenge, [refusing] to punish a crime . . . because you could not add eternal perdition to the present penalty."[13] Hamlet acquits himself of the first two charges but remains silent on the third, and Theseus explains why: "It is usual for guilt to elude enquiry when it cannot defend its content." "What can I say?" is Hamlet's rejoinder, and he ends up thrusting the blame on Shakespeare's "fiery genius" whose faults must be excused if not justified.

Toward the end of the century a more ingenious solution emerges, based on recent developments in the nascent study of the operations of the mind shortly to be named *psychology*.[14] The study developed primarily in Scotland, following the ground-breaking lead of Thomas Reid and David Hume, and it is two Scottish critics – William Richardson, a Professor of Humanity at Glasgow, and Thomas Robertson, a Doctor of Divinity at Edinburgh – who turn to this new study to champion the passage considered "the most difficult to be defended in the whole character of Hamlet."[15] Confronted by the ostensible contradiction between the abhorrent speech and the virtuous speaker, "We are . . . bound, in justice and candour, to look for some hypothesis that shall reconcile [the two]."[16] Both critics light upon the same "hypothesis." What Hamlet says is not what he means; the diabolical wishes he utters "are not his real sentiments."[17] What Hamlet really feels as he prepares to strike is not ferocity but its precise opposite: "the ascendant of a gentle disposition." He responds by putting up his sword, yet cannot admit that it is his "extreme sensibility" which compels him to do so. He "looks about for a motive," and comes up with the appalling excuse he offers. To disguise a "delicate disposition," Hamlet pretends to "a savage enormity."[18]

Hamlet's lines had caused critics similar embarrassment in both the nunnery and closet scenes. Here, too, in order to exonerate Hamlet, it was necessary to dissociate him from the insulting and injurious words he speaks. Because Hamlet in both scenes was in the company of others, this was easily done. As Johnson had maintained of the nunnery scene, Hamlet speaks only one of his lines in his own person: "Nymph, in thy orisons / Be all my sins remember'd" (3.1.89–90).[19] He speaks the rest in the Antic's guise, not to hurt Ophelia, but to convince her, or the eavesdropping King and councilor, of his madness. Upon entering his mother's quarters, Hamlet himself explains why he adopts such scathing language in addressing his mother: "I must be cruel only to be kind" (3.4.180). In the prayer scene, however, Hamlet is effectively alone. Claudius is on stage, but because absorbed in prayer, he neither sees nor hears Hamlet. For whose sake, then, does Hamlet feign to be "cruel" when he is in truth "kind"? With no one to deceive either on stage or off, for whom could Hamlet's deception in the prayer scene be intended?

According to the two Scottish critics, the pretense is for no one but Hamlet. He at first intends to strike, "now I'll do't," but then his characteristic sensitivity holds him back; rather than admit to such a weakness, "he endeavours to hide it from himself";[20] he "shelters himself under the subterfuge" of a monstrous intention.[21] The soliloquy, rather than disclosing a character's true intents to the audience, in this instance gives voice to a new form of deceit: *the deceit of the self.* The most "difficult lines to be defended" prove defensible after all: they are a cover-up for Hamlet's real feelings, spoken to himself to convince himself that he is capable of taking revenge – indeed, *more* than revenge – when in fact he shies from the very prospect. What had previously appeared a "grievous fault" in his character is thus transformed to a "genuine beauty" of characterization: "a most exquisite picture of amiable self-deceit," though admittedly "not very obvious to cursory observation."[22]

Richardson assumes that his readers, on the basis of their own experience and observation, would not be unfamiliar with the psychological phenomenon.

I would ask then, whether on many occasions we do not alledge those considerations as the motives of our conduct which really are not our motives? Nay, is not this sometimes done almost without our knowledge? Is it not done when we have no intention to deceive others; but when, by the influences of some present passion, *we deceive ourselves* [italics added]?

For corroboration, he refers them to a popular eighteenth-century moral philosopher and theologian:

Consult Bishop Butler, your favourite and the favourite of every real enquirer into the principles of human conduct, and you will be satisfied concerning the truth of this doctrine. Consult Bishop Butler and then apply it to the case of Hamlet.[23]

Joseph Butler's works were widely read in Scottish universities, particularly his sermons, three of which are on the subject of self-deceit or "internal hypocrisy."[24] In one of his examples from the Bible, David rashly condemns a man to death for killing another man's beloved lamb; in order to do so, according to Butler, David had to deceive himself by denying his own greater guilt in having committed both adultery and murder.[25] In another example, from English history, the supporters of Charles I's execution were self-deceived in believing that they were defending liberty when in fact they were destroying the constitution.[26] For Butler, self-deceit involves the attempt to delude one's conscience on matters of right and wrong. But when, as for Butler, conscience is the inner presence of God in the individual, the attempt to delude God is indistinguishable from self-deception. Had Claudius arisen from prayer confident that he had truly repented when in truth his thoughts remained insincerely below ("My words fly up, my thoughts remain below," 3.3.97), he would have perfectly illustrated Butler's understanding of self-deceit.

In a form of mimesis based on disguise and impersonation, there certainly is nothing unfamiliar about deceit. It is at the very heart of the theatrical enterprise, as the antitheatrical polemicists never tired of pointing out: William Prynne, for example, insisted that hypocrisy and playing are "one and the same substance."[27] *Hypocrite* derives from the Greek for actor, *hupocritēs*. Players pretend to be characters they are not; men play women, the low play the high, all players play someone other than themselves, and those parts may well call for further dissimulation, as the plot requires. In this play, the hypocrite *par excellence* is Claudius. He appears a jovial king when he is in reality a guilt-ridden murderer. After the Ghost's harrowing appearance and disclosure, Hamlet jots down only one aphorism on his newly cleansed tablebook: "One may smile, and smile, and be a villain" (1.5.108). The play contains numerous variants on the "smiling villain" topos: the devil sugared over (3.1.48–9), the harlot beautified with cosmetics (3.1.51–3), women given one face and wearing another (3.1.144–6), the tongue as hypocrite to the soul (3.2.388), the face without a heart (4.7.107–8). Any and all of these figures for deceit and hypocrisy would have been suitable tags for theater-goers to set down in the tablebooks they took to the theatre.[28] Instances of deceit also abound: Hamlet announces his intention to feign madness (1.5.179–80), Ophelia is instructed to pretend to be reading devoutly upon a book (3.1.44–6), Hamlet determines to speak brutally to his mother while intending her no harm ("My tongue and soul in this be hypocrites," 3.2.388), Laertes enters a duel he knows is rigged as if it were fair play ("And yet it is almost against my conscience," 5.2.300).

But hypocrisy or deceit is quite different from the self-deceit discovered in Hamlet. A character hiding something from the knowledge of others is not the same as one who hides it from himself. In ordinary deception, the deceiver knows that there is a discrepancy between how he seems and how he is. Claudius knows all too well that he is deceitful, and admits his deceit, in an aside (3.1.51–4), as well as in his private prayer when he acknowledges the rift between his words and thoughts (3.3.97–8). The self-deceiver, however, has no such knowledge, for he is also the self-deceived. Characters who deceive know full well they are deceiving, and could at any point make their deceit known to other characters or to the audience, just as they might disclose any secret they were keeping to themselves.

A "tragedy of thought," as both Schlegel and Coleridge famously dubbed the play, is hard enough to enact. But how to perform a "tragedy of self-deception"? When the character himself has no knowledge of his intent to deceive – when he is both deceiver and deceived – how can his deception be staged? Perhaps other characters could discuss his state. (Horatio might ask Gertrude if her son had any history of such behavior.) Perhaps a stage convention might indicate that a character is deceiving himself. (Hamlet might rub his eyes.) Or perhaps in soliloquy the self-deceived might disclose his state, though he would no longer be self-deceived if he could. Short of such indicators, is there any way to distinguish a character who speaks monstrous words which he intends from one who speaks monstrous words in order to deceive himself? There is no equivalent in the drama to the novel's omniscient authorial voice which might choose to inform the reader of such complex psychological phenomena. Only in a post-Freudian world might an audience turn to mechanisms of repression, resistance, or denial to account for otherwise inexplicable language and behavior.

And yet the new hermeneutic catches on quickly, at least in commentary on the play. It is epitomized nicely by Schlegel: "[Hamlet] is a hypocrite towards himself."[29] Coleridge, familiar with both Schlegel's lectures and Butler's sermons, turned to this same psychological mechanism, and once again to salvage the three notorious lines from Johnson's denunciation: "Dr. Johnson did not understand the character of Hamlet, and censured accordingly."[30] Johnson had taken Hamlet's words at face value, not recognizing them as "a pretext for not acting" and "the excuse Hamlet made to himself."[31] As a result, Johnson mistook for "horror-striking fiendishness" words that were in fact "marks" of another condition altogether. For Coleridge, they did not signify "gentleness" or "delicacy" as for Robertson and Richardson: Hamlet's problem lay in not *hyper*sensitivity but *in*sensitivity. Wrapped in a world of thought, Hamlet was sealed off from outward impressions: "all real objects are faint and dead to him." His "enormous intellectual activity" pulls him out of the world of action, and proportionally, for the more he thinks, the less he acts: "great enormous intellectual activity, and a consequent proportionate aversion to real action."[32] Rather than acknowledge this disequilibrium or "overbalance in the contemplative activity," Hamlet admits to an opposite extreme, professing a resolve not only to act but to over-react, not only by killing Claudius but by damning him. By the time of the 1821 variorum, the theory has assumed the status of dogma: "[Hamlet] attempts by a pretended refinement of revenge, *to hide from his own knowledge* his incurable habits of procrastination" [emphasis added].[33]

The possibility that the mind does not have access to its own processes opens up a whole new prospect for hermeneutic interpretation. Characters move out of a world in which they possess motives of which they are aware (and can reveal or conceal, as they choose). This is not to say that Hamlet's "interiority" was not discovered until around 1800. Hamlet always possessed an area within, hidden from the other characters, and has good reason for keeping it to himself, as noted in Chapter 3. But what Hamlet does not possess until around 1800 is an area of consciousness which he cannot reveal even to himself. A new model of mind becomes available to theatrical characters, in criticism if not in performance. It is no longer a cogitating Cartesian mind observing its own workings: Descartes' thoughts, as he sits alone in his study doubting the reality of wax on his desk, are entirely accessible to Descartes. In the *cogito*, his very existence depends upon their accessibility, as do his transcriptions of those thoughts or *The Meditations on First Philosophy* (1641). But by 1800 we are in a Kantian world in which relations to the self are mediated by categories of time and space, just as are relations to others and to the external world; the immediate and certain have given way to the framed and hypothetical. There are recesses of the mind that consciousness cannot tap, even the mind of the character known for his introspective powers. According to Freud's disciple Ernest Jones, Freud's theory of repression was what gave his analysis the edge over all others. The inaccessibility of the unconscious to consciousness explained why the pensive Hamlet could not himself understand the cause of his delay. Nor, according to Freud, was it understood by anyone else – not even Shakespeare – until some 300 years after the play's first production, when in 1900 Hamlet's unconscious workings were brought to light in a footnote to Freud's *Interpretation of Dreams*. Once the repressive force of the unconscious has been revealed, Hamlet's expressed wish to damn Claudius ceases to shock. It is lumped together with his other "alleged motives" for delaying – that he is a coward, for example, or that he mistrusts the Ghost's intentions – all of which, according to Jones, can be dismissed "as being more or less successful attempts on his part to blind himself with self-deception." The self-deceit first emerging at the end of the eighteenth century as defense of Hamlet's vicious three lines is by the end of the next century undermining the "last stronghold" of the belief dominating philosophy, theology, and psychology: the belief in self-consciousness, in the mind's capacity to know its own desires and processes. The introspective Hamlet is also the hero who reveals the limitations of introspection, dramatizing "powers of self-deception in the human mind to which a limit has yet to be found."[34]

Once emptied of its execrable intent, Hamlet's excuse for sparing Claudius at prayer becomes one among many stalling tactics. Procrastination becomes his salient, indeed his defining trait.[35] Through most of the eighteenth century, Hamlet was judged "the most difficult [of Shakespeare's characters] to be reduced to any fixed or settled principle," "an apparent heap of inconsistency."[36] His aversion to action provided a unifying "ruling passion" or "leading idea."[37] Coleridge extended his irresolution at the prayer scene to cover his behavior throughout the play: "perpetual solicitation of the mind to act, but as constant an escape from action."[38] Prompted to immediate action by the Ghost's commandment, he hesitates, even after the Ghost's disclosure has been confirmed by the Mousetrap play. His repeated willingness to be diverted from his task further confirms the analysis: he lets himself be conveyed to England, consents to a duel with Laertes, and converses aimlessly with the courtier Osric and the grave-maker Goodman Delver. The traits once found incoherent now appeared facets of the same irresolution; and the irresolution was no longer circumstantial but chronic: an "incurable procrastination," the "infirmity of his disposition."[39]

The same hesitation also gave shape to the plot. Indeed it was hard to distinguish the hesitant disposition of the one from the halting course of the other. In Goethe's description, familiar in England in the early decades of the nineteenth century, the hero's inability to act resembles the play's difficulty moving toward a catastrophe: "How he twists and turns, trembles, advances and retreats, always being reminded, always reminding himself, and finally almost losing sight of his goal."[40] Coleridge's summary suggests the same overlap: "after still resolving, and still refusing, still determining to execute, and still postponing execution."[41] After the prayer scene, as Schlegel also noted, both Hamlet and the plot come to a halt: "the main action either stands still or appears to retrograde."[42] His characteristic trajectory of starts and stops in the struggle to move forward against obstacles also interests Hegel, providing him with an apt allegory for the dialectical movement of the spirit of consciousness. Hamlet's irresolution suggests the movement of spirit, warring against itself, as it struggles toward self-realization, progressing but then retreating on a linear trajectory strewn with impediments. The play dramatizes his being "bandied from pillar to post," encountering a series of "colliding factors," before yielding up his self-determining power to contingency in consenting to both the voyage to England and the duel with Laertes.[43] Hamlet only gets so far on his onward self-oppositional course until his infinite spirit is mired in what Hegel terms "the sandbank of his finite condition."[44]

A. C. Bradley, the younger brother of the Hegelian idealist philosopher F. H. Bradley and himself the author of four lectures on Hegel's *Theory of Tragedy*, gives the fullest and most influential demonstration of how character informs the plot of this play. As in all four of the great tragedies, plot is of interest only insofar as it manifests character: "Action is essentially the expression of character."[45] Although other factors may influence the outcome of the plot – for example, insanity, the supernatural, and chance – the dictum "Character is destiny" remains "a vital truth" (29): "the dominant factor consists in deeds which issue from character" (32). The fact that, for Bradley, Hamlet's distinction resides in what he *does not do* rather than what he *does* required a significant modification of Hegel's theory. Tragic action is the emanation of character, but in the exceptional case of Hamlet, character is expressed by two discrete kinds of actions: *performed* and *avoided* (164). Both "acts or *omissions* [are] thoroughly expressive of the doer" [italics added] (29).

At the beginning of his first lecture on *Hamlet*, Bradley bypasses "the splendours of the whole tragedy" in order "to proceed at once to the central question of Hamlet's character" (95). He rejects as "fatally untrue" (116) Schlegel and Coleridge's view that inaction is the result of Hamlet's speculative nature. As Bradley illustrates through his speculation on Hamlet's experience before the start of the play, if not for the "violent shock" of the Ghost's revelation Hamlet "would have been perfectly equal to his task" (116). That "shock," as he repeatedly calls it, comes from the disclosure of his mother's sensuality and leads to "a state of mind quite abnormal" (109), a "pathological condition" that takes the form of world-weariness and a longing for death. Bradley identifies it as "melancholy" or "melancholia" and describes its symptoms as speculation and inaction. Hamlet's hesitation in the prayer scene is pivotal – "the turning point of the tragedy" (133) – but it is in no way exceptional. His once notorious excuse is only one among "many unconscious excuses for delay" (101), as "is now pretty generally agreed" (132).

For Bradley, his own explanation for Hamlet's "melancholic paralysis" ranks above all others because it comes closest to explaining all aspects of the play, "all the relevant facts presented by the text of the drama" (127). The character must be grasped before approaching the rest of the play. Thus his first chapter on Hamlet establishes his character while the second examines its expression in plot: "to follow rapidly the course of the action in so far as it specially illustrates the character." The plot would be unintelligible without comprehending his character; there would be no answer to the question which surfaces, according to Bradley, at every single first experience of the play: "why in the world did not Hamlet obey the Ghost at once?" (93). In his extended account of the plot, that question never stops throbbing, as the following abridgment suggests:

After encountering the Ghost, Hamlet vows to take revenge, but "within an hour" he has "relapse[d] into the weariness . . . which is the immediate cause of his later inaction" (127). "[A] considerable time has elapsed" before we next see him. "What has Hamlet done? . . . Hamlet has done absolutely nothing" (128), "Now he takes a further step . . . He must act," (128); but then, just when the perfect opportunity arises – Claudius is at his prayers – he passes it up, his "determination led to nothing" (138), we find Hamlet right back where he started, "Hamlet . . . is here, in effect, precisely where he was at the time of his first soliloquy . . . two months ago" (129): "how is it possible for us to hope that . . . Hamlet will be any nearer to his revenge?" (130). "He *feels* that he is doing something towards his end . . ." (130). The clock is advancing all the while: "a considerable time has elapsed . . . as much as two months" (127), "night passes, and the day that follows" (129), "evening comes" (130), "we must again suppose an interval" (138), but still "no plan of action" (141), and then "change comes too late" (139) – "at the latest hour" (142) – and finally Fate or Providence steps in to do the job. Punctuating Hamlet's inaction are his soliloquies glossing his delay, "showing the state of mind which caused Hamlet to delay his vengeance" (153).

For Bradley, the plot gives articulation to the delaying character he has just analyzed in the previous chapter: "The whole story turns upon the peculiar character of the hero" (93).

Around the same time that Bradley was writing his lectures, Freud was working out his Oedipal theory through the example of Hamlet. An 1897 letter contains both his first explanation of Hamlet's delay and his first mention of the Oedipus complex. Like Bradley, Freud begins his discussion with the assumption that the play is "based upon Hamlet's hesitation" and with the dismissal of all earlier attempts to explain it. They had all been founded on "the still prevailing conception" that Hamlet is incapable of action, when in fact "Hamlet is able to do anything but take vengeance upon the man who did away with his father and has taken his father's place with his mother."[46] The prayer scene highlights the precise nature of Hamlet's difficulty. The sight of Claudius in the act of penance awakens the faint memory of his own incestuous and parricidal desire: "His arm was paralyzed by his own obscure sense of guilt."[47] As for Bradley, the cause of Hamlet's delay explains other peculiarities of his character: his hatred of women, his sexual revulsion, his murder of Ophelia's father rather than the man who murdered his own father, and his own fatal entrapment. But for Freud and his disciple Ernest Jones, the greatest triumph of Freud's theory is that it explains not only why Hamlet delays, but also why he himself cannot explain why he delays, "I do not know / Why yet I live to say this thing's to do" (4.4.43–4). As Jones emphasizes in his monograph *Hamlet and Oedipus*, while such an explanation might well be expected from a character with a penchant for self-examination, Hamlet can offer only "pretended excuses for his hesitation" (48). The real cause could be determined only through the newly discovered mechanism of repression: in addition to providing the "cornerstone" of psychoanalysis, the theory solved the 300-year mystery of *Hamlet*: "I have here translated into consciousness what had to remain unconscious in the mind of the hero," as well as in the mind of his creator, and in the minds of all who had experienced the play before Freud.[48] Once translated into the recently available terms of Oedipal guilt, his delay could be identified with a new range of staying mechanisms: repression, but also trauma, denial, obsession, fixation, and cathexis.

In his 1958–9 lectures, abridged in English under the title "Desire and the Interpretation of Desire in *Hamlet*," Lacan revises Freud's theory of subjectivity in the process of revising Freud's interpretation of *Hamlet*.[49] (He has also read Bradley.) The same question of Hamlet's delay motivates his account, but with his new "symbolic apparatus" (37) he aims to surpass his master. His understanding of "the function of the object in desire," for example, "definitely does enable us to go much further than anyone has ever gone by any route" (29). "Route" is the operative word, for his commentary traces "the winding paths that lead Hamlet to the completion of the act" (20); "the hero's progress toward his mortal rendezvous with his act" (12); "the unrelenting movement of the subject" (25). The route, path, or progress of "the man who has lost the way of his desire" (12) can hardly be straightforward, for it depends on the ambiguous "desire of the Other" (in particular, his mother's errant sexuality). Hamlet, therefore, repeatedly submits to the timetables of others, suspended "at the hour of the Other," whether it be his mother's request that he remain in Elsinore or Claudius' invitation to duel with Laertes (18–20), when like a dog "he seems just to lie down and roll over, one more time" (30). In Lacan's colloquial rendering, Hamlet "just doesn't know what he wants" (26); he is "constantly and fundamentally at somebody else's beck and call" (30). In sum, what brings Hamlet to a halt is his subjection to the signifier of desire: the phallus.

Lacan's discussion ends not with the play's final debacle, but with that same old challenge to critical ingenuity. The moment of truth arrives in the prayer scene when Claudius turns out not to be Hamlet's target after all. His deplorable reason is once again irrelevant; the truth is "he wanted something or someone better" (51). The play ends not as a tragedy of revenge but as a "tragedy of desire" (11) – and not with the attainment of its end but with the disclosure of its unattainability. The very attempt proves absurd, for the phallus is "a ghost." As the watch discovers when they try with their partisans to stop the Ghost, "it is as the air, invulnerable" (1.1.150). The play's great mystery is embedded in Hamlet's enigmatic chiasmus: "The body is with the king, but the king is not with the body" (4.2.26–7). Substitute "phallus" for "king," and both the passage and the tragedy of desire itself lose their opacity. We are bound to the signifier of the phallus but "the phallus, on the contrary, is bound to nothing." Hamlet's quest has been a wild goose chase, as he learns, but only too late, at the moment of death.

There is now a long tradition in which critics identify Hamlet's delay as the play's problem and propose a new disorder to account for it, often drawing upon the latest theories in philosophy, psychology, and psychoanalysis, discrediting the proposals of their predecessors by showing how more or different aspects of Hamlet's behavior can be accounted for by their diagnosis of the problem. Nietzsche found in Hamlet the enervating effects not of speculation but of "insight into the truth"; having penetrated into the absurd and cruel reality of things, Hamlet recoils in disgust: "Knowledge kills action; action requires that one be shrouded in a veil of illusion – this is the lesson of Hamlet."[50] For Benjamin, too, there is a lesson to be learned from Hamlet's "contemplative paralysis." In the wake of the Reformation, "the philosophy of Wittenberg" taught the renunciation of good works: "Human actions were deprived of all value" and a numbing *acedia* set in.[51] So, too, for Adorno, Hamlet marks the historical moment when self-reflection (the subject's turning into a "being-for-itself") introduces an inhibiting distance between insight and action.[52] And something of the same constriction sets in with Lévinas' Hamlet: over-invested in himself and the lineage that is an extension of himself, he cannot respond to the claim of another that is the basis of ethical responsibility.[53]

Answers to the question of Hamlet's delay keep piling up, from sensitivity, to excessive meditation, to melancholia, to guilt, to the wound of castration. The list could be extended indefinitely to include poststructuralist psychoanalysis, as in Abraham's analysis of the paralyzing encryptment of the father's guilt or Zizek's account of the inhibiting effects of confrontation with the Other. Deconstruction has also contributed in the form of Derrida's reading of Hamlet's delay as a waiting for an apocalyptic form of justice beyond the commensurability of a revenge ethos. However theoretically informed the reading, Hamlet remains answerable to that old question. Through this question, Hamlet is continually reopened to yield a different problem which can in turn account differently for varying textual details. When organized around it, the play lends itself to infinite reprogramming: any theory of what makes a subject, however construed, tick (or stop ticking) can be fed into the machinery of the play to set into motion some measure of its inexhaustible verbal energies.

Our most sophisticated literary critics are still contributing answers to the question, whatever the focus of their discussion, as if no reading were valid unless it could speak to the issue. Janet Adelman attributes Hamlet's paralysis to "the psychic domination of the mother."[54] Terry Eagleton determines that Hamlet's delay marks the indeterminacy of his selfhood: "he is pure deferral and diffusion, a hollow void which offers nothing determinate to be known."[55] Jonathan Goldberg sees Hamlet's "delays and deferrals" as the result of his identification (through reiteration and inscription) with his father's command which leaves him in a state of "Being divided by non-being."[56] For Catherine Belsey, on the other hand, it is precisely his resistance to his father's deadly injunction that holds him back, as he seeks to make "ethical sense of the Ghost's command."[57] Marjorie Garber argues that Hamlet's inability to forget the paternal command impedes his action, for "action is inextricably bound with forgetting."[58] Richard Halpern discusses Hamlet's "dilatory tactics" or "internal entropy" as a resistance to Oedipal law – which if overcome would yield "a space for new productivities"; the lapse signaled by hesitation is no telic failure but rather the opportunity for new organizations of energy.[59] John Guillory sees in Hamlet's interrupted revenge a dynamic of sublimation that seeks to civilize the aggressive faction-alism of the armigerous elite.[60] Stephen Greenblatt explicitly raises the question, "What has intervened to deflect a direct course of action . . . ?" and proposes a complicated response, at once psychological and theological, in which Hamlet's struggle to extricate himself from the "embarrassments of matter" is bound up with the Reformation's difficulty abrogating the incar-national and eucharistic beliefs and rituals of the Old Faith.[61] Linda Charnes, in the conclusion to her reading of *Hamlet* as a radical critique of patriline-ality, recasts the old question of Hamlet's "pathological delay" in terms not of his inability to perform his dead father's command, but of his inability to *refuse* to do so; as a result, the generational deadlock remains.[62]

   Thus *Hamlet* continues to be read as if it were, in the words of the play's foremost twentieth-century editor, "a play about a man with a deed to do who for most of the time conspicuously fails to do it."[63] Philosophy, psychology, psychoanalysis, critical theory, history, and theology continue to provide new explanations for the old problem. And no end is in sight. In his recent biography of Shakespeare, Greenblatt has proposed an explanation that promises to open up the question indefinitely. With the writing of *Hamlet*, Shakespeare discovered that character could be deepened and intensified by "a new technique of radical excision." By withholding Hamlet's motive, Shakespeare created a "strategic opacity" that interpretation can never conclusively penetrate.[64]

   And yet there was a time when Hamlet's delay was simply not an issue.[65] For almost two hundred years – for about half the play's lifetime – the "question of questions" was not raised. None of the eighteenth-century

editors from Rowe in 1709 through Malone in 1790 is troubled by it.
Johnson in his 1765 edition actually commends the play's action as being
largely "in continual progression."⁶⁶ This is not to say that no one
noticed that there was delay. Clearly there was a long lag between
Hamlet's breathless resolution to swoop to his revenge at the play's start
and his eventual killing of Claudius at its end. The Ghost draws
attention to it when it chides Hamlet for his tardiness (3.4.107–9); so,
too, does Hamlet in soliloquy (4.4.32–66, Q2 only). In his seminal 1736
essay, George Stubbes registers his complaint: "To speak the truth, our poet
has fallen into an absurdity: there appears no reason at all in nature why
this young Prince did not put the usurper to death as soon as possible."⁶⁷ But the problem for him is with *plot* not *character*. Shakespeare
turned to the "old wretched Chronicler" (the recently discovered Saxo
Grammaticus) rather than to one of "the noble Originals of Antiquity"
(Sophocles or Aeschylus) and followed the "Ground-work" so closely
as to produce "an Absurdity in the Plot": "Had [Hamlet] gone naturally
to work . . . there would have been an End of our Play." He, therefore,
"was obliged to delay his Hero's Revenge" (27). In Saxo, Hamlet's
counterpart must wait for years – until he has grown up – before he
can exact revenge, and he bides his time for this long span; so, too, in
the anonymous *The Hystorie of Hamblet*, Hamlet revenges his father's
death "many yeres after the act committed." In both narratives, the time
is filled up with the pranks, ruses, and riddles that are the signs of
the idiocy implied by his name in Old Norse: *Amlodi*, "a fool, ninny,
an idiot, trickster feigning simplicity."⁶⁸ Shakespeare follows the same
expedient: he ekes out the play through Hamlet's feigning of an "antic
disposition." While unhappy with the solution, Stubbes sympathizes:
"I must confess, nothing is more difficult than to draw a real Madness
well, much more a feign'd one" (28). Johnson, in the endnote to his edition
of the play, notes that after having determined the King's guilt through the
Mousetrap play, Hamlet takes no action. But this is not Hamlet's doing;
"rather an instrument than an agent," he does as the plot requires.⁶⁹ George
Steevens similarly spares Hamlet in criticizing the lack of "Progress in
the Fable"; he wonders if Shakespeare had not nodded off after the prayer
scene, exhausted after the labors of the first three acts.⁷⁰ But Hamlet's
revenge, he allowed, must necessarily be "stagnated" if the play is not to end
immediately. During the standstill, Hamlet's antics are given free reign:
"he goes from Act to Act playing the Fool, always *talking, threatening,*
but never *executing*."⁷¹ As even the sober-minded Johnson appreciated,
"the pretended madness of Hamlet causes much mirth."⁷²

Thus on the rare occasions before the end of the eighteenth century when the delay is noted, the problem resides in the plot, and Shakespeare is thought to have addressed it in his drama as Saxo and Belleforest had in narrating the Hamlet legend: by eking out the time lag with his hero's antics. From a neo-classical point of view, the solution led to a serious indecorum: the Prince was reduced to playing a fool. By 1800, however, the problem had migrated from plot to character. No longer is it the plot that drags but the character who hesitates. The job of the critic was to determine why the protagonist does not move ahead, not only in the prayer scene, but from the time he vows "swoopstake" to revenge.

In the twentieth century, no less a critic than William Empson entertained the possibility that delay was a dramaturgical rather than a psychological problem. In his long essay on the play, he proposes that Shakespeare, in response to the popularity of revenge plays, turned his hand to the revision of the so-called *Ur-Hamlet*, an earlier play known only through several references predating Shakespeare's version.[73] On the basis of two of these references, Empson infers that the *Ur-Hamlet* was something of "an old laughingstock" by 1600.[74] Both suggest that the play had been mocked for the long waiting periods before its predictable climax. Thomas Nashe in 1589 described the play as one long diatribe after another: "whole Hamlets, I should say handfuls, of tragical speeches."[75] Thomas Lodge in 1596 compared "the ghost which cried so miserably at the Theatre . . . *Hamlet, revenge*" to an oyster wife, implying that the injunction was repeated like the sales pitch of street-criers until it was at long last satisfied.[76] As Empson observes, "You had a hero howling out 'Revenge' all through the play, and everybody knew the revenge wouldn't come till the end." Were anyone in the course of the play to cry out "Hurry up" (82), the play's ludicrous secret would be out: a huge gap exists in the middle of the play.

Empson imagines that what "the first audiences came to see was whether the Globe could revamp the old favourite without being absurd" (85). In other words, what could Shakespeare make of that long stretch between the command and its performance? Shakespeare rose to the dramaturgical challenge by having his hero conceal the problem by exaggerating it: "The only way to shut this hole is to make it big" (84). Hamlet "walks out to the audience and says 'You think this an absurd old play, and so it is, *but I'm in it*, and what can I do?'" (104). He repeatedly berates himself for the delay he is at a loss to explain, "I don't know why I'm delaying any more than you do; the motivation of this play is just as blank to me as it is to you; but I can't help it" (84). By anticipating the audience's recognition of the plot's structural problem, Hamlet co-opts their laughter: "instead of reducing the old play to farce, [Shakespeare] made it thrillingly life-like and profound" (84). He made the play "life-like" by exposing it for the stage craft that it is, dramatizing not the Prince's irresolvable dilemma but the play's implausible structure. And he made it "profound" by taking occasion to probe the complexities of theatrical performance. According to Empson, such a strategy would have presupposed a sophisticated audience that had attended the play with the express purpose of observing the technical ingenuity expended in converting an absurd plot into a respectable play. For him, the play grows out of the original *donnée*, which is that between the endpoints of a revenge tragedy lies a yawning interval.[77] The question, then, would have been not, "What in Hamlet's character causes him to delay?", but rather, "What will Shakespeare do with the wide hole in the middle?" Shakespeare held the audience's attention by raising metatheatrical questions, inviting the audience to wonder, for example, "who is crawling among the trestles" when they hear "Swear" repeatedly intoned from the cellarage below the stage (85). "In spite of its great variety of incident, the play sticks very closely to discussing theatricality" (85), providing occasion for disquisitions on the rivalry between theatrical companies, the proper method of acting, the moral force of mimesis.

Stubbes and Empson both take for granted that the revenge tragedy dictated a certain structure. Once the command to revenge was issued – "Revenge his foul and most unnatural murder" (1.5.25) – it was only a matter of time before it was satisfied, "Here, thou . . . damned Dane, / Drink off this potion" (5.2.330–1). The challenge for the dramatist was to find some way to fill the interval. Stubbes assumes that Shakespeare found the solution in the kind of jests that filled out his Latin narrative source; Empson sees Shakespeare filling up the time with reflections on theatricality and performance. From the vantage of popular theatrical tradition, the two accounts are not so far apart. For the role of the antic or clown filled up the time, and typically by breaking the representational surface of the play to allow for the metatheatrical effects highlighted by Empson. As Patricia Parker has pointed out, a long history associates folly with the wasting of time, encouraged by the phonetic overlap between the Latin *mora* or delay and Greek *moria* or folly.[78] The semantic connection between the *moronic* and *moratory* is easily grasped: the fool slows things down, sometimes by being stupidly slow, but more often by wasting time through clever and eruptive interjections. Clowning, like other forms of festivity (juggling, tumbling, mumming, dancing) interrupts the workaday continuum, inserting periods of release between the duty-filled routines of the year. *Farce*, as its etymology attests, is filler: *enfarcir*, to stuff.[79] Interludes were a form of light entertainment stuffed between the acts of a medieval morality or mystery play, like the *intermezzi* of popular tragedy on the Continent. Hamlet's "pranks" (3.4.2), "antic[s]" (1.5.180), "idle[ness]" (3.2.90, 3.4.10), "confusion" (3.1.2), "lunacy" (2.2.49, 3.1.4), "wild-ness" (3.1.40), "liberty" (2.1.32, 4.1.14), "madness . . . in craft" (3.4.189–90), "distemp'r[ature]" (Q1), "ecstasy" (3.4.140), "mere madness" (5.1.279), and "sore distraction" (5.2.225) eke out the *meantime* or *meanwhile* between the injunction to revenge and its fulfillment. That they are politically motivated in no way lessens their entertainment value.

Hamlet's great classical model deployed the same strategy. As Livy recorded in *The Romane Historie*, Junius Brutus was kept in attendance by the Tarquins "as their laughing stock to make them pastime by the way" until he found occasion to end their rule.[80] As the English rendering of the Norse legend specified, Hamblet learned to bide his time by playing the fool: though all the while scheming, he appeared unthreat-eningly "fitte for nothing but to make sport to the pages and ruffling courtiers that attended in the court."[81] As we saw in Chapter 4, for Shakespeare's prince, the ruse of being *non compos mentis* does more than deflect suspicion. It gives Hamlet license to express equivocally what it would have been fatal to express directly: his resentment at having been defrauded of his imperial expectation.

"They are coming to the play," says Hamlet to Horatio, as the audience assembles for the performance of *The Murder of Gonzago*; "I must be idle" (3.2.90). And between the court's arrival and the beginning of the play, he does just that, passing the time through dilatory punning, on "fares," "Brutus," "Capitol," "metal", "lie," and other "country matters" (3.2.92–133). The Players cannot begin the play until their prince and sponsor is finished: "they stay upon your patience" (106). At the beginning of this scene, in his advice to the Players, Hamlet had singled out such stalling tactics as the particular vice of the clown. In order to get laughs, the clown extemporizes, and thereby holds up the action of the play, by both his interpolated jokes and the laughter they trigger, his own as well as the audience's:

And let those that play your Clowns speak no more than is set down for them – for there be of them that will themselves laugh, to set on some quantity of barren spectators to laugh too, though in the meantime some necessary question of the play be then to be considered. (38–43).

But, of course, this is precisely what clowns had been put on stage to do. Three decades later, in Richard Brome's *The Antipodes*, when a Lord berates a Clown for adding his own "free fancy" to what was scripted, the Clown counters by pointing out that customarily such license was allowed for the purpose of moving "mirth and laughter," and the Lord grants him that this had been so "in the days of Tarlton and Kempe," the clowns of the Queen's Men and the Lord Chamberlain's men.[82] Identified with "free fancy," the clown had no binding allegiance to the script and its necessary questions. His skills of improvisation, song, dance, piping, drumming, and tumbling were extratextual. Even his customary position on the stage, as Weimann has reconstructed it, bespoke his independence from the plot: he routinely stepped out from the center or *locus* of the stage to its edge or *platea* from where he could directly address the audience.[83] From the vantage of the represented fiction, his extemporized lines were indeed dispensable. Consisting largely of proverbs, jests, riddles, and scurrilities they contributed nothing to the movement of the plot. Were a clown to follow Hamlet's advice and stick to the script (and the point), his performance would be no different from that of the other members of the acting company. In effect, Hamlet would revoke the very license on which the clown's function and popularity depended.

Hamlet's objection to clowns might well be applied to the two performers called *Clowns* in all three of the early *Hamlet* texts at the opening of Act 5: "Enter Clowne and an other" (Q1); "Enter two Clownes" (Q2, F). Eighteenth-century critics faulted these clowns for holding up the tragic dénouement with untimely levity. Voltaire's aggravation with their *quodlibets* convinced Garrick to cut the entire scene from his production: "The Grave-diggers were absolutely thrown out of the play."[84] Though the cut proved untenable (the scene was too popular on stage), it is not hard to justify, for the Clowns contribute nothing to the "necessary question of the play." Even the pit they are digging is, after all, already there. They do debate whether Ophelia's death was a suicide, but since that issue is also raised at Ophelia's burial service, it, too, is superfluous. And it takes up time. Clown 1 protests that Ophelia killed herself not in her own defense but in her own offense, *se offendendo*, and then proceeds to argue the point circularly, concluding with a tautology that supports the opposite verdict: "Argall, he that is not guilty of his own death shortens not his own life" (5.1.19–20). He then moves on to tease out another riddle, Adam was the first gentleman. And he follows it up with a third, "What is he that builds stronger than either the mason, the shipwright, or the carpenter?" (41–2). Clown 2 guesses wrong, the riddle is repeated verbatim, he prepares to venture another guess, "Marry, now I can tell" (53) but then gives up, "Mass I cannot tell" (55). Pauses were no doubt intended to precede each of Clown 2's responses, for he is decidedly slow-witted, as Clown 1 makes clear: "Cudgel thy brains no more about it, for your dull ass will not mend his pace with beating" (56–7). In addition to the drawn-out verbal matches, physical stunts drag out the scene. According to J. O. Halliwell, a stage tradition perhaps dating back to Shakespeare's players had Clown 1 strip off about a dozen waistcoats before beginning to dig.[85] The text also encourages this kind of bodily slapstick when it calls for Clown 1 to act out, with self-appointed props, his argument regarding Ophelia's drowning. He introduces his presentation, "Give me leave" (15) and "mark you that" (18). And he points to his props: "Here lies the water [indicating the pit? his coat?] – good. Here stands the man [indicating his spade? a skull or bone?] – good" (15–16). No doubt he acts out the two scenarios he entertains: "if the man go to this water and drown himself" (16–17) he is an agent and a suicide, and "if the water come to him and drown him" (18–19) he is a victim and no suicide. The play's approaching catastrophe would be further postponed by whatever laughter his skits provoked.

There is one occasion for laughter that only the Folio provides. Only in the Folio does one of Clown 1's jokes, concerning Adam's armiger gentility, appear in its entirety. In both Q2 and F, in response to Clown 1's claim that the oldest lineage descends from Adam, Clown 2 asks if Adam was a gentleman. Clown 1 informs him that "he was the first that ever bore armes." But only F gives him the opportunity to unpack the punch line.

CLO.   What, ar't a Heathen? How does thou understand the Scripture?
        The Scripture sayes *Adam* dig'd; could hee digge without Armes?
                                                              (35–7)

That the joke is extended in only one text suggests that the number and length of jokes may have been adjustable. A clown could take the occasion to tell one joke or two or more, stretching them out or holding them back, depending on the duration of the audience's laughter, in a routine now known as an elastic gag. Commonplaces possessed the same flexibility. Self-contained modular units, *sententiae* could be piled on or held back as time, audience, or other actors allowed. As we have seen, in Laertes' counsel to Ophelia (see Illustration 7), Q2 marks three such sayings with the typographical sign for maxims, the quotation mark.

"The chariest maide is prodigall inough
If she unmaske her butie to the Moone
"Vertue it selfe scapes not calumnious strokes
"The canker gaules the infants of the spring
Too oft before their buttons be disclos'd
(1.3.36–40)

But it gives an additional unmarked three:

And in the Morne and liquid dew of Youth,
Contagious blastments are most imminent.
Be wary then, best safety lies in feare. (41–3)

The actor playing Laertes has a choice as to whether to buttress his warning with one saying or six or none at all. Q1 gives him only three. So, too, in an exchange Q1 omits, Q2 gives Claudius seven *sententiae* in order to fortify Laertes' resolution to avenge his father; F, however, provides him with only two. The number of jokes a clown delivers is also variable, as is suggested by Hamlet's advice to the Players in Q1. At one point alone is the notoriously truncated Q1 text longer than either Q2 or F, and by ten lines. In his advice to the actors, after warning the Clown not to ad lib, Hamlet indulges the routine he would abolish by himself rattling off one stock jest after another.

Cannot you stay till I eate my porrige? *And*, you owe me
A quarters wages: *and*, my coate wants a cullison:
And, your beere is sowre: *and*, blabbering with his lips,
And thus keeping in his cinkapase of ieasts,
When, God knows, the warme Clowne cannot make a iest
Unlesse by chance, as the blinde man catcheth a hare.
(F2r–F2v [italics added])

Four jests are topped off with a fifth at the expense of the jest-maker to complete a "cinkapase of jests" – five (cinque) stinking (sink-a-piss) jests. That the jests are linked together with *and*s suggests that in performance additional ones could be strung on indefinitely, as long as the audience kept laughing. In railing against the Clown for "blabbering with his lips," Hamlet himself blabbers. If he also laughs at his jokes, as clowns are wont to do (3.2.39–41), he will be in double violation of his own precepts.

It is generally believed that the supernumerary lines in Q1 record interpolations by the actor-playing-Hamlet which subsequently found their way into the Q1 text.[86] Discovered in 1823 and existing in only two copies, the Q1 text bears witness to a practice that must have been quite routine: a player holds on to the spotlight, as it were, by taking flight

Ham. And doe you heare ? let not your **Clowne** speake
More th'n is set downe, there be of them I can tell you
That will laugh themselues, to set on some
Quantitie of barren spectators to laugh with them,
Albeit there is some necessary point in the Play
Then to be obserued: O t'is vile, and shewes
A pittifull ambition in the foole that vseth it.
And then you haue some agen, that keepes one sute
Of ieasts, as a man is knowne by one sute of
Apparell, and Gentlemen quotes his ieasts downe
                    F 2   In

The Tragedy of Hamlet

In their tables, before they come to the play, as thus:
Cannot you stay till I eate my porrige? and, you owe me
A quarters wages: and, my coate wants a cullison:
And, your beere is sowre: and, blabbering with his lips,
And thus keeping in his cinkapase of ieasts,
When, God knows, the warme Clowne cannot make a ieft
Vnlesse by chance, as the blinde man catcheth a hare:
Maisters tell him of it.

Illustration 17. Marginal pointing finger, in *The Tragicall Historie of Hamlet,*
fol. F2r, F2v.

from the script and saying "more than is set down" (3.2.39). Like all forms
of grand-standing, it "shows a most pitiful ambition" (3.2.44). In this case,
Hamlet (or the actor-playing-Hamlet) drags out the time between the
scripted lines assigned to him and those of the next speaker (the deferential First Player) by stringing together jests, some of which can be found
in jest books that in turn had been heard at the theater and jotted down
in tablebooks.[87] The seventeenth-century reader's markings in the
British Library's copy of Q1 indicate further recycling: the jokes are both
underlined and indicated by two pointing fingers (Illustration 17).

By taking the liberty of exceeding his scripted part, Hamlet (or rather
the actor-playing-Hamlet) in Q1 decidedly holds up the show – as well as
the show-within-the-show – for the Mousetrap play is scheduled to begin.
As if to make up for lost time after his lengthy lecture, Hamlet rushes off
the actors, "Go make you ready," and instructs Polonius to do the same,

"Bid the players make haste," as well as Rosencrantz and Guildenstern, "Will you two help to hasten them?" (3.2.45, 49, 50).

Among the itinerant "tragedians" (2.2.327), there is no clown to receive the caveat Hamlet expressly addresses to "those that play your Clowns" (3.2.38–9). But the clown's closest theatrical kin is there. "That's villainous" (43–4) concludes Hamlet of clowns who impertinently hold up a play's climax. By charging clowns with villainy, Hamlet recalls the close association between the roles of the Clown and the Vice in the medieval moralities.[88] The Antic-Vice remained the dominant stage figure through the middle of the sixteenth century, very much kept alive on the commercial stage by the celebrated clown Richard Tarlton. At his death in 1588, more than the loss of a clown was lamented: "Now Tarlton's dead, the Consort lackes a Vice."[89] His dual role as Clown and Vice survived him into Shakespeare's time through his successor, Will Kempe, known as "Jest monger and Viceregentgenerall to the Ghost of Dick Tarlton."[90] That the two roles coalesced was quite natural for both were grounded in knavery, the Clown's concentrated in jest and the Vice's in scheming.

In the *Murder of Gonzago*, the Vice figure appears in the character of Lucianus. Though there is no reason to think he speaks more than is set down, he certainly brings action to a standstill, and just before the climactic act that is intended to "unkennel" Claudius' "occulted guilt" (3.2.80–1) – the pouring of poison into the Player-king's ear. Hamlet's impatient Senecan outburst indicates that Lucianus (or rather the actor-playing-Lucianus) has been taking his time.

> Begin, murderer. Leave thy damnable faces and begin.
> Come, the croaking raven doth bellow for revenge.
>
> (3.2.246–8)

Between his entrance and his first speech, Lucianus has been on stage (or rather on the stage-within-the stage) for ten lines while Hamlet banters bawdily with Ophelia. For this duration, Lucianus has the stage to himself, all eyes (of the court audience) are upon him, and he takes the opportunity to ham it up ("a most pitiful ambition"), apparently by making "damnable faces." Clowns were known for their mugging or grimacing. Tarlton famously contorted what is imagined to have been a naturally ugly face when he routinely poked his head out of the tiring-house to make "a scurvey face" at the audience, stretching out the time before his entrance for as long as the laughs kept coming (perhaps laughing himself).[91] The stunt turns grotesque in a contemporary anti-theatrical diatribe which complains of how the Clown enters and shows "his teeth in double rotten row."[92] In the graveyard, Hamlet seems to remember such grinning on the face of the jester Yorick, and, when perusing his skull, registers its loss, "Quite chop-fallen" (5.1.186). If Lucianus were playing the scene for laughs by pulling faces, at once fiendishly grotesque and ludicrously comical, we have another instance of the dilational Clowning censured by Hamlet.

The Vice's antics obviously do not delight Hamlet, and the feeling might well be mutual: Lucianus has cause to grow impatient with Hamlet for holding up show-time with his off-color repartee with Ophelia. Indeed the two may be in competition for the on-stage audience or the off-stage audience, or both. With his "damnable faces," the actor-playing-the-player-playing Lucianus may be trying (or pretending to try) to upstage or out-clown the scurrilities of the actor-playing-Hamlet-playing-the-antic. Up until now, antic Hamlet has been the only Clown on stage. As commentators have long noted, his feigned madness in no way helps him to accomplish his assigned task. On the contrary, as many commentators have noted, rather than concealing his purpose, it draws attention to it, rousing the suspicions of the King, Queen, and councilor. But it is a good pretext for gratuitous prolixity. Hamlet speaks more than half of the lines in the play, and, as we have seen in Chapter 5, when addressed to anyone other than his confidante Horatio they are typically rude, offensive, or unintelligible. Like Lucianus with his "damnable faces" and like the graveyard Clowns with their jokes and slapstick, Hamlet routinely holds up the show with his desultory and dilatory remarks. But they are not altogether impertinent, for they pertain, however elusively and opaquely, not merely to "some necessary question of the play," but to *the* question. Like Lucianus' sinister faces and the Clown's complaints against the uneven dispensation among "even-Christen" (5.1.28–9), they give voice to the political resentment and aggression that dares – during Claudius' regime – risk no other outlet.

It is quite possible that Hamlet also makes "damnable faces." Ophelia describes him barging into her closet, "As if he had been loosed out of hell/ To speak of horrors" (2.1.83–4). And perhaps when striking an antic pose, he like Lucianus makes ugly faces, in imitation of the grotesque masks or false-heads called "antics."[93] Such grinning or grimacing might be designed to mimic the play's arch-villain, the "vice of kings" (3.4.98). Claudius must be all smiles in the opening court scene to make sense of Hamlet's vituperative apostrophe: "O villain, villain, smiling damned villain!" (1.5.106). Certainly his response to Hamlet's concession to remain in Denmark calls for an ear-to-ear grin: "This gentle and unforc'd accord of Hamlet/ Sits smiling to my heart" (1.2.123–4). And a smile might also attend his expressed pleasure upon hearing of Hamlet's ostensibly harmless enthusiasm for the Players' entertainment: "it doth much content me" (3.1.24). Claudius is the example who proves the rule which Hamlet jots into his newly wiped tablebook, "One may smile, and smile, and be a villain" (1.5.108). While recording it, Hamlet might himself illustrate it by baring his teeth in sinister imitation of Claudius.

Hamlet's "antic disposition" seems to call for a particular disposal of the body as well as the face. Claudius comments that since Hamlet's transformation, "nor th'exterior nor the inward man/ Resembles what it was" (2.2.6–7). Ophelia, the first to witness him in his antic persona, describes it in detail. He has lost control of his body: his knees knock, his head shakes, indeed his whole frame heaves, making it impossible to maintain a dignified and erect princely posture, "thrice his head waving up and down,/ He rais'd a sigh so piteous and profound/ As it did seem to shatter all his bulk / And end his being" (2.1.93–6). His convulsive movements have been hard on his clothing: his braces tear apart, his cap flings off, his garters snap. (One early allusion has him stripped of constraining outer clothes, so his "shirt he onely weares."[94]) Although he can recompose his face and body when he switches out of his antic persona – to speak *solus* or to Horatio, for example – he cannot so readily alter his clothes. In modern performances, Hamlet usually retains the dashing mourning garb or "inky cloak" (1.2.77) of his first appearance, but there is just as much textual warrant to keep him in dishabille for the duration of his antic act, until he is en route to England (4.4).

Hamlet's lines often invite a correspondent gesture, especially in the movements of the limbs so exaggerated that they throw the body off its stately vertical axis. For example, to illustrate the difference between a hawk and a handsaw, Hamlet might gesticulate wildly (flapping his arms for the former and "saw[ing] the air too much" for the latter, 3.2.4); or to ridicule women's jigging and ambling ("you jig and amble," 3.1.146) he might mimic their fancy footwork; his satirical description of old men with "weak hams" (2.2.200) invites him to splay out both arms and legs in imitation of a crab which, unlike old men, can "go backward" (2.2.203–4); his claim to still love Rosencrantz "by these pickers and stealers" (3.2.327) would seem to call for some kind of groping or snatching gesture, perhaps in the private area of Rosencrantz's purse. So, too, before the *Murder of Gonzago*, it is hard to imagine that, from his reclining position in Ophelia's lap, he would have resisted the infamously lewd motions of the hobby-horse ("For o, for o, the

Hobby-horse is forgot," 3.2.133), the equestrian figure banned from the Morris dancing of the May Games for its obscene cavorting.⁹⁵ Finally, the references collected in Chapter 1 to his *running mad* indicate that Hamlet must have taken numerous entrances and exits in a frenzy, just as he is said to have entered Ophelia's closet as if "loosed out of hell." The text quite explicitly calls for at least two such exits. Hamlet obviously breaks away from his companions in order to follow the Ghost ("Hold off your hands"; "unhand me gentlemen," 1.4.80, 84), and violently, as his companions comment, "He waxes desperate" (87). In the Folio, he also shoots off stage when Rosencrantz and Guildenstern are sent by the King to fetch him. First he indicates that he will comply – "Bring me to him" (4.2.29) – but then does an abrupt about-face and darts off shouting "Hide fox and all after," the cry of a children's game, forcing his hunters to follow in pursuit.⁹⁶

These disfiguring facial expressions, gestures, movements, and attire are trappings of his antic role. The First Player gives a demonstration of the bodily investment acting requires when in his recitation of "Priam's slaughter" he takes the pitiful part of Hecuba:

> his visage wann'd,
> Tears in his eyes, distraction in his aspect,
> A broken voice, and his whole function suiting
> With forms to his conceit. (2.2.548–51)

Hamlet calls the transformation "monstrous" (2.2.545): like any extreme of passion, grief contorts the aspect and function of the body; so, too, does its performance. Also monstrous is Hamlet's antic guise. It bends him out of shape, like grotesques in manuscripts, antics in masques, madmen in the Bedlam asylum, and devils on stage. In keeping with his stipulation that acting "[s]uit the action to the word, the word to the action" (3.2.17–18), Hamlet's antics have a verbal counterpart. "Put your discourse into some frame" (3.2.300), Rosencrantz urges. As Weimann has brilliantly demonstrated, Hamlet's antic idiom derives largely from the stock figure of the Antic-Vice.⁹⁷ It may not be possible to determine whether Hamlet frequented the outer rim of the stage, as the Vice figure did the *platea*, but he certainly speaks as if he did. A large proportion of his lines are not intended for the ears of the other characters. Much of what they hear, they ignore or cannot understand. Wordplay is "the Vice's hallmark," and Hamlet has more puns to his credit than any other Shakespearean character, no less than ninety.⁹⁸ Typically they float over the heads of the other characters and so go unremarked. As with his first three punning utterances, the dialogue continues as if they had not been spoken.

KING   But now, my *cousin* Hamlet, and my *son* –
HAM.   A little more than *kin*, and less than *kind.*
KING   How is it that the clouds still hang on you?
HAM.   Not so, my lord, I am too much in the *sun.*
QUEEN   . . . .
        Thou know'st 'tis *common*: all that lives must die
        . . . .
HAM.   Ay, madam, it is *common.*

                                    (1.2.64–74) [italics added]

Also in the tradition of the Antic-Vice, he speaks insolently or impertinently to his interlocutors, often talking down to his betters or elders. He
addresses the likeness of his father as "old mole" (1.5.170), talks back to his
king and stepfather, mocks the old chief councilor, accuses Ophelia of
harlotry, prescribes sexual behavior to his mother. As the exasperated
Rosencrantz notes, his conduct belies his breeding, "this courtesy is not
of the right breed" (3.2.306). On several occasions, his abuse takes the
homiletic form typifying the Vice. He inveighs against the custom of
drinking in Denmark, tottering old men, the excesses of theatrical performance, the sensuality of women, the sycophancy of courtiers. That he
has a tablebook on his person is appropriate, for his satire often takes
pithy proverbial form. Credited with seventy-one proverbs, he is nothing
if not sententious: "Frailty, thy name is woman" (1.2.146); "Assume a
virtue if you have it not" (3.4.162); "Use every man after his desert, and
who shall scape whipping?" (2.2.524–5).[99] The other characters repeatedly
complain of the difficulty of communicating with him. Says the King, "I
have nothing with this answer, Hamlet. These words are not mine"
(3.2.95–6); and Guildenstern, "Good my lord, put your discourse into
some frame, and start not so wildly from my affair" (3.2.300); and
Rosencrantz, "I understand you not, my lord" (4.2.21). All these reactions
attest to the Antic-Vice's familiar tactic of thwarting the give-and-take of
dialogue. This is most obvious in question- and-answer exchanges.

OPH.   What means your lordship?
HAM.   That if you be honest and fair, your honesty should admit
            no discourse to your beauty.

                                                        (3.1.106–8)

OPH.   What means this, my lord?
HAM.   Marry, this is miching malicho. It means mischief.
                                                        (3.2.134–5)

POL.   What do you read, my lord?
HAM.   Words, words, words.
                        (2.2.191–2)

KING   Now, Hamlet, where's Polonius?
HAM.   At supper.
KING   At supper? Where?
HAM.   Not where he eats, but where a is eaten.

(4.3.16–19)

Hamlet, as he explains, will not give "wholesome answer," for, as he insists, "my wit's diseased" (3.2.313).

Hamlet's unframed discourse cuts his words off from the dialogue of the other characters. In this respect it is not so different from the words they cannot even hear, his asides and soliloquies, for his interlocutors understand no more when he speaks over their heads than they do when he is out of hearing range. In the nineteenth century, to sustain the impression that the play was "a tragedy of thought," Hamlet had to give the frequent impression of thinking aloud. To Charles Lamb, that nine-tenths of Hamlet's lines consisted of "solitary musings" presented a problem in performance: he "comes and mouths [words] before an audience, making four hundred people his confidants at once." How can Hamlet be in solitude (*solus*) when standing before an audience? How can he be thinking when words are coming out of his mouth? William Hazlitt was troubled by the same absurdity. Hamlet seeks out isolation – retiring "to holes and corners and the most sequestered parts of the palace" – in order to spill out his ruminations to a crowd of auditors.[100] The presence of the audience becomes an embarrassment, despite the effort of the Restoration theatre to conceal it by raising the stage high above the ground level of the audience and cordoning it off on three sides. To be life-like, the illusion of Hamlet thinking requires privacy and silence, but the presence of an audience precludes both.

The Globe's open stage would have allowed Hamlet no such illusion of exclusionary self-absorption. His need to pull away from the centrally located court may well have taken him to the outer rim of the stage, the area closest to the standing audience. It is from there, perhaps, that Hamlet would have highlighted the pretense of solitude by announcing, "Now I am alone" (2.2.543). The stage has just cleared – *Exeunt Polonius and Players. Exeunt [Rosencrantz and Guildenstern]* – but the audience is all ears; at the Globe, approximately one-third of it would be standing at his feet. "Now I am alone" is not a cue to the audience to pretend not to be there. On the contrary, it is a signal that Hamlet will be speaking for its benefit alone. The "solitary musings" Lamb and Hazlitt found "hardly capable of being performed" may have been consummately performative on Shakespeare's stage, giving occasion for virtuoso self-display. In this context, "Now I am alone" (2.2.543) means not "Now no one is looking or listening," but rather "Now I have the audience's undivided attention, all eyes and ears are on me." The exiting of the other characters clears a space not for pure solipsistic thought but for direct contact with the audience.

Weimann's multiple discussions of *Hamlet* go far toward establishing Hamlet's affiliation with the traditional Vice figure. Yet they curiously overlook the trait for which the Vice is named. As the adversary of Virtue in the perennial contest over human souls, the Vice is vicious. In his advice to the Players, Hamlet refers to the theatrical tradition that dramatized their opposition: "[T]he purpose of playing, whose end, both at the first and now, was and is to hold as 'twere the mirror up to nature; to show virtue her feature, scorn her own image" (3.2.20–3). The stage should work to represent "virtue" and "Vice" (or, in Hamlet's metonym, "scorn") in such a way that the one will be loved and imitated and the other contemned and avoided. When taking up the avenger's role, Hamlet does his best to show "scorn her own image" by looking frightful and behaving cruelly. The role does not come naturally; he has to whip himself into villainy, "Bloody, bawdy villain!/ Remorseless, treacherous, lecherous, kindless villain!" (2.2.576–7). Claudius is the subject of the apostrophe, but it occurs in a monologue in which Hamlet berates himself for not being sufficiently bloodthirsty. It is Claudius, "a Vice of kings" (3.4.98), who possesses the villainous qualities Hamlet lacks and needs in order to chill and spill blood. When Hamlet asks, "Who calls me villain?", he is using the word in a different though related sense:

> Who calls me villain, breaks my pate across,
> Plucks off my beard and blows it in my face
> Tweaks me by the nose, gives me the lie i'th'throat
> As deep as to the lungs – who does me this?
>
> (2.2.567–70)

Claudius' villainy is apparent in his crime; Hamlet's in his cowardice. Both senses of the word stem from *villein*, the term used in the Domesday Book for persons bound to the soil, like serfs or churls. In his self-debasement, Hamlet also refers to himself as a "*peasant* slave." The negative connotations of *peasant*, like those of *villain*, *serf*, and *churl*, derive from bondage to the land. So, too, do those of another of Hamlet's self-styled epithets: "muddy-mettled *rascal*" (2.2.562), from the French word for mud, *rasque*. These rustic terms have domestic equivalents. Hamlet calls himself not only *peasant* and *rascal*, but also "drab" and "scullion," servants who perform menial household chores. He equates himself with those whose labor puts them in routine contact with either outside or inside dirt. Like the proverbially meek peasant, he is "pigeon-liver'd" (2.2.573) and therefore too timid to protest his subservience: he lacks the "gall to make oppression bitter" (573–4). So debased, he imagines himself suffering the indignity of having his beard plucked, his nose tweaked. Incapable of striking back, he is like those who meekly suffer their subjection. Like a foul-mouthed wretch, his only recourse is to "unpack [his] heart with words" (581), and "fall a-cursing like a very drab,/ A scullion" (582–3). In this speech, Hamlet would convert one kind of villainy to another, menial scullery to savage butchery, by making a meal of Claudius, carving and serving up his intestines to ravenous appetites: "[E]re this/ I should ha' fatted all the region kites / With this slave's offal" (2.2.574–6). This is the kind of carnage he admired in the Player's account of "the hellish Pyrrhus" (2.2.459) who made mincemeat of Priam: "mak[ing] malicious sport,/ In mincing with his sword her husband's limbs" (2.2.509–10). Hamlet, in imagination, does him one better, not only slicing up his victim, but serving him up to birds of prey.

There may be evidence in this monologue that the actor-playing-Hamlet got carried away with viciousness much as he did with clowning in his advice to the Players in Q1: "Bloody, bawdy villain!/ Remorseless, treacherous, lecherous, kindless villain!/ [O Vengeance!]" (2.2.576–8). Editors have considered the possibility that the final short line, found only in the Folio, represents an actor's addition, "O Vengeance!"[101] But this string of extra-metrical abuses might also be interpolation, signaled, perhaps, by Hamlet's immediate self-reproach for his need to "like a whore unpack my heart with words" (581). The diatribe might be an instance of where the actor-playing-Hamlet, in another fit of "pitiful ambition," got carried away with his villainy as he did with his clowning in the extended passage in Q1. Like the series of jokes, the string of epithets could go on indefinitely, or at least as long as it takes to work up the audience (or give up on doing so). After hearing the Player's passionate delivery of "Priam's slaughter," Hamlet wonders, "What would he do had he the motive and the cue for passion/ That I have?" (2.2.554–6). And he gives the answer, "He would drown the stage with tears,/ And cleave the ear with horrid speech,/ Make mad the guilty and appal the free" (556–8). His non-metrical invective represents his attempt to work himself into the bloodthirsty rage that would stun and craze an audience.

The Murder of Gonzago rouses similar ambitions in Hamlet. He and the villain Lucianus have comparable roles in their respective plots. Hamlet like Lucianus is "nephew to the king" (3.2.239) he would murder. Lucianus pours poison in the king's ear; Hamlet pours "[p]oison in jest" (229) in the King's ear. After witnessing Lucianus' villainy, Hamlet formulates his own ghoulish fantasies:

> 'Tis now the very witching time of night,
> When churchyards yawn and hell itself breathes out
> Contagion to this world. Now could I drink hot blood.
>
> (3.2.379)

Both assassins deliver what Jenkins terms "the traditional night-piece, apt prelude to a deed of blood."[102] If Lucianus has "[t]houghts black" (3.2.249), Hamlet could "drink hot blood." If Lucianus' infernal poison is distilled in a little flask, Hamlet's contagion would blast the whole world. If Lucianus makes damnable faces in anticipation of trickling poison into his victim's ear, Hamlet might also make them while contemplating the drinking of hot blood. Like a mask, the grin is as easily doffed as donned: Hamlet drops it before approaching his mother, "Soft, now to my mother" (3.2.383), though perhaps not quite – "Let me be cruel" and "speak daggers" (386, 387).

Hamlet's desire in the prayer scene to damn a soul to eternal pain is the most extreme form of evil imaginable in a society that gave even its most heinous felons the opportunity to repent before execution. By a tradition dating back to the early Church, the desire belongs exclusively to devils; consigning souls to eternal damnation is their business in this world as well as the next. In manuals on the art of dying, they are depicted hovering around the deathbed in hope of snatching up a despairing soul. In illustrations of the Last Judgment, devils lurk at the left hand of Christ tugging the wretched souls of the damned down to searing tortures. In recent years, scores of wall paintings dating from the fifteenth and early-sixteenth centuries have been discovered on the chancels of English parish churches, beneath Reformation or Victorian white-wash. The most frequently depicted scene is the Doom or Last Judgment, represented as the weighing of souls. The blessed rise or are swooped up by angels; Horatio's prayer over Hamlet's dead body – "flights, of angels sing thee to thy rest" (5.2.365) – alludes to the same determination, as does Hamlet's dying wish in Q1, "heauen receiue my soule" (I3v). The damned are yanked down into hell's mouth by gleefully grinning devils;[103] it is to them that Laertes would consign Hamlet, "The devil take thy soul" (5.1.251). In the early-nineteenth century, a wall painting of the Doom was discovered beneath white-washing over the chancel arch in the Guild Chapel at Stratford, and carefully copied before the church was restored.[104] As illustrated in the drawing, numerous maniacally grinning devils appear, some tormenting sinners with clubs, fleshhooks, and horns, others corralling a group of them with a chain, and dragging them into a wide-open hell's mouth, the upward curves of the devils' mouths contrasting with the down-turned ones of the miserable sinners (Illustration 18).[105]

The Ghost's appearance in "questionable shape" (1.4.43) casts doubt on its allegiance, and Hamlet's urgent questions go unanswered.

> Be thou a spirit of health or goblin damned?
> Bring with thee airs from heaven or blasts from hell?
> Be thy intents wicked or charitable?   (1.4.40–2)

As Hamlet acknowledges, the fact that it bears the endearing form of his father's likeness offers no reassurance.

> The spirit that I have seen
> May be a devil, and the devil hath power
> T'assume a pleasing shape[.]   (2.2.594–6)

When the Ghost beckons Hamlet to follow him alone to "more removed ground" (1.4.61), Horatio and the guards do their utmost to prevent him: "But do not go with it. No by no means . . . Do not, my lord . . . You shall not go, my lord . . . Be rul'd; you shall not go" (62, 64, 80, 81). They fear for Hamlet's soul:

> What if it tempt you toward the flood, my lord,
> Or to the dreadful summit of the cliff
> That beetles o'er his base into the sea,
> And there assume some other horrible form
> Which might deprive your sovereignty of reason
> And draw you into madness?   (69–74)

The fiend legendarily singles out those weakened by melancholy or guilt and further unsettles them with images of the abysmal void prompting "thoughts beyond the reaches of [their] souls" (56), impelling them to despair and suicide. From the vantage of that "dreadful summit," "every brain/ That looks so many fathoms to the sea/ And hears it roar beneath" (76–7) feels a touch of despair, the demonic sublime; and if the devil were there to "assume some other horrible form" – some monstrous phantasma – the weak-minded would renounce all faith and topple over

Illustration 18. *Doomsday Devils*, in Thomas Fisher, *A Series of Ancient Allegorical, Historical, and Legendary Paintings . . . on the Walls of the Chapel of the Trinity, at Stratford upon Avon* (1807).

the precipitous edge, into the clutches of the devil. (Edgar in *King Lear* convinces his guilt-ridden father that such a hideously fiendish figure drove him to his suicidal leap from the cliffs of Dover.[106]) Hamlet's reckless response to the alarm of his companions only justifies it.

> Why, what should be the fear?
> I do not set my life at a pin's fee,
> And for my soul, what can it do to that,
> Being a thing immortal as itself? (64–7)

The immortality of his soul is precisely what should cause him fear, as he later realizes: "The spirit that I have seen / May be a devil . . ., yea, and perhaps, / Out of my weakness and my melancholy, / As he is very potent with such spirits, / Abuses me to damn me" (2.2.594–9).

"The devil take thy soul" (5.1.251), bids Laertes, when Hamlet, the slayer of his father, reveals himself at Ophelia's grave. Hamlet invokes no infernal agent in his plan to send Claudius' soul headlong to hell. The eighteenth-century scholars who saw his resolve as fiendish were exactly right. His wish is pure diabolism. Indeed it may well be that Hamlet was the first secular character to have given voice to such a desire on stage. As we have seen, though keen to attribute his fiendish intention to theatrical convention, scholars could find no precedents. They would have had no trouble had they looked for them among stage devils. As John Cox has established, devils from before *Mankind* to long after Marlowe, indeed all the way up to the closing of the theaters, appeared on stage, often at the final hour, to seize the souls of those who had abjured God, hilariously abducting them by dragging or lugging them off stage, riding them off piggyback, or yanking them into the gaping mouth of hell.[107] The memory of those devils lingered in the trap of the stage itself, the opening to the traditional theatrical location of hell, the area beneath the scaffolding. At the Globe, this area would have been activated by the Ghost's descent and eerie intonations from below. The Arden editor suggests that the epithets with which Hamlet addresses the Ghost – "boy," "truepenny" (1.5.158), "fellow" (159) – recall the familiar manner in which the stage Vice traditionally addressed the Devil. He also notes the applicability of "*hic et ubique*" (164), "old mole" (170), and "worthy pioner" (171) to the ubiquitous subterranean activity of devils.[108]

When confronted with the perfect opportunity to "[t]o quit [Claudius] with this arm" (5.2.68), Hamlet decides to postpone the requital. The terms are not right. Were he to take Claudius' soul in the act of penance, he would have blood for blood, but not soul for soul. His father's soul at death was "Unhousel'd, disappointed, unanel'd" (1.5.77), while his murderer's would be, by Hamlet's inference, "fit and season'd for his passage" to everlasting bliss (3.3.86).

> That would be scann'd:
> A villain kills my father, and for that
> I, his sole son, do this same villain send
> To heaven.
> Why, this is hire and salary, not revenge.
>
> (3.3.75–9)

For having killed his father, Hamlet would secure for Claudius eternal reward: grace in return for guilt. Yet an even settlement is not what he wants either: the Mosaic *lex talionis* of "an eye for an eye," "a tooth for a tooth."[109] As John Marston in *Antonio's Revenge* reminded his audience by quoting Seneca, revenge must go beyond justice. "*Scelera non ulcisceris, nisi vincis*": Crimes are not avenged unless they are exceeded.[110] While his father was killed in the harmless act of sleeping in the garden, his uncle must be taken in "some act/ That has no relish of salvation in't" (3.3.91–2),

> that his heels may kick at heaven
> And that his soul may be as damn'd and black
> As hell, whereto it goes.   (93–5)

This is overkill, not retaliation, and a reminder that both iniquity and inequity have incommensurability at their semantic root.[111] By the Ghost's report, the state of King Hamlet's soul at death sent him to purgatory, not hell, and between the two destinations there is a world of difference. Punishment in purgatory may be long and hard, but it is finite.[112] As the Ghost reveals, he has been sentenced for a definite period – "Doom'd for a certain term . . . Till the foul crimes done in my days of nature/ Are burnt and purg'd away" (1.5.10–13). That is bad enough: "O horrible! O horrible! Most horrible!" (80). But Hamlet wishes upon Claudius the "more horrid hent" (3.3.88) of everlasting punishment, the eternal agony of fiery hell. With such fiendishness, he surpasses his rival, the smiling "[b]loody, bawdy villain" (2.2.576) or "vice of kings" (3.4.98), whose malice is merely of this world. So, too, at least in his imagination he proved more wicked that his Greek model, "the hellish Pyrrhus" (2.2.459), outdoing his carnage by not only slaughtering his victim but tossing his innards to scavenging "kites" (2.2.575).

On Shakespeare's stage, Hamlet's atrocious lines may well have been intended to give an audience what it came to a revenge play to see: how far the avenger will go. Laertes is also committed to this retributional excess, vowing after his father's murder and Ophelia's ruin that the damage "shall be paid with weight/ Till our scale turn the beam" (4.5.156–7). Baited by Claudius' question, "[W]hat would you undertake/ To show yourself in deed your father's son?" (4.7.123–4), he sets his limit; "To cut his throat i'th'church" (125), responds Laertes, happy to commit sacrilege. "Revenge should have no bounds" (127) commends Claudius. Neither character gives thought to damning his victim. In fact, Laertes' willingness to slay Hamlet in church, perhaps at prayer, suggests an indifference to the circumstances that stay Hamlet's hand, for surely there is some "relish of salvation" in church attendance. Laertes' revenge, then, *does* remain within bounds, for it is limited to the here and now, blood for blood.

Hamlet's sentiment, however, goes beyond the pale of the human. Like grotesque visors and black costumes, such extreme malice on the early stage was the devil's hallmark.[113] Sir Thomas Browne could not believe the report of the Italian who after tricking his enemy to renounce Christ in order to escape with his life, stabbed him before he could repent to assure his eternal agony: "our bad wishes and malevolous desires proceed no further than this life: it is the Devil and uncharitable *votes* of hell that desire our misery in the world to come."[114] In uttering the devil's sentiments, Hamlet crosses the divide between the natural and the unnatural, the human and the monstrous, in egregious violation of the "special observance" he has imposed upon the Players to "o'erstep not the modesty of nature." His own violation, it must be stressed, is a studied one. The prayer scene is framed to set it off. Its conspicuous forestalling of the climactic action gives Hamlet the opportunity to show off his villainy, ratcheting it up to the point of devilry. Like its theatrical flipside of folly, it is mischievously inserted just at the point when "some necessary question of the play be then to be considered" (3.2.42–3).

Stage devils may have survived the Reformation, but not the closing of the theaters. Once the devil had disappeared from the stage, Hamlet's grotesque malice lost its point of reference. Or rather, it became self-referential, and as such had no excuse. The most effective solution was to excise offending lines. When retained, they could only be read as an abominable expression of their speaker's intent. Later criticism found a way of preserving both the speech and Hamlet's character by turning to psychology; Hamlet's performative monstrosity was thereby naturalized as deep-seated emotional or psychological disturbance. It was not the old stage devil speaking in Hamlet, but rather the unconscious expressing itself in words Hamlet did not mean. Yet when Hamlet's lines hearkened back to the age-old tradition of devilry there was no need for such ingenious defenses. Hamlet himself alludes to this tradition when told that his father has been dead for many months, "So long? Nay then, let the devil wear black, for I'll have a suit of sables" (3.2.127–8). In an attempt to differentiate the devil's "black" from Hamlet's "sable," editors have gone so far as to deny that sable is black, even though both mourning garb and heraldic black were called *sable*. But their synonymity may be the point. In the attiring-house, Hamlet's "inky cloak" or "customary suits of solemn black" (1.2.77, 78) might have doubled as the devil's black robe listed in several stage inventories. "Damnable faces" and "devil-wear" may have been as much part of his antic repertoire as his clownish jig-making and pipe-playing (3.3.123, 341–2).

After the Restoration, Hamlet's antics become the target of neo-classical censure. As we have seen, Stubbes recognized that Shakespeare used Hamlet's antic disposition to fill the gap between the command to "Revenge." (1.5.25) and its execution, "Then, venom, to thy work" (5.2.327). The expedient was, from his neo-classical point of view, an unhappy one: "The whole Conduct of Hamlet's Madness, is, in my Opinion, too ludicrous." His essay extracts comic stretches from the play to censure them: "all things tending to raise a Laugh, are highly offensive in Tragedies" (19). Hamlet's advice to the Players is applauded, particularly its silencing of the Clown. The Grave-digger scene comes under particular censure for putting the Prince in conversation with a peasant or, in Philip Sidney's famous formulation, "mingling kings and Clowns."[115] Particularly objectionable in this same scene was the singing of the rustic grave-digger just before the solemn ceremony of the court funeral, a flagrant instance of generic mixing. But it was the leading character who offended more than individual scenes, through his repeated collapsing of high and low, "as if we were to dress a Monarch in all his Robes, and then put a Fool's Cap upon him" (19). Prince Hamlet as Antic was a walking generic outrage, and it fell to the critic to distinguish his generic components: praising his princely manner and locution and faulting his lowbrow antics.

Later in the century, critics lose sight of the dilational function of Hamlet's antics, and acknowledge only their entertainment value. Charlotte Lennox considers Hamlet's feigned madness "of no Consequence to the principal Design of the Play" and "certainly a Fault": "It is of no other use than to enliven the Dialogue."[116] So, too, her great friend Johnson maintains that "of the feigned madness of Hamlet there appears no adequate cause."[117] Francis

Gentleman considers it in violation of "decorum and consistence [sic]," and saw no benefit except in its "giving great scope for capital acting."[118] The most serious objections raised against Hamlet's antics are based less on their degradation of the tragic genre than on their marring of the tragic character: "it hurts the Reputation of his Heroe."[119] Hamlet's moral stature suffered in particular from his antics. George Steevens complained of "the immoral tendency of his character," including his abuse of Ophelia, his "outrage of decency" at her graveside, and his notorious desire to damn a man's soul, and thought him woefully undeserving of Horatio's requiem, "And flights of angels sing thee to thy rest."[120]

Steevens was also the first to consider a previously unexplored rationale for both Hamlet's indecorous buffoonery and his moral failures. As we saw in Chapter 5, a physician had proposed to him "that the conduct of Hamlet was every way unnatural and indefensible, unless he were to be regarded as a young man whose intellects were in some degree impaired by his own misfortunes."[121] Subsequent critics eagerly embrace this new defense, including the Scots critics who sought his exculpation in the psychological theory of self-deceit. Richardson saw his feigned madness as an extension of a real one: Hamlet counterfeits "an insanity which in part exists." Robertson in addition to his counterfeited madness allowed him "a degree of real phrenzy."[122] For these critics, the explanation for Hamlet's bizarre behavior lies not in feigned antics but in real instability. Mackenzie forgives his giddiness as the manifestation of a "delicate sensibility" which when suffering from melancholy allows itself "without feeling any degradation from the indulgence, a smile with the cheerful, and a laugh with the giddy." In such a personality, "gravity and elevation" often go hand in hand with "pleasantry and gaiety."[123] In his notes to the 1821 edition, Boswell maintained that the combination of levity and reflection occurred with particular frequency in "men of genius."[124] Coleridge is able to explain their concurrence by appealing to "a law of the human mind." Hamlet's "wild transition to the ludicrous" is the result of his encounter with the terrible: the "overwhelming and supernatural" appearance of the Ghost. The natural tendency of the mind after experiencing terror, explains Coleridge, is to seek relief. And so Hamlet does, by putting on a "cunning bravado," in the first instance with his eccentric, "Hillo, ho, ho, boy! Come, bird, come" (1.5.118). But this bluster is only "half false." The other half borders on "flights of delirium." Hamlet adopts the disguise of madness only when on the brink of madness: "he plays that subtle trick of pretending to act only when he is very near really being what he acts."[125]

Thus the role of the impertinent Antic-Vice gives way first to neo-classical judgment and then to psychological analysis. Decorum and psychology are both particularly challenged by the three scenes on which this book has focused: Hamlet's zaniness after the appearance of the Ghost, his frenzy at Ophelia's grave, and his fiendishness at the prayer scene. All three moments of high theatricality are recast as violations of decorum or psychopathological symptoms. Certainly, after the twenty-year shut-down of the theaters, it was not possible to access the traditional idioms of the moralities and mysteries which Hamlet deploys in giving vent to his biting disappointment. Standards of decorum at least preserved an allegiance to the theatre, a concern for what should and should not be enacted and spoken on stage. In a tragic hero, "sport" (3.4.208), "idle[ness]" (3.2.90, 3.4.10), "madness . . . in craft" (3.4.189–90), and "pranks" (3.4.2) are all indecorous. But psychology de-theatricalizes Hamlet's stunts, converting his pranks to symptoms, the result of "shock," "wound," "neurosis," or "pathology." After two hundred years, Hamlet's complex, elusive, and opaque interiority is so much a given of the play that it is assumed, even by the scholar who has done most to ground Hamlet's disposition in earlier popular stage traditions. "Hamlet, of course, is no Vice figure," Weimann insists, and repeatedly, "Hamlet, however, is no Vice."[126] Despite his emphasis on the affinities between Hamlet and the Antic-Vice, Hamlet remains the modern hero of consciousness: "Hamlet himself ultimately assumes the image of a more poetically unified individuality."[127] In this play above all, Weimann maintains, Shakespeare is working to synthesize into a fuller artistic unity the irregularities he had inherited from the medieval theatrical tradition, as if his career were following a Hegelian trajectory toward higher consciousness and a more integrated aesthetic. Despite all the evidence in theatrical practice to the contrary, Hamlet's status as the inaugural modern character remains unshaken.

Hamlet begins with the command to revenge ("Revenge his foul and most unnatural murder," 1.5.25), and ends with the satisfaction of the command ("Here, thou . . . damned Dane, / Drink off this potion," 5.2.330–1). Once the command (or vow) has been uttered, the deed is as good as done: the dictates of the convention demand it. From the start, the end is both imminent and immanent. The extremes are set, and the middle – the meantime – is all that remains. That meantime takes the form not of a telic advance from start to finish, but rather of a filling up between those two endpoints.[128] The play's multiple acts of revenge all conform to this structure. A pause invariably intervenes between the resolution to act and its execution. On the verge of striking Priam, Pyrrhus' sword sticks midair; about to pour poison in the sleeping king's ear, Lucianus bides his time; just before stabbing Hamlet with the envenomed rapier, Laertes wavers; and most centrally (indeed at the dead center of the play), Hamlet poised to exact his revenge: delays.

"Priam's slaughter" occurs in the speech Hamlet "chiefly loved" – "Aeneas' tale to Dido" describing the Fall of Troy (2.2.444, 442, 442–3). Hamlet may be right in claiming that this speech "was never acted, or if it was, not above once" (430–1), though Tacitus records that the Emperor Nero gave an impromptu performance of the Fall of Troy to the backdrop of burning Rome in the nine-day Great Fire of AD 64.[129] Whatever its history on stage, it was certainly reproduced in textual form, and copiously. Throughout the sixteenth century, Aeneas' long narration of the Fall of Troy that extends over two books of the *Aeneid* was the primary set-piece from which students learned the rhetorical skill of *copia* – of dilation or expansive embellishment through the generation of text.[130] Erasmus, in his influential *De Copia* recommends that the Fall of Troy be used in order to teach both brevity and copiousness and himself illustrates how the event can be either reduced to a mere six words ("And the fields, where Troy was") or expanded indefinitely (he gives a version of eight lines).[131] Shakespeare expands it to 217 lines when Lucrece fills up the hours between the dispatch of a messenger and his return with a long meditation on the "skilful painting" of the Fall of Troy hanging in her quarters.[132] It is from this tale that Hamlet selects one detail: "Priam's slaughter." The bloody avenger Pyrrhus locates his prey, strikes wide with a blow by whose mere "whiff and wind . . . Th'unnerved father falls" (2.2.469–70).

Pyrrhus then raises his sword as if to finish off the old king, but is arrested by the crash of Troy's topless towers. At this point the narrative itself pauses, punctuated by the interjection "For lo," and action comes to a tableau-like standstill.

> For lo, his sword,
> Which was declining on the milky head
> Of reverend Priam, seem'd i'th'air to stick;
> So, as a painted tyrant, Pyrrhus stood,
> And like a neutral to his will and matter,
> Did nothing.   (2.2.473–8)

Suspended between the intent and its execution, Pyrrhus is "like a neutral." His declining sword remains uplifted through a long periodic sentence of sixteen lines which postpones the fatal blow until its end: "Now falls on Priam" (488). The speech takes place in real time: it takes Pyrrhus' sword as long to fall on Priam as it does to deliver the dilation. (And the duration might be marked by the slow descent of the Player's upraised arm.). We have then a dilated passage, rendered in slow motion, drawn from the narrative "Aeneas' tale to Dido," that is the *locus classicus* of dilation, to mark the pause – "Pyrrhus's pause" – between the rise of the sword and its fall. "This is too long" (2.2.483), complains Polonius with some justification (though he grows impatient even in Q1's two-line rendition of the slaughter), and Hamlet orders it sent to the barber's to be cut, along with Polonius' beard.

Laertes' revenge also occurs after a pause. There is a long wait between his impetuous vow in the middle of Act 4 ("I'll be reveng'd/ Most thoroughly for my father," 4.5.135–6) and its performance in the final duel. He gets off to a roaring start when he storms the royal palace, but is then checked by the King ("forbeare a while," enjoins Claudius in Q1), and renews his vow ("But my revenge will come," 4.7.29), but not before he hears out Claudius' elaborate scheme. This is made even longer by the addition of several maxims (two in F, six in Q2) warning against the waning of passion over time: the "abatements and delays" (4.7.119) that come between what we *would* do and what we *do* do. When the time finally does come, Laertes hesitates. About to stab Hamlet with unbaited and poisoned sword, he pauses, "And yet it is almost against my conscience" (5.2.300). His hesitation is visible – that is, *staged* – so that Hamlet notices it and eggs him on, "You do but dally" (301).

All the play's assassins – Lucianus, Pyrrhus, Laertes, and Hamlet – hesitate before the act they intend. So, too, does Jepthah, the subject of the popular ballad Hamlet sings to Polonius. His story was one of the best known in the Bible (Judges 11:30–40), related in the homily "Against Swearing and Perjury" which was regularly read in all Anglican churches and the subject of several plays as well as ballads.[133] Jepthah, the captain of the Israelite forces against the Ammonites, vows to God that if victorious in battle he would sacrifice "the first quick thing" that he met upon returning home: it turns out to be his only child.

> O Jephthah, judge of Israel, what a treasure hadst thou! . . .
> One fair daughter and no more,
> The which he loved passing well.
>
> (2.2.399–400, 403–4)

The time between Jepthah's vow and its fulfillment is filled up with a two-month respite during which his virginal daughter with her maidens bemoans her fate in the wilderness. The ballad's narrative follows the same structure as the play: beginning with a vow and ending with its satisfaction, the interim is taken up with the dilational filler not of clowning but of complaint. Within Shakespeare's play, the ballad itself serves an intermissive function. Hamlet sings this stanza (or more, if the actor-playing-Hamlet so chooses) between the announcement of the Players' arrival ("My lord, I have news to tell you . . . The actors are come hither," 385–8) and their actual entrance ("Enter the Players," 416). When they arrive, he calls them his "abridgement" (416): they cut him off from his antics.

There is no assassin to blame for Ophelia's death, though in the eyes of the Church she is a *felo da se* who receives the abbreviated funeral rites of one who "did with desp'rate hand/ Fordo it own life" (5.1.213–14). "Your sister's drown'd" (4.7.163) announces Gertrude, and then in her account draws out the time between Ophelia's fall into the brook and her sinking to muddy death. "Her clothes spread wide" (174) and for "awhile they bore her up" (175), long enough for her to sing snatches of old tunes; but "long it could not be" (179) before her saturated garments pull her down to the bottom of the river bed. Gertrude's narrative has her buoyant above the water, "mermaid-like" (175), for six lines, and then by the force of gravity, like the poised swords of Pyrrhus, Hamlet, and Laertes, she eventually, after a melodious interlude, drops, in a periodic sentence that follows the same suspenseful trajectory.

A pause also occurs when Hamlet in his most famous soliloquy considers "self-slaughter" (1.2.132). As he contemplates whether "To be, or not to be" (3.1.56) and the easy solution of making his "quietus . . . [w]ith a bare bodkin" (3.1.75–6), his own dagger may be bared and raised, like the sword he holds over the praying Claudius or the one that seemed to "stick" (2.2.475) in the air over Priam's head. Indeed in considering whether "To be or not to be," Hamlet seems at first to favor the second alternative. Rather than suffer further "[t]he heart-ache and the thousand natural shocks that flesh is heir to" (3.1.62–3), he is tempted to finish himself off, embracing the "consummation devoutly to be wish'd" (63–4). Preferable to life's jolts and pains is the *requiem aeternum* to which the dead are consigned at burial, the sleep of death: "To die, to sleep" (64). (At his death, Horatio will bid angels deliver him to this heavenly rest, 5.2.365.) But then second thoughts occur, "To die, to sleep; to sleep, perchance to dream" (64–5) and he stops short, like a ball in a game of bowls blocked by a "rub" or obstacle: "ay, there's the rub." Hamlet makes it very clear what that "rub" is:

> For in that sleep of death what dreams may come,
> When we have shuffled off this mortal coil,
> Must give us pause.   (3.1.66–8)

We pause at the fearful prospect of posthumous dreams, the "dread of something after death" (78). While Hamlet has no trouble imagining the afterlife of the body (to Horatio's mind, he does so only "too curiously," 5.1.199), his mind balks at thoughts of what happens after death to the soul. Like the "thoughts beyond the reaches of our souls" (1.4.56) excited by the Ghost's appearance, they cannot be grasped, only vaguely indicated through nondescript substantives: "the respect," "ills . . . we know not of," "pale cast of thought," "regard" (3.1.68, 81–2, 85, 87). The Ghost has experienced those dreaded dreams – they are, as it were, his reality – but is forbidden to tell their "secrets" (1.5.14). He describes not the secrets, therefore, but the effect they would have if disclosed:

> I could a tale unfold whose lightest word
> Would harrow up thy soul, freeze thy young blood,
> Make thy two eyes like stars start from their spheres,
> Thy knotted and combined locks to part,
> And each particular hair to stand an end
> Like quills upon the fretful porpentine.   (1.5.15–20)

As the sight of the Medusa turned spectators to stone, the mere mention of that dreadful "something after death" (3.1.78) would petrify auditors: their blood would freeze, their hair stiffen. If it were to enter "ears of flesh and blood" (1.5.22) it would mortify, like the "leperous distilment" (1.5.64) poured into the sleeping king's ears.

The Ghost's postmortem existence is living proof that death is less an end than a long repose prior to the final end, what Q1 terms the "General ending" (Bv) or Doomsday. When dying, Hamlet imagines Death as a stern officer of the law: "this fell sergeant, Death/ Is strict in his arrest" (5.2.341–2). Once arrested, the dead, like the Ghost, remain "confin'd" as in a "prison-house" (1.5.11, 14). Q1 specifies the limit of that confinement: the dreams that begin in the "sleep of death" will end at Judgment Day, "when wee awake, / And borne before an everlasting Iudge"; "The happy smile, and the accursed damn'd" (D4v). The Old Faith gave form and color to that long sleep, that "something after death" (3.1.78) through the fiction of purgatory, the place where the guilty dead, "for a certain term" (1.5.10) depending on their record, eked out the interval between this world and the next in excruciating pain – the eschatological version of the "law's delay" – while awaiting the verdict of the Last Judgment. In 1645,

when Archbishop Laud, impeached for High Treason, approached the
scaffold, observers noted his sanguine confidence. But once on the block,
according to one eye-witness, "he trembled every joint of him; the sense of
something after death, and the undiscovered country unto which his soul
was wandering startling his resolution, and possessing every joint of him
with an universal palsy of fear."[134] From Hamlet's most famous soliloquy
comes the rhetoric for that "palsy" or seizure that takes hold between the
anticipation of death and its arrival, between the rise and fall of the
executioner's axe.

Only one of the play's last-minute hiatuses has received critical attention, Pyrrhus' "pause" before slaying Priam, and mainly as an analogue for
Hamlet's delay in the prayer scene, the tableau of Hamlet's problem.[135]
But there is a much grander model for the medial structure of the play's
central action and its many reenactments. Salvational history begins with
the Fall in Genesis and is to end at Doomsday as forecast in Revelation.
The intervening books of the Bible represent the history between the
recorded beginning and the promised but indeterminate end. After Adam
and Eve break God's commandment, their end is set before them: "For in
the day that thou eatest thereof thou shalt surely die" (Gen. 2:17). As
exegetes explained, however, death did not occur on that specific "day,"
but was deferred, so that "the day that thou eatest thereof" was expanded
to comprehend "all the days of Adam's life" which ended only at the ripe
age of 930 years. Milton with exquisite compression describes this remit-
tance: Christ sentences the fallen Adam and Eve to death, but "th'instant
stroke of Death denounc't that day/ Remov'd far off." Death was not
instantaneous (as feared) but deferred indefinitely.[136] As the angel Michael
explains, the very day of Death's "seizure" is postponed; Adam and Eve
are given an extension – "many days/ [are] Giv'n thee of Grace." This is
the first grace period, extra time between the sentence and its execution,
granted for the purpose of making amends: "wherein thou mayst repent/
And one bad act with many deeds well done/ May'st cover."[137]

But the pronouncement was not only deferred; in time, it was also
converted, from a sentence of death to a promise of everlasting life. This is
the good news of the Gospel. From St. Paul onward, the structure of the
promise provided the typological relation between the Old and New
Testaments. The events of Israel's history narrated in the earlier testament
were types prefiguring the promise of Christ delivered by the later. As
Milton's account also emphasized, that promise was implicit in the
original sentence of Genesis, in the form of the *protoevangelum*, the "first
gospel" or news of the Messiah, addressed to the offending serpent: "I will

put enmity between you and the woman, and between your offspring and hers; He will crush your head, while you strike at his heel" (Gen. 3:15). These words were taken as prophecy that Christ would defeat Sin and Death through his own sacrifice. (According to Luther, Adam and Eve precipitously expected Abel, woman's first offspring, would be the one to deal the blow.[138]) What took many generations to unfold in time was implied from the start in the mystical wording of that pronouncement. One foreclosed structure superseded the other: the promise overtook the sentence. And between the termini of the sentence-turned-promise and its execution-turned-fulfillment, stretched a middle of indefinite duration known as world history.

How readily the dilational and dilatory parousial structure translated into dramatic form is apparent from the late-fifteenth-century *Everyman* which begins when Everyman is summoned by the "strict sergeant Death" and ends in the anticipation of "the day of doom," and in the middle is his pilgrimage toward that final reckoning of Last Judgment. Although ordered to appear "Without delay or any tarrying," Everyman does his best to bide his time before the final reckoning: "To give a reckoning longer leisure I crave"; "defer this matter till another day"; "Alas, shall I have no longer respite?"[139] Like *Everyman*, *Hamlet* is structured in the shadow of the *katechon*, the participle of *katechein*, the verb signifying both to "delay" as well as to "encompass." It is used by Paul to describe the power that at once holds back and maintains the end of time (2 Thess. 2:6).[140]

In *Hamlet*, the revenge command sets the two termini in place and the interim is filled with the heap of events reported by Horatio. The first act reports of a serpent in a garden, the last act opens in a graveyard foreshadowing Doomsday. In the middle is the messy stuff of Horatio's promised summary: "carnal, bloody, and unnatural acts," "accidental judgments, casual slaughters," "purposes mistook / Fall'n on th'inventors' heads" (5.2.386, 387, 389–90). In the middle of that medial span is the prayer scene (often considered the play's turning-point) in which the sinful Claudius takes time to fall to his knees in prayer. Hamlet gives him still more time, though hardly to repent: "This physic but prolongs thy sickly days" (3.3.96). In another refinement of diabolic iniquity, he allows Claudius a reprieve, giving him additional time not to strengthen his chances of salvation but utterly to destroy them.

Ultimately it is Hamlet's end and not his victim's that is the focus of the tragedy. His death is first deferred by his thoughtful suicidal pause or rub. Before the play's close, he will receive two other deadlines. As Hamlet recounts, Claudius issues "an exact command" that "[m]y head should be struck off" (25). This is Claudius' missive to the King of England, voiced with a special urgency when addressed to an English audience, "Do it, England" (4.3.68). Hamlet intercepts Claudius' command with a forgery which substitutes the heads of the emissaries for his own: "An earnest conjuration . . . He should those bearers put to sudden death" (5.2.38–46). The substitution allows Hamlet not to escape death but to postpone it. As Horatio points out, the revised command gives him only as much time as it takes for Rosencrantz and Guildenstern to sail to England, be executed, and then for word of the execution to reach Denmark. Hamlet's time will then be up, for the report of the messengers' execution will expose his forgery. Claudius will know what he has until now only feared and suspected: that Hamlet is not mad but scheming against him. As Hamlet allows, this deadline leaves him little leeway: "It will be short. The interim is mine" (5.2.73). But when Hamlet accepts Laertes' challenge to a duel, another deadline is interposed. In Q2, an emissary enters with no purpose except to ask Hamlet if he would like to postpone the match. "Now or whensoever" (5.2.199), replies Hamlet. And repeats the sentiment, as if bracing himself for Death's imminent arrest, "The readiness is all" (5.2.218), an echo of passages in Matthew and Luke which urge preparation for the unknown time of the Second Coming: "Be ye therefore ready also; For the Son of man cometh at an hour when you think not." Like the "General ending" (Q1, Bv) of the world, the particular ending of a man's life is either now or later, and an indefinite span occurs between these points: "If it be not now, yet it will come" (5.2.217–18). There is, however, no further extension. The English ambassadors arrive and announce that the "commandment is fulfill'd" (5.2.375): Rosencrantz and Guildenstern are dead. But they are too late ("And our affairs from England come too late," 373) to receive thanks from its issuer. Death has already made its "strict . . . arrest" (5.2.342).[141]

"In thee there is not half an hour's life" (321), warns Laertes after wounding Hamlet with the poison which Claudius predicts in Q1 "[s]hall be his period" (H4). Half an hour is the time between the delivery of the fatal wound and death, the time it takes the poison from the envenomed sword to run through the bloodstream. With that deadline before him, Hamlet manages to cram in a great deal: he kills the king twice-over, exchanges forgiveness with Laertes, prevents Horatio's suicide, secures his own good report, and endorses Fortinbras's succession. Half an hour is a short time to have left to live in real life but a very long time to be dying on stage. Hamlet draws out his expiration, as if to claim every instant of his allotment: "I am dead, Horatio" (5.2.338); "Horatio, I am dead"

204

Hamlet without Hamlet

The potent poyſon quite ore-crowes my ſpirit,
I cannot liue to heare the Newes from England,
But I do propheſie th'election lights
On *Fortinbras*, he ha's my dying voyce,
So tell him with the occurrents more and leſſe,
Which haue ſolicited. The reſt is ſilence. O,o,o,o. *Dyes*

Illustration 19. Hamlet's "dying voice," *The Tragedie of Hamlet*, in *Mr. William Shakespeares Comedies, Histories, & Tragedies* (London, 1623).

(343); "O, I die, Horatio" (357); "The potent poison quite o'ercrows my spirit" (358); and finally, "The rest is silence" (363). But not quite. In the Folio, Hamlet's final sentence is followed by a series of interjections (Illustration 19). The notation in F, like an etcetera, may well signal the opportunity for the actor to drag out his dying moment still further with some form of utterance: a moan or gasp, perhaps, or a profounder kind of exhalation like the "sigh" with which Hamlet in Ophelia's closet pretended to "end his being" (2.1.94, 96). (Richard Burbage, the great tragedian who first played Hamlet, was remembered in his elegy for his virtuoso performance of death.[142]) Hamlet is certainly keenly aware of the histrionics of the moment and takes note of his spellbound audience, both on the stage and off: "You that look pale and tremble at this chance,/ That are but mutes or audience to this act" (5.2.339–40). Between the "silence" (363) that is his last word and the cardiac "crack" (364) that sounds his final passing, he is given his last chance to exceed the script. "O, o, o, o" reserves for the player-playing-Hamlet a final opportunity to indulge that "most pitiful ambition" of holding on to the stage, just before the imperially ambitious Fortinbras stakes out his ancestral claim to the realm.[143]

In his final tribute to Hamlet, Fortinbras acknowledges the possibility that never materialized: "he was likely, had he been put on/ To have prov'd most royal" (5.2.402–3). It is the possibility which, once foreclosed, both precipitates the plot and individuates the main character. It is also the possibility which the 200-year-old critical tradition has slighted, in its enshrinement of Hamlet at the forefront of the modern, over and above the very worldly preoccupations of the play whose name he shares.

Notes

INTRODUCTION

1 Harold Jenkins, ed., *Hamlet*, Arden edn. (London and New York: Methuen, 1982), 1.2.159. Subsequent references to the play are keyed to this edition and will appear parenthetically in the text.

2 Sir Edward Coke, *The Second Part of the Institutes of the Lawes of England*, in Steve Sheppard, ed., *The Selected Writings and Speeches of Sir Edward Coke*, 3 vols. (Indianapolis: Liberty Fund, 2003), II:962.

CHAPTER 1: MODERN HAMLET

1 Harold Bloom, *Shakespeare: The Invention of the Human* (New York: Riverhead, 1998), 409; Jonathan Bate, *The Genius of Shakespeare* (London: Picador, 1997), 261; Alexander Welsh, *Hamlet in His Modern Guises* (Princeton, NJ: Princeton University Press, 2001), x; Marjorie Garber, *Shakespeare After All* (New York: Pantheon Books, 2004), 4.

2 For evidence of an *Ur-Hamlet*, see Harold Jenkins, ed., *Hamlet*, Arden edn. (London and New York: Methuen, 1982), 82–5. William Empson discusses Shakespeare's challenge of having to revamp "an out-of-date object," in *Essays on Shakespeare*, ed. David B. Pirie (Cambridge: Cambridge University Press, 1986), 79.

3 Thomas Nashe, Preface to Greene's *Menaphon* (1589), quoted in Jenkins, ed., *Hamlet*, 83.

4 Thomas Lodge, *Wit's Miser* (1596), cited in *ibid.*, 83.

5 *Ibid.*, 1.2.72, 1.3.78, 5.2.10. Unless otherwise noted, all quotations from the play follow Jenkins' Arden edition and appear parenthetically in the text.

6 For a transcription of this manuscript note in Gabriel Harvey's 1598 copy of Chaucer's *Workes*, see Appendix, in *ibid.*, 573–4.

7 Paul S. Conklin counts twenty-three allusions to the ghost in the seventeenth century; see his *A History of "Hamlet" Criticism, 1601–1821* (London: F. Cass, 1968), 10, n. 6.

8 Anthony Scoloker, *Diaphantus; or, the Passions of Love* (1604), in *Critical Responses to "Hamlet": 1600–1900*, ed. David Farley-Hills, 4 vols. (New York: AMS Press, 1995–), I:2. Hereafter cited as *CR*.

9 Conklin, *History*, 18–19.

10 *Eastward Ho*, in G. A. Wilkes, ed., *The Complete Plays of Ben Jonson*, 4 vols. (Oxford: Clarendon Press, 1981), II (3.2.3–6).

11 The line appears only in the 1623 Folio and therefore is omitted from Jenkins' edition, which follows the 1604 Second Quarto.

12 "A Funeral Elegy on the Death of Richard Burbage" (1618), in E. K. Chambers, *The Elizabethan Stage*, 2 vols. (Oxford: Oxford University Press, 1923), II:309.

13 For evidence of the popularity of Hamlet's antics in the seventeenth century, see Conklin, *History*, 16–20; for reports of Hamlet's hyperactivity in seventeenth- and eighteenth-century productions, see John A. Mills, *"Hamlet" on Stage: The Great Tradition* (WestPort, CT: Greenwood Press, 1985), 4–5. For Hamlet's participation in the antic traditions of popular festival and guild productions, see Robert Weimann, *Shakespeare and the Popular Tradition in the Theater: Studies in the Social Dimension of Dramatic Form and Function*, ed. Robert Schwartz (Baltimore: Johns Hopkins University Press, 1978), esp. 125–33, and *"Hamlet* and the Purposes of Playing," in Weimann, *Author's Pen and Actor's Voice: Playing and Writing in Shakespeare's Theatre*, ed. Helen Higbee and William West (Cambridge: Cambridge University Press, 2000), esp. 166–79. For the upstaging of Hamlet's antics by the modern preoccupation with his inner state, see Margreta de Grazia, "Hamlet the Intellectual," in *The Public Intellectual*, ed. Helen Small (Oxford and Malden, MA: Blackwell, 2002), 89–109.

14 John Evelyn, diary entry of 26 November 1661, in *CR*, I:14.

15 On the use of "the last age" in the late seventeenth and eighteenth centuries, see Jack Lynch, *The Age of Elizabeth in the Age of Johnson* (Cambridge and New York: Cambridge University Press, 2003).

16 Samuel Johnson, Preface to edition of Shakespeare (1765), in *Shakespeare: The Critical Heritage*, ed. Brian Vickers, 6 vols. (London and Boston: Routledge and Kegan Paul, 1974–81), V:74. Hereafter cited as *CH*.

17 David Hume, *The History of Great Britain* (1754), in *CH*, IV:173.

18 Thomas Rymer, *A Short View* (1693), quoted in Weimann, *Popular Tradition*, 185.

19 Thomas Warburton, Preface to Shakespeare (1747), in *CR*, I:154.

20 Alexander Pope, ed., *The Works of Shakespeare*, 6 vols. (London: J. Tonson, 1723–5), The Preface, I:xxiii.

21 See note 6 above.

22 Shakespeare himself uses "modern" interchangeably with "recent" to imply a comparison with something prior. When Jaques refers to "wise saws and modern instances" (*As You Like It*, 2.7.155), a contrast is assumed between the former (axioms formulated of old) and the latter (recent examples that confirm their truth). Similarly "the modern friends" for whom the captive Cleopatra sets aside a few trifling jewels are of slight and passing importance, we must assume, compared to tried-and-true-alliances (*Antony and Cleopatra*, 5.2.163). So, too, the "modern grace" by which Bertram claims Diana seduced him is the result, to his mind, of makeshift superficial artifice as opposed to

the inbred attraction of aristocratic lineage (*All's Well That Ends Well*, 5.3.218). In all these instances, "modern" suggests the derivative and ephemeral, generally implying a decline from what came before. This is especially so when poetry is the subject. In Sonnet 83, when Shakespeare disparages the "modern quill" that falls short of its subject, he undoubtedly intends it to be measured against the more skillful pen of an Ovid or a Horace. (See John Kerrigan, ed., *The Sonnets and "A Lover's Complaint"* [Harmondsworth: Penguin, 1986], 277, n. 7.) Sonnet 59 explicitly invokes the contrast when the poet looks "in some antique book" to determine "Whether we are mended, or whe'er better they." With the exception of *Hamlet*, all works by Shakespeare are cited from Stephen Greenblatt et al., eds., *The Norton Shakespeare* (New York: Norton, 1997).

23 *Oxford English Dictionary*, 2nd edn., A1. For similar uses of the Latin *modernus* from the fifth century through the middle ages, see Hans Ulrich Gumbrecht, *Making Sense in Life and Literature*, trans. Glen Burns (Minneapolis, MN: University of Minnesota Press, 1992), 81–2.

24 Earl of Shaftesbury, *Characteristicks of Men, Manners, Opinions, Times* (1710), in *CR*, I:38.

25 Lewis Theobald, *Shakespeare Restored* (London, 1726), v.

26 James Drake, *The Antient and Modern Stages Survey'd* (1699), in *CR*, I:22.

27 See Margreta de Grazia, *Shakespeare Verbatim: The Reproduction of Authenticity and the 1790 Apparatus* (Oxford: Clarendon Press, 1991), 44–6.

28 David Hume, *History*, in *CH*, IV:174; Voltaire, "Dissertation sur la Tragédie" (1752), quoted in Conklin, *History*, 88.

29 John Dennis, *An Essay upon the Genius and Writings of Shakespeare* (1711), in *CR*, I:50.

30 *Ibid.*

31 Johnson, Preface to edition of Shakespeare (1765), in *CH*, V:55.

32 Brian Vickers, "The Emergence of Character Criticism, 1774–1800," *Shakespeare Survey* 34 (1981), 11–12.

33 Aristotle, *Poetics*, trans. Richard Janko (Indianapolis, IN: Hackett, 1987), 3.1.3.

34 Pope, Preface, v.

35 Nicholas Rowe, *Life of Shakespeare* (1709), in *CR*, I:30–1.

36 For a summary of the *Querrelle des anciens et des modernes*, see Robert J. Nelson, "The Ancients and the Moderns," in *A New History of French Literature*, ed. Denis Hollier (Cambridge, MA: Harvard University Press, 1989), 364–9.

37 Charles Gildon, *Remarks on the Plays of Shakespeare* (1710), in *CR*, I:41.

38 George Stubbes, *Some Remarks on "The Tragedy of Hamlet"* (1736 facs. rpt.; New York: AMS Press, 1975), 24, 41. Boswell/Malone in 1821 reproduce much of the essay at the end of their edition of *Hamlet*, in *The Plays and Poems of William Shakspeare*, ed. Edmond Malone and James Boswell, 21 vols. (1821; New York: AMS Press, 1966). Other eighteenth-century writers who draw the Orestes/Hamlet parallel are Jean-Bernard Le Blanc, *Letters on the English and French Nations* (1747), the anonymous author of *Observations on the "Tragedy*

of Hamlet" (1752), John Upton, *Critical Observations on Shakespeare* (1748), and William Richardson, *A Philosophical Analysis* (1774).

39 For an account of how this controversy contributed to the definition of ancient and modern as distinct historical periods, see Gumbrecht, *Making Sense*, 84–5, and Fredric Jameson, *A Singular Modernity: Essay on the Ontology of the Present* (London and New York: Verso, 2002), 20–2.

40 Henry Mackenzie, No. 99, *Mirror*, 18 April 1780, in *CR*, I:270.

41 William Richardson, *Essay on Shakespeare's Dramatic Characters* (1798).

42 Thomas Robertson, *An Essay on the Character of Hamlet* (1790), in *CR*, II:13.

43 S. T. Coleridge, "1811–12 Lectures on Shakespeare & Milton," in Coleridge, *Lectures 1808–1819 on Literature*, ed. R. A. Foakes, Bollingen Series, 2 vols. (London: Routledge and Kegan Paul, and Princeton, NJ: Princeton University Press, 1987), 1:386. Passage in square brackets is from Collier's report on this lecture, in *CR*, II:54. Unless otherwise indicated, subsequent references to Coleridge are from Foakes' edition and appear parenthetically in the text.

44 Coleridge, "Notes on *Hamlet*", in *CR*, II:72. Shakespeare, he maintained, "regarded his stories little more than a painter does his canvas," Foakes, ed., *Lectures*, II:456.

45 In the passage quoted in text from Lecture 5, Coleridge ends mid-sentence, as indicated by the square brackets. I have inserted Foakes' suggestion for the sequel (1:466–7, n. 5), taken verbatim from John Black's English translation of Schlegel's *Course of Lectures on Dramatic Art and Literature* (Philadelphia: Hogan and Thompson, 1833), 275.

46 Coleridge, *S. T. Coleridge's Treatise on Method*, ed. Alice D. Snyder (London: Constable, 1934), 26. The treatise was first published as the General Introduction to *The Encyclopaedia Metropolitana* (1818).

47 Coleridge, *Treatise*, 32, n. 3.

48 *Ibid.*, 30. According to Foakes, the earliest record of Coleridge's use of the term is in *Essays on His Times* (1800). Foakes also notes Coleridge's use of *psycho-analytical* in 1818, almost a century before the *OED*'s first citation. For both references, see Coleridge, *Lectures*, ed. Foakes, II:94, n. 14. For the German origins of the word, and its first use in English in 1748 by David Hartley, the philosopher after whom Coleridge named his son, see Jacob Isaacs, "Coleridge's Critical Terminology," *Essays and Studies* 21 (1936), 94–5.

49 Coleridge, *Treatise*, 30. For Friedrich Schlegel's opinion that *Hamlet* was "the first and greatest of the *psychologische Romane*," see William Kerrigan, *Hamlet's Perfection* (Baltimore: Johns Hopkins University Press, 1994), 7 and 155, n. 10. For Coleridge's borrowings and adaptations from Schlegel, mainly unacknowledged, see Foakes' introduction to *Lectures*, 1:lix-lxi.

50 Coleridge contrasts Hamlet's report with Hostess Quickly's account in *2 Henry IV* (2.1.78–94) in order to demonstrate the difference between recollection mediated by reflection and recollection based on impressions, in *Treatise*, 27–30.

51 *Ibid.*, 31.

52 *Ibid.*, 29–30.

53 *Ibid.*, 31.

54 Coleridge, "Notes on *Hamlet*," in *CR*, II:60.

55 G. W. F. Hegel, *Aesthetics: Lectures on Fine Art*, trans. T. M. Knox, 2 vols. (Oxford and New York: Clarendon Press, 1998), II:1158. Subsequent page references are included in text.

56 Because conditions in the East did not, according to Hegel, allow for individual freedom and therefore accountability, "the whole Eastern outlook inhibits *ab initio* an adequate development of dramatic art," *ibid.*, II:1205.

57 On plot as so many "acts or omissions thoroughly expressive of the doer," see A. C. Bradley, *Shakespearean Tragedy: Lectures on "Hamlet", "Othello", "King Lear", "Macbeth"* (1904; Harmondsworth: Penguin, 1991), 29. In discussing *Hamlet*'s plot in Lecture 4, he follows "the course of the action in so far as it specially illustrates the character," 127.

58 William Hazlitt, *Characters of Shakespear's Plays* (1817), in *CR*, II:114.

59 G. G. Gervinus, *Shakespeare Commentaries*, trans. F. E. Bunnètt, rev. edn. (1877 facs. rpt; New York: AMS Press, 1971), 575.

60 Ralph Waldo Emerson, *Representative Men: Seven Lectures*, ed. Douglas Emory Wilson (Cambridge, MA: Harvard University Press, 1996), 117.

61 Georg Brandes, *William Shakespeare: A Critical Study* (New York: Macmillan, 1902), 388.

62 Bradley, *Tragedy*, 95. Subsequent references to Bradley appear in the text. For the view that *Hamlet* criticism did not properly begin until about 1800, see Empson, *Essays*, 80. William Kerrigan begins *Hamlet's Perfection* with the claim that Hamlet's history "begins in Romantic Germany" and accordingly omits seventeenth- and eighteenth-century critics from his survey of "*Hamlet* in History" (1–33). For the view that Hamlet's interiority exists from the start, though lacking a vocabulary of interiority until Hazlitt, see John Lee, *Hamlet and the Controversies of the Self* (Oxford: Clarendon Press, 2000), esp. Part 2, 95–145.

63 For J. G. Herder, see Horace Howard Furness, ed., *Hamlet*, Variorum edn., 2 vols. (1877; New York: Dover, 1963), II:276–8. For Schlegel, see Hans Eichner, *Friedrich Schlegel* (New York: Twayne, 1970), 25.

64 Sigmund Freud, "An Autobiographical Study," in *The Freud Reader*, ed. Peter Gay (New York: Norton, 1989), 38.

65 Ernest Jones, *Hamlet and Oedipus* (New York: Norton, 1976), 68.

66 Freud, "Autobiographical Study", 18.

67 Freud, *The Interpretation of Dreams*, in *The Basic Writings of Sigmund Freud*, ed. and trans. A. A. Brill (New York: Modern Library, 1938), 309.

68 Jacques Lacan, "Desire and the Interpretation of Desire in *Hamlet*," trans. James Hulbert, in *Literature and Psychoanalysis: The Question of Reading, Otherwise*, ed. Shoshana Felman (Baltimore: Johns Hopkins University Press, 1982), 39. Subsequent page references appear in the text. For a discussion of Lacan's reading of *Hamlet* as a rehabilitation of Freud's that "both propagates and distends the Freudian legacy," see Richard Halpern,

Shakespeare Among the Moderns (Ithaca, NY: Cornell University Press, 1997), 254.

69 Julia Reinhard Lupton and Kenneth Reinhard discuss the continuing relevance of *Hamlet* to developments within psychoanalysis, and themselves extend the Lacanian trajectory by introducing the mother as the bearer of loss. See *After Oedipus: Shakespeare in Psychoanalysis* (Ithaca, NY: Cornell University Press, 1993), 1–33. For a more lucid account of this progression, see Jean-Michel Rabaté, "*Hamlet* and the Desire of the Mother," in his *Jacques Lacan: Psychoanalysis and the Subject of Literature* (Basingstoke, Hampshire and New York: Palgrave, 2001), 54–68, 61.

70 Nicolas Abraham and Maria Torok, *The Shell and the Kernel: Renewals of Psychoanalysis*, ed. and trans. Nicholas T. Rand (Chicago: University of Chicago Press, 1994), 190.

71 *Ibid.*, 188.

72 Jacques Derrida, *Specters of Marx: The State of Debt, the Work of Mourning, and the New International*, trans. Peggy Kamuf (New York: Routledge, 1994), xix, 25, 168.

73 *Ibid.*, 12.

74 On the modernist imperative to avoid reproducing the stereotypical Hamlet, see Halpern's "Hamletmachines," in *Among the Moderns*, 227–88.

75 Compare Paul de Man's identification of the modern with "a desire to wipe out whatever came earlier, in the hope of reaching at last a point that could be called a true present, a point of origin that marks a new departure," in "Literary History and Literary Modernity," in *Blindness and Insight: Essays in the Rhetoric of Contemporary Criticism*, 2nd edn. (Minneapolis: University of Minnesota Press, 1983), 143, 148.

76 Terry Eagleton, *William Shakespeare* (Oxford and New York: Blackwell, 1986), 75; compare Francis Barker's observation that Hamlet's "promise of essential subjectivity remains unfulfilled," in his *The Tremulous Private Body: Essays on Subjection* (London and New York: Methuen, 1984), 38.

77 Harold Bloom, *Shakespeare: The Invention of the Human* (New York: Riverhead, 1998), 429; Bloom, *"Hamlet": Poem Unlimited* (New York: Riverhead, 2003), 7.

CHAPTER 2: "OLD MOLE": THE MODERN *TELOS* AND THE RETURN TO DUST

1 Harold Jenkins, ed., *Hamlet*, Arden edn. (London and New York: Methuen, 1982), 1.5.157, 163. Unless otherwise specified, all citations from the play follow this edition and appear parenthetically in the text.

2 G. W. F. Hegel, *Lectures on the History of Philosophy*, trans. E. S. Haldane and Frances H. Simson, 3 vols. (Lincoln, NE and London: University of Nebraska Press, 1995), III:547.

3 Virgil, *Aeneid*, in *Virgil*, trans. H. Rushton Fairclough, rev. G. P. Goold, 2 vols. (Cambridge, MA: Harvard University Press, 1999–2000), I:33.

4 Hegel, *The History of Philosophy*, 546.

5 Hegel, *The Philosophy of History*, trans. J. Sibree (New York: Dover Publications, 1956), 110, 109. All subsequent references to this work are included parenthetically in the text.

6 Karl Marx, *Capital: A Critique of Political Economy*, trans. Ben Fowkes (New York: Penguin, 1976), 925. All subsequent references are included parenthetically in text.

7 Karl Marx, *The German Ideology: Part I*, in *The Marx-Engels Reader*, 2nd edn., ed. Robert C. Tucker (New York and London: Norton, 1978), 166.

8 Marx, *The Eighteenth Brumaire of Louis Bonaparte*, in *Marx-Engels*, ed. Tucker, 606. Marx also identifies the "old mole" with "the Revolution" in his speech of 14 April 1856 on the anniversary of the Chartist *People's Paper*, as cited by S. S. Prawer, *Karl Marx and World Literature* (Oxford: Clarendon Press, 1967), 246. For the philosophical moles of his doctoral dissertation on Democritus and Epicurus (1830), see Hans Blumenberg, *The Legitimacy of the Modern Age*, trans. Robert M. Wallace (Cambridge, MA and London: MIT Press, 1991), 142. For further discussion of the mole's importance to Marx's materialism, see Peter Stallybrass, "'Well Grubbed, Old Mole': Marx, Hamlet, and the (Un)Fixing of Representation," *Cultural Studies* 12:1 (1998), 3–14.

9 Friedrich Engels, *The Condition of the Working Classes in England*, ed. David McLellan (Oxford and New York: Oxford University Press, 1993), "The Miners," 274–94, esp. 282.

10 On the attachment of *Quem queritis in sepulchro, Christicole* to the liturgy and its subsequent dramatization, see Karl Young, ed., *The Drama of the Medieval Church*, 2 vols. (Oxford: Clarendon Press, 1967), I:201–491.

11 Hegel, *History of Modern Philosophy*, III:547.

12 Marx, *Manifesto of the Communist Party*, in *Marx-Engels*, ed. Tucker, 500; Marx, *Eighteenth Brumaire*, in *ibid.*, 598.

13 *Ibid.*, 597.

14 Hegel, *Aesthetics: Lectures on Fine Art*, trans. T. M. Knox, 2 vols. (Oxford and New York: Clarendon Press, 1998), II:1225.

15 *Ibid.*, II:1226.

16 *Ibid.*, II:1231, and Hegel, *The Philosophy of Fine Art*, trans. F. P. B. Osmaston, 4 vols. (New York: Hacker Art Books, 1975), IV:342.

17 Hegel, *Aesthetics*, II:1214.

18 William Camden, *Remaines concerning Britain* (1657 facs. rpt.; New York: AMS Press, 1972), 19.

19 See Ovid, *Ovid's Metamorphoses*, trans. Arthur Golding, ed. Frederick Nims (1603; Philadelphia: Paul Dry Books, 2000), 1.101–2.

20 Plutarch, *The Philosophie, commonlie called, The Morals*, trans. Philemon Holland (London, 1603), 671.

21 Lucretius, *On the Nature of Things*, trans. Martin Ferguson Smith (Indianapolis, IN and Cambridge: Hackett Publishing, 2001), 5.927–8.

22 Andrew Boorde, *The Breviary of Health* (1552), in Jenkins, ed., *Hamlet*, 528.

23 Gail Kern Paster, *The Body Embarrassed: Drama and the Disciplines of Shame in Early Modern England* (Ithaca, NY: Cornell University Press, 1993), 69.

24 Robert Alter draws out the cognates in his translation of Genesis, "then the Lord God fashioned the human, humus from the soil," in *The Five Books of Moses: A Translation with Commentary* (New York: Norton, 2004).

25 Sir Walter Raleigh, *The History of the World* (London, 1614), 1.2.4.

26 For the formula provided in William Weste's *Simboleography, which may be termed the Art, or Description, of Instruments and Presidents* (1615), see Samuel Schoenbaum, *William Shakespeare: A Documentary Life* (New York: Oxford University Press and the Scholar Press, 1975), 246.

27 In Geoffrey Bullough, ed., *Narrative and Dramatic Sources of Shakespeare*, 8 vols. (London: Routledge and Kegan Paul, and New York: Columbia University Press, 1957–75), VII:62, 90.

28 See Jenkins, ed., *Hamlet*, 89 and 234, n. 2.1.79.

29 First introduced by John Dover Wilson in his 1934 edition of the play, "sullied" is the favored emendation for "sallied flesh" (Q1, Q2) and "solid Flesh" (F), but the interchangeability of "sullied" (and "soiled") and "sallied" in the early texts has been demonstrated by Patricia Parker, "Black *Hamlet*: Battening on the Moor," *Shakespeare Studies* 31 (2003), 131.

30 Andrew Gurr and Mariko Ichikawa suggest that the Q2 spelling "Ostricke" may reference an ostrich feather, "the supreme ornament of late Elizabethan gallantry," in *Staging in Shakespeare's Theatres* (Oxford: Oxford University Press, 2000), 154.

31 For "chuff" (F *chough* and Q2 *Chowgh*) as *churl* or *rustic* and its identification with farmers' sons aspiring to the ranks of the landed, see G. R. Hibbard, ed., *Hamlet* (Oxford and New York: Oxford University Press, 1994), 340, n. 5.2.89.

32 John Nowden, *Speculum Britanniae* (1593), cited by *OED*, 2nd edn., *hide sb* 2:1.

33 Andrew Gurr, *The Shakespearean Stage 1574–1642* (Cambridge: Cambridge University Press, 1994), 187.

34 Derived from *ortus* or *hortus*, orchard [Q2], like *arbor* [Q1], was used interchangeably with *garden* to designate an enclosed piece of ground for flowers as well as flowering trees.

35 The relevance of Cain to a plot triggered by fratricide is even more obvious when entitled *Der Bestrafte Brudermord* or *Fratricide Punished*, as was the early spin-off from the play (or from its postulated source, the putative *Ur-Hamlet*), thought to have been performed by touring players in Germany during the seventeenth century, though surviving only in a late-eighteenth-century edition. See Jenkins, ed., *Hamlet*, 112–22.

36 This pun, ignored by Peter Brooks in his unfolding of the term in *Reading for the Plot: Design and Intention in Narrative* (New York: Vintage, 1984), is foregrounded in Martin Brückner and Kristen Poole, "The Plot Thickens: Surveying Manuals, Drama, and the Materiality of Narrative Form in Early Modern England," *English Literary History* (2002), 617–48.

37 The Argument to the anonymous *The Hystorie of Hamblet* (1608) gives numerous instances of fratricide committed for rule of the polis, from Romulus and Remus to the Roman Tarquins to the contemporary Turkish court, before considering "what tragedies have bin plaid to the like effect in the memorie of our ancestors," in Bullough, ed., *Sources of Shakespeare*, VII:81–4.

38 In Beaumont and Fletcher's *Philaster* (1608–10), a play strongly influenced by *Hamlet*, the stage floor is quite explicitly identified with estate: Claudius' counterpart asks how his trespasses can be forgiven when he is "Praying upon the ground I hold by wrong"; Hamlet's counterpart maintains to his rival, "This earth you tread upon . . . was not left / By my dead Father / To your inheritance," in *Philaster: or, Love Lies A-Bleeding*, ed. Andrew Gurr (Manchester and New York: Manchester University Press, and New York: Palgrave, 2003), 2.4.66, 1.1.176–80. For *Philaster*'s many liftings from *Hamlet*, see Donald Joseph McGinn, *Shakespeare's Influence on the Drama of His Age* (New Brunswick, NJ: Rutgers University Press, 1938), 56–63.

39 See Richard Dutton, "*Hamlet, An Apology for Actors*, and the Sign of the Globe," *Shakespeare Survey* 41 (1989), 35–43. It is worth noting that while liveried and in possession of their own stage, Shakespeare's acting company never owned the land on which their stages were erected. They were evicted from Shoreditch when their 21-year lease expired in 1597 and moved to Bankside where they built the Globe on land with a longer lease; the problem recurred in 1630. They were also evicted from Blackfriars when that lease expired, though James Burbage appears eventually to have secured the freehold in perpetuity. For the Globe and Blackfriars tenancy respectively, see Andrew Gurr, *Shakespearean Stage*, 41–9 and *The Shakespeare Company, 1594–1642* (Cambridge and New York: Cambridge University Press, 2004), 4–12, and Appendix 2, "Documents about the Company," 247–70.

40 See Paul S. Conklin, *A History of "Hamlet" Criticism: 1601–1821* (London: Frank Cass, 1968), 8, n. 4.

41 Conklin, has counted twenty-three allusions to the Ghost in the seventeenth century; see his *History*, 10, n. 6.

42 Nicholas Rowe, "Life of Shakespeare" (1709), in *Critical Responses to "Hamlet": 1600–1900*, ed. David Farley-Hills, 4 vols. (New York: AMS Press, 1995–), 1:30.

43 John Manningham, *The Diary of John Manningham of the Middle Temple, 1602–1603*, ed. Robert Parker Sorlien (Hanover, NH: University Press of New England, 1976), entry for 13 March 1601, 29b–30.

44 On ubiquity as the exclusive property of God and the devil, see Jenkins, ed., *Hamlet*, 458.

45 On *Hamlet*'s referencing of the tripartite stage of the miracle plays, see E. M. W. Tillyard, *Shakespeare's Problem Plays* (Toronto: University of Toronto Press, 1950), 29–30.

46 For this hoax "plot" scheduled at the Swan in 1602, see Tiffany Sterne, "'On each Wall / And Corner Post': Playbills, Title-pages, and Advertising in Early Modern London," *English Literary Renaissance* 36:1(2006), 87–9.

47 For an illustration of the Ghost's presence above and below the stage floor, see C. Walter Hodges' drawing in *Enter the Whole Army: A Pictorial Study of Shakespearean Staging, 1576–1616* (Cambridge: Cambridge University Press, 1999), 120.
48 Edward Coke, *The First Part of the Institutes or the Laws of England* (1628), in *The Selected Writings of Sir Edward Coke*, ed. Steve Sheppard, 3 vols. (Indianapolis, IN: Indiana University Press, 2003), II:629. Coke gives this principle in Latin; the translation is the editor's.
49 Sir Edward Coke, *First Part of the Institutes of the Lawes of England; Or, A Commentarie upon Littleton* (London, 1628), 110b.
50 Schoenbaum, *William Shakespeare*, 243.
51 John Minsheu, *"Ductor in linguas" and "Vocabularium hispanicolatinum"* (1617 facs. rpt.: Delmar, NY: Scholars' Facsimiles and Reprints, 1978), 227.

CHAPTER 3: EMPIRES OF WORLD HISTORY

1 Anon., *Sir Thomas Smithes Voiage and Entertainment in Rushia. With the tragicall ends of two Emperors, and one Empresse, within one Moneth during his being there* (London, 1605), sig. K.
2 *Ibid.*, sig. M2.
3 Harold Jenkins, ed., *Hamlet*, Arden edn. (London and New York: Methuen, 1982), 5.2.385–6. Unless otherwise indicated, all subsequent quotations from the play follow this edition and appear parenthetically in the text.
4 For pagan precedents, Eastern as well as Western, to the schema as established by Jerome and Orosius, see Joseph Ward Swain, "The Theory of the Four Monarchies: Opposition History under the Roman Empire," *Classical Philology* 35:1 (1940), 1–21.
5 This dream was borne out by a later vision of four great beasts rising from the sea to be destroyed by a greater beast; see G. W. Trompf, *The Idea of Historical Recurrence in Western Thought: From Antiquity to the Reformation* (Berkeley, CA: University of California Press, 1979), 186, 222–9, 282, 343–5.
6 For Luther's use of Daniel's Four Monarchies scheme, see Robin Bruce Barnes, *Prophecy and Gnosis: Apocalypticism in the Wake of the Lutheran Reformation* (Stanford: Stanford University Press, 1988), 39–41. For Milton's use of it, see Andrew Barnaby, "'Another Rome in the West?': Milton and the Imperial Republic, 1654–1670," *Milton Studies* 30 (1993), 67–84. For the Fifth Monarchists' self-legitimization in Daniel 2, see James Holstun, *A Rational Millennium: Puritan Utopias of Seventeenth-Century England and America* (New York and Oxford: Oxford University Press, 1987), 149–50.
7 John Sleidan, *A Briefe chronicle of the foure principall Empyres: To witte, of Babilon, Persia, Grecia, and Rome*, trans. Stephan Wythers (London, 1563).
8 Thomas Heywood, *Troia Britanica: or, Great Britaines Troy* (1609 facs. rpt.; Hildesheim, NY: G. Olms, 1972), *Proemium*.
9 Walter Raleigh, *The History of the World* (London, 1614), 5.6.12, p. 775.

10 See also John Stow, *The Annales of England* (London, 1601), 4r–8r, and Thomas Lanquet, *Epitome of cronicles conteining the whole discourse of the histories as well of this realme of England, as all other countreis* (London, 1549), fol. 89r.

11 Norman Cohn, *The Pursuit of the Millennium: Revolutionary Millenarians and Mystical Anarchists of the Middle Ages* (1957; rev. edn. London: Pimlico, 1993), 21.

12 Jean Bodin, *Method for the Easy Comprehension of History*, trans. Beatrice Reynolds (New York: Octagon, 1966), 291.

13 Louis Leroy explicates Daniel's dream of both the statue and the four sea beasts, in *Of the Interchangeable Course or Variety of Things in the whole world*, trans. Robert Ashley (London, 1594), 120r–121v.

14 *Ibid.*, 32v, 126r–126v.

15 Bodin, *Method*, 293.

16 Quoted by Reinhart Koselleck, *Futures Past: On the Semantics of Historical Time*, trans. Keith Tribe (Cambridge, MA and London: MIT Press, 1979), 6.

17 Raleigh, *History*, 5.6.12, p. 775.

18 See, for example, Daniel Vitkus, *Turning Turk: English Theater and the Multicultural Mediterranean, 1570–1630* (New York: Palgrave Macmillan, 2003), and Jane Degenhardt, *Faith, Embodiment, and "Turning Turk": Islamic Conversion and the Production of Religious and Racial Identity on the Renaissance Stage*, University of Pennsylvania PhD Thesis (2005).

19 Quoted from *The Tragedie of Hamlet*, in *The First Folio of Shakespeare*, prepared by Charlton Hinman (New York: Norton, 1968), TLN 2150–1.

20 Q1 and Q2 both term the play a *Tragicall Historie* on their title-page, but give *The Tragedie of Hamlet* in their running titles.

21 The opening line of *1 Henry VI* – "Hung be the heavens with black!" – suggests that the black hangings draped over the stage for the performance of tragedies may also have been present for histories; see Michael Neill, *Issues of Death: Mortality and Identity in English Renaissance Tragedy* (Oxford: Clarendon Press, and New York: Oxford University Press, 1997), 282–3.

22 On the ambiguity of the term "history," especially as a dramatic genre, see Paulina Kewes, "The Elizabethan History Play: A True Genre?," in *A Companion to Shakespeare's Works: The Histories*, ed. Richard Dutton and Jean E. Howard, 3 vols. (Malden, MA and Oxford: Blackwell, 2003), II:170–93.

23 D. R. Woolf, *The Idea of History in Early Stuart England* (Toronto, London, and Buffalo, NY: University of Toronto Press, 1990), 16–17.

24 Sir Philip Sidney, *An Apology for Poetry*, ed. Geoffrey Shepherd (Manchester and New York: Manchester University Press, 1965), 110.

25 On "narrative tragedy," see Willard Farnham, *The Medieval Heritage of Elizabethan Tragedy* (New York: Barnes and Noble, 1956), esp. 340–5.

26 Francis Meres, *Francis Meres's Treatise "Poetrie": A Critical Edition*, ed. Don Cameron Allen (Urbana, IL: University of Illinois Press, 1933), 76.

27 Raphael Holinshed, *Chronicles of England, Scotland, and Ireland*, 3 vols. (London, 1587), III:title-page.

28 Stephen Orgel, *The Authentic Shakespeare and Other Problems of the Early Modern Stage* (New York and London: Routledge, 2002), 33–4.

29 Holinshed, *Chronicles*, III:32, bk. 3, ch. 18.
30 *Ibid.*, III:51–2, bk. 4, ch. 19.
31 John Foxe, *The Acts and Monuments of John Foxe*, ed. George Townsend, 8 vols. (1859 facs. rpt.; New York, AMS Press, 1965), 1:305–6.
32 Holinshed, *Chronicles*, "A notable aduertisement touching the summe of all the foresaid historie," III:202, bk. 8.
33 Both of these title-pages are reproduced in Richard Helgerson, *Forms of Nationhood: The Elizabethan Writing of England* (Chicago and London: University of Chicago Press, 1992), 119, 123; Gordon McMullan considers the images in terms of a new interest in Britain's colonial past prompted by its own colonial ventures in the late-sixteenth and early-seventeenth centuries, in "Early Britain / Late Writing: Jacobean Drama and the Colonisation of the Atlantic Archipelago," in *Reading the Medieval in Early Modern England*, ed. David Matthews and Gordon McMullan (forthcoming from Cambridge University Press). I thank him for showing me the essay before publication.
34 Samuel Daniel, *The Collection of the Historie of England*, (1618; facs. rpt. Delmar, NY: Scholars' Facsimiles and Reprints, 1986), 22.
35 *Ibid.*, 22.
36 Fulke Greville, *A Treatise on Monarchy*, in *The Remains Being Poems of Monarchy and Religion*, ed. G. A. Wilkes (Oxford: Oxford University Press, 1965), 169, stanza 534.
37 For Foxe, there are "Five Conquests of Britain," with the Scots and Picts coming between the Roman and Saxon, in *Acts and Monuments*, II:107.
38 On Malone's "Attempt to Ascertain the Order in which the Plays of Shakspeare Were Written," see Margreta de Grazia, *Shakespeare Verbatim* (Oxford: Clarendon Press, 1991), 141–52.
39 Edmond Malone and James Boswell, eds., *The Plays and Poems of William Shakspeare*, 21 vols. (1821; New York: AMS Press, 1966), 1:xvii, XV:189.
40 See the Table of Contents by Genre, in *The Norton Shakespeare*, ed. Stephen Greenblatt et al. (New York: Norton, 1997), ix.
41 *King John*, 5.7.116–17. With the exception of *Hamlet*, all references to Shakespeare's work are quoted from the *Norton Shakespeare*.
42 To the contrary, Leah Marcus holds that the Folio set out to lift the plays from their topical and historical situation into a universalized realm of transcendent art, in *Puzzling Shakespeare: Local Reading and Its Discontents* (Berkeley: University of California Press, 1988), 2–32.
43 Alexander Pope, ed., *The Works of Shakespeare*, 6 vols. (1725 facs. rpt.; New York: AMS Press, 1969).
44 For Theobald's discovery of Saxo Grammaticus, see Lewis Theobald, ed., *The Works of Shakespeare*, 7 vols. (1733; New York: AMS Press, 1968), VII:225–6; for Edward Capell's of Belleforest, see Capell, ed., *Mr. William Shakespeare his Comedies, Histories, and Tragedies*, 10 vols. (1767–8 facs. rpt.; New York: AMS Press, 1968), 1:52–3.
45 Philip Edwards, ed., *Hamlet, Prince of Denmark* (Cambridge: Cambridge University Press, 1985), 64.

46 *The Hystorie of Hamblet* (1608), in *Narrative and Dramatic Sources of Shakespeare*, ed. Geoffrey Bullough, 8 vols. (London: Routledge and Kegan Paul, and New York: Columbia University Press, 1957–75), VII:85.

47 *Ibid.*, VII:103.

48 Compare Foxe's characterization of Britain's subjection to the Danes: "through all England, if an Englishman had met a Dane upon a bridge, he might not stir one foot before the Lord Dane (otherwise Lurdane) were past. And then if the Englishman had not given low reverence to the Dane at his coming by, he was sure to be sharply punished," *Acts and Monuments*, II:107.

49 In his generic reconfiguration of Shakespeare's canon, Leonard Tennenhouse groups *Hamlet* with the chronicle histories because of their shared "strategies of representation," in *Power on Display: The Politics of Shakespeare's Forms* (New York and London: Methuen, 1986), 72.

50 Stow, *Annales*, 41.

51 Harry Levin, *The Question of Hamlet* (New York: Oxford University Press, 1959), 95; and Margaret W. Ferguson, "Hamlet: Letters and Spirits," in *Shakespeare and the Question of Theory*, ed. Patricia Parker and Geoffrey Hartman (New York and London: Methuen, 1985), 303.

52 Heywood, *Troia*, 15.93, 406.

53 Appian, *Punica*, cited by Trompf, *Recurrence*, 79. For Shakespeare's knowledge of Appian, see Ernest Schanzer, ed., *Shakespeare's Appian: A Selection from the Tudor Translation of "Appian's Civil Wars"* (Liverpool: Liverpool University Press, 1956), xix–xxviii.

54 Appian, *Appian's Roman History*, trans. Horace White (London: William Heinemann, and New York: Macmillan, 1912), xix, 637–8.

55 Raleigh, *History*, 1.2.314.

56 Gyles Godet's *A briefe Abstract of the Genealogy of All the Kinges of England* (1560) opens with Priam's fall, and situates it within salvational history between the Creation and the Incarnation, tracing Priam's descent back beyond the Flood to Japthet, founder of Europe, and son of Noah. For "Shakespeare and the Troy legend," see Heather James, *Shakespeare's Troy: Drama, Politics, and the Translation of Empire* (Cambridge and New York: Cambridge University Press, 1997), 7–41.

57 Lily B. Campbell, ed., *The Mirror for Magistrates* (New York: Barnes and Noble, 1960).

58 Jeffrey Knapp, *An Empire Nowhere: England, America, and Literature from "Utopia" to "The Tempest"* (Berkeley: University of California Press, 1992), 42–8.

59 Holinshed, *Chronicles*, I:202.

60 See Jenkins, ed., *Hamlet*, 294, n. 104.

61 Stephen Orgel, *Authentic Shakespeare*, 241–3.

62 For the likelihood that Burbage played both Hamlet and Brutus and John Heminge both Caesar and Polonius, see E. A. J. Honigmann, "The Date of *Hamlet*," *Shakespeare Survey* 9 (1956), 27–9.

63 *The Hystorie of Hamblet* (1608), in Bullough, ed., *Sources of Shakespeare*, VII:90.

64 Hamlet assumes an "Anticke" (Q1 Dv, Q2 D4v, F 258) disposition; Priam
   wields his "antike" (Q1 E4v) or "anticke" (Q2 F 3v, F 263) sword; and Horatio
   is more an "antike" (Q1 I 3v), "anticke"(Q2 O), or "Antike" (F 281) Roman
   than a Dane.

65 See Bullough, ed., *Sources of Shakespeare*, VII:90 and n. 4. The note also
   recommends reading Dionysius of Halicarnassus who relates how Junius
   feigned stupidity after Tarquin had killed his father and brother and confis-
   cated the ancient family's inheritance, in *Roman Antiquities*, trans. Ernest
   Cary, 7 vols. (London: William Heinemann, and Cambridge, MA: Harvard
   University Press, 1937), II, IV:68–9.

66 From *The Romane Historie by Titus Livius*, trans. Philemon Holland (1600),
   in Bullough, ed., *Sources of Shakespeare*, VII:80.

67 Shakespeare, *The Rape of Lucrece*, 1810, 1814, 1815.

68 See also the comparison of Prince Hal's vanities to "the outside of the Roman
   Brutus, / Covering discretion with a coat of folly," in *Henry V*, 2.4.37–8.

69 Niccoló Machiavelli, *Discourses upon Livy*, trans. Harvey C. Mansfield and
   Nathan Tarcov (Chicago: University of Chicago Press, 1996), 216–18.

70 Plutarch, "The Life of Marcus Brutus," in *The Lives of the Noble Grecians and
   Romanes*, trans. Thomas North (1579; New York: AMS Press, 1967), 182.

71 David Norbrook, *Writing the English Republic: Poetry, Rhetoric and Politics,
   1627–1660* (Cambridge: Cambridge University Press, 1999), 451.

72 Woolf, *Idea*, 180.

73 *Julius Caesar*, 2.1.160 and 53–4.

74 On the study of Roman history, particularly Tacitus, for the instability of its
   constitutional forms, see R. Malcolm Smuts, *Culture and Power in Early
   Stuart England, 1585–1685* (New York: St. Martin's Press, 1999), 39, 70–2.

75 Jenkins transcribes Harvey's manuscript note in his edition of *Hamlet*,
   Appendix, 573–4. For evidence of Harvey's reading of Livy with the "wiser
   sort," including members and associates of the Sidney circle, see Lisa Jardine
   and Anthony Grafton, "'Studied for Action': How Gabriel Harvey Read his
   Livy," *Past and Present* 129 (November 1990), 30–78, esp. 54–5.

76 For Hamlet's republican leanings as derived from Tacitus' *History* and
   Annals and especially Livy's *History of Rome*, see Andrew Hadfield's discussion of *Hamlet* as "a distinctly republican play," in *Shakespeare and
   Republicanism* (Cambridge: Cambridge University Press, 2005), 189. I am
   grateful to the author for sharing Chapter 6, "The Radical *Hamlet*" with me
   before publication.

77 On "innovation" as a synonym for "rebellion" or "insurrection" as well as the
   identification of the "late innovation" with the recent Essex rebellion, see
   Jenkins, ed., *Hamlet*, 4, 471–2.

78 For the grave-digger in *Hamlet* and the Diggers, see Annabel Patterson,
   Shakespeare and the Popular Voice (Oxford: Blackwell, 1989), 101, 179, n. 22.

79 Jenkins provides the reference to Matthew (Jenkins, ed., *Hamlet*, 174, n. 123);
   John Parker in conversation provided parallels from Isaiah and Mark.

80 For Eusebius, the two events converged "not by mere human accident" but "of God's arrangement," as proven by the prophecies they fulfill; Augustine, however, passes over this coincidence with a mere sentence, eager to dissociate the eternal City of God from recently sacked Rome, Christian History from Roman History. See Theodor Ernst Mommsen, "St. Augustine and the Christian Ideal of Progress: The Background of *The City of God*," in *Medieval and Renaissance Studies*, ed. Eugene F. Rice, Jr. (Ithaca, NY: Cornell University Press, 1966), esp. 282; 296.

81 On this providentially driven transfer of imperial power, see Ernst Robert Curtius, *European Literature and the Latin Middle Ages*, trans. Willard R. Trask (New York: Pantheon, 1953), 28–30. On its destination after Charles V's abdication, and England's prospects, see Frances A. Yates, *Astraea: The Imperial Theme in the Sixteenth Century* (London and Boston: Routledge and Kegan Paul, 1975), 20–8, 51–9.

82 See "The Murder of Francesco Maria I, Duke of Urbino," in Bullough, ed., *Sources of Shakespeare*, 172–3.

83 Foxe, *Actes and Monuments*, IV:260.

84 "The Acts and Doings of Martin Luther Before the Emperor, at the City of Worms," *ibid.*, IV:281–92, 252.

85 Samuel Lewkenor, *A Discourse . . . of forraine cities* (London, 1600), 15–16.

86 Foxe, *Actes and Monuments*, IV:293.

87 On the celebrated gun emplacements overlooking the strait leading to the Baltic, see Martin Rivington Holmes, *The Guns of Elsinore* (London: Chatto and Windus, 1964), 51, 181.

88 Daniel, *Collection*, 21.

89 *Ibid.*, 22.

90 Sir John Smythe, *Certain Discourses Military* (1590), ed. J. R. Hale (Ithaca, NY: Cornell University Press, 1964), 7, 9. Paul A. Jorgensen discusses the necessity for war as the antidote to the "impostume of peace," and notes a decline in England's militarism from Elizabeth to James, in *Shakespeare's Military World* (Berkeley: University of California Press, 1956), 202–3; see also Smuts, *Culture and Power*, 85–7.

91 For the association of peace with degeneracy in the wake of the English translations of Tacitus in the 1590s, as well as in Machiavelli, see Smuts, *Culture and Power*, 37.

92 James I, "To the Reader," *A Counter-blaste to Tobacco* (1604; rpt. Amsterdam: Theatrum Orbis Terrarum, and New York: Da Capo Press, 1969).

93 Francis Bacon, *The Essays*, ed. John Pitcher (London and New York: Penguin, 1985), 152.

94 For *pursy* as "fat," "puffy," and "swollen like a purse," see *OED* a.1, 1, 2.

95 Greville, *The Remains*, 178, stanza 573, n. 25.

96 Claudius proclaims Hamlet his successor before the court (1.2.108–9), and Rosencrantz reminds Hamlet of the proclamation (3.2.331–2). Claudius' dropping into Hamlet's chalice of a union pearl "Richer than that which

8851 82028

four successive kings / In Denmark's crown have worn" (5.2.270), also seems calculated to symbolize the nomination.

97 See, for example, Janet Adelman, *Suffocating Mothers: Fantasies of Maternal Origin in Shakespeare's Plays* (New York: Routledge, 1992), 28–9.

98 Patricia Parker takes issue with the editorial bias against Q1's "guyana" in "Murder in Guyana," *Shakespeare Studies* 28 (2000), 169.

CHAPTER 4: GENERATION AND DEGENERACY

1 See A. C. Bradley, *Shakespearean Tragedy: Lectures on "Hamlet", "Othello", "King Lear", "Macbeth"* (1904; London and New York: Penguin, 1991), 373.

2 For nineteenth-century editions that replaced "thirty years" with "twenty," see Horace Howard Furness, ed., *Hamlet*, A New Variorum Edition, 2 vols. (1877; New York: Dover, 1963), I:391, n. 153, 395, n. 163, 377–8.

3 Lewis Theobald, ed., *The Works of Shakespeare*, 7 vols. (1733; New York: AMS Press, 1968), VII:236.

4 Yet for Goethe, Hamlet was less the model for Wilhelm Meister than his foil. Wilhelm is released to be himself after his father's death (he drops his surname, retaining only the name connecting him to Shakespeare, and transfers his inheritance to his brother-in-law. Hamlet, however, is crushed by the genealogical imperative to avenge his father's death, as is revealed by Goethe's famous metaphor for his plight, "An oak tree is planted in a precious pot which should only have held delicate flowers. The roots spread out, the vessel is shattered." See Goethe's *Wilhelm Meister's Apprenticeship*, in *Goethe's Collected Works*, ed. and trans. Eric A. Blackall, 9 vols. (Princeton: Princeton University Press, 1995), IX:146. For a similar account, see Jonathan Bate, *Shakespeare and the English Romantic Imagination* (Oxford: Clarendon Press, 1986), 223–4.

5 See Barbara Everett, *Young Hamlet: Essays on Shakespeare's Tragedies* (Oxford: Clarendon Press, 1989), 28–30. For the enduring importance of the play to novels after Goethe influenced by the *Bildungsroman* – by Scott, Dickens, Melville, and Joyce – see Alexander Welsh, *Hamlet in His Modern Guises* (Princeton, NJ: Princeton University Press, 2001).

6 See Edward Dowden, *Shakspeare: A Critical Study of His Mind and Art* (London: Routledge and Kegan Paul, 1967), 132–3.

7 See Bradley's extended meditation "concerning Hamlet as he was just prior to his father's death," *Tragedy*, 109–20.

8 See Annabel Patterson, *Shakespeare and the Popular Voice* (Cambridge, MA and Oxford: Blackwell, 1989), 31.

9 Everett, *Young Hamlet*, 30.

10 For the use of the thirty-year unit in Elizabethan drama, see Jenkins, ed., *Hamlet*, 553; and Bradley, *Tragedy*, 375. For Augustine's division of salvational time into generational epochs, see Herschel Baker, *The Race of Time: Three Lectures on Renaissance Historiography* (Toronto: University of Toronto Press, 1967), 56; for Joachim of Flora's reliance on the generational

unit of thirty years, see Frank Kermode, *The Sense of an Ending: Studies in the Theory of Fiction* (Oxford: Oxford University Press, 1967), 13.

11 For Polybius' use of the generational interval to mark constitutional alternation, see G. W. Trompf, *The Idea of Historical Recurrence in Western Thought: From Antiquity to the Reformation* (Berkeley: University of California Press, 1979), 29–30, 33–7.

12 For Machiavelli's redaction of Polybius in his *Discourses*, see Trompf, *ibid.*, 252–9, and J. G. A. Pocock, *The Machiavellian Moment: Florentine Political Thought and the Atlantic Republican Tradition* (Princeton, NJ: Princeton University Press, 1975), 49–80.

13 See, for example, Genesis 5:32, 1 Chronicles, and Matt. 1:1–17.

14 For patterns of generational alternation throughout Deuteronomy, see Trompf, *Recurrence*, 156–60.

15 For generations of varying lengths in Hesiod, Plato, Meno, and Aristotle, see *ibid.*, 37, n. 114.

16 On Shakespeare's frequent location of dramatic conflict at the point of familial, social, and political transition, particularly moments of marriage and death, see Louis Adrian Montrose, *The Purpose of Playing: Shakespeare and the Cultural Politics of the Elizabethan Theatre* (Chicago: University of Chicago Press, 1996), 33.

17 For the play's use of the generational divide between Hamlet I and Hamlet II to represent the transition from Catholicism to Protestantism, see Anthony Low, "Hamlet and the Ghost of Purgatory: Intimations of Killing the Father," *English Literary Renaissance* 29 (1999), 456.

18 Michael Neill, *Issues of Death: Mortality and Identity in English Renaissance Tragedy* (Oxford: Clarendon Press, 1997), 443–67.

19 From James Howell, *Familiar Letters* (1645), quoted in Jenkins, ed., *Hamlet*, 434. As David Norbrook has pointed out, Scotland was also ruled by an elective monarchy until the beginning of the eleventh century, "*Macbeth* and the Politics of Historiography," in *Politics of Discourse: The Literature and History of Seventeenth-Century England*, ed. Kevin Sharpe and Steven N. Zwicker (Berkeley: University of California Press, 1987), 78–116.

20 Questions of patrimony have not figured in the numerous studies of mourning in *Hamlet* published since the 1990s; for example, Neill, *Issues*; Low, "Hamlet and the Ghost;" and Stephen Greenblatt, *Hamlet in Purgatory* (Princeton, NJ: Princeton University Press, 2001), all of which focus on the loss of compensatory rites and rituals during the Reformation. See also, Steven Mullaney, "Mourning and Misogyny: *Hamlet*, *The Revenger's Tragedy*, and the Final Progress of Elizabeth I, 1600–1607," *Shakespeare Quarterly* 45:2 (1994), 139–62; and Julia Reinhard Lupton and Kenneth Reinhard, *After Oedipus: Shakespeare in Psychoanalysis* (Ithaca, NY: Cornell University Press, 1993), 1–33.

21 On paternal negligence as the source of Hamlet's defrauding, see Linda Charnes, *Hamlet's Heirs: Shakespeare and the Politics of a New Millennium* (New York and London: Routledge, 2006), esp. 60–6; on the matrilineal and matrimonial impediment to Hamlet's coming into his own, see Lisa

Jardine, *Reading Shakespeare Historically* (London and New York: Routledge, 1996), 35–47.

22 For the expectation from the twelfth through the seventeenth century that a man should not be free to disinherit or alienate his heir, and the various legal instruments for both bypassing and enforcing this constraint, see J. H. Baker's discussion of "Alienation," in his *An Introduction to English Legal History*, 4th edn. (London and Edinburgh; Butterworths, 2002), 260–5.

23 On the similarity between the laws governing inheritance and succession, see William Blackstone, *Commentaries on the Laws of England*, 4 vols. (1765–9 facs. rpt.; Chicago: University of Chicago Press, 1979), I:184–9.

24 For Blackstone's comments, see Edmond Malone and James Boswell, eds., *The Plays and Poems of William Shakspeare*, 21 vols. (1821 facs. rpt; New York: AMS Press, 1966), VII:200.

25 For a discussion of the play's references to this constitutional form, see E. A. J. Honigmann, "The Politics in *Hamlet* and 'The World of the Play,'" *Stratford-Upon-Avon Studies* 5 (1964), 129–47.

26 A. P. Stabler, "Elective Monarchy in the Sources of *Hamlet*," *Studies in Philology* 62:5 (January 1965) 654–61; see esp. Belleforest's comment on the principle and process of elective monarchy quoted on 658, n. 12.

27 That "[t]he crown of Denmark was elective" is first noted by George Steevens, and confirmed by William Blackstone; see Malone and Boswell, eds., *Shakspeare*, VII: 199–200, n. 1.

28 John Dover Wilson, *What Happens in "Hamlet"* (1935; Cambridge: Cambridge University Press, 1995), 28.

29 Thus Leonard Tennenhouse does not mention Denmark's specific form of monarchy in maintaining that the play stages a problematic transfer of power involving conflicting sources of authority, in *Power on Display: The Politics of Shakespeare's Forms* (New York and London: Methuen, 1986), 88–90. Eric Mallin notes the unusual constitutional form, but argues for Shakespeare's purposeful obfuscation of the succession process to distance it from the sensitive issue of Queen Elizabeth's imminent death without an heir, and it plays no role in his detailed reading of the Q2 *Hamlet* as an embedded allegory of the sexual and political intrigue leading to James' succession to the Scottish throne, *Inscribing the Time: Shakespeare and the End of Elizabethan England* (Berkeley: University of California Press, 1995), 112–14.

30 On the complexly inflected exchange between Hamlet and the King's two spies in this scene, see Wilson, *What Happens*, 122–3.

31 In Q1, in response to the Queen's poisoning, it is Hamlet who cries out "Treason, ho" (I3v).

32 Coke, *Institutes*, ed. Sheppard, II:980.

33 According to the statute of the reign of Edward III (c. 1350), it is treason "when a man doth compass or imagine the death of our lord the king." John Barrell remarks that until the treason trials at the end of the eighteenth century, "there was no punishment in English law for killing the king, only for intending his death"; "Imaginary Treason, Imaginary Law," in his *The*

Birth of Pandora and the Division of Knowledge (Philadelphia: University of Pennsylvania Press, 1992), 123.

34 In explicating the statute pertaining to High Treason – "*Fait compasser ou imaginer la mort*" (25 EIII.cap 2) – Coke argues that "he that is *non compos mentis* and totally deprived of all compassings, and imaginations, cannot commit High Treason by compassing or imagining the death of the King," *Institutes*, ed. Sheppard, II: 962.

35 On the Latin *testes* as both male genitalia and juridical instruments (and the play's "failure to properly testificate or testiculate"), see Charnes, *Hamlet's Heirs*, 56. The two cognates conjoin in Hamlet's slick description of how he seized the pouch or "packet" on the unindividuated person of Rosencrantz-and-Guildenstern: "Up from my cabin, / My sea-gown scarf'd about me, in the dark, / Grop'd I to find out them, had my desire, / Finger'd their packet, / And in fine withdrew / To mine own room again" (5.2.12–16). Mallin deftly unpacks the narrative's homoerotic charge: "His condition of being 'up' (erect), his groping to find them, the fulfillment of his desire, his fingering of their packet (letters, but also slang for genitalia), and his satisfied withdrawal all suggest homoerotic dalliance, intercourse, or in this case rape, stealthily mounted," *Inscribing*, 117. Hamlet's fingering of their "packet" may be in retaliation for their fingering of his: Hamlet has his father's testamentary and testicular seal or signet in his packet or "purse" (5.2.49), and accuses Rosencrantz-and-Guildenstern of fingering him as if he were a pipe or "little organ" (F, 3.2.359). Hamlet's confession "Man delights not me" (2.2.309) may be relevant here; for Horatio as the delightful exception, however, see Jeffrey Masten, "Toward a Queer Address: The Taste of Letters and Early Modern Friendship," *GLQ: A Journal of Lesbian and Gay Studies* 10:3 (2004), 367–84.

36 The proverb, which Hamlet does not quote in full, is glossed in Morris Palmer Tilley, *A Dictionary of the Proverbs in England in the Sixteenth and Seventeenth Century* (Ann Arbor: University of Michigan Press, 1950), G423.

37 Steven Mullaney, "Lying Like Truth: Riddle, Representation, and Treason," in his *The Place of the Stage: License, Play, and Power in Renaissance England* (Chicago: University of Chicago Press, 1988), 116–21.

38 Charnes sees "*symbolic filicide*" occurring in the combat between Fortinbras I and Hamlet I in which both fathers, by staking crown lands, demonstrated their willingness "capriciously to gamble away their son's patrimonies," in *Hamlet's Heirs*, 61, 66.

39 In Q1, "Full fortie yeares are past" since the marriage (F3).

40 In entertaining the vexed question of who first bore arms, Edmund Bolton confidently excludes the heroes of both Homer and Virgil, in *The Elements of Armories* (London, 1610), 9–10.

41 John Guillim, *A Display of Heraldrie* (London, 1611), 118.

42 *Ibid.*, 101.

43 In the *Aeneid* (2.506–8), Pyrrhus enters chasing Priam's son and kills him before his father's eyes at the ancestral altar. On this shift of locale and emotional focus, see David Lee Miller, *Dreams of the Burning Child:*

Sacrificial Sons and the Father's Witness (Ithaca, NY: Cornell University Press, 2003), 52–91.

44 Sir William Segar, *Honor Military, and Civill, Contained in Foure Bookes* (1602), quoted by Neill, *Issues*, 272.

45 The College of Arms was charged from the end of the fifteenth century with properly preserving the heraldic status of the deceased; see Neil, *Issues*, 40, 272–3.

46 Guillim, *Heraldrie*, 34.

47 *Ibid.*, 31–2.

48 See *OED*, 2nd edn., *sb* 2 1.

49 On the threat posed by the "aerie of children" to the King's Men, see Roslyn Lander Knutson, *Playing Companies and Commerce in Shakespeare's Time* (Cambridge and New York: Cambridge University Press, 2001), 120–6.

50 The *locus classicus* for this battle is Virgil, *Georgics* 1:281; for its proverbial status, see Tilley, *Dictionary of Proverbs*, O81. See, also, Ovid's account in *Metamorphoses*, 1:171–8.

51 See Robert Weimann, *Shakespeare and the Popular Tradition in the Theater: Studies in the Social Dimension of Dramatic Form and Function*, ed. Robert Schwartz (Baltimore: Johns Hopkins University Press, 1978), 68, 72.

52 For Herod's ranting and raving in the medieval mystery cycles, see *ibid.*, 64–72.

53 Patricia Parker has traced out the play's numerous references to blackness in "Black *Hamlet*: Battening on the Moor," *Shakespeare Studies* 31 (2003), 127–64. She does not, however, connect Hamlet with Ham whose curse was thought to have resulted in black skin color and who in representations of the three continents was identified with Africa, as his brothers Shem and Japhet were with Asia and Europe respectively. For an account of how Ham's transgression and curse were seen in the seventeenth and eighteenth centuries to justify the taking possession of land in the East and West Indies as well as the institution of slavery generally, see Werner Sollors, *Neither Black nor White yet Both: Thematic Explorations of Interracial Literature* (New York and Oxford: Oxford University Press, 1997), "The Curse of Ham, or From 'Generation' to 'Race,'" 78–111.

54 Sir Walter Raleigh, *The History of the World* (London, 1614), 1.1.8, p. 129.

55 On the variable ages for both menarche and menopause in the early modern period, see Patricia M. Crawford, *Blood, Bodies and Families in Early Modern England* (New York: Longman, 2004), 49, n. 112, 50, n. 114.

56 Both Saxo and Belleforest bestialize Gertrude's appetite; see Jenkins, ed., *Hamlet*, 88, 91.

57 According to Roland Frye, the typical interval between a husband's death and his widow's marriage was over a year; see *The Renaissance Hamlet: Issues and Responses in 1600* (Princeton: Princeton University Press, 1984), 86.

58 See Frye, *Renaissance Hamlet*, 85, and David Cressy, *Birth, Marriage, and Death: Ritual, Religion, and the Life-Cycle in Tudor and Stuart England* (New York: Oxford University Press, 1997), 398. On *trentals* and *trigintals*,

see Stephen Greenblatt, *Hamlet in Purgatory* (Princeton: Princeton University Press, 2001), 21, 267–8, n. 26, and 306–7, n. 34.

59 See Crawford, *Blood*, 53.

60 On the predominantly female gendering of *shoe* in the early modern period, see Peter Stallybrass, "Footnotes," in *The Body in Parts: Fantasies of Corporeality in Early Modern Europe*, ed. David Hillman and Carla Mazzio (New York and London: Routledge, 1997), 313–25, esp. 324, n. 23. *Foot*, however, is typically gendered male, like that other standard of measurement, *yard*. In *Eastward Ho*, Jonson, Chapman, and Marston target Shakespeare by featuring an incompetent "footman" named Hamlet, who fails properly to attend to the "coach" or "case" of his lubricious mistress Gertrude, when "She comes, she comes, she comes." She is advised to provide him with a "Hobby horse" so he might "have something betwixt his legs to ease them," in *The Complete Plays of Ben Jonson*, ed. G. A. Wilkes (Oxford: Clarendon Press, 1981), 3.2.24, 44–5.

61 On the Levitical prohibition against copulation during "the time of separation" or menses, see Crawford, *Blood*, 29–30.

62 On male and female seed and sperm, see Gail Kern Paster, *The Body Embarrassed: Drama and the Disciplines of Shame in Early Modern England* (Ithaca, NY: Cornell University Press, 1993), 81.

63 On the intimacy of the closet, see Alan Stewart, *Close Readers: Humanism and Sodomy in Early Modern England* (Princeton, NJ: Princeton University Press, 1997), 161–87; see, also, Lisa Jardine's application of Stewart to the closet scene, *Reading*, 150–4.

64 The legends of Agrippina's murder are based on Tacitus, *Tacitus the Annals*, trans. A. J. Woodman (Indianapolis: Hackett, 2004), ch. 14, 8–9; Shakespeare alludes to Nero's matricide in *King John*: "You bloody Neros, ripping up the womb / Of your dear mother England, blush for shame," in *The Norton Shakespeare*, ed. Stephen Greenblatt et al. (New York: Norton, 1997), 5.2.152–3.

65 See Margaret Ferguson's discussion of the matter/mater homonym in "*Hamlet*: Letters and Spirits," in *Shakespeare and the Question of Theory*, ed. Patricia Parker and Geoffrey Hartman (New York and London: Methuen, 1985), 295.

66 See Neill, *Issues*, 139.

67 For several anatomical engravings of the female body torn open or écorché, to reveal the womb, see Jonathan Sawday, *The Body Emblazoned: Dissection and the Human Body in Renaissance Culture* (London: Routledge, 1995), 84–5.

68 Katharine Park, *Secrets of Women: Gender, Generation, and the Origins of Human Dissection* (New York: Zone Books, 2006), 234–49.

69 See the illustrations of the child shielding his eyes in the womb in Paster, *Body Embarrassed*, 176, 177.

70 For evidence of mossy and flowery banks as stage properties, see Andrew Gurr's discussion of Henslowe's inventories as well as of stage directions

specifying props, in *The Shakespearean Stage, 1574–1642* (Cambridge: Cambridge University Press, 1970), 187–93.

71 William Percy's *The Faery Pastorall* calls for "A greene Bank being Pillow to the Hed," in Gurr, *Shakespearean Stage*, 193. On the motif of the male head in woman's lap, see Mary Nyquist, "Textual Overlapping and Dalilah's Harlot-Lap," in *Literary Theory / Renaissance Texts*, ed. Patricia Parker and David Quint (Baltimore: Johns Hopkins University Press, 1986), 341–72.

72 One of the pageants presented before Queen Elizabeth on her first procession included two "hylles or mountaynes," one of them "cragged, barreyn, and stonye, in the which was erected one tree . . . all withered and deade" representing "*Ruinosa Respublica*, a decayed common weale," while the other "was made fayre, fresche, grene, and beawtifull, the grounde thereof full of flowers" standing for "*Respublica bene institute*. A florishyne commonweale"; see *The Quenes Maiesties Passage through the Citie of London to Westminster the day before her Coronacion* (1559), ed. James M. Osborn (New Haven: Yale University Press, 1960), 46–7.

73 Patricia Parker includes jointures and jointresses in her discussion of joints and joinery in "'Rude Mechanicals,'" in *Subject and Object in Renaissance Culture*, ed. Margreta de Grazia, Maureen Quilligan, and Peter Stallybrass (Cambridge: Cambridge University Press, 1996), 71–2.

74 In both Saxo and Belleforest, Jutland passes to Amleth's father as well as to his uncle through Gerutha, daughter of Roric King of Denmark. See Jenkins, ed., *Hamlet*, 179, n. 9 and Longer Notes, 434. On Gertrude's holding of "jointure or life interest in the crown," see Wilson, *What Happens*, 38.

75 For this passage in the anonymous English translation and Belleforest's French original, see Israel Gollancz, ed., *The Sources of "Hamlet"*, (London: Humphrey Milford, Oxford University Press, 1926), 292–3.

76 The free bench widow's right to continue in possession of land was usually conditional on her not remarrying. For the need in the event of the mother's remarriage to watch over the children's inheritance, see E. P. Thompson, "The Grid of Inheritance: A Comment," in *Family and Inheritance: Rural Society in Western Europe, 1200–1800*, ed. Jack Goody, Joan Thirsk, and E. P. Thompson (Cambridge and New York: Cambridge University Press, 1976), 350.

77 Sir Walter Raleigh, *Instructions to His Son and to Posterity*, in *Advice to a Son: Precepts of Lord Burghley, Sir Walter Raleigh, and Francis Osborne*, ed. Louis B. Wright (Ithaca, NY: Cornell University Press, 1962), 22.

78 See Jardine, *Reading*, 35–47, esp. 40–1, and Mallin, *Inscribing*, 112–14.

79 On the sexualized politics of Claudius' "popp[ing] in," see Mallin, *Inscribing*, 116–17. The parallel between the incestuous marriage of Claudius and Gertrude and that of Henry VIII and Catherine of Aragon (widow of his brother Arthur) has long been noted. Mallin revisits the question of Scottish succesion and relates the play to the adulterous second marriage of James' mother to a second husband who had murdered the first, *ibid.*, 124–66.

80 Jack Goody, *The Development of the Family and Marriage in Europe* (Cambridge: Cambridge University Press, 1983), 134–46, 174–82. On the particular prerogatives endogamy conferred upon women in this period, see Maureen Quilligan, *Incest and Agency in Elizabeth's England* (Philadelphia: University of Pennsylvania Press, 2005).

81 T. S. Eliot, "Hamlet," in *Selected Prose of T. S. Eliot*, ed. Frank Kermode (London: Faber and Faber, 1975), 45–9.

82 Indeed, toward the end of the essay, Eliot allows for such incommensurability in the psychopathology of everyday life: "The intense feeling, ecstatic or terrible, without an object or exceeding its object, is something which every person of sensibility has known," in "Hamlet," 49.

83 Ernest Jones, "The Oedipus Complex as an Explanation of Hamlet's Mystery: A Study in Motive," *The American Journal of Psychology* 21:1 (January 1910), 72–113.

84 The pudendal button is also relevant to the bantering between Hamlet and Rosencrantz and Guildenstern about their relation to Fortune. Modern editions, following F, have consistently thought the most desirable place to be on Fortune was the "button" on her "cap": "on Fortune's cap we are not the very button" (2.2.228–9). But Q2's "lap" is also possible; indeed most of the dialogue concerns the advantage of being in the middle parts of the "strumpet" Fortune – "about her waist," "in the middle of her favours," in her "secret parts," the special prerogative of "her privates" (232–5).

85 See Louis Adrian Montrose's remarkable note on "flowers" as the commonest term for "menses" in Shakespeare's time, in "Shaping Fantasies: Figuration of Gender and Power in Elizabethan Culture," in *Representing the English Renaissance*, ed. Stephen Greenblatt (Berkeley and Los Angeles: University of California Press, 1988), n. 44, 62–3.

86 See G. K. Hunter, "The Marking of *Sententiae* in Elizabethan Printed Plays, Poems, and Romances," *The Library* 5th series 6:3–4 (1951), 171–88. I am grateful to William Sherman for sharing his unpublished study of these indexical digits, "Toward a History of the Manicule."

87 Lord Burghley, Henry Sidney, Sir Walter Raleigh, King James, and Henry Percy all passed books on to their sons containing such maxims.

88 On the mechanics and use of tablebooks in the early modern period, see H. R. Woudhuysen, "Writing-Tables and Table-Books," *The Electronic British Library Journal* (2004), article 3, 1–11; and Peter Stallybrass, Roger Chartier, et al., "Hamlet's Tables and the Technologies of Writing in Renaissance England," *Shakespeare Quarterly* 55:4 (2004), 379–419.

89 A fishmonger's daughter (2.2.174) seems similarly predisposed to conception: the salacious salt from saltwater fish was thought to rub off on female flesh; see Jenkins, ed., *Hamlet*, 465–6.

90 On the promiscuity of bakers' daughters, see *ibid.*, 533.

91 For the most commonly accepted identification of "long purples," see the description of the *Orchis mascula*, popularly known as "dead man's finger,"

"cuckoo cock," "dog stones," and "priest's pintel," in Gregory Grigson, *The Englishman's Flora* (London: Phoenix House, 1955), 425–7.

92 Charlton Hinman, ed., *The Norton Facsimile: The First Folio of shakespeare* (1623 facs. rpt.; New York: Norton, 1968), 782, line 2918.

93 According to Alan C. Dessen and Leslie Thomson, "disheveled hair is one way of signaling *enter ravished*," in *Dictionary of Stage Directions in English Drama, 1580–1642* (Cambridge and New York: Cambridge University Press, 1999), 107.

94 Lear's apostrophe to the ailment suggests that he, too, beats his heart when gripped by its emotional surge: "O, how this mother swells up toward my heart! *Hysterica passio*, down, thou climbing sorrow, / Thy element's below!" (2.4.54–6). See Janet Adelman, *Suffocating Mothers: Fantasies of Maternal Origin in Shakespeare's Plays, "Hamlet" to "The Tempest"* (New York and London: Routledge, 1992), 114, 300–1, n. 27.

95 On the *florilegium* as "flower-culling," see Mary Carruthers and Jan M. Ziolkowski, eds., *The Medieval Craft of Memory: An Anthology of Texts and Pictures* (Philadelphia: University of Pennsylvania Press, 2002), 5.

96 Isabella Whitney, *A Sweet Nosgay* (1573), in *The Floures of Philosophie (1572) by Hugh Plat and A Sweet Nosgay (1573) and The Copy of A Letter (1567) by Isabella Whitney*, ed. Richard J. Panofsky (Delmar, NY: Scholars' Facsimiles and Reprints, 1982), The Auctor to the Reader, The Epistle Dedicatory. For a legal florilegium, see Thomas Ashe, *Fasciculus Florum or A Handfull of Flowers Gather out of the severall Bookes of . . . Sir Edward Coke* (London, 1618).

97 For the punning use of pansies for *pensées* in Elizabethan embroidery, including Elizabeth's, see Lisa M. Klein, "Your Humble Handmaid: Elizabethan Gifts of Needlework," *Renaissance Quarterly* 50 (1997), 459–93.

98 For the "dissembling daisy," "the cornuted columbine" and fennel "for flatterers," see Jenkins, ed., *Hamlet*, 538–41.

99 Isabella Whitney, *Nosgay*, The Auctor to the Reader.

100 On the eroticizing overtones of Ophelia's spreading "clothes," see Patricia Parker, *Shakespeare from the Margins: Language, Culture, Context* (Chicago and London: University of Chicago Press, 1996), 255, 366 n. 65. A "close" is also an enclosed area of land (*OED*, sb1).

101 The actress Jane Lessingham played Ophelia for the first time in Covent Garden Theatre in 1772. An engraving of her in the role is among the thirty-six plates of contemporary actors and actresses printed in John Bell, ed., *Bell's Edition of Shakespeare's Plays* (London, 1775–6).

102 Of the virgin nymph Chloris' transformation to the goddess Flora after she was raped by Zephyrus, see Ovid's *Fausti*, trans. Betty Rose Nagle (Bloomington: Indiana University Press, 1995), 5, 195–378. Frederick Kiefer reproduces four sixteenth- and seventeenth-century engravings of Flora or Spring and discusses the draping of the figure with flowers in several court masques of the period in *Shakespeare's Visual Theatre: Staging the Personified Characters* (Cambridge: Cambridge University Press, 2003), 26–31. For an alternative version of the myth, deriving from Plutarch and Boccaccio,

in which Flora's natural fertility is recast in mercenary and meretricious terms, see Julius Held, "Flora, Goddess and Courtesan," in *De Artibus Opuscula XL: Essays in Honor of Erwin Panofsky*, ed. Millard Meiss, 2 vols. (New York: Pantheon, 1961), 1:201–18. Bridget Gellert Lyons applies Held's account of the two Flora narratives in order to read the flower-dispensing nymph iconographically as a figure of pastoral innocence who cannot survive the "political intrigue and sexual danger" of the court, "The Iconography of Ophelia," *English Literary History* 44:1 (1977), 72.

103 On Le Moyne's painting and de Bry's engraving of the Pictish maiden as well as William Camden's account of the "Britannorum stigamata" of the ancient Britons or Picts, see Juliet Fleming, *Graffiti and the Writing Arts of Early Modern England* (Philadelphia: University of Pennsylvania Press, 2001), 99–106. See, also, the arboreal and fructifying landscape of Great Britain's gown in the *Poly-Olbion* frontispiece engraving (Illustration 3).

104 As Sir Philip Sidney learned from Plutarch, even the abominable tyrant Alexander Pheraeus wept at the tragedy of Hecuba in a performance of Euripides' *Troades*; see *An Apology for Poetry*, ed. Geoffrey Shepherd (Manchester and New York: Manchester University Press, 1965), 118. On Hecuba as the image of insuperable grief, see Harry Levin, *The Question of "Hamlet"* (New York: Oxford University Press, 1959), 143–7.

105 Ovid, *Ovid's Metamorphoses*, trans. Arthur Golding, ed. Frederick Nims (1603 facs. rpt.; Philadelphia: Paul Dry Books, 2000), 6.258, 241.

106 *Ibid.*, 6.392–5.

CHAPTER 5: DOOMSDAY AND DOMAIN

1 Harold Jenkins, ed., *Hamlet*, Arden edn. (London and New York: Methuen, 1982). Unless otherwise noted, all quotations from this play follow this edition.

2 A. C. Bradley, *Shakespearean Tragedy: Lectures on "Hamlet," "Othello," "King Lear," "Macbeth"* (1904; London and New York: Penguin, 1991), 141.

3 Shakespeare, *The Tragicall Historie of Hamlet Prince of Denmarke* (1603), H3v. Quotations from Q1 are from the facsimile reprint of the British Library's copy (London: British Library, 2003).

4 As has been noted since the Johnson-Steevens 1793 edition, the grave-digger's explanation of the coroner's inquest law parodies a famous legal case following upon a suicide by drowning, *Hales* v. *Petit* (1562). The case involved the competing claims of the suicide's widow and the Crown over his property, including the leasehold to 200 acres of marshland. For a full analysis of the case and its relation to questions of agency in *Hamlet*, see Luke Wilson, *Theatres of Intention: Drama and the Law in Early Modern England* (Stanford: Stanford University Press, 2000), 39–60.

5 For a discussion of the Dance of Death tradition in printed books, see Michael Neill, *Issues of Death: Mortality and Identity in English Renaissance Tragedy* (Oxford: Clarendon Press, 1997), 53–7.

6 For an account of the paintings, including a description of them in 1576 by John
   Stow, see Clifford Davidson, *The Guild Chapel Wall Paintings at Stratford-
   upon-Avon* (New York: AMS Press, 1988), 6–12, 33–4. Unlike the religious
   paintings in the Chapel, the Dance of Death series were not white-washed
   after the iconoclastic royal injunctions of 1559. A reconstruction of the schema
   was made in the 1950s and is reproduced in Davidson, *Guild Chapel,* figure 19.
7 Vanessa Harding, *The Dead and the Living in London and France 1500–1670*
   (Cambridge: Cambridge University Press, 2002), 46.
8 *Ibid.,* 127–8.
9 *Ibid.,* 55.
10 *Ibid.,* 64.
11 Thomas Dekker, "Gods Tokens," in *The Plague Pamphlets of Thomas Dekker,*
   ed. F. P. Wilson (Oxford: Clarendon Press, 1925), 158–9.
12 Harding, *The Dead,* 174.
13 See David Cressy, "Death and the Social Order: The Funerary Preferences of
   Elizabethan Gentlemen," *Continuity and Change* 5:1 (1989), 99–119.
14 See Philippe Ariès, *The Hour of Our Death,* trans. Helen Weaver (New York:
   Oxford University Press, 1991), 215.
15 For the association of the sexton with plebian protest and egalitarianism, see
   Robert Weimann, *Shakespeare and the Popular Tradition in the Theater:
   Studies in the Social Dimension of Dramatic Form and Function,* ed. Robert
   Schwartz (Baltimore: Johns Hopkins University Press, 1978), 239–40 and
   Annabel Patterson, *Shakespeare and the Popular Voice* (Cambridge, MA and
   Oxford: Blackwell, 1989), 93–106. Patterson argues for limiting the classification *peasant* to "the urban underclasses," claiming that the term is "not
   specific to agricultural labor, still less (unlike 'serf') in precise relationship
   to feudal agriculture," 32.
16 In glossing Ben Jonson's reference to "A Midlesex Clowne" in *A Tale of a
   Tub,* the editors refer to Thomas Fuller's derivation of clown from "*colonus,
   one that plougheth the ground*" in *Worthies of England* (1662) as well as a
   similar etymology from Raphael Holinshed's *Chronicles* (1587). See C. H.
   Herford and Percy Simpson, eds., *The Works of Ben Jonson,* 11 vols. (Oxford:
   Clarendon Press, 1925–52), IX:280, n. 34.
17 Richard Helgerson, *Forms of Nationhood: The Elizabethan Writing of England*
   (Chicago: University of Chicago Press, 1992), 216. See also Robert Weimann,
   Author's Pen and Actor's Voice, ed. Helen Higbee and William West
   (Cambridge: Cambridge University Press, 2000), 101.
18 His pun would have been familiar from heraldic manuals which often begin,
   as does John Guillim's *A Display of Heraldrie* (London, 1611), by explaining
   that "*Armes* in English, and in Latine, *Arma*" are terms of "aequivocation or
   ambiguitie"; as Guillim explains, the word refers to three types of instruments: "naturall" (the limbs of the body), "mechanicall" (the implements of
   farming and building), and "militarie" (weapons). But the word also "by way
   of figure called *Metonymic subiecti*" refers to the surfaces on which ensigns
   were engraved as well as to the ensigns themselves, 2.

19 God also approves the inverse: "They shall beat their swords into plough-shares, And their spears into pruning-hooks" (Micah 4:3).

20 John Stow, *A Survey of London*, 2 vols. (1603 rpt.; Oxford: Clarendon Press, 1908), II:77.

21 "Robert Scarlett," in *Oxford Dictionary of National Biography*, ed. H. C. G. Matthew and Brian Harrison (Oxford: Oxford University Press, 2004), 191.

22 The mural was painted on the south side of the Cathedral's west door. It apparently was mutilated by Cromwell's soldiery in 1643, and then in 1665 covered by a commissioned oil painting of Scarlett; the mural was not discovered until 1961 when the painting was removed for restoration. See George Dixon, *Old Scarlett* (1980; Glossop: Paul Bush, 1997). Roland Mushat Frye reproduces an early nineteenth-century engraving of the portrait and entertains the possibility that Scarlett was the model for the grave-digger in *Hamlet*, in *The Renaissance "Hamlet": Issues and Responses in 1600* (Princeton: Princeton University Press, 1984), 226.

23 See Andrew Gurr and Mariko Ichikawa, *Staging in Shakespeare's Theatres* (Oxford: Oxford University Press, 2000), 57.

24 Gerard Leigh, *Accedence of Armorie* (1591) cited in Horace Howard Furness, ed., *Hamlet*, A New Variorum Edition (1877; New York: Dover, 1965), 377–8, n. 30.

25 In the eighteenth century, the graveyard scene was repeatedly criticized for its mixing of dramatic kinds, an instance of Shakespeare's sacrificing the classical rules to popular taste. After Voltaire's criticism of the exchange, it was cut from production by Garrick, Kemble, and Kean. See Philip Edwards, ed., *Hamlet, Prince of Denmark* (Cambridge: Cambridge University Press, 1985), 64.

26 Morris Palmer Tilley, *A Dictionary of the Proverbs in England in the Sixteenth and Seventeenth Century* (Ann Arbor, MI: University of Michigan Press, 1950), C933.

27 Sir Philip Sidney, *An Apology for Poetry*, ed. Geoffrey Shepherd (Manchester and New York: Manchester University Press, 1965), 136.

28 *Ibid.*, 135.

29 Since 1870, the collection has gone by the title of *Tottel's Miscellany*. See H. E. Rollins, ed., *Tottel's Miscellany*, 2 vols. (Cambridge, MA: Harvard University Press, 1965), 1:165–6. For the many versions of the song in manuscript and print, see Jenkins, ed., *Hamlet*, 548–50. Patterson also mentions its anomalous courtly provenance, noting that "from Hamlet's perspective, the song in the gravedigger's mouth means only that a laborer has mistaken his place in the world," *Popular Voice*, 103. The title Patterson assigns the song and the page number in Rollins' edition is incorrect, as is her description of the song as "jumbled," 179, n. 26, 103.

30 The radical sect known as the Diggers drew their name from the association of the digging of the land with the upheaval of the landed. According to Patterson, the name first appeared in the Midland Risings of 1607, *ibid.*, 179, n. 22.

31 In his 1765 edition of *Hamlet*, Samuel Johnson notes the indecorum of a prince putting himself in the shoes of those who "fardels bear": "Hamlet, in

his enumeration of miseries, forgets, whether properly or not, that he is a prince, and mentions many evils to which inferior stations only are exposed," in David Farley-Hills, ed., *Critical Responses to "Hamlet": 1600–1900*, 4 vols. (New York: AMS Press, 1995–), I:189. Hereafter cited as *CR*.

32 For the conflict between the country clown and the court jester, see Helgerson, *Forms*, 215–28. Helgerson follows Weimann in arguing that Shakespeare's theater by 1600 was moving from a "player's theater" to an "author's theater."

33 The term *knave* referred to a relation of service until well into the seventeenth century. While editors typically follow sixteenth-century lexicographers in glossing "absolute" with its now obsolete sense of "complete" or "perfect," Christopher Hill demonstrates the word's association with unlimited monarchic power, as in Essex's allegation that Queen Elizabeth was aspiring toward "an infinite absoluteness," in *A Nation of Change and Novelty: Radical Politics, Religion, and Literature in Seventeenth-Century England* (New York: Routledge, 1990), 84–5.

34 On the impertinence of clowns, see Weimann, *Popular Tradition*, 119–33.

35 On the association of ambiguity with political subversion, see Steven Mullaney, *The Place of the Stage: License, Play, and Power in Renaissance England* (Chicago: University of Chicago Press, 1988), 119–20.

36 For the belief based on Revelation that Christ's Second Coming would establish a messianic kingdom on earth, see Norman Cohn, *The Pursuit of the Millennium: Revolutionary Millenarians and Mystical Anarchists of the Middle Ages* (London: Pimlico, 1993), particularly his discussion of the Peasants' Revolt (198–204) and the Anabaptist movement (252–88). For a refinement of Cohn, see Bernard McGinn, *Visions of the End: Apocalyptic Traditions in the Middle Ages* (New York: Columbia University Press, 1998), esp. 28–36. On the duration of millenarian and egalitarian prospects into the period of the English Revolution, see Christopher Hill, *The World Turned Upside Down: Radical Ideas during the English Revolution* (New York: Viking Press, 1972), 19–38.

37 Cohn, *Pursuit*, 265.

38 Thomas Cooper, "An Admonition to the People of England" (1589), quoted in Hill, *World Turned Upside Down*, 115.

39 Raphael Holinshed, *Chronicles of England, Scotland, and Ireland*, 3 vols. (London, 1587), III:437. For other uses of the proverb, see Patterson, *Popular Voice*, 39, 46, 100–1.

40 For the use of the Domesday Book to determine questions of land and rights during Elizabeth's reign, see Elizabeth M. Hallam, *Domesday Book through Nine Centuries* (London: Thames and Hudson, 1986), 71. The classic study on this survey is Frederic William Maitland, *Domesday Book and Beyond: Three Essays in the Early History of England* (Cambridge: Cambridge University Press, 1921).

41 It has been suggested that William had the survey made in anticipation of invasion in 1085 from Onut II of Denmark who planned to assert his claim to

the throne of England. See Frank Barlow, "Domesday Book," in *Domesday Essays*, ed. Christopher Holdsworth (Exeter: University of Exeter Press, 1986), 23.

42 Samuel Daniel, *The Collection of the Historie of England* (1618 facs. rpt.; Delmar, NY: Scholars' Facsimiles and Reprints, 1986), 40.

43 See Jenkins, ed., *Hamlet*, 286, n. 172.

44 J. G. A. Pocock, *The Ancient Constitution and the Feudal Law: A Study of English Historical Thought in the Seventeenth Century: A Reissue with Retrospect* (Cambridge: Cambridge University Press, 1987), esp. Ch. 2, "The Common-Law Mind," 30–55.

45 *The Life and Death of Jack Straw* (1593), quoted by Patterson, *Popular Voice*, 46.

46 Richard fitz Nigel, *Dialogus de Scaccario: The Course of the Exchequer*, quoted by David Bates, "Domesday Book 1086–1986," in *Domesday Essays*, ed. Holdsworth, 1.

47 On the existence of the common law "since time out of mind," see Pocock, *Ancient Constitution*, esp. Ch. 2, 30–55.

48 For the association of *Domesday* with peasant movements, see Hallam, *Domesday Book*, 100–5.

49 *Ibid.*, 104.

50 See G. R. Owst, *Literature and Pulpit in Medieval England: A Neglected Chapter in the History of English Letters and of the English People* (New York: Barnes and Noble, 1961), 294–302.

51 See the formula provided in William Weste's *Simboleography, which may be termed the Art, or Description, of Instruments and Presidents* (1615), quoted by Samuel Schoenbaum, *William Shakespeare: A Documentary Life* (New York: Oxford University Press and the Scholar Press, 1975), 246.

52 Stephen Greenblatt, *Hamlet in Purgatory* (Princeton: Princeton University Press, 2001), 70–1.

53 On the shared semantics and mechanics of generational and textual imprints, see Margreta de Grazia, "Shakespeare, Gutenberg, and Descartes," in *Alternative Shakespeares*, vol. II, ed. Terence Hawkes (London and New York: Routledge, 1996), esp. 74–82.

54 On the exceptional appearance of a ghost in armor, see Ann Rosalind Jones and Peter Stallybrass, *Renaissance Clothing and the Materials of Memory* (Cambridge and New York: Cambridge University Press, 2000), 251.

55 R. S. Guernsey, *Ecclesiastical Law in "Hamlet"* (New York: The Shakespeare Society of New York, 1885), 8, 14.

56 For classical, medieval, and Renaissance examples from collections of paternal precepts, see Jenkins, ed., *Hamlet*, 440–1.

57 On this unit, varying from 10 to 120 acres, see Maitland's 200-page essay, "The Hide," in his *Domesday Book and Beyond*, 357–520. See, also, T. M. Charles-Edwards, "Kinship, Status, and the Origins of the Hide," *Past and Present* 55 (1972), 3–33.

58 Holinshed, *Chronicles*, I:13.

59 Upon arrival in Libya, Dido asked for a small bit of land, only as much as could be encompassed by an ox-hide, for a temporary refuge. When granted this, she cut the ox-hide into a thong so fine that she was able to surround the plot of land which became Carthage. See Virgil, *Aeneid*, in *Virgil*, trans. H. Rushton Fairclough, rev. G. P. Goold, 2 vols. (Cambridge, MA: Harvard University Press, and London: William Heinemann, 1974), I, 1.365–8; and Christopher Marlowe, *Dido Queen of Carthage*, in *"Dido Queen of Carthage" and "The Massacre at Paris"*, ed. H. J. Oliver (Cambridge, MA: Harvard University Press, 1968), 4.2.13.

60 On the puffed-up or swollen rhetoric of the Shakespearean upstart and its relation to the inflation of titles, honors, and money, see Patricia Parker's comments on Parolles, Oswald, and Osric, in *Shakespeare from the Margins: Language, Culture, Context* (Chicago: University of Chicago Press, 1996), esp. 213–20.

61 The stage directions for Q2 call for "a corse" and for Q1 and F "a coffin." Frye argues that the former was "far more frequent" in the period, *Renaissance "Hamlet"*, 351, n. 63.

62 See Edwards, ed., *Hamlet*, 222, n. 225, and Jenkins, ed., *Hamlet*, 433.

63 In his apology to Laertes, Hamlet refers to him as "my brother" (5.2.239) and calls the duel a "brothers' wager" (5.2.249). This would make him loving brother to Ophelia as well: "Forty thousand brothers / Could not with all their quantity of love / Make up my sum" (5.1.264–6).

64 "A Funeral Elegy on the Death of Richard Burbage" (1619), in E. K. Chambers, *The Elizabethan Stage*, 2 vols. (Oxford: Oxford University Press, 1923), II:309; but see Weimann on Burbage as the model for self-contained impersonation rather than non-representational clowning, *Author's Pen*, 136.

65 See Simon Shepherd, "Revels End, and the Gentle Body Starts," *Shakespeare Survey* 55 (2002), 237–56.

66 Weimann, *Author's Pen*, 101.

67 Some modern productions heroize Hamlet's leap by postponing it until the final scene. Robert Hapgood reports that Sir Laurence Olivier, by jumping down from a fifteen-foot height to kill Claudius, outdid John Barrymore's ten-foot leap: "the King's burly stuntman was knocked unconscious and lost two teeth." See Robert Hapgood, ed., *Hamlet Prince of Denmark* (Cambridge: Cambridge University Press, 1999), 70.

68 See, for example, Harley Granville-Barker, *Prefaces to Shakespeare* (Princeton: Princeton University Press, 1946), 139, n. 19; and C. Walter Hodges' illustration and discussion of the scene, *Enter the Whole Army: A Pictorial Study of Shakespearean Staging, 1576–1616* (Cambridge: Cambridge University Press, 1999), 156, 158.

69 J. Dover Wilson, *What Happens in "Hamlet"* (Cambridge: Cambridge University Press, 1995), 300.

70 *Ibid.*, 268.

71 Samuel Johnson, Annotation to *Hamlet* (1765), in *CR*, I:191.

72 George Steevens, Annotation to *Hamlet* (1793), in *CR*, I: 228–9.

73 Henry Mackenzie, *Mirror* 100 (1780), in *CR*, I:272.
74 William Richardson, *Essays on Shakespeare's Dramatic Characters . . . and Additional Observations on the Character of Hamlet* (1783), in *Shakespeare: The Critical Heritage*, ed. Brian Vickers, 6 vols. (London and Boston: Routledge and Kegan Paul, 1979–81), VI:368–9.
75 Wilson, *What Happens*, 92.
76 Ernest Jones, *Hamlet and Oedipus* (New York: Norton, 1976), 82.
77 *Ibid.*, 85.
78 Jacques Lacan, "Desire and the Interpretation of Desire in *Hamlet*," trans. James Hulbert, in *Literature and Psychoanalysis: The Question of Reading, Otherwise*, ed. Shoshana Felman (Baltimore: Johns Hopkins University Press, 1982), 20. Page references to Lacan henceforth appear parenthetically in text.

CHAPTER 6: HAMLET'S DELAY

1 As early as 1898, A. H. Tolman identified eighteen different explanations for Hamlet's delay, "A View of the Views about Hamlet," *PMLA* 13:2 (1898), 155–84.
2 For a list of eighteenth-century critics offended by Hamlet's diabolical desire for revenge, see Brian Vickers, "The Emergence of Character Criticism, 1774–1800," *Shakespeare Survey* 34 (1981), 14–15, and Vickers, ed., *Shakespeare: The Critical Heritage*, 6 vols. (London and Boston: Routledge and Kegan Paul, 1979–81), vol. VI:24; henceforth cited as *CH*.
3 George Stubbes, *Some Remarks on "The Tragedy of Hamlet"* (1736 facs. rpt.; New York: AMS Press, 1975), 33.
4 William D'Avenant, ed., *The Tragedy of Hamlet, Prince of Denmark: As it is now Acted at His Highness the Duke of York's Theatre* (London, 1676), "To the Reader." In the German prose play *Der Bestrafte Brudermord oder Prinz Hamlet aus Dännemark*, a version of *Hamlet* thought to have been taken to the Continent by English actors sometime before 1626, Hamlet refrains from killing Claudius because he does not want the penitent's sins upon his own head. For a translation of this play, see *Fratricide Punished*, in *Narrative and Dramatic Sources of Shakespeare*, ed. Geoffrey Bullough, 8 vols. (London: Routledge and Kegan Paul, and New York: Columbia University Press, 1957–75), VII:128–58.
5 For an account of how these lines were neutralized or cut throughout this period, see Philip Edwards' introduction to his edition of *Hamlet* (Cambridge: Cambridge University Press, 1993), 63–7. Edwin Booth in his 1870 performance appears to have been the first actor since before the Restoration to speak the infamous lines; a contemporary account reports that "he smile[d] savagely with shut teeth" and looked "terrible, almost ferocious, and *inhumanly* malignant;" see Charles H. Shattuck, *The Hamlet of Edwin Booth* (Urbana, IL: University of Illinois Press, 1969), 222–3.
6 Thomas Davies, *Life of Garrick* (1784), in *Critical Responses to "Hamlet" 1600–1900*, ed. David Farley-Hills, 4 vols. (New York: AMS Press, 1995–), I:285; hereafter cited as *CR*.

7 George Steevens, *St. James Chronicle* (1782), in *CR*, I:221
8 Samuel Johnson, ed., *The Plays of William Shakespeare*, 8 vols. (1765 facs. rpt.; New York: AMS Press, 1968), VIII:236, n. 7.
9 Francis Gentleman, *The Dramatic Censor* (1770), in *CR*, I:2
10 Joseph Ritson, *Remarks* (1783), in *CH*, VI:342.
11 Thomas Davies, *The Life of Garrick*, in *CR*, I:285.
12 The post-*Hamlet* analogues are: Webster's *White Devil* (1612), S.S.'s *The Honest Lawyer* (1616), Beaumont and Fletcher's *Four Plays in One* (c. 1608), and Lewis Machin's *The Dumb Knight* (1633); see Edmond Malone and James Boswell, eds., *The Plays and Poems of William Shakspeare*, 21 vols. (1821 facs. rpt.; New York: AMS Press, 1966), VII:382–3. Eleanor Prosser lists twenty-three instances of similar fiendishness in stage avengers, but none in drama before Shakespeare; see her *Hamlet and Revenge* (Stanford: Stanford University Press, 1971), 265–79.
13 Anonymous, "A Dialogue between Two Theatrical Heroes of Shakespeare and Corneille," *London Magazine* (1782), in *CH*, VI:316–20.
14 For "psychology," the *OED* cites Blancard's 1693 *Physical Dictionary* which divides "*Anthropologia or the Description of Man*" into two parts: "Anatomy, which treats of the Body, and *Psycology* [sic], which treats of the Soul." In 1800 Coleridge introduces the term to literary criticism, "we have no single term to express the Philosophy of the Human Mind"; Alice D. Snyder, ed., *S. T. Coleridge's "Treatise on Method"* (London: Constable, 1934), 32, n. 3.
15 Thomas Robertson, "An Essay on the Character of Hamlet" (1788), in *CH*, VI:486. Thomas Sheridan anticipated this evasive critical move: if spoken "really from the heart," he argued, the lines would make Hamlet "the most black, revengeful man"; it would be more consistent with his character "to suppose him here endeavouring to make an excuse to himself"; as recorded in Boswell's journal (1763), cited by Vickers, in *CH*, IV:8.
16 William Richardson, *Essays on Shakespeare's Dramatic Characters . . . and Additional Observations on the Character of Hamlet* (1783), in *CH*, VI:367.
17 *Ibid.*
18 Richardson, *Characters*, in *CH*, VI:368.
19 Johnson, ed., *Plays of William Shakespeare*, VIII:209, n. 9.
20 Robertson, *Character*, in *CH*, VI:486.
21 Richardson, *Characters*, in *CH*, VI:368.
22 *Ibid.*
23 *Ibid.*, VI:367–8.
24 Joseph Butler, "Upon the Character of Balaam," "Upon Self-Deceit," "'And not using your liberty for a cloak of maliciousness,'" in W. E. Gladstone, ed., *The Works of Joseph Butler*, 3 vols. (Bristol: Thoemmes Press, 1995), II:121–35, 168–84, 317–38. According to Ernest Mossner, by the late eighteenth century, Butler was widely read in Scottish universities; *Bishop Butler and the Age of Reason* (New York: Macmillan, 1936), 196–7.
25 Butler, *Works*, II:118–20.
26 Butler, *Works*, I:259–67.

27 William Prynne, *Histrio-Matrix* (1633), quoted in Ramie Targoff, "The Performance of Prayer: Sincerity and Theatricality in Early Modern England," *Representations* 60 (1997), 51. For an illuminating discussion of the importance of hypocrisy to both theatrical impersonation and religious conformity, see Targoff, "Performance," 49–69; and Katharine Eisaman Maus, "Introduction: Inwardness and Spectatorship," in her *Inwardness and Theater in the English Renaissance* (Chicago and London: University of Chicago Press, 1995), 1–34.

28 For evidence of this practice, see Douglas Bruster, *Quoting Shakespeare: Form and Culture in Early Modern Drama* (Lincoln: University of Nebraska Press, 2000), 23, 217–18, n. 28.

29 August Wilhelm von Schlegel, *Course of Lectures on Dramatic Art and Literature*, trans. John Black (Philadelphia: Hogan and Thompson, 1833), 329.

30 J. P. Collier's report of Lecture 12 of S. T. Coleridge's *Lectures on Shakespeare and Milton* (1811–12), in *CR*, II:58.

31 S. T. Coleridge, "1811–12 Lectures on Shakespeare & Milton," in Coleridge, *Lectures 1808–1819 on Literature*, ed. R. A. Foakes, 2 vols. (London: Routledge and Kegan Paul, and Princeton: Princeton University Press, 1987), I:389.

32 Coleridge, "1813 Lectures on Shakespeare and Education," in Coleridge, *Lectures 1808–1819 on Literature*, ed. Foakes, I:539.

33 Malone and Boswell, eds., *Plays and Poems of Shakspeare*, VII:537. Nathan Drake in *Shakespeare and His Times* (1817) also discusses Hamlet's "exquisite self-deceit" in this scene, "affording a striking proof of that hypocrisy which . . . he was constantly exercising on himself," in *CR*, II:128. For Byron's condemnation of Hamlet's fiendishness in this scene, and Shelley's appeals to prevarication in his defense, see Jonathan Bate, *Shakespeare and the English Romantic Imagination* (Oxford: Clarendon Press, 1986), 223–4.

34 Ernest Jones, *Hamlet and Oedipus* (New York: Norton, 1976), 52.

35 On the emergence of character criticism from the search for the Horatian ideals of consistency and morality, particularly in *Hamlet*, see Vickers, "Emergence of Character Criticism," 11–21.

36 Henry Mackenzie, *The Mirror* (1780), in *CR*, I:268; Francis Gentleman, *The Dramatic Censor* (1770), in *CR*, I:213.

37 Mackenzie, *Mirror*, in *CR*, I:268.

38 Coleridge, "1811–12 Lectures," in Coleridge, *Lectures 1808–1819 on Literature*, ed. Foakes, I:386.

39 Thomas Sheridan located the consistency of Hamlet's character in his irresolution: "His timidity being once admitted, all the strange fluctuations which we perceive in him may be easily traced to that source"; as recorded by Boswell (1763), quoted by Vickers, in *CH*, IV:8.

40 Johann Wolfgang von Goethe, *Wilhelm Meister's Apprenticeship*, ed. and trans. Eric A. Blackall, Goethe's Collected Works no. 9 (Princeton: Princeton University Press, 1995), 146.

41 Coleridge, "1811–12 Lectures," in Coleridge, *Lectures 1808–1819 on Literature*, ed. Foakes, 1:390.

42 Schlegel, *Course*, 42.

43 G. W. F. Hegel, *The Philosophy of Fine Art*, trans. F. P. B. Osmaston, 4 vols. (New York: Hacker Art Books, 1975), IV:335, 338.

44 *Ibid.*, IV:342.

45 A. C. Bradley, *Shakespearean Tragedy: Lectures on "Hamlet," "Othello," "King Lear," "Macbeth"* (1904; London and New York: Penguin, 1991), 35. Page references to Bradley will henceforth appear in the text.

46 Sigmund Freud, *Interpretation of Dreams*, in *The Basic Writings of Sigmund Freud*, ed. and trans. A. A. Brill (New York: Modern Library, 1938), 163–4.

47 Freud, "An Autobiographical Study," in *The Freud Reader*, ed. Peter Gay (New York: Norton, 1989), 38.

48 Freud, *Interpretation*, 310.

49 Jacques Lacan, "Desire and the Interpretation of Desire in *Hamlet*," trans. James Hulbert, in *Literature and Psychoanalysis: The Question of Reading, Otherwise*, ed. Shoshana Felman (Baltimore: Johns Hopkins University Press, 1982), 11–52. Subsequent page references to Lacan appear parenthetically in the text. For a discussion of Lacan's reading of *Hamlet* as a rehabilitation of Freud that "both propagates and distends the Freudian legacy," see Richard Halpern, *Shakespeare Among the Moderns* (Ithaca, NY: Cornell University Press, 1997), 254. See also Jean-Michel Rabaté, *Jacques Lacan: Psychoanalysis and the Subject of Literature* (Basingstoke, Hampshire and New York: Palgrave, 2001), 54–68.

50 Friedrich Nietzsche, *The Birth of Tragedy and Other Writings*, ed. Raymond Geuss and Ronald Speirs, trans. Ronald Speirs (Cambridge: Cambridge University Press, 1999), 40.

51 Walter Benjamin, *The Origin of German Tragic Drama*, trans. John Osborne (London and New York: Verso, 1985), 140, 138.

52 Theodor W. Adorno, *Negative Dialectics*, trans. E. B. Ashton (New York: Continuum, 1966), 228.

53 Emmanuel Lévinas, *Otherwise Than Being, or Beyond Essence*, trans. Alphonso Lingis (Pittsburgh: Duquesne University Press, 1981), 117, 124.

54 Janet Adelman, *Suffocating Mothers: Fantasies of Maternal Origin in Shakespeare's Plays* (New York: Routledge, 1992), 30.

55 Terry Eagleton, *William Shakespeare* (Oxford and New York: Blackwell, 1986), 72.

56 Jonathan Goldberg, *Voice Terminal Echo: Postmodernism and English Renaissance Texts* (New York: Methuen, 1986), 99, 100.

57 Catherine Belsey, *Shakespeare and the Loss of Eden: The Construction of Family Values in Early Modern Culture* (London: Palgrave, 2000), 173.

58 Marjorie Garber, *Shakespeare's Ghost Writers: Literature as Uncanny Causality* (New York: Methuen, 1987), 156. For a reversal of Garber's reading, see John Kerrigan's argument that remembering, not forgetting, dulls revenge, in *Revenge Tragedy: Aeschylus to Armageddon* (Oxford and New York: Clarendon Press, 1996), 186–7.

59 Halpern, *Shakespeare Among the Moderns*, 284, 287–8.

60 John Guillory, "'To Please the Wiser Sort': Violence and Philosophy in *Hamlet*," in *Historicism, Psychoanalysis, and Early Modern Culture*, ed. Carla Mazzio and Douglas Trevor (New York and London: Routledge, 2000), 82–109.

61 Catherine Gallagher and Stephen Greenblatt, *Practicing New Historicism* (Chicago: University of Chicago Press, 2000), 158, and Greenblatt, *Hamlet in Purgatory* (Princeton: Princeton University Press, 2001), 243. For the centering of Eucharistic debates on the "embarrassments of matter" in the Reformation, see Greenblatt, "Remnants of the Sacred in Early Modern England," in *Subject and Object in Renaissance Culture*, ed. Margreta de Grazia, Maureen Quilligan, and Peter Stallybrass, (Cambridge: Cambridge University Press, 1996), 337–45.

62 Linda Charnes, *Hamlet's Heirs: Shakespeare and the Politics of a New Millennium* (New York and London: Routledge, 2006), 115–23.

63 Jenkins, ed., *Hamlet*, 139–40.

64 Stephen Greenblatt, *Will in the World: How Shakespeare Became Shakespeare* (New York and London: Norton, 2004), 324.

65 As Paul Werstine has argued, delay is much more a feature of the eighteenth-century composite text than of any of the three early texts of the play; see "The Textual Mystery of *Hamlet*," *Shakespeare Quarterly* 39 (1988), 1–26. Leah S. Marcus, quoting Peter Guinness, refers to Q1 as "*Hamlet* with the brakes off," in *Unediting the Renaissance: Shakespeare, Marlowe, Milton* (New York and London: Routledge, 1996), 145. In the anonymous *Fratricide Punished*, the presence of the King's bodyguards is repeatedly given as the cause of Hamlet's delay; see Bullough, ed., *Sources of Shakespeare*, VII:138, 154.

66 See Samuel Johnson, "Annotations on Shakespeare" (1765), in *CR*, I:192.

67 Stubbes, *Some Remarks on "The Tragedy of Hamlet"*, 5. Subsequent page references to this work appear parenthetically in the text. Goethe refers to this view when observing that even the English have admitted that the plot "doesn't move along at all," the "last two [acts] lagging sorrily on," the play "seems to stand stock-still," *Wilhelm Meister*, 151.

68 J. V. Jensen, "Hamlet," *The London Mercury* (March 1925), quoted by Harry Levin, *The Question of Hamlet* (New York: Oxford University Press, 1959), 124 and 128, n. 17.

69 Johnson, "Annotations," in *CR*, I:192.

70 George Steevens, "Commentary and Annotations on *Hamlet*" (1772), in *CR*, I:221.

71 *Ibid.*, I:220.

72 Johnson, "Annotations," in *CR*, I:192.

73 See Chapter 1, above, 7, n. 2.

74 William Empson, *Essays on Shakespeare*, ed. David B. Pirie (Cambridge and New York: Cambridge University Press, 1986), 82. Page references to Empson will henceforth appear in text.

75 Thomas Nashe, Preface to *Menaphon* (1589), as quoted in Jenkins, ed., *Hamlet*, 83.

76 Thomas Lodge, *Wit's Misery* (1596), as quoted in *ibid.*, 83.

77 In *Will in the World*, Greenblatt argues that Shakespeare bracketed the play between two endpoints ("revelation and revenge") and used "the queasy interval" in order "to focus almost the entire tragedy on the consciousness of the hero," 304–5.

78 Patricia Parker includes *mora* and *moria* in her discussion of the proliferative verbal networking mulberries, moors, and more, in "What's In a Name: And More," *Sederi: Revista de la Sociedad Española de Estudios Renacentistas Ingleses* 11 (2002), 101–50. See also her *Shakespeare from the Margins: Language, Culture, Context* (Chicago: University of Chicago Press, 1996), 275, n. 11.

79 Parker relates "farce" to material to be stuffed, crammed, or forced between two endpoints, *Margins*, 76, 301, n. 33.

80 Livy, *The Romane Historie by Titus Livius*, trans. Philemon Holland (1600), in Bullough, ed., *Sources of Shakespeare*, 80.

81 *The Hystorie of Hamblet* (1608), in *ibid.*, 95.

82 Richard Brome, *The Antipodes*, ed. Ann Haaker (Lincoln: University of Nebraska Press, 1966), 40. A number of scholars have followed David Wiles in arguing that Hamlet's reprimand reflects the Clown's waning popularity after Kempe in 1600, *Shakespeare's Clown* (Cambridge: Cambridge University Press, 1987), vii–viii. Richard Preiss challenges this view, in "Robert Armin Do the Police in Different Voices," in *From Stage to Print in Early Modern England*, ed. Peter Holland and Stephen Orgel (New York and Basingstoke, Hampshire: Palgrave Macmillan, 2006), 208–27.

83 Robert Weimann, *Shakespeare and the Popular Tradition in the Theater: Studies in the Social Dimension of Dramatic Form and Function*, ed. Robert Schwartz (Baltimore: Johns Hopkins University Press, 1978), 224.

84 Thomas Davies, *The Life of Garrick* (1784), in *CR*, 1:295.

85 J. O. Halliwell, cited in the Variorum *Hamlet*, ed. Horace Howard Furness, A New Variorum Edition of Shakespeare, 2 vols. (1877; New York: Dover, 1963), 1:375.

86 See Marcus, *Unediting the Renaissance*, 173–4 and Robert Weimann, *Author's Pen and Actor's Voice: Playing and Writing in Shakespeare's Theatre*, ed. Helen Higbee and William West (Cambridge: Cambridge University Press, 2000), 23–5.

87 For the use of writing tables by characters in plays, see Alan C. Dessen and Leslie Thomson, *A Dictionary of Stage Directions in English Drama, 1580–1642* (Cambridge and New York: Cambridge University Press, 1999), 224–5; for evidence of their use by the audience, see Laurie E. Maguire, *Shakespearean Suspect Texts: The "Bad" Quartos and Their Contexts* (Cambridge and New York: Cambridge University Press, 1996), 125–35.

88 On the Clown's origin in the Tudor Vice, see Wiles, *Clown*, 1–10.

89 From the anonymous *A Whip for an Ape* (1589), quoted by Weimann, *Popular Tradition*, 158.

90 *Ibid.*, 191.
91 See *Pilgrimmage to Parnassus*, in *The Three Parnassus Plays, 1598–1601*, ed. J. B. Leishman, (London: Nicholson and Watson, 1949), 129, 223.
92 Joseph Hall, *Virgidemiarum* (1597), cited by Weimann, *Popular Tradition*, 287.
93 See Jenkins, ed., *Hamlet*, 226, n. 180, and Weimann, *Author's Pen*, 167–8.
94 Anthony Scoloker, *Diaphantus: Or, The Passions of Love* (1604), in *CR*, I:2.
95 For the theatrical tradition of vulgarity in the play scene, see John A. Mills, *"Hamlet" on Stage: The Great Tradition* (Westport, CT: Greenwood Press, 1985), 83.
96 For Weimann, this shift – from decorous compliance to grotesque evasion – epitomizes the recurrent clash in early modern theatre between the "mirror of representation" and its antic "deformation," *Author's Pen*, 174–6.
97 Weimann, *Popular Tradition*, 116–60.
98 From M. M. Mahood, *Shakespeare's Wordplay* (1957), cited by Weimann in his *Popular Tradition*, 130 and *Author's Pen*, 177.
99 Weimann, *Popular Tradition*, 130.
100 Charles Lamb, *The Tragedies of Shakespeare* (1818), in *CR*, II:102–3.
101 See Harold Jenkins, ed., *Hamlet*, 272, n. 577, and his "Playhouse Interpolations in the Folio Text of *Hamlet*," *Studies in Bibliography* 13 (1960), 31–47.
102 Jenkins, ed., *Hamlet*, 511.
103 These remarkable images can be seen in the developing catalogue of "Medieval Wall Painting in the English Parish Church," at http://www. paintedchurch.org./conpage.htm. A wall painting of the Doom existed on the chancel currently being restored at Holy Trinity Church in Coventry.
104 The Stratford Guild Hall Chapel also included illustrations of the legend of the cross, a Crucifix, Saints Modwena and Ursula, and the martyrdom of St. Thomas Becket. The Guild Chapel stands across the street from New Place, the property purchased by Shakespeare in 1597. In 1563–4, John Shakespeare, William's father, then Chamberlain, oversaw the defacing of these images after the Royal Injunctions of 1559 that all signs of "superstition" and "idolatry" be removed from places of worship. For a discussion of the wall paintings and reproductions of the early-nineteenth-century drawings, see Clifford Davidson, *The Guild Chapel Wall Paintings at Stratford-upon-Avon* (New York: AMS Press, 1988).
105 On the devil's "laughing, grinning, and gnashing his teeth," see Stephen Greenblatt's discussion of John Foxe's ridicule of "ye merry Antiques" of Sir Thomas More, *Hamlet in Purgatory* (Princeton: Princeton University Press, 2001), 251.
106 *King Lear* (Conflated Text), in *Norton Shakespeare*, ed. Greenblatt et al. 4.6.69–72. With the exception of *Hamlet*, all works by Shakespeare are quoted from this edition.
107 For the ubiquity of devils in the medieval mysteries and moralities as well as their surprising longevity on the London public stage up to the closing of

the theaters, see John D. Cox, *The Devil and the Sacred in English Drama, 1350–1642* (Cambridge and New York: Cambridge University Press, 2000).

108 Jenkins, ed., *Hamlet*, 458.

109 Francis Bacon, "Of Revenge," in *The Essays*, ed. John Pitcher (London and New York: Penguin, 1985), 72. The law of retaliation is three times stated in the Old Testament (Exodus 22:24; Lev. 24:20; Deut. 19:21) and once quoted (to be overturned) in the New (Matt. 5:39).

110 Seneca, *Thyestes*, in *Tragedies of Seneca*, trans. Frank Justus Miller (Cambridge, MA: Harvard University Press, 1968), 2.104; John Marston, *Antonio's Revenge*, ed. W. Reavley Gair (Manchester: Manchester University Press, and New York: St. Martin's Press, 1999), 3.1.51.

111 Christ's mercy is also inequitable, as Hamlet notes, "Use every man after his desert, and who shall scape whipping?" (2.2.524–5). (Laertes' "exchange of forgiveness" with Hamlet, the play's only instance of forgiveness, is also uneven: "Mine and my father's death come not upon thee, / Nor thine on me" [5.2.335–6]). I am indebted to John Parker for noting the uneasy kinship between *inequity* and *iniquity*, particularly as instantiated by Christ himself; see *The Aesthetics of Antichrist: From Christian Drama to Christopher Marlowe* (Ithaca, NY: Cornell University Press, forthcoming).

112 For the distinction between the eternal pains of hell and the determinate ones of purgatory, see Greenblatt, *Hamlet in Purgatory*, 230.

113 See Cox, *Devil*, 5–6.

114 Sir Thomas Browne, *Religio Medici*, in *"Religio Medici," "Hydriotaphia," and "The Garden of Cyrus,"* ed. Robin Robbins (Oxford: Clarendon Press, 2001), 72.

115 Sir Philip Sidney, *An Apology for Poetry*, ed. Geoffrey Shepherd (Manchester and New York: Manchester University Press, 1965), 135.

116 Charlotte Lennox, *Shakespear Illustrated* (1753), in *CR*, I:178.

117 Johnson, "Annotations," in *CR*, I:192.

118 Francis Gentleman, *The Dramatic Censor* (1770), in *CR*, I:212

119 Lennox, in *CR*, I:178.

120 George Steevens, "Commentary and Annotations on *Hamlet*," in *CR*, I:229, 228.

121 *Ibid.*, I:229.

122 William Richardson, *Essays on Shakespeare's Dramatic Characters* (1783), in *CH*, VI:368; Thomas Robertson, *An Essay on the Character of Hamlet* (1788), in *CH*, VI:482.

123 Mackenzie, *The Mirror*, in *CR*, I:274.

124 Malone and Boswell, eds., *Plays and Poems of Shakspeare*, VII:535.

125 S. T. Coleridge, "Marginalia," in *CR*, II:73–4.

126 Weimann, *Popular Tradition*, 128–9, 150.

127 *Ibid.*, 126.

128 On the time of the "middest," see Frank Kermode, *The Sense of an Ending: Studies in the Theory of Fiction* (Oxford and New York: Oxford University Press, 1967), esp. 43–8; on the traditional novel "as a complex gloss upon the

word *meanwhile*," see Benedict Anderson, *Imagined Communities: Reflections on the Origin and Spread of Nationalism* (London: Verso, 1983), 25.

129 Tacitus, *The Annals*, trans. A. J. Woodman (Indianapolis: Hackett, 2004), 15.39.

130 See T. H. Baldwin, *Small Latine and Lesse Greeke*, 2 vols. (Urbana, IL: University of Illinois Press, 1944), II:484–7, 495.

131 Erasmus, *On Copia of Words and Ideas*, trans. Donald B. King and H. David Rix (Milwaukee, WI: Marquette University Press, 1963), 13.

132 *The Rape of Lucrece*, in *The Norton Shakespeare*, ed. Stephen Greenblatt et al. (New York and London: Norton, 1997), line 1367.

133 For the popularity of the biblical passage as legend, sermon, drama, and ballad, see Jenkins, ed., *Hamlet*, Longer Notes, 475–7.

134 An anonymous report, *The London Post* (January 1645), in *CR*, I:12.

135 On Pyrrhus' mirroring of Hamlet's inaction, see Levin's richly informed reading of the Player's speech, in *The Question of Hamlet*, 151. See also Christopher Pye's oedipal account of the standstill in *The Vanishing: Shakespeare, the Subject, and Early Modern Culture* (Durham, NC: Duke University Press, 2000), 110–11.

136 John Milton, *Paradise Lost*, 10.210–11, in John Milton, *Complete Poems and Major Prose*, ed. Merritt Y. Hughes (Indianapolis: The Odyssey Press, 1980).

137 *Ibid.*, 11.254–5, 255–7.

138 "When Eve had given birth to her first-born son, she hoped that she already had that Crusher," in Martin Luther, *Lectures on Genesis: Chs. 1–5*, in *Luther's Works*, ed. Jaroslav Pelikan, 55 vols. (Saint Louis: Concordia Publishing House, 1958), 1:193.

139 Anon., *Everyman*, in *Medieval Drama*, ed. David Bevington (Boston: Houghton Mifflin, 1975), lines 71, 101, 123, 131.

140 On the centrality of the *Katechon* to the Pauline notion of Messianic time, see Giorgio Agamber, *The Time That Remains: A Commentary on the Letter to the Romans*, trans. Patricia Daily (Stanford: Stanford University Press, 2005), 108–11.

141 On the figure of Death as a sergeant making arrests without bail in anticipation of the summoning and sentencing to occur at the final judgment, see Michael Neill, *Issues of Death: Mortality and Identity in English Renaissance Tragedy* (Oxford: Clarendon Press, and New York: Oxford University Press, 1997), 59.

142 For life-like representations of death as the epitome of the tragedian's art, see Tobias Doëring, "Writing Performance: How to Elegize Elizabethan Actors," *Shakespeare Survey* 58 (2005), 60–71.

143 For the debate over whether these "Os" were scripted by Shakespeare or interpolated by actors, see Peter Holland, "*Hamlet*: Text in Performance," in *Hamlet*, ed. Peter J. Smith and Nigel Wood, (Buckingham and Philadelphia: Open University Press, 1996), esp. 66–70.

Selected bibliography

PRIMARY SOURCES (BEFORE 1800)

Alter, Robert, *The Five Books of Moses: A Translation with Commentary* (New York: Norton, 2004)

Anon., *The Mirror for Magistrates*, ed. Lily B. Campbell (New York: Barnes and Noble, 1960)

Anon., "A Funeral Elegy on the Death of Richard Burbage" (1618), in E. K. Chambers, *The Elizabethan Stage*, vol. II (Oxford: Oxford University Press, 1923)

Anon., *Fratricide Punished*, in Geoffrey Bullough, ed., *Narrative and Dramatic Sources of Shakespeare*, 8 vols., vol. VII (London: Routledge and Kegan Paul, and New York: Columbia University Press, 1957–75)

Anon., *Everyman*, in *Medieval Drama*, ed. David Bevington (Boston: Houghton Mifflin, 1975)

Anon., *Pilgrimmage to Parnassus*, in J. B. Leishman, ed., *The Three Parnassus Plays, 1598–1601* (London: Nicholson and Watson, 1949)

Anon., *Sir Thomas Smithes voiage and entertainment in Rushia. With the tragicall ends of two Emperors, and one Empresse, within one Moneth during his being there* (London, 1605)

Appian (trans. Horace White), *Appian's Roman History* (London: William Heinemann, and New York: Macmillan, 1912)

Shakespeare's Appian: A Selection from the Tudor Translation of Appian's "Civil Wars", ed. Ernest Schanzer (Liverpool: Liverpool University Press, 1956)

Aristotle (trans. Richard Janko), *Poetics* (Indianapolis, IN: Hackett, 1987)

Ashe, Thomas, *Fasciculus Florum or A Handfull of Flowers Gathered out of the severall Bookes of . . . Sir Edward Coke* (London, 1618)

Bacon, Francis, *The Essays*, ed. John Pitcher (London and New York: Penguin, 1985)

Beaumont, Francis and John Fletcher, *Philaster: or, Love Lies A-Bleeding*, ed. Andrew Gurr (Manchester and New York: Manchester University Press Press, and New York: Palgrave, 2003)

Belleforest, François de (trans. anon.), *The Hystorie of Hamblet* (1608), in Geoffrey Bullough, ed., *Narrative and Dramatic Sources of Shakespeare*, 8 vols., vol. VII (London: Routledge and Kegan Paul, and New York: Columbia University Press, 1957–75), 81–124

Blackstone, William, *Commentaries on the Laws of England*, 4 vols. (1765–9 facs. rpt.; Chicago and London: University of Chicago Press, 1979)

Bodin, Jean (trans. Beatrice Reynolds), *Method for the Easy Comprehension of History* (New York: Octagon, 1966)

Bolton, Edmund, *The Elements of Armories* (London, 1610)

Brome, Richard, *The Antipodes*, ed. Ann Haaker (Lincoln: University of Nebraska Press, 1966)

Browne, Sir Thomas, *"Religio Medici", "Hydriotaphia", and "The Garden of Cyrus"*, ed. Robin Robbins (Oxford: Clarendon Press, 2001)

Butler, Joseph, *The Works of Joseph Butler*, ed. W. E. Gladstone, 3 vols. (Bristol: Thoemmes Press, 1995)

Camden, William, *Remaines concerning Britain* (1657 facs. rpt.; New York: AMS Press, 1972)

Coke, Sir Edward, *The First Parte of the Institutes of the Lawes of England; Or, A Commentarie upon Littleton* (London, 1628)

The Selected Writings of Sir Edward Coke, ed. Steve Sheppard, 3 vols. (Indianapolis, IN: Liberty Fund, 2003)

Daniel, Samuel, *The Collection of the Historie of England* (1618 facs. rpt.; Delmar, NY: Scholars' Facsimiles and Reprints, 1986)

Dekker, Thomas, *The Plague Pamphlets of Thomas Dekker*, ed. F. P. Wilson (Oxford: Clarendon Press, 1925)

Drayton, Michael, *Poly-Olbion* (London, 1612)

Erasmus, Desiderius (trans. Donald B. King and H. David Rix), *On Copia of Words and Ideas* (Milwaukee, WI: Marquette University Press, 1963)

Foxe, John, *The Acts and Monuments of John Foxe* (1563), ed. George Townsend, 8 vols. (1859 facs. rpt.; New York: AMS Press, 1965)

"The Story of M. Symon Fish," in Frank Manley, Germain Marc'hadour, Richard Marius, and Clarence Miller, eds., *The Complete Works of St. Thomas More*, vol. VII (New Haven: Yale University Press, 1990)

Godet, Gyles, *A Briefe Abstract of the Genealogy and Race of All the Kinges of England* (London, 1562)

Greville, Fulke, *A Treatise on Monarchy*, in *The Remains Being Poems of Monarchy and Religion*, ed. G. A. Wilkes (Oxford: Oxford University Press, 1965)

Guillim, John, *A Display of Heraldrie* (London, 1611)

Heywood, Thomas, *Troia Britanica: or, Great Britaines Troy* (1609 facs. rpt.; Hildesheim and New York: G. Olms, 1972)

Holinshed, Raphael, *Chronicles of England, Scotland, and Ireland*, 3 vols. (1587 facs. rpt.; London: J. Johnson et al., 1808).

James I, *A Counterblaste to Tobacco* (1604 facs. rpt.; Amsterdam: Theatrum Orbis Terrarum, and New York: Da Capo Press, 1969)

Jonson, Ben, Eastward Ho, *in The Complete Plays of Ben Jonson*, ed. G. A. Wilkes, vol. II (Oxford: Clarendon Press, 1981)

The Works of Ben Jonson, ed. C. H. Herford and Percy Simpson, 11 vols. (Oxford: Clarendon Press, 1925–52)

Leroy, Louis (trans. Robert Ashley), *Of the Interchangeable Course or Variety of things in the whole world . . . from the beginning of civility and memory of Man to this present* (London, 1594)

Lewkenor, Samuel, *A Discourse . . . of forraine cities* (London, 1600)

Livius, Titus (trans. Philemon Holland), *The Romane Historie by Titus Livius* (1600), in Geoffrey Bullough, ed., *Narrative and Dramatic Sources of Shakespeare*, 8 vols., vol. VII (London: Routledge and Kegan Paul, and New York: Columbia University Press, 1957–75)

Lucretius (trans. Martin Ferguson Smith), *On the Nature of Things* (Indianapolis, IN: Hackett Publishing, 2001)

Luther, Martin, *Lectures on Genesis: Chapters 1–5*, in Jaroslav Pelikan, ed., *Luther's Works*, vol. I (Saint Louis, MO: Concordia Publishing House, 1958)

Machiavelli, Niccolò (trans. Harvey C. Mansfield and Nathan Tarcov), *Discourses upon Livy* (Chicago: University of Chicago Press, 1996)

Manningham, John, *The Diary of John Manningham of the Middle Temple, 1602–1603*, ed. Robert Parker Sorlien (Hanover, NH: University Press of New England, 1976)

Marlowe, Christopher, *"Dido Queen of Carthage" and "The Massacre at Paris"*, ed. H. J. Oliver (Cambridge, MA: Harvard University Press, 1968)

Marston, John, *Antonio's Revenge*, ed. W. Reavley Gair (Manchester: Manchester University Press, and New York: St. Martin's Press, 1999)

Meres, Francis, *Francis Meres's Treatise "Poetrie": A Critical Edition*, ed. Don Cameron Allen (Urbana, IL: The University of Illinois Press, 1933)

Milton, John, *Paradise Lost*, in Merritt Y. Hughes, ed., *Complete Poems and Major Prose* (Indianapolis: The Odyssey Press, 1980)

Minsheu, John, *"Ductor in linguas" and "Vocabularium hispanicolatinum"* (1617 facs. rpt.; Delmar, NY: Scholars' Facsimiles and Reprints, 1978)

More, Thomas, *The Supplication of Souls*, in Frank Manley, Germain Marc'hadour, Richard Marius, and Clarence Miller, eds., *The Complete Works of St. Thomas More*, vol. VII (New Haven: Yale University Press, 1990)

Norden, John, *Speculum Britanniae* (London, 1593)

Ovid (trans. Betty Rose Nagle), *Fasti* (Bloomington: Indiana University Press, 1995)

Ovid (trans. Arthur Golding), *Ovid's Metamorphoses* ed. Frederick Nims (1603 facs. rpt.; Philadelphia: Paul Dry Books, 2000)

Peele, George, *The Araygnement of Paris* (1584 facs. rpt.; Oxford: Oxford University Press: The Malone Society Reprints, 1910)

Plutarch (trans. Sir Thomas North), "The Life of Marcus Brutus," in *The Lives of the Noble Grecians and Romanes Compared* (London, 1579)

Plutarch (trans. Philemon Holland), *The Philosophie, commonlie called, The Morals* (London, 1603)

Raleigh, Sir Walter, *The History of the World* (London, 1614)

    Instructions to His Son and to Posterity, in Louis B. Wright, ed., *Advice to a Son: Precepts of Lord Burghley, Sir Walter Raleigh, and Francis Osborne* (Ithaca, NY: Cornell University Press, 1962)

Richardson, William, *A Philosophical Analysis of Some of Shakespeare's Remarkable Characters* (1774), in David Farley-Hills, ed., *Critical Responses to "Hamlet": 1600–1900*, 4 vols., vol. I (New York: AMS Press, 1995), 230–52

Essays on Shakespeare's Dramatic Characters of Richard the Third, King Lear, and Timon of Athens. To which are added, An Essay on the Faults of Shakespeare: and Additional Observations on the Character of Hamlet (1783), in Brian Vickers, ed., *Shakespeare: The Critical Heritage*, 6 vols., vol. VI (London: Routledge and Kegan Paul, 1979–81), 351–70

Robertson, Thomas, "An Essay on the Character of Hamlet" (1788), in Brian Vickers, ed., *Shakespeare: The Critical Heritage*, 6 vols., vol. VI (London: Routledge and Kegan Paul, 1979–81)

Rowe, Nicholas, *Life of Shakespeare* (1709), in David Farley-Hills, ed., *Critical Responses to "Hamlet": 1600–1900*, 4 vols., vol. I (New York: AMS Press, 1995–)

Saxo Grammaticus (trans. O. Elton), *Historiae Danicae*, in Geoffrey Bullough, ed., *Narrative and Dramatic Sources of Shakespeare*, 8 vols., vol. VII (London: Routledge and Kegan Paul, and New York: Columbia University Press, 1957–75)

Scoloker, Anthony, *Diaphantus; or, the Passions of Love* (1604), in David Farley-Hills, ed., *Critical Responses to "Hamlet": 1600–1900*, 4 vols., vol. I (New York: AMS Press, 1995–)

Seneca (trans. Frank Justus Miller), *Thyestes*, in *Tragedies of Seneca* (1907; Cambridge, MA: Harvard University Press, 1968)

Shakespeare, William, *Bell's Edition of Shakespeare's Plays*, ed. John Bell (London, 1775–6)

The Tragicall Historie of Hamlet Prince of Denmarke (1603 facs. rpt.; London: British Library, 2003)

The Tragicall Historie of Hamlet, Prince of Denmarke, in Michael J. B. Allen and Kenneth Muir, eds., *Shakespeare's Plays in Quarto* (1604/5 facs. rpt.; Berkeley: University of California Press, 1981)

The Tragedy of Hamlet, Prince of Denmark: As it is Now Acted at His Highness the Duke of York's Theatre, [ed. William D'Avenant] (London, 1676)

Hamlet, ed. Horace Howard Furness, A New Variorum Edition of Shakespeare, vols. I–II (1877; New York: Dover, 1963)

Hamlet, ed. Harold Jenkins (London: Methuen, The Arden Shakespeare, 1982)

Hamlet, Prince of Denmark, ed. Philip Edwards (Cambridge: Cambridge University Press, 1985)

Hamlet, ed. G. R. Hibbard (Oxford and New York: Oxford University Press, 1994)

Hamlet Prince of Denmark, ed. Robert Hapgood (Cambridge: Cambridge University Press, 1999)

The Sonnets and "A Lover's Complaint", ed. John Kerrigan (Harmondsworth: Penguin, 1986)

Mr. William Shakespeares Comedies, Histories, & Tragedies (1623 facs. rpt.; Washington, DC: Folger Library Publications, 1991)

The Works of Mr. William Shakespeare, ed. Nicholas Rowe, 6 vols. (London, 1709)

The Works of Shakespeare, ed. Alexander Pope, 6 vols. (1723–5 facs. rpt.; New York: AMS Press, 1969)

The Works of Shakespeare in Seven Volumes, ed. Lewis Theobald (1733 facs. rpt.; New York: AMS Press, 1968)

The Plays of William Shakespeare, ed. Samuel Johnson, 8 vols. (1765 facs. rpt.; New York: AMS Press, 1968)

Mr. William Shakespeare, his Comedies, Histories, and Tragedies, ed. Edward Capell, 10 vols. (1767–8 facs. rpt.; New York: AMS Press, 1968)

The Plays of William Shakespeare, ed. Samuel Johnson and George Steevens, revised and augmented by Isaac Reed, 10 vols. (London, 1793)

The Plays and Poems of William Shakspeare, ed. Edmond Malone and James Boswell, 21 vols. (1821 facs. rpt.; New York: AMS Press, 1966)

The Norton Shakespeare, ed. Stephen Greenblatt et al. (New York: Norton, 1997)

Sidney, Sir Philip, *An Apology for Poetry*, ed. Geoffrey Shepherd (Manchester and New York: Manchester University Press, 1965)

Sleidan, John (trans. Stephan Wythers), *A Briefe chronicle of the foure principall Empyres. To witte, of Babilon, Persia, Grecia, and Rome* (London, 1563)

Smythe, Sir John, *Certain Discourses Military* (1590), ed. J. R. Hale (Ithaca, NY: Cornell University Press, 1964)

Steevens, George, "Commentary and Annotations on *Hamlet*" (1772), in David Farley-Hills, ed., *Critical Responses to "Hamlet": 1600–1900*, 4 vols., vol. I (New York: AMS Press, 1995)

St. James Chronicle (1782), in David Farley-Hills, ed., *Critical Responses to "Hamlet": 1600–1900*, 4 vols., vol. I (New York: AMS Press, 1995–)

Stow, John, *A Survey of London*, 2 vols. (1603 facs. rpt.; Oxford: Clarendon Press, 1908)

The Annales of England (London, 1601)

Stubbes, George, *Some Remarks on "The Tragedy of Hamlet"* (1736 facs. rpt.; New York: AMS Press, 1975)

Tacitus (trans. A. J. Woodman), *The Annals* (Indianapolis, IN: Hackett Publishing, 2004)

Tottel, Richard, *Tottel's Miscellany*, ed. H. E. Rollins, 2 vols. (Cambridge, MA: Harvard University Press, 1965)

Virgil (trans. H. Rushton Fairclough), *Aeneid*, in *Virgil*, rev. G. P. Goold, vol. I (Cambridge, MA: Harvard University Press, 1999–2000)

Virgil (trans. H. Rushton Fairclough), *Georgics*, in *Virgil*, rev. G. P. Goold, vol. I (Cambridge, MA: Harvard University Press, 1999–2000)

Whitney, Isabella, *A Sweet Nosgay* (1573), in Richard J. Panofsky, ed., *The Floures of Philosophie (1572) by Hugh Plat and A Sweet Nosgay (1573) and The Copy of A Letter (1567) by Isabella Whitney* (Delmar, NY: Scholars' Facsimiles and Reprints, 1982)

SECONDARY SOURCES (AFTER 1800)

Abraham, Nicolas and Maria Torok, *The Shell and the Kernel: Renewals of Psychoanalysis*, ed. and trans. Nicholas T. Rand (Chicago: University of Chicago Press, 1994)

Adelman, Janet, *Suffocating Mothers: Fantasies of Maternal Origin in Shakespeare's Plays, "Hamlet" to "The Tempest"* (New York: Routledge, 1992)

Adorno, Theodor W. (trans. E. B. Ashton), *Negative Dialectics* (New York: Continuum, 1966)

Agamben, Giorgio (trans. Patricia Dailey), *The Time that Remains: A Commentary on the Letter to the Romans* (Stanford: Stanford University Press, 2005)

Alexander, Peter, *Hamlet: Father and Son* (Oxford: Clarendon Press, 1955)

Anderson, Benedict, *Imagined Communities: Reflections on the Origin and Spread of Nationalism* (London: Verso, 1983)

Ariès, Philippe (trans. Helen Weaver), *The Hour of Our Death* (New York: Oxford University Press, 1991)

Baker, Herschel, *The Race of Time: Three Lectures on Renaissance Historiography* (Toronto: University of Toronto Press, 1967)

Baker, J. H., *An Introduction to English Legal History*, 4th edn. (London and Edinburgh: Butterworths, 2002)

Baldwin, T. H., *Small Latine and Lesse Greeke*, 2 vols. (Urbana, IL: University of Illinois Press, 1944)

Barker, Francis, *The Tremulous Private Body: Essays on Subjection* (London and New York: Methuen, 1984)

Barlow, Frank, "Domesday Book," in Christopher Holdsworth, ed., *Domesday Essays* (Exeter: University of Exeter Press, 1986), 17–29

Barnaby, Andrew, "'Another Rome in the West?': Milton and the Imperial Republic, 1654–1670," *Milton Studies* 30 (1993), 67–84

Barnes, Robin Bruce, *Prophecy and Gnosis: Apocalypticism in the Wake of the Lutheran Reformation* (Stanford: Stanford University Press, 1988)

Barrell, John, *The Birth of Pandora and the Division of Knowledge* (Philadelphia: University of Pennsylvania Press, 1992)

Bate, Jonathan, *The Genius of Shakespeare* (London: Picador, 1997)
  Shakespeare and the English Romantic Imagination (Oxford: Clarendon Press, 1986)

Bates, David, "Domesday Book 1086–1986," in Christopher Holdsworth, ed., *Domesday Essays* (Exeter: University of Exeter Press, 1986), 1–15

Belsey, Catherine, *Shakespeare and the Loss of Eden: The Construction of Family Values in Early Modern Culture* (London: Palgrave, 2000)

Benjamin, Walter (trans, John Osborne), *The Origin of German Tragic Drama* (London and New York: Verso, 1985)

Bloom, Harold, *"Hamlet": Poem Unlimited* (New York: Riverhead, 2003)
  Shakespeare: The Invention of the Human (New York: Riverhead, 1998)

Blumenberg, Hans (trans. Robert M. Wallace), *The Legitimacy of the Modern Age* (Cambridge, MA: MIT Press, 1991)

Bradley, A. C., *Shakespearean Tragedy: Lectures on "Hamlet", "Othello", "King Lear", "Macbeth"* (1904; London and New York: Penguin, 1991)

Brandes, Georg, *William Shakespeare: A Critical Study* (New York: Macmillan, 1902)

Brooks, Peter, *Reading for the Plot: Design and Intention in Narrative* (New York: Vintage, 1984)

Brückner, Martin and Kristen Poole, "The Plot Thickens: Surveying Manuals, Drama, and the Materiality of Narrative Form in Early Modern England," *English Literary History* (2002), 617–48

Bruster, Douglas, *Quoting Shakespeare: Form and Culture in Early Modern Drama* (Lincoln: University of Nebraska Press, 2000)

Bullough, Geoffrey, ed., *Narrative and Dramatic Sources of Shakespeare*, 8 vols. (London: Routledge and Kegan Paul, and New York: Columbia University Press, 1957–75)

Carruthers, Mary and Jan M. Ziolkowski, eds., *The Medieval Craft of Memory* (Philadelphia: University of Pennsylvania Press, 2002)

Charles-Edwards, T. M., "Kinship, Status, and the Origins of the Hide," *Past and Present* 55 (Nov. 1972), 3–33

Charnes, Linda, *Hamlet's Heirs: Shakespeare and the Politics of a New Millenium* (New York and London: Routledge, 2006)

Cohn, Norman, *The Pursuit of the Millennium: Revolutionary Millenarians and Mystical Anarchists of the Middle Ages* (1957; rev. edn. London: Pimlico, 1993)

Coleridge, Samuel Taylor, "1811–12 Lectures on Shakespeare & Milton", in R. A. Foakes, ed., *Lectures 1808–1819 on Literature*, 2 vols., vol. I (London: Routledge and Kegan Paul, and Princeton: Princeton University Press, 1987)

  S. T. Coleridge's "Treatise on Method" (1818), ed. Alice D. Snyder (London: Constable, 1934)

Conklin, Paul S., *A History of "Hamlet" Criticism, 1601–1821* (London: F. Cass, 1968)

Cox, John D., *The Devil and the Sacred in English Drama, 1350–1642* (Cambridge and New York: Cambridge University Press, 2000)

Crawford, Patricia M., *Blood, Bodies and Families in Early Modern England* (New York: Longman, 2004)

Cressy, David, *Birth, Marriage, and Death: Ritual, Religion and the Life-Cycle in Tudor and Stuart England* (New York: Oxford University Press, 1997)

  "Death and the Social Order: The Funerary Preferences of Elizabethan Gentlemen," *Continuity and Change* 5:1 (1989), 99–119

Curtius, Ernst Robert (trans. Willard R. Trask), *European Literature and the Latin Middle Ages* (New York: Pantheon, 1953)

Davidson, Clifford, *The Guild Chapel Wall Paintings at Stratford-upon-Avon* (New York: AMS Press, 1988)

Degenhardt, Jane, *Faith, Embodiment, and "Turning Turk": Islamic Conversion and the Production of Religious and Racial Identity on the Renaissance Stage*, University of Pennsylvania PhD Thesis (2005)

de Grazia, Margreta, "Hamlet the Intellectual," in Helen Small, ed., *The Public Intellectual* (Oxford and Malden, MA: Blackwell, 2002), 89–109

  "Shakespeare, Gutenberg, and Descartes," in Terence Hawkes, ed., *Alternative Shakespeares*, vol. II (London and New York: Routledge, 1996), 63–94

  Shakespeare Verbatim: The Reproduction of Authenticity and the 1790 Apparatus (Oxford: Clarendon Press, 1991)

de Man, Paul, "Literary History and Literary Modernity," in his *Blindness and Insight: Essays in the Rhetoric of Contemporary Criticism*, 2nd edn. (Minneapolis: University of Minnesota Press, 1983), 142–65

Derrida, Jacques (trans. Peggy Kamuf), *Specters of Marx: The State of Debt, the Work of Mourning, and the New International* (New York: Routledge, 1994)

Dessen, Alan C. and Leslie Thomson, *A Dictionary of Stage Directions in English Drama, 1580–1642* (Cambridge and New York: Cambridge University Press, 1999)

Dixon, George, *Old Scarlett* (Glossop: Paul Bush, 1997)

Doëring, Tobias, "Writing Performance: How to Elegize Elizabethan Actors," *Shakespeare Survey* 58 (2005), 60–71

Dowden, Edward, *Shakspeare: A Critical Study of his Mind and Art* (London: Routledge and Kegan Paul, 1967)

Dutton, Richard, "*Hamlet, An Apology for Actors*, and the Sign of the Globe," *Shakespeare Survey* 41 (1989), 35–43

Eagleton, Terry, *William Shakespeare* (Oxford and New York: Blackwell, 1986)

Eichner, Hans, *Friedrich Schlegel* (New York: Twayne, 1970)

Eliot, T. S., "Hamlet," in Frank Kermode, ed., *Selected Prose of T. S. Eliot*, (London: Faber and Faber, 1975), 45–9

Emerson, Ralph Waldo, *Representative Men: Seven Lectures*, ed. Douglas Emory Wilson (Cambridge, MA and London: Harvard University Press, 1996)

Empson, William, *Essays on Shakespeare*, ed. David B. Pirie (Cambridge: Cambridge University Press, 1986)

Engels, Friedrich, *The Condition of the Working Classes in England*, ed. David McLellan (Oxford and New York: Oxford University Press, 1993)

Everett, Barbara, *Young Hamlet: Essays on Shakespeare's Tragedies* (Oxford: Clarendon Press, 1989)

Farley-Hills, David, ed., *Critical Responses to "Hamlet": 1600–1900*, 4 vols. (New York: AMS Press, 1995–)

Farnham, Willard, *The Medieval Heritage of Elizabethan Tragedy* (New York: Barnes and Noble, 1956)

Ferguson, Margaret W., "*Hamlet*: Letters and Spirits," in Patricia Parker and Geoffrey Hartman eds., *Shakespeare and the Question of Theory* (New York and London: Methuen, 1985), 292–309

Fleming, Juliet, *Graffiti and the Writing Arts of Early Modern England* (Philadelphia: University of Pennsylvania Press, 2001)

Freud, Sigmund, "An Autobiographical Study," in Peter Gay, ed., *The Freud Reader* (New York: Norton, 1989), 3–41
    The Interpretation of Dreams, in A. A. Brill, ed. and trans., *The Basic Writings of Sigmund Freud* (New York: Modern Library, 1938)

Frye, Roland, *The Renaissance "Hamlet": Issues and Responses in 1600* (Princeton: Princeton University Press, 1984)

Gallagher, Catherine and Stephen Greenblatt, *Practicing New Historicism* (Chicago: University of Chicago Press, 2000)

Garber, Marjorie, *Shakespeare After All* (New York: Pantheon Books, 2004)
    Shakespeare's Ghost Writers: Literature as Uncanny Causality (New York: Methuen, 1987)

Gervinus, G. G. (trans. F. E. Bunnètt), *Shakespeare Commentaries* (1877 facs. rpt.; New York: AMS Press, 1971)

Goethe, Johann Wolfgang von, *Wilhelm Meister's Apprenticeship*, ed. and trans. Eric A. Blackall, Goethe's Collected Works no. 9 (Princeton: Princeton University Press, 1995)

Goldberg, Jonathan, *Voice Terminal Echo: Postmodernism and English Renaissance Texts* (New York: Methuen, 1986)

Gollancz, Israel, ed., *The Sources of "Hamlet"* (London: Humphrey Milford, Oxford University Press, 1926)

Goody, Jack, *The Development of the Family and Marriage in Europe* (Cambridge: Cambridge University Press, 1983)

Granville-Barker, Harley, *Prefaces to Shakespeare* (Princeton: Princeton University Press, 1946)

Greenblatt, Stephen, *Hamlet in Purgatory* (Princeton: Princeton University Press, 2001)

"Remnants of the Sacred in Early Modern England," in Margreta de Grazia, Maureen Quilligan, and Peter Stallybrass, eds., *Subject and Object in Renaissance Culture* (Cambridge: Cambridge University Press, 1996), 337–45

Will in the World: How Shakespeare Became Shakespeare (New York and London: Norton, 2004)

Grigson, Gregory, *The Englishman's Flora* (London: Phoenix House, 1955)

Guernsey, R. S., *Ecclesiastical Law in "Hamlet"* (New York: The Shakespeare Society of New York, 1885)

Guillory, John, "To Please the Wiser Sort: Violence and Philosophy in Hamlet," in Carla Mazzio and Douglas Trevor, eds., *Historicism, Psychoanalysis, and Early Modern Culture* (New York and London: Routledge, 2000), 82–109

Gumbrecht, Hans Ulrich (trans. Glen Burns), *Making Sense in Life and Literature*, (Minneapolis: University of Minnesota Press, 1992)

Gurr, Andrew, *The Shakespeare Company, 1594–1642* (Cambridge and New York: Cambridge University Press, 2004)

The Shakespearean Stage 1574–1642 (Cambridge: Cambridge University Press, 1970, rpt. 1994)

Gurr, Andrew and Mariko Ichikawa, *Staging in Shakespeare's Theatres* (Oxford: Oxford University Press, 2000)

Habermas, Jurgen (trans. Thomas Burger), *The Structural Transformation of the Public Sphere* (Cambridge, MA: MIT Press, 1995)

Hadfield, Andrew, *Shakespeare and Republicanism* (Cambridge: Cambridge University Press, 2005)

Hallam, Elizabeth M., *Domesday Book through Nine Centuries* (London: Thames and Hudson, 1986)

Halpern, Richard, *Shakespeare Among the Moderns* (Ithaca, NY: Cornell University Press, 1997)

Harding, Vanessa, *The Dead and the Living in London and France 1500–1670* (Cambridge: Cambridge University Press, 2002)

Hegel, G. W. F. (trans. T. M. Knox), *Aesthetics: Lectures on Fine Art*, vol. II (Oxford and New York: Clarendon Press, 1998)

Hegel, G. W. F. (trans. E. S. Haldane and Frances H. Simson), *Lectures on the History of Philosophy*, 3 vols. (Lincoln: University of Nebraska Press, 1995)

Hegel, G. W. F. (trans. F. P. B. Osmaston), *The Philosophy of Fine Art*, 4 vols. (New York: Hacker Art Books, 1975)

Hegel, G. W. F. (trans. J. Sibree), *The Philosophy of History* (New York: Dover Publications, 1956)

Held, Julius, "Flora, Goddess and Courtesan," in Millard Meiss, ed., *De Artibus Opuscula XL: Essays in Honor of Erwin Panofsky*, 2 vols., vol. 1 (New York: Pantheon, 1961), 201–18

Helgerson, Richard, *Forms of Nationhood: The Elizabethan Writing of England* (Chicago: University of Chicago Press, 1992)

Hill, Christopher, *A Nation of Change and Novelty: Radical Politics, Religion, and Literature in Seventeenth-Century England* (New York: Routledge, 1990)
  The World Turned Upside Down: Radical Ideas during the English Revolution (New York: Viking Press, 1972)

Hodges, C. Walter, *Enter the Whole Army: A Pictorial Study of Shakespearean Staging, 1576–1616* (Cambridge: Cambridge University Press, 1999)

Holland, Peter, "Hamlet: Text in Performance," in Peter J. Smith and Nigel Wood, ed., *Hamlet* (Buckingham and Philadelphia: Open University Press, 1996), 55–82

Holmes, Martin Rivington, *The Guns of Elsinore* (London: Chatto and Windus, 1964)

Holstun, James, *A Rational Millennium: Puritan Utopias of Seventeenth-Century England and America* (New York and Oxford: Oxford University Press, 1987)

Honigmann, E. A. J., "The Date of *Hamlet*," *Shakespeare Survey* 9 (1956), 24–34
  "The Politics in *Hamlet* and 'The World of the Play,'" *Stratford-Upon-Avon Studies* 5 (New York, 1964), 129–47

Hunter, G. K., "The Marking of *Sententiae* in Elizabethan Printed Plays, Poems, and Romances," *The Library* 5th series 6:3–4 (1951), 171–88

Isaacs, Jacob, "Coleridge's Critical Terminology," *Essays and Studies* 21 (1936), 86–104

James, Heather, *Shakespeare's Troy: Drama, Politics, and the Translation of Empire* (Cambridge and New York: Cambridge University Press, 1997)

Jameson, Fredric, *A Singular Modernity: Essay on the Ontology of the Present* (London and New York: Verso, 2002)

Jardine, Lisa, *Reading Shakespeare Historically* (London and New York: Routledge, 1996)

Jardine, Lisa and Anthony Grafton, "'Studied for Action': How Gabriel Harvey Read His Livy," *Past and Present* 129 (November 1990), 30–78

Jenkins, Harold, "Playhouse Interpolations in the Folio Text of *Hamlet*," *Studies in Bibliography* 13 (1960), 31–47

Johnson, Samuel, Preface to his edition of Shakespeare (1765), in Brian Vickers, ed., *Shakespeare: The Critical Heritage*, 6 vols., vol. V (London: Routledge and Kegan Paul, 1979)

Jones, Ann Rosalind and Peter Stallybrass, *Renaissance Clothing and the Materials of Memory* (Cambridge and New York: Cambridge University Press, 2000)

Jones, Ernest, *Hamlet and Oedipus* (New York: Norton, 1976)

"The Oedipus Complex as an Explanation of Hamlet's Mystery: A Study in Motive," *The American Journal of Psychology* 21:1 (January 1910), 72–113

Jorgensen, Paul A., *Shakespeare's Military World* (Berkeley: University of California Press, 1956)

Kermode, Frank, *The Sense of an Ending: Studies in the Theory of Fiction* (Oxford and New York: Oxford University Press, 1967)

Kerrigan, John, *Revenge Tragedy: Aeschylus to Armageddon* (Oxford and New York: Clarendon Press, 1996)

Kerrigan, William, *Hamlet's Perfection* (Baltimore: Johns Hopkins University Press, 1994)

Kewes, Paulina, "The Elizabethan History Play: A True Genre?" in Richard Dutton and Jean E. Howard, eds., *A Companion to Shakespeare's Works: The Histories*, 3 vols., vol. II (Malden, MA and Oxford: Blackwell, 2003), 170–93

Kiefer, Frederick, *Shakespeare's Visual Theatre: Staging the Personified Characters* (Cambridge: Cambridge University Press, 2003)

Klein, Lisa M., "Your Humble Handmaid: Elizabethan Gifts of Needlework," *Renaissance Quarterly* 50 (1997), 459–93

Knapp, Jeffrey, *An Empire Nowhere: England, America, and Literature from "Utopia" to "The Tempest"* (Berkeley: University of California Press, 1992)

Knutson, Roslyn, *Playing Companies and Commerce in Shakespeare's Time* (Cambridge and New York: Cambridge University Press, 2001)

Koselleck, Reinhart (trans. Keith Tribe), *Futures Past: On the Semantics of Historical Time* (Cambridge, MA and London: MIT Press, 1979)

Lacan, Jacques (trans. James Hulbert), "Desire and the Interpretation of Desire in *Hamlet*," in Shoshana Felman, ed., *Literature and Psychoanalysis: The Question of Reading, Otherwise* (Baltimore: Johns Hopkins University Press, 1982), 11–52

Lamb, Charles, *The Tragedies of Shakespeare* (1818), in David Farley-Hills, ed., *Critical Responses to Hamlet: 1600–1900*, 4 vols., vol. II (New York: AMS Press, 1995–)

Lee, John, *Hamlet and the Controversies of the Self* (Oxford: Clarendon Press, 2000)

Levin, Harry, *The Question of "Hamlet"* (New York: Oxford University Press, 1959)

Lévinas, Emmanuel (trans. Alphonso Lingis), *Otherwise Than Being, or Beyond Essence* (Pittsburgh: Duquesne University Press, 1981)

Low, Anthony, "Hamlet and the Ghost of Purgatory: Intimations of Killing the Father," *English Literary Renaissance* 29:3 (1999), 443–67

Lupton, Julia Reinhard and Kenneth Reinhard, *After Oedipus: Shakespeare in Psychoanalysis* (Ithaca, NY: Cornell University Press, 1993)

Lynch, Jack, *The Age of Elizabeth in the Age of Johnson* (Cambridge and New York: Cambridge University Press, 2003)

Lyons, Bridget Gellert, "The Iconography of Ophelia," *English Literary History* 44:1 (1977), 60–74

Mackenzie, Henry, The Mirror (1780), in David Farley-Hills, ed., *Critical Responses to "Hamlet": 1600–1900*, 4 vols., vol. I (New York: AMS Press, 1995–)

Maguire, Laurie E., *Shakespearean Suspect Texts: The "Bad" Quartos and Their Contexts* (Cambridge and New York: Cambridge University Press, 1996)

Maitland, Frederic William, *Domesday Book and Beyond: Three Essays in the Early History of England* (Cambridge: Cambridge University Press, 1921)

Mallin, Eric, *Inscribing the Time: Shakespeare and the End of Elizabethan England* (Berkeley: University of California Press, 1995)

Marcus, Leah, *Puzzling Shakespeare: Local Reading and Its Discontents* (Berkeley: University of California Press, 1988)

  Unediting the Renaissance: Shakespeare, Marlowe, Milton (New York and London: Routledge, 1996)

Marx, Karl (trans. Ben Fowkes), *Capital: A Critique of Political Economy* (New York: Penguin, 1976)

  The Eighteenth Brumaire of Louis Bonaparte, in Robert C. Tucker, ed., *The Marx-Engels Reader*, 2nd edn. (New York: Norton, 1978)

  The German Ideology: Part I, in Robert C. Tucker, ed., *The Marx-Engels Reader*, 2nd edn. (New York: Norton, 1978)

  Manifesto of the Communist Party, in Robert C. Tucker, ed., *The Marx-Engels Reader*, 2nd edn. (New York: Norton, 1978)

Masten, Jeffrey, "Toward a Queer Address: The Taste of Letters and Early Modern Friendship," *GLQ: A Journal of Lesbian and Gay Studies* 10:3 (2004), 367–84.

Maus, Katharine Eisaman, *Inwardness and Theater in the English Renaissance* (Chicago and London: University of Chicago Press, 1995)

McGinn, Bernard, *Visions of the End: Apocalyptic Traditions in the Middle Ages* (New York: Columbia University Press, 1998)

McGinn, Donald Joseph, *Shakespeare's Influence on the Drama of His Age* (New Brunswick, NJ: Rutgers University Press, 1938)

McKisack, May, *Medieval History in the Tudor Age* (Oxford: Clarendon Press, 1971)

Miller, David Lee, *Dreams of the Burning Child: Sacrificial Sons and the Father's Witness* (Ithaca, NY: Cornell University Press, 2003)

Mills, John A., *"Hamlet" on Stage: The Great Tradition* (Westport, CT: Greenwood Press, 1985)

Mommsen, Theodor Ernst, "St. Augustine and the Christian Ideal of Progress: The Background of *The City of God*," in Eugene F. Rice Jr., ed. *Medieval and Renaissance Studies* (Ithaca, NY: Cornell University Press, 1966)

Montrose, Louis Adrian, *The Purpose of Playing: Shakespeare and the Cultural Politics of the Elizabethan Theatre* (Chicago: University of Chicago Press, 1996)

  "Shaping Fantasies: Figuration of Gender and Power in Elizabethan Culture," in Stephen Greenblatt, ed., *Representing the English Renaissance* (Berkeley and Los Angeles: University of California Press, 1988), 31–64

Mossner, Ernest, *Bishop Butler and the Age of Reason* (New York: Macmillan, 1936)

Mullaney, Steven, "Mourning and Misognyny: *Hamlet, The Revenger's Tragedy*, and the Final Progress of Elizabeth I, 1600–1607," *Shakespeare Quarterly* 45:2 (1994), 139–62

   The Place of the Stage: License, Play, and Power in Renaissance England (Chicago: University of Chicago Press, 1988)

Neill, Michael, *Issues of Death: Mortality and Identity in English Renaissance Tragedy* (Oxford: Clarendon Press, and New York: Oxford University Press, 1997)

Nelson, Robert J., "The Ancients and the Moderns," in Denis Hollier, ed., *A New History of French Literature* (Cambridge, MA: Harvard University Press, 1989), 364–9

Nietzsche, Friedrich (trans. Ronald Speirs), *The Birth of Tragedy and Other Writings*, ed. Raymond Geuss and Ronald Speirs (Cambridge: Cambridge University Press, 1999)

Norbrook, David, "*Macbeth* and the Politics of Historiography," in Kevin Sharpe and Steven N. Zwicker, eds., *Politics of Discourse: The Literature and History of Seventeenth-Century England* (Berkeley: University of California Press, 1987), 78–116.

   Writing the English Republic: Poetry, Rhetoric and Politics, 1627–1660 (Cambridge: Cambridge University Press, 1999)

Nyquist, Mary, "Textual Overlapping and Dalilah's Harlot-Lap," in Patricia Parker and David Quint, eds., *Literary Theory/Renaissance Texts* (Baltimore: Johns Hopkins University Press, 1986), 341–72

Orgel, Stephen, *The Authentic Shakespeare and Other Problems of the Early Modern Stage* (New York and London: Routledge, 2002)

Owst, G. R., *Literature and Pulpit in Medieval England: A Neglected Chapter in the History of English Letters and of the English People* (New York: Barnes and Noble, 1961)

Park, Katharine, *Secrets of Women: Gender, Generation, and the Origins of Human Dissection* (New York: Zone Books, 2006)

Parker, Patricia, "Black *Hamlet*: Battening on the Moor," *Shakespeare Studies* 31 (2003), 127–64

   "Murder in Guyana," *Shakespeare Studies* 28 (2000), 169–74

   "'Rude Mechanicals,'" in Margreta de Grazia, Maureen Quilligan, and Peter Stallybrass, eds., *Subject and Object in Renaissance Culture* (Cambridge: Cambridge University Press, 1996), 43–82

   Shakespeare from the Margins: Language, Culture, Context (Chicago: University of Chicago Press, 1996)

   "What's In a Name: And More," *Sederi: Revista de la Sociedad Española de Estudios Renacentistas Ingleses* 11 (2002), 101–50

Paster, Gail Kern, *The Body Embarrassed: Drama and the Disciplines of Shame in Early Modern England* (Ithaca, NY: Cornell University Press, 1993)

Patterson, Annabel, *Shakespeare and the Popular Voice* (Cambridge, MA and Oxford: Blackwell, 1989)

Pocock, J. G. A., *The Ancient Constitution and the Feudal Law: A Study of English Historical Thought in the Seventeenth Century: A Reissue with Retrospect* (Cambridge: Cambridge University Press, 1987)

The Machiavellian Moment: Florentine Political Thought and the Atlantic Republican Tradition (Princeton: Princeton University Press, 1975)

Prawer, S. S., *Karl Marx and World Literature* (Oxford: Clarendon Press, 1967)

Preiss, Richard, "Robert Armin Do the Police in Different Voices," in Peter Holland and Stephen Orgel, eds., *From Stage to Print in Early Modern England* (New York and Basingstoke, Hampshire: Palgrave Macmillan, 2006), 208–27.

Prosser, Eleanor, *Hamlet and Revenge* (Stanford: Stanford University Press, 1971)

Quilligan, Maureen, *Incest and Agency in Elizabeth's England* (Philadelphia: University of Pennsylvania Press, 2005)

Rabaté, Jean-Michel, "Hamlet and the Desire of the Mother," in his *Jacques Lacan: Psychoanalysis and the Subject of Literature* (Basingstoke and New York: Palgrave, 2001)

Sawday, Jonathan, *The Body Emblazoned: Dissection and the Human Body in Renaissance Culture* (London: Routledge, 1995)

Schlegel, August Wilhelm von (trans. John Black), *Course of Lectures on Dramatic Art and Literature* (Philadelphia: Hogan and Thompson, 1833)

Schoenbaum, Samuel, *William Shakespeare: A Documentary Life* (New York: Oxford University Press and the Scholar Press, 1975)

Shattuck, Charles H., *The Hamlet of Edwin Booth* (Urbana, IL: University of Illinois Press, 1969)

Shepherd, Simon, "Revels End, and the Gentle Body Starts," *Shakespeare Survey* 55 (2002), 237–56

Sherman, William, "Toward a History of the Manicule" [unpublished study]

Smuts, R. Malcolm, *Culture and Power in Early Stuart England, 1585–1685* (New York: St. Martin's Press, 1999)

Sollors, Werner, *Neither Black, nor White, yet Both: Thematic Explorations of Interracial* (New York and Oxford: Oxford University Press, 1997)

Stabler, A. P., "Elective Monarchy in the Sources of *Hamlet*," *Studies in Philology* 62:5 (January 1965), 654–61

Stallybrass, Peter, "Footnotes," in David Hillman and Carla Mazzio, eds., *The Body in Parts: Fantasies of Corporeality in Early Modern Europe* (New York and London: Routledge, 1997), 313–25

"'Well Grubbed, Old Mole': Marx, Hamlet, and the (Un)Fixing of Representation," *Cultural Studies*, 12: 1 (1998), 3–14

Stallybrass, Peter, Roger Chartier, et al., "Hamlet's Tables and the Technologies of Writing in Renaissance England," *Shakespeare Quarterly* 55:4 (2004), 379–419

Sterne, Tiffany, "'On each Wall / And Corner Post': Play bills, Title-pages and Advertising in Early Modern London," *English Literary Renaissance* 36:1 (2006), 57–89

Stewart, Alan, *Close Readers: Humanism and Sodomy in Early Modern England* (Princeton, NJ: Princeton University Press, 1997)

Swain, Joseph Ward, "The Theory of the Four Monarchies: Opposition History under the Roman Empire," *Classical Philology* 35:1 (1940), 1–21

Targoff, Ramie, "The Performance of Prayer: Sincerity and Theatricality in Early Modern England," *Representations* 60 (Autumn 1997), 49–69

Tennenhouse, Leonard, *Power on Display: The Politics of Shakespeare's Forms* (New York and London: Methuen, 1986)

Thompson, E. P., "The Grid of Inheritance: A Comment," in Jack Goody, Joan Thirsk, and E. P. Thompson, eds., *Family and Inheritance: Rural Society in Western Europe, 1200–1800* (Cambridge and New York: Cambridge University Press, 1976), 328–60

Tilley, Morris Palmer, *A Dictionary of the Proverbs in England in the Sixteenth and Seventeenth Century* (Ann Arbor: University of Michigan Press, 1950)

Tillyard, E. M. W., *Shakespeare's Problem Plays* (Toronto: University of Toronto Press, 1950)

Tolman, A. H., "A View of the Views about Hamlet," PMLA 13:2 (1898), 155–84

Trompf, G. W., *The Idea of Historical Recurrence in Western Thought: From Antiquity to the Reformation* (Berkeley: University of California Press, 1979)

Vickers, Brian, "The Emergence of Character Criticism, 1774–1800," *Shakespeare Survey* 34 (1981), 11–21

ed., *Shakespeare: The Critical Heritage*, 6 vols. (London and Boston: Routledge and Kegan Paul, 1979–81)

Vitkus, Daniel, *Turning Turk: English Theater and the Multicultural Mediterranean, 1570–1630* (New York: Palgrave Macmillan, 2003)

Weimann, Robert, *Author's Pen and Actor's Voice*, ed. Helen Higbee and William West (Cambridge: Cambridge University Press, 2000)

"Mimesis in *Hamlet*," in Patricia Parker and Geoffrey Hartman, eds., *Shakespeare and the Question of Theory* (New York and London: Methuen, 1985), 275–91

Shakespeare and the Popular Tradition in the Theater: Studies in the Social Dimension of Dramatic Form and Function, ed. Robert Schwartz (Baltimore: Johns Hopkins University Press, 1978)

Welsh, Alexander, *Hamlet in His Modern Guises* (Princeton, NJ: Princeton University Press, 2001)

Werstine, Paul, "The Textual Mystery of *Hamlet*," *Shakespeare Quarterly* 39 (1988), 1–26

Wiles, David, *Shakespeare's Clown* (Cambridge: Cambridge University Press, 1987)

Wilson, John Dover, *What Happens in "Hamlet"* (1935; Cambridge: Cambridge University Press, 1995)

Wilson, Luke, *Theatres of Intention: Drama and the Law in Early Modern England* (Stanford: Stanford University Press, 2000)

Woolf, D. R., *The Idea of History in Early Stuart England* (Toronto, London, and Buffalo, NY: University of Toronto Press, 1990)

Woudhuysen, H. R., *Sir Philip Sidney and the Circulation of Manuscripts, 1558–1640* (New York: Clarendon Press, 1996)

"Writing-Tables and Table-Books," *The Electronic British Library Journal* (2004), 1–11, http://www.bl.uk/collections/eblj/2004/article3.html

Yates, Frances A., *Astraea: The Imperial Theme in the Sixteenth Century* (London and Boston: Routledge and Kegan Paul, 1975)

Young, Karl, ed., *The Drama of the Medieval Church*, 2 vols., vol. 1 (Oxford: Clarendon Press, 1967)

Index

Mirror for Magistrates 66
modern 10–18, 22
modern age 25, 26, 28, 43
mole 23–9
  "vicious mole" 30–1
  and world history 28, 29, 43
  as break with the past 26–7
  as coal-miner 24, 30
  as Hamlet 28–9
  as Hamlet's father 42, 43, 184
  as revolution 211 n. 8
  as spirit of consciousness 23
  as teleology 26, 29
  interchangeable with *mold* and *mould* 3, 6,
    29–31, 43
  velocity of 27
Mommsen, Theodor Ernst 219 n. 80
Montrose, Louis Adrian 221 n. 16, 227 n. 85
Mossner, Ernest, 236 n. 24
"mother" 31, 103
mountains 39, 97, 105, 148, 226 n. 72
mountebank 127
mourning 86, 100–1, 123–5
Mousetrap play 36, 71, 91, 97, 104, 127, 175, 188
Mullaney, Steven 90, 221 n. 20, 223 n. 37, 232 n. 35
Munday, Anthony 49
Murder of Gonzago, see Mousetrap play

Nashe, Thomas 173
Neill, Michael 103, 108, 215 n. 21, 229 n. 5,
  243 n. 141
Nelson, Robert 207 n. 36
neo-classicism 11, 14, 194
Nero 102–3, 197
Nietzsche 170
Niobe 3, 6, 123–5, 149
Norbrook, David 218 n. 71, 221 n. 19
Norman Conquest 55–6, 63–5, 72, 73, 80, 139,
  140, 142; *see also* epochal divides
Norman horseman 63–4, 82
Normandy 63–4
Nyquist, Mary 226 n. 71

obscenity 101, 113, 115–16, 139, 140
  "long purples" 115
Oedipal complex 19–20, 108, 154, 168–9
Oedipus 11, 20
old-fashioned 7–9
Ophelia
  as fairy isle 127–8
  as flower 108–10, 113, 145
  as flowerbed 34, 126
  burial of 32, 39–40, 118, 130, 148–50
  drowning 119–23, 127–8, 199
  father's death 113–19

fertility 34, 100
flowers 116–28, 145, 148
flower-strewn corpse 123, 145, 156
grave 37–8, 129–30, 145, 148–50, 154–5
lap 104, 116
like Laertes 118–19
madness 113–14, 153–4
mind 115, 112–13, 116–18
Pict daughter 123, 125
songs 114–16, 119, 199
undoing of 115, 118–19, 122–8
virginity 108–12, 148
orchard 212, *see also* garden
Orestes 11–12, 20
Orgel, Stephen 55, 67
Osric 34, 147
Ovid 30, 123

parchment 35, 146
Park, Katharine 103, 225 n. 68
Parker, John 242 n. 111, 218 n. 79
Parker, Patricia 174, 212 n. 29, 220 n. 98,
  224 n. 53, 226 n. 73, 228 n. 100, 234 n. 60,
  240 n. 78, 79
parliament, *see* Council
Paster, Gail Kern 103, 212 n. 23
pathology 19, 167, 196
patrimony 81, 96, 98
patronymic 1, 86, 98, 143
Patterson, Annabel 83, 218 n. 78, 230 n. 15,
  231 n. 29, n. 30, 232 n. 39
pax Romana 71
Percy, William 226 n. 71
persons and land 3, 6, 31–2, 34, 43–4, 147
  "sullied flesh" 33
  Adam and *adamath* (clay) 31–2, 44
  Crown and peasant 132, 186
  contraction at death 34–5, 146
  dermatology and topography 30–1, 149
  deracination 26–8
  emperors and empires 51
  flesh and clay 33–4, 146
  Hamlet and kingdom 2
  king and kingdom 52
  return to dust 25, 26, 32–4
    "quintessence of dust" 33
  self-extension through land 34, 37, 147
  villein 186
Philaster 213 n. 38
Philomela 115
Plat, Hugh 116
Pliny 67
plot 12–13, 35–7, 172–3
Plutarch 30, 67, 70, 149
Pocock, J. G. A. 221 n. 12, 233 n. 44